D1569426

Sports and Society

Series Editors
Benjamin G. Rader
Randy Roberts

A SPORTING TIME

A
SPORTING
TIME

New York City and
the Rise of Modern Athletics,
1820–70

MELVIN L. ADELMAN

UNIVERSITY OF ILLINOIS PRESS
Urbana and Chicago

Publication of this work has been supported by a grant from the Oliver M. Dickerson Fund. The fund was established by Mr. Dickerson (Ph.D., Illinois, 1906) to enable the University of Illinois Press to publish selected works in American history, designated by the executive committee of the Department of History.

Acknowledgment is also made of support received from the Research Contingency Fund of the School of Health, Physical Education, and Recreation of the Ohio State University.

Library of Congress Cataloging in Publication Data

Adelman, Melvin L. (Melvin Leonard), 1944–
   A sporting time.

   (Sports and society)
   Bibliography: p.
   Includes index.
   1. Athletics—New York (N.Y.)—History—19th century.
   2. Sports—New York (N.Y.)—History—19th century.
   I. Title. II. Series.
   GV584.5.N4A34   1986   796'.09747'1   85-13967
   ISBN 0-252-01250-X (alk. paper)

To
Earle F. Zeigler and Robert M. Sutton
mentors and friends

Contents

Preface

A goodly number of historical studies originate from questions raised in graduate seminars or insightful points made by mentors and other scholars. This work did not. While I profited from my experiences in graduate school, the roots of this book go back to youthful experiences and my fascination with a baseball team that once played at Ebbets Field. My love of sport as both a participant and a fan often distracted me from my schoolwork, to the dismay of my teachers and principals, but it stimulated my curiosity about the meaning of sport and its hold on people. This curiosity later evolved into an interest in the history of sport. I was fortunate to enter graduate school at a time when there was growing acceptance of sport as a legitimate area of scholarly inquiry.

In this book I seek to redirect historical scholarship on when the rise of sport in America occurred and to offer a new framework for analyzing sports change in nineteenth-century America. I argue that contrary to previous thinking the rise of sport began prior to the later decades of the nineteenth century. Between 1820 and 1870 American athletics became increasingly organized and commercialized, marked by the emergence of national standards and competition, specialized player roles, a burgeoning sports information system, and ideological sanctions promoting the moral and social benefits of sport. The transformation of American athletics from its premodern to modern form was nowhere more evident than in New York City—the nation's largest, wealthiest, and most dynamic city. It was there that sport—paralleling the rise of the modern city—first assumed its modern shape and set the tone and direction for the development of sport nationally.

I employ the concept of modernization as an analytic framework for investigating the cause of sports change. I believe that this approach enables the historical study of sport to move beyond the current tendency to see sport as a mirror of society and to perceive sports change as solely a by-product of larger societal alterations. The modernization framework directs us beyond these limitations by promoting a dual approach to analyzing the metamorphosis of sport. While this approach continues to examine the relationship between sports and society, it also facilitates an analysis of the critical question of how the institutional and structural requirements of sports contributed to the profound athletic changes that occurred in nineteenth-century America.

A project of this length would have been impossible had it not been for the help and cooperation of many people. My parents, Sylvia and Harry Adelman, were always and continue to be a source of inspiration. They were there whenever I needed them, and my love for them will never diminish.

I received kind assistance from people at the New York Public Library, the Brooklyn Public Library, and the New-York Historical Society. The librarians at the University of Illinois, Urbana-Champaign, provided their usual outstanding service. Librarians at the University of Illinois, Chicago, and The Ohio State University were also helpful. The New York Yacht Club and the New York Racquet and Tennis Club kindly allowed me to use their libraries. I would especially like to thank Robert W. Henderson, the librarian of the New York Racquet and Tennis Club, for his assistance.

During the course of my doctoral studies at the University of Illinois, Urbana-Champaign, I profited from the assistance I received from various professors. Frederic C. Jaher helped me frame my initial questions and encouraged my research. Members of my dissertation committee—Robert Waller, Wallace Farnham, Marianna Trekell, and John Loy—were generous with their time and provided stimulating insights. I also received cogent criticism and positive encouragement from a host of friends with whom I shared my graduate experience: Jeff Brown, James Ducker, Dave Dunning, James Farrell, Dim Lazo, John C. Rouff, Gregory Schmidt, and Phil VanderMeer. I think we all know the debts we owe one another.

I have been fortunate to belong to a community of scholars interested in the study of sport history. Numerous members of the North American Society for Sport History raised thought-provoking questions about my work, but I am especially grateful to Steven Riess, who from the outset was always willing to listen to me discuss my work and to offer many helpful comments; to Stephen Hardy, who read the entire manuscript and whose questions and usual perceptive insights made the final product that much better. The two editors of the Sports and Society series, Benjamin G. Rader and Randy Roberts, also contributed useful suggestions.

Susan L. Hunsdon read the entire manuscript more times than she would like to remember and offered more criticism than I frequently wanted to hear. I hope that she will always know the special feeling I have for her. Lawrence J. Malley, editor-in-chief of the University of Illinois Press, was constantly helpful and throughout was an author's editor. Theresa L. Sears, who copyedited the manuscript, provided invaluable service in making this book a more polished work.

There are two people to whom I am especially indebted: Professor Earle F. Zeigler served as the advisor to my master's thesis, and Professor Robert M. Sutton chaired my doctoral dissertation committee. Both of these gentlemen provided unlimited help and constant encouragement, and both were generous with their time throughout my graduate years. Their contribution to this work, however, goes beyond scholarly and professional considerations. Their thoughtfulness, patience, and warmth will always be deeply appreciated and well remembered. Dedicating this book to them is only a small repayment for all the kindnesses they have shown me.

Introduction

Since the early 1970s there has been a growing interest in sport as an area of historical scholarship. Professional historians have provided us with a number of books and journal articles to enhance our understanding of sports developments and their meanings for American life, yet wide gaps in the literature remain.[1] Of particular importance is the need to place the changes in sports behaviors and patterns within the context of a more comprehensive analytic framework.

In this book I examine the development of sport in America between 1820 and 1870, employing the concept of modernization to analyze the nature of and reasons for the significant changes that occurred. It is my intent to demonstrate that the basic structure of modern sport and the ideological sanctions of modern athletics evolved during this half-century. References to the somewhat earlier modernization of sport in England are discussed only as it directly impinged on developments in this country. I also hope to provide a more coherent explanation of the relationship between urban change and sports change, and to offer new insights into the class and ethnic backgrounds of sports participants.

Sporting developments in New York City are examined as a means of understanding the modernization of sport in America. New York was the nation's wealthiest and most populated city during the nineteenth century, and the first urban area to feel the impact of modernizing influences. It had a rich sports heritage even during the colonial period and was America's sports capital between 1820 and 1870, with all the major sports journals located there. More significantly, the characteristics associated with modern athletics in America initially appeared in New York; hence, that city set the tone and direction for the development of sport nationally.

My discussion, then, will focus on the changing sports patterns in New York, although I will occasionally tie this in with similar developments taking place nationally.

Historians are in agreement that the rise of sport in America occurred during the last three decades of the nineteenth century and that urbanization/industrialization was the major impetus. In the post–Civil War years Americans witnessed a tremendous expansion of interest and participation in athletics, including the development of new sporting activities and the increasing organization and commercialization of sport. By 1900 organized sport had become one of the nation's major sources of recreation.[2] In contrast to this view, the antebellum years are portrayed as ones of limited sports activity, although some historians have noted antecedents to the later athletic surge during this period, especially after 1850. This perspective derives from a paucity of scholarly work, most of which examines the changing attitudes toward sport.[3] These limited studies distort our understanding of the evolution of nineteenth-century athletic practices, however. While the popularity of sport markedly increased in the last decades of the nineteenth century, it is my contention that the basic framework of modern sport was established during the period 1820–70.

An examination of sport in New York City in the mid-nineteenth century reveals not only a much more active sporting life in this country than was previously thought to exist, but also the extent to which competitive and recreational sports already had become organized. By 1850, both horse and harness racing were in their third decade as organized sporting events, and there was a host of cricket, rowing, racquet, gymnastics, yachting, and shooting clubs in the Empire City. In particular, the surge in the number of baseball clubs in the metropolitan area in the late 1850s symbolized the trend toward participation in organized sport. New Yorkers also were turning out, with increasing fervor and in ever-expanding numbers, to watch various sporting events. Horse and harness racing were the first spectator sports, and several others soon followed on their heels.

This period, 1820–70, was selected for study because it permits a sweeping examination of the transformation of athletics from a premodern to a modern pattern. Since modernization is a process, not a single event, it is obviously impossible to fix a precise date for the inception of modern sport in America; however, from the standpoint of societal and sports developments in New York and nationally, the year 1820 can serve to mark the beginning. In the decades immediately following the War of 1812, profound economic and societal changes spurred the onset of modern America. Richard Brown claims that by the 1820s the prevailing personality type in America was a modern one, although he recognizes that various factors inhibited this type from reaching full maturation until after the Civil War.[4] This was also the decade when New York City firmly solidified its position as the country's preeminent urban area. While possessing many of the characteristics of the premodern city, it also held the seeds that gave rise to the modern city. Finally, and most importantly, the return of legalized horse racing in New York during this decade ushered in a new sports era. Like other aspects of American life, horse racing retained many of its earlier characteristics while also encouraging significant innovations. The intersectional horse race in 1823 between Eclipse and Henry, before a reported crowd of 50,000 spectators, symbolized the onset of modern sport.

The study ends in 1870 because that year marks the end of an era for both New York and modern athletics. Although the city would continue to be viewed as America's sports capital, its dominant role (at times one might say stranglehold) declined with the growth and expansion of athletics on a national level, as evidenced by the increasing number of national organizations to regulate and control all forms of sports activities. While it is not my intent to argue that all sports became fully modern by 1870, the essential framework, both structural and ideological, had been established by that date.

In this study I seek to establish modernization as an analytic framework for comprehending changes in the structures, attitudes toward, and functions of sport in the nineteenth century, and within this framework to explore the relationship between sport and the urban environment. In the past historians have examined the rise of sport coincident with the urbanization/industrialization of America. Clearly, these factors were critical, but the urban/industrial model suffers from a variety of drawbacks, not the least of which is the inappropriate way this particular framework has been used. Historians have yet to distinguish between the impact of industrialization and of urbanization; they too easily use the terms as catchalls to describe the changing climate of American life; and they treat the two processes as mere abstractions whose influence should be self-evident. Moreover, when discussing the impact of industrialization on sport, historians tend to concentrate on the stimulus provided by its end products — improved standards of living, reduced working hours, technological innovations (which should not be confused with industrialization). Their analyses lack an appreciation of the impact of industrialization on human behavior. Similar problems exist with their explanations of the urban impact on sport (to be discussed later). As a result of these deficiencies, historians have thus far not explained adequately how urbanization and industrialization facilitated the transformation of athletics.[5]

The inadequacies of the urban/industrial model go beyond inappropriate usage. Rather, since both urbanization and industrialization are, by definition, concerned with specific, but not all-inclusive, forms of societal change,[6] even if the variables are combined and applied in a more insightful manner, use of the urban/industrial model is at best a piecemeal, one-dimensional approach. The conceptual nature of the model is such that its variables (and by extension, society), assumed to be critical to the transformation, meaning, and character of athletics, lead scholars to examine the development of sport solely in terms of its connection to society. While this approach can and has produced useful and interesting material—obviously, the study of sport cannot ignore societal influences—this particular orientation nevertheless fails to provide a comprehensive picture because it is not designed to explore both the institutional character and the structure of sport on their own terms, or to explain the vital role they play in the transformation of athletics. As a result of this deficiency historians have tended to parallel sporting and societal developments. Sport in their works emerges as a by-product of societal conditions, the all too frequent and simple view that sport is a mirror of society. The causal connection between athletic and societal change is thereby missing, as is an appreciation of sports structures and behaviors as both part of and expressing a cultural process, not merely a reflection or extension of it.[7]

Historians seem to have a love-hate relationship with modernization as an analytic framework for their studies. Although entering into the discussion may well be nonproductive, since much has already been written, a few comments are necessary because mine is the first study I know of to apply modernization to the history of sport.

Critics of modernization theory charge that it suffers dramatically from cultural bias, that it has been used too easily as a catchall, and that it has been applied in a manner that is both reductive and deterministic. Supporters of the theory do not deny these assertions, but they accurately claim that misuse does not inherently invalidate its application; that historians continue to use the theory in a variety of ways despite the ongoing charge that it has been fully discredited; and that critics have failed to present a coherent alternative. More significantly, proponents of modernization theory assert that it can be applied as a heuristic device to organize material on cultural developments during a specific time period, particularly within the context of the experience of Western society, and then to relate these developments to broader societal change.[8]

My use of modernization as an analytic framework draws on the works of Richard Brown, Allen Guttmann, and Eric Dunning.[9] Brown applies the concept of modernization to an examination of the transformation of American life. He distinguishes between two ideal societal types—traditional and modern—although he concedes that neither type has ever existed in its ideal form. These societal types possess polar characteristics.

Traditional society is marked by stability, localism, an ascriptive paternalistic hierarchy both in the family and society, an absence of specialized roles, and a dependence on muscle power. The past, present, and future are the same, and time moves in endless cycles. Traditional society is further characterized by the weaving together of family and community in labor, leisure, and religion. Ritual flows through the entire experience of traditional society, and no precise boundaries exist between the secular and religious life, or between work and leisure. The prevailing outlook is one of acceptance or of resignation toward life as it is; the repetition of past ways rather than innovative action is encouraged.

By contrast, modern society is dynamic, cosmopolitan, technological, and marked by a functional social structure that conforms to shifting political and economic structures; most of all, it is rational. The desire for change and the belief that it can be achieved through the application of rational analysis is central to modern society. From this set of assumptions flows many of the distinctive elements of modern society, especially the belief that the rational mode can be used to manipulate objects, the environment, people, and ideas. The modern personality type thus exhibits a significant drive for individual autonomy, initiative, and achievement. For Brown, modernization entails movement in the direction of this ideal type, which conceptually rests on patterns of thought, behavior, and organization and which may be applied to any sphere of social life.

The efforts of Guttmann and Dunning to differentiate the characteristics of modern sport and folk games (or premodern sport)[10] facilitate an application of the concept of modernization to the study of athletics. While I have been influenced by their discussions and classifications, I differentiate premodern and modern sport in terms of six polar characteristics (see Table 1). The modernization of sport, like the modernization of society, entails movement from the premodern to the modern pattern.

As an analytic framework, modernization facilitates an examination of sport on two distinct, but interrelated and interacting, levels: the relationship between sport and the modernization of society and/or its component parts; and the evolution of modern sports structures and ideology. What both levels share, and what in fact unifies them, is the dominant role of rationalism in modern society. The increasing emphasis on rationalism and its logical extension, the desire to establish rational order, provides an important missing link in the analysis of modern sport. David Voigt correctly notes that "the appearance of a formal sport reflects man's rational attempt at channeling fun, and the rise of many formal sports in industrial society testifies to this faith in rationalism—a faith which values the formalization of most patterns of behavior."[11] While scholars point to the emergence of the institutional character of athletics,

TABLE 1. The Characteristics of Premodern and Modern Ideal Sporting Types

Premodern Sport	Modern Sport
1. *Organization*—either nonexistent or at best informal and sporadic; contests are arranged by individuals directly or indirectly (e.g., tavern owners, bettors) involved.	1. *Organization*—formal; institutionally differentiated at the local, regional, and national levels.
2. *Rules*—simple, unwritten, and based on local customs and traditions; variations exist from one locale to another.	2. *Rules*—formal, standardized, and written; rationally and pragmatically worked out and legitimated by organizational means.
3. *Competition*—locally meaningful only; no chance for national reputation.	3. *Competition*—national and international, superimposed on local contests; chance to establish national and international reputations.
4. *Role differentiation*—low among participants; loose distinction between playing and spectating.	4. *Role differentiation*—high; emergence of specialists (professionals) and strict distinctions between playing and spectating.
5. *Public information*—limited, local, and oral.	5. *Public information*—reported on a regular basis in local newspapers, as well as national sports journals; appearance of specialized magazines, guidebooks, etc.
6. *Statistics and records*—nonexistent.	6. *Statistics and records*—kept and published on a regular basis; considered important measures of achievement; records sanctioned by national associations.

in the past their studies have merely traced the growing presence of the structural components of rationality, the organization of sport, and the codification of its rules. The result is more a description of what occurred than a coherent explanation of how and why it occurred or what it means.

The problems with historians' treatments of sport are nowhere more clearly revealed than in their discussions of the impact of the city. The philosopher Jacques Ellul noted that "sport has been conditioned by the organization of the great cities; apart from city life its very invention is inconceivable. 'Country sport' is but a pale imitation of city sport and has none of the characteristics of what we know as sport."[12] However, with the exception of Stephen Hardy's recent study of sports developments in Boston between 1865 and 1915, historians have not adequately clarified the connection between the changing nature of the city and the changing nature of sport. They examine "urban" in the context of "site" rather than "process"; hence, the city emerges merely as the setting for the transformation of sport. At best, such work illustrates parallel developments—as the city became increasingly complex and organized, so did sport—but the causal relationship is missing.[13]

The now classic articles of Oscar Handlin and Louis Wirth on the nature and evolution of the modern city provide an excellent starting point for analyzing the relationship between sport and the city. Handlin noted that the generative impulse of the modern city emerged from three dramatic and interrelated societal changes that were external to it: the centralized national state, the new productive system, and the vastly improved communication system. These combined to increase the city's population, to endow it with a novel economic function, and to impose on it a fresh conception of order. While demographic increments had important ramifications for city life, the significant changes that took place in the modern city flowed from its role as the economic and communication center of the new productive system. These new tasks required the establishment of a rational order within the boundaries of the city. Both the desire and ability of the modern city "to impose a rational order upon the relations created by the new productive system" provided the city with its modern identity and resulted in "a thoroughgoing transformation in the urban way of life." This need to establish a rational order is the critical connection between the changing nature of the city and the changing structure of sport and can be examined in terms of Wirth's three components of urban society: physical space, organizational structures, and collective behavior.[14]

The modern productive system required a new division of urban space based solely on the criteria of economic utility and value. This alteration resulted in the removal of traditional recreational areas and required that users of new and specifically designated sports areas compete economically for the land. The shift in land allocation thereby stimulated the creation of voluntary associations, private entrepreneurs, and even municipal government, all with greater amounts of capital, to become increasingly involved with sport. The emergence of these agencies dramatically illustrates that the complexities of urban life made it increasingly difficult for sport to exist on its previous informal and spontaneous basis.[15]

The establishment of numerous voluntary sporting associations was at the heart and soul of the organized sports movement, but it was more than just a response to shifts in the physical contours of the city. Demographic increments, changes in the nature of social relations, shifts in urban social structure, the creation of new concepts of class, and the erosion of the former basis of status also stimulated the emergence of modern sports structures.

The increasing size and heterogeneous nature of the nineteenth-century urban population produced significant alterations in the form and function of social relations. Scholars have long recognized that the tremendous rise of urban voluntary associations during this period resulted from the emergence of the impersonal and fragmented city. Such associations performed important integrative functions by helping to stitch together diverse communal factions. With the various changes within the structure and meaning of the urban community, sporting clubs, similar to other organizations, acted at one level to promote an activity among individuals who shared a common interest but did not know each other on a personal basis.[16]

Class structure also strongly influenced the formation of sports clubs.[17] The initial thrust of organized sport came largely from the upper and upper-middle classes. While elite sports clubs were tied to the efforts of their members to institutionalize their status and disassociate themselves from the masses, the social backgrounds of individual members reflected the changing composition of New York's upper class during the half-century between 1820 and 1870. The middle class provided the organizational leadership for the two major spectator sports—harness racing and baseball—as well as several other sports. Ethnic groups promoted certain sports as a means of unifying their respective immigrant communities and preserving national identity in a foreign land. Artisans were not responsible for initially organizing any sport, but they engaged in a variety of organized sports and established their own clubs. Their participation in athletics was an expression of the tension created in the worker community by the onset of the modern productive system. On the one hand, involvement in sport was an extension of their desire to preserve traditional values and their ongoing veneration of physical prowess. On the other hand, artisan participation in certain sports, most notably baseball, was a reflection of their efforts to demonstrate their middle-class status. The lower class was conspicuous by its absence from organized sport. While the city's bottom strata engaged in boxing and no doubt participated in a variety of physical recreations, they neither sought nor had the financial wherewithal to formalize and institutionalize these behavioral patterns.

The most significant influence of the new rational order emerged via the role the city played in the construction of the ideology of modern sport. The growing fear that urban residents were physically degenerating and that the urban social order was decaying sparked the emergence of a new and more positive view of athletics. Spokesmen for the newer attitudes asserted that sport helped combat the problems created by the modern city in three specific, interrelated ways: by promoting good health, by encouraging morality, and by instilling positive character values.

While shifting attitudes toward athletics were a response to the rising concern about the changes in urban society, the desire to channel sport into socially productive outlets was at the heart of the new sports ideology. The claims that athletics promoted positive social benefits provided sport with greater dignity and importance but also illustrated that the fundamental justification of sport remained its utilitarian benefits. At a time when work and play emerged as distinct entities in urban life, proponents increasingly viewed the two as interrelated. The new relationship, however, was hardly one of equality. By training and adjusting urban men to the new social system, sport as a promoter of rational order became a servant of its creator, the modern productive system.

While the modern city was both a setting and a stimulant for the transformation of athletics, the creation of modern sports structures was not solely a by-product of societal change. The institutional needs of the various sports to establish their own order were equally responsible for the modernization of athletics. Since the modernization of each sport was in part a response to its particular requirements, the rate varied from sport to sport. Internal growth, competition, and commercialization combined to directly affect the degree to which modern sports structures evolved.

The increasing number of units within each particular sport and their emergence at more and different geographical locations made the older, local rules, norms, and sanctions inoperative. To facilitate the athletic experience within a growing sports universe required the development of uniform rules and the creation of governing agencies to administer the sport and provide a mechanism for rational change. The expansion of sport, moreover, produced an increased desire and need for more information, the result being burgeoning local coverage, the emergence of national sports journals, the creation of guidebooks and other sports manuals, and the developing importance of statistics.

The growing emphasis on competitive sport acted as a further stimulant for the transformation of athletics. A desire to demonstrate superiority — which is the essence of competition, particularly among individuals who do not know each other on a personal basis — required the formalization of behavioral patterns and contributed to the professionalization of sport, with a concomitant emphasis on training and specialized roles. The emergence of sports information and statistics and records was largely associated with the growth of competitive-professional athletics.

The commercialization of sport contributed to the modernization of sport in two ways: by facilitating the growth of competitive athletics beyond local boundaries and by aiding the rise of professional sports. In neither case was commercialization the cause of these developments, since both flowed from the search for superiority; in fact, the presence of competitive and professional elements within a particular sport always preceded commercialization. Rather, commercialization served as a catalyst for the expansion of competition and professionalism by providing a more rational and productive method of financing these developments. In addition, the increase in the number of commercial units nationally required that the various sports entrepreneurs coordinate and rationalize their business practices to maximize their profits. Critical to this process was equality of competition, uniform rules, systematic scheduling, and increased organization.

My examination of the transformation of sport from premodern to modern takes place within the context of a specific orientation and approach, namely, an effort to investigate sports developments in terms of the class and ethnic backgrounds of participants. During the last several years scholars have paid more attention to the role of class and ethnicity in their examinations of sport, but the number of studies focusing on this theme has not kept pace with the overall growth of sport history as a field of inquiry. Moreover, only a handful of sport historians have applied quantification techniques to their studies. The ongoing reliance on the impressionistic and often inaccurate data left by contemporary observers impairs our development of a more penetrating analysis of sport.

Limited available sources (and space in this already lengthy study) unfortunately restricted the application of quantification methods to the study of baseball players and one cricket club.[18] This approach has led to a reinterpretation of social class among early baseball players and has also facilitated a more accurate assessment of the initial stage of organized baseball. Despite the limited usage of quantification techniques, every effort was made to assess the class and ethnic backgrounds of sports participants. Significant bits of information did exist to permit such a portrait, albeit incomplete. The result, I believe, is a clearer understanding of the motivations and sports behaviors of nineteeth-century New Yorkers.

To understand what constitutes sport, I follow the lead of a number of scholars who have examined its character and nature by distinguishing it from other activities which share certain similar characteristics, most notably play and games. While sport includes elements of both, two characteristics essentially differentiate it from these activities: the greater degree to which sport demands the demonstration in a competitive-contest situation of some kind of physical prowess and skill; and the greater degree to which sport has institutionalized and rationalized structural patterns.[19] In this study sport is conceived as a range of activities that are instrumental (rather than expressive), somewhat utilitarian, highly regulated, and institutionalized; as a demonstration of physical prowess or skill; and as subject to recorded histories and traditions.

While scholars believe that a conceptual approach to understanding sport is useful for an empirical study of this phenomenon, they recognize that certain ambiguities and borderline cases exist in their construction of a continuum between play and sport. One such area concerns the intent of the participant. Richard Gruneau has analyzed the distinction between leisure and competitive sport and notes that the former refers to recreational activities "which are not necessarily oriented to outcome or production as their prime objective," while the latter "are always oriented towards outcomes and production (i.e., skill mastery or winning) as a prime function." These categories are not mutually exclusive, but "there do seem to be important variations in their degrees of regulation, organization and purpose."[20]

Although I will concentrate on competitive athletics, a brief examination of leisure sports is necessary for three reasons. First, while for several sports, such as baseball, the competitive aspect did play a critical role in their modernization and maturation, the majority of participants engaged in these sports on a recreational level. To neglect this dimension of leisure would make it exceedingly difficult to comprehend the development of the sport. Second, the modernization of leisure sports did begin to take place in 1820–70, although to a lesser extent than among competitive sports. Moreover, the emergence of modern characteristics in leisure sports reveals the impact that changing social conditions had on the transformation of athletics in a way that an examination of competitive sport alone cannot. Finally, since contemporary New Yorkers did not, in their discussions of athletics, seek to create the refined distinctions between competitive and recreational sports as made by sociologists, an understanding of their perceptions of the changing sports experience in the city requires an examination of both forms.

I will examine the material topically rather than chronologically because such an approach facilitates a more coherent discussion of the changes in the institutional structure of each sport. The book is divided basically into three sections: turf sports (horse and harness racing), ball games (cricket and baseball), and a myriad of New York sporting experiences (boating, professional and leisure sports). A concluding chapter examines the creation of the ideology of modern athletics, especially as influenced by the New York press.

A panorama of New York City and vicinity, 1866. Note in the left foreground a baseball game in progress at the Elysian Fields, in Hoboken, N.J. From a drawing by John Bachman.

1

The Changing Character
of New York City

The city of New York has almost always been in the midst of change.[1]
After the departure of British troops in 1783 a variety of demographic,
political, economic, and social forces undermined the character of colonial
New York. By 1820 the commercial vigor that had elevated the city to
its premier economic position in America had produced, by contemporary
standards, a fairly cosmopolitan life-style. Despite the significant alterations,
however, Manhattan retained many of the crude and rustic characteristics
of a preindustrial city; it was still a provincial port, more like Bristol or
Liverpool than Paris or London.

New York continued to change significantly during the next half-
century. By 1870 it had been transformed from a mercantile city into a
worldly metropolis. Now the undisputed commercial and financial hub
of the country, the city's economic gains furthered its cosmopolitan
reputation and fostered a luxurious life-style for its richest residents.
However, such rapid urbanization and economic expansion carried the
price of poverty, crime, and a host of other social problems. Frightened
that former institutions of social order were decaying, New Yorkers
established by the post–Civil War years an ever-increasing number of
modern organizations to deal with the growing complexities of urban life.

The population explosion following independence most immediately
transformed New York. Between 1790 and 1820 the city's population
almost quadrupled, from 33,131 to 123,706; by 1810 New York had
replaced Philadelphia as the most populous American city. While the
normal birthrate obviously contributed to this growth, New York's ability
to attract and keep newcomers was really the key to its swelling ranks.

People arrived there from a variety of places but especially from New England. These New Englanders, inclined toward a more conservative life-style, had a profound impact on the city's economic, religious, and social life. Despite the cultural differences between them and the native Knickerbockers, New York in the period 1783–1812 "was more truly an American city, in the sense that the ethnic background of its population reflected the national composition, than in any other period of its history."[2]

While the majority of newcomers were American citizens, New York continued to attract sufficient numbers of European immigrants to sustain its reputation as a polyglot community. The lion's share of foreigners came from the British Isles, especially Ireland; German and French immigrants also constituted a major addition to the existing settlements of Danes, Swedes, Italians, Portuguese, and Spaniards. By the 1820s these newcomers made up 11.3 percent of New York's population, with perhaps as many as one in five residents being of foreign birth.[3]

During the colonial period political and economic troubles had instigated the revival of ethnic and religious loyalties. For the most part, however, intermarriage among the families of English, Dutch, and Huguenot leaders, the process of acculturation, and the relative ease of assimilation softened the effects of nationality on the city's social structure. After the Revolution, although only a handful of new immigrants reached the upper echelons, the city continued to make room for the thrifty foreign-born merchant or mechanic. By the 1820s, however, the increasing number of new arrivals began to strain the city's social institutions. Consternation among local citizens mounted, as more and more New Yorkers came to believe that foreigners, especially Irish Catholics, were the source of many of the problems confronting the city.[4]

The population explosion was accompanied by rapid expansion of the economy. Despite its natural and geographical advantages, New York was overshadowed by its northeastern seaport rivals during the colonial period. Following independence, however, the city began a period of unprecedented growth as its merchants rearranged their trade routes to adjust to new commercial conditions. Taking bold and aggressive action, New Yorkers sent their vessels around the world, although the major portion of their trade was divided among the Caribbean, Europe, and the coast of North America. By 1797 New York had surpassed Philadelphia in both imports and exports and assumed the position of America's mercantile center.[5]

For the next two decades the city's margin of economic leadership over its commercial rivals remained narrow. Yet because it provided greater opportunity than other urban centers, it also attracted a larger share of the talented and ambitious, who further stimulated economic growth. By the early 1800s few people failed to comment on the city's preoccupation with business. One visitor remarked in 1807 that every "thought, word, look and action of the multitude seemed to be absorbed by commerce." Although New York's prosperity vanished under the impact of the Embargo Act and a second war with Great Britain, the ensuing peace brought a new surge of economic growth. Between 1815 and 1825 New York left its commercial rivals "almost hopelessly far behind."[6]

The willingness of New York merchants to break with traditional business practices was the most important factor in its economic expansion. In particular, the formation of the auction system was a crucial and aggressive entrepreneurial decision. Six auctions existed as early as 1790, and by 1817 that number had increased sixfold. The auction system allowed British manufacturers to consign a ship's cargo to American auctioneers, retaining ownership of the merchandise until it was sold and eliminating the middlemen while reducing the price of goods. Regular ocean voyages by the Black Ball Packet Line, beginning in 1817, were also vital to New York's economic advancement. Although many merchants were skeptical initially, the advantages of punctuality and dependability quickly became obvious to the business community and extensive imitation readily followed.[7]

The formation of specialized business institutions of capital accumulation was closely tied to the city's commercial success, and by 1820 New York had become America's financial center as well. Between 1790 and 1825 the number of New York banks increased from one to fourteen, with New York bankers being the first to organize a commercial money market. These financial institutions were initially a response to the increasing demand for commercial capital, but by 1815 they began to pursue alternative investments to shipping. Capital accumulation, even more than foreign trade, became a more accurate indicator of New York's economic preeminence. Although the city's leadership role was firmly established prior to 1820, the completion of the Erie Canal in 1825 solidified this dominance in providing unmatched access to western markets. A great entrepôt of goods, migrants, and talent, New York had become the Empire City.[8]

Change within the context of structural stability marked New York's governmental and political institutions in the generation following the Revolution. The structure of the city's corporate status, although now based on the state constitution of 1777, continued to function much as it had throughout most of the colonial period. Power was vested in the common council, which consisted of aldermen and their assistants, along with the mayor and recorder; the state governor continued to appoint members of the executive office. Thus, although the structure of government did not undergo any radical alterations, important changes occurred in the nature and extent of power exercised by the different offices, as well as the formation of new agencies to handle the enlarging scope of municipal affairs.[9]

Political power still rested firmly, although not absolutely, with wealthy men. The elite provided leadership for both the Federalist and Democratic-Republican parties. Differences in the social backgrounds of the members of these two political parties were overshadowed by their similarities. Maintenance of political control by the city's most prominent citizens emanated from a degree of restricted sufferage, the continuation of deferential politics, and their ability both to manage the varying political factions and monopolize the selection of candidates through the creation of ad hoc nominating committees.[10]

The municipal government continued to function much as it had in earlier times, even while the growth of New York necessitated its becoming involved in several new areas. The city government's financial outlays were still small, but they increased in the generation following the Revolution as a result of an expansion in social services. Despite the rise in New York's expenditures, the city still found it increasingly difficult to finance the basic needs of its swelling population.[11]

This inability to keep pace with an expanding population stemmed in part from a governmental structure that was more appropriate to a large town than an emerging city. Of even greater significance was the fact that the business elite had control of New York. While they neither formed a monolithic economic class nor totally dictated policy, they were adamant about not taxing themselves. In this regard they were not simply motivated by self-gain; rather, they collectively acted on the widely held economic belief that the prosperity of the city was closely allied to the success of its most prosperous residents.[12]

New York's physical structure in 1820 reflected its population and commercial growth. In the forty years since the Revolution the city had recovered fully from the destruction of the war and expanded beyond the confines of its colonial boundaries. In what became a perennial struggle, New Yorkers adjusted in various ways to the rapidly changing conditions. A housing boom that started in the first decade of the nineteenth century was temporarily halted by the War of 1812, but it later resumed with even greater vigor. Yet by 1825 there were still claims that no vacant houses existed in New York, despite the fact that some 3,000 dwellings were under construction.[13]

Corresponding expansion took place in the street system as new streets were laid out and others extended. In 1811 New York adopted its famous gridiron pattern, solely for reasons of practicality and economy. The farsighted plan offered a ready solution for expanding the city in an orderly fashion well beyond its current boundaries. However, it robbed New York of its former individuality and charm, put an end to neighborhood gathering places such as parks and squares, and had, according to one scholar, "a socially disintegrating effect."[14]

Increasing segregation of land based on economic function coincided with New York's physical expansion. Broadway, already the main thoroughfare and the setting for some of the finest homes in the city, had become the center of the dry and fancy goods retail business by 1805. Pearl Street, the site of many of the leading shops, served as the locus for the wholesaling of dry goods. Williams Street catered to the fashionable retailing of dry goods, although establishments on Maiden Lane, Chatham Street, and the lower part of Greenwich Street were challenging its supremacy. The city's largest warehouses were located on Water and Front streets, while insurance companies, merchant exchanges, and banking houses were concentrated in the Wall Street area. The section of the city near the river and along South Street was devoted to sea and sailor.[15]

Despite all these changes New York retained many of the elements of a compact, preindustrial city. Manhattan's long and narrow shape made it difficult to cope with the city's growing population. The absence of a transportation system generally restricted settlement to an area south of Potter Field (currently Washington Square). With the boundaries extending to Fourteenth Street, the overwhelming portion of the populace resided within two miles of City Hall, then the heart of the city. Some of the leading families began a gradual northward movement, and the most prosperous merchants lived in large, comfortable homes in exclusive residential districts. But for the majority, workplace and home were closely situated, if not actually interspersed.[16]

The physical environment of preindustrial New York imposed a certain degree of familiarity among its residents and led to greater interaction among all social classes than is found in modern urban areas. Yet New York, which had been a part of one of the most aristocratic North American colonies, remained a highly structured society. Although class lines had loosened somewhat in the immediate post-Revolutionary period, by the 1820s the city's richest residents held an even greater portion of the wealth than their predecessors had.

By 1820 a relatively new merchant class had mounted the social ladder. The withdrawal of the Loyalists and, more importantly, changing economic opportunities opened the upper echelons of New York society to men of new wealth. In fact, nearly 40 percent of the city's most affluent citizens represented first-generation wealth. While mobility to the upper class was still possible in the 1820s, the new economic forces enabled wealthy New Yorkers to further increase their share of the financial rewards. In 1789 less than one-third of the population controlled three-quarters of the city's wealth in terms of personal property; by 1815 just one-tenth owned that amount.[17]

Social interactions remained exclusively class-bound. While urban social clubs were a thing of the future, prominent New Yorkers did establish formal and informal institutions to perpetuate their status and hegemony. The elite also created patterns of residential segregation. Scattered throughout the city's wards, they nonetheless clustered on certain streets. By the 1820s more than half of the wealthiest New Yorkers lived on just 8 of the city's 250 streets.[18]

Most New Yorkers fell into the middle class, comprised of lesser merchants, small-scale entrepreneurs, and the more prosperous artisans, and their economic and social positions varied considerably. The majority shared the benefits of the city's prosperity and lived comfortably, albeit far below the life-style accorded the wealthy. This large, diverse middle class had acquired a consciousness of themselves as a class in the years just prior to the Revolution and had long expressed antiaristocratic sentiments. They were not levelers, however; quite the contrary, they shared many of the elite's ideological beliefs, most notably the fundamental right to private property. They accepted the virtues of the Protestant ethic and advocated a society in which opportunity was equally accessible to all.[19]

New York's artisans also appear to have benefited from the economic growth of the city, although fluctuations existed among the various crafts. Despite the gains, new economic conditions resulting from improvements in transportation, the broadening of markets, the expansion of credit, and the emergence of the merchant-capitalist began to erode the position of the city's artisans in the 1820s. While they remained committed to republican ideals, they also were becoming increasingly apprehensive that changing economic conditions would undermine these principles. They were especially concerned with the growing inegalitarian society emerging from the capitalist economy. Although the thrust of the workers' movement would not occur for some time, their concern was such that the New York Workingman's party was established by the end of the 1820s in an effort to maintain a competitive position.[20]

Socioeconomic gradations existed even among those on the bottom rung of New York's social ladder, although the bulk of the lower class lived collectively on the fringes of poverty. During the colonial period New York had its share of urban poor, but the crisis of poverty intensified in the decade following the Revolution as a result of changing economic, social, and demographic conditions. In conjunction with other factors, at the start of the nineteenth century the swelling population gave rise to high-density urban slums, the worst of which, though not atypical, was the section known as Five Points, at the southernmost tip of Manhattan. There, among dilapidated buildings, filthy streets, basement saloons, and dance halls, lived a majority of the city's Irish immigrants. Respectable

New Yorkers viewed this area as a breeding ground for vice, crime, and disease, "the most depraved few acres in North America."[21]

The emergence of urban slums symbolized the host of social problems that beset New York during this period of metamorphosis. By 1820 some of these difficulties had already crystallized, while others just beginning to emerge would become serious only in subsequent decades. New Yorkers increasingly complained of the hazards and harassments of city life, but their greatest concern was that middle-class values and norms had little meaning for immigrants, blacks, and other inhabitants of the slums. Already fearful that urban change was undermining the institutions of social order, they created numerous voluntary associations both to deal with the perplexities of urban life and as a means of preserving a stable, well-ordered society. By 1825 there were over a hundred benevolent associations in New York.[22]

Despite these difficulties New Yorkers remained generally optimistic about themselves and their future. They continued to see themselves as residents of a burgeoning commercial and financial metropolis, an outlook largely absent among citizens of other leading cities. While increased congestion and numerous public nuisances disturbed New Yorkers, they simultaneously saw these as indicators of the city's economic superiority. Commentators in the 1820s "more than ever before detected a dynamism in the life of New York that derived in part from the vitality of its fluid, effervescent society, in part from the rapid accelerating vigor of its commercial life."[23]

Self-confident New Yorkers continued to pursue an active intellectual, cultural, and social life. Intellectual endeavors showed great vitality in the first quarter of the nineteenth century as the Knickerbocker school, led by James Fenimore Cooper, William Cullen Bryant, and Washington Irving, established Manhattan as America's literary capital. While the city's leadership in this area soon passed to Boston, it did assume and maintain a preeminent position in the field of journalism, centered, not surprisingly, around the practical, mundane, and financial. New York had eleven newspapers by 1800, and as early as 1817 the ability of the city's aggressive journalists to get the European news first established for New Yorkers an "informational hegemony." Even with the declining importance of foreign news by the 1820s, New York retained its position as the communication center by dominating the flow of domestic information.[24] New Yorkers also engaged in a variety of cultural, charitable, and religious endeavors in the generation following independence. Newly created voluntary associations fostered philanthropic, educational, and religious works. Frequently established and led by New York elites, these associations were designed to inculcate discipline and compliance on the part of the masses, even as they permitted the wealthy to exercise and display class leadership and provide them with rationales for their holding wealth and wielding power.[25]

The cosmopolitan nature of New York has been part of the city's heritage almost from its inception. In colonial days this spirit derived from the blending of different cultures and languages, the greater degree of religious tolerance, the life-style of the aristocracy, and the generally favorable attitude of public officials toward pastimes and amusements. The social and economic developments of the post-Revolutionary period further enhanced the city's cosmopolitan reputation. In both tone and setting New York's cultural activities differed from their northeastern competitors. Whereas Bostonians, for example, viewed their city as the "Athens of America," New Yorkers likened Manhattan to London economically and Paris socially.[26] The mercantile community in New York often sought respite from their devotion to the countinghouse in a variety of light amusements and the gaiety of nightlife. The social activities of the upper class were largely exclusive. Dancing was very popular with New York's fashionable set, and concerts, lectures, and the theater attracted many from the upper class. While club life was not in vogue until the mid-1830s, several exclusive fraternal and patriotic societies already catered to the connoisseurs of good food, drink, and conversation. For all the fullness of the social life of the elite, they abstained from the ostentatious display that had characterized New York's colonial aristocracy and would eventually distinguish the "smart set" of the Gilded Age.[27]

Recreational diversions were not the prerogative of the wealthy. Since colonial days the middle class had pursued an active social life, and their diversions were often the same as those of the city's elite. While the recreational patterns of New Yorkers had a certain class orientation, their relative inexpensiveness and the absence of legalistic barriers prevented any social group from obtaining exclusive control of most amusements. Class differences were seen more in terms of the form the activity took, the extent of participation, and the people with whom one chose to participate. Although a combination of factors mitigated against any extensive recreational pursuits by the lower class, they were not without their moments of leisure. Most of their activities tended to center around the tavern; however, they appear to have joined in several recreations having wide community appeal.[28]

By 1820 New Yorkers had inherited a rich sports heritage. Almost from the immediate settlement of New Amsterdam the seeds of sport fell on fertile ground. The city's first residents brought with them a love of physical activity and pursued a variety of outdoor amusements. The arrival of the English augmented sports participation and injected a new set of diversions. During the 1700s the economic prosperity of the city, its cosmopolitan nature, the cavalier spirit of crown officials, the emergence of a wealthy aristocracy, and the favorable attitudes toward amusements in general all stimulated the growth of sport. By the outbreak of the Revolution New Yorkers led a very active sporting life by existing standards. With only Charleston, South Carolina, as its rival, New York was able to call itself America's leading sports city.[29]

The War for Independence had little impact on sport in New York. Although the Continental Congress tried to suppress numerous recreations, British control of New York and the surrounding area following the campaign of 1776 made the edict useless there. For the duration of the war a constant round of sporting events took place for the diversion of English officers and their troops. However, several factors did mitigate against the growth of sport in the generation following independence. The evacuation of English officers and their Loyalist companions removed many of the leading sports figures from colonial New York, and their places were not filled by the new social leaders, in part because of their efforts to adjust to the frenzied tempo of New York created by the changing economic conditions, their somewhat more conservative life-style, and the increasing opposition to certain sports because of their association with the colonial aristocracy, gambling, or violation of the Sabbath. The decline of horse racing and its legal banning in 1802 were the clearest expression that the golden age of colonial sport had passed. Although less active than their earlier counterparts, New Yorkers in the generation following the Revolution did continue to pursue a variety of physical recreations.[30]

A host of demographic, economic, social, and political changes continued to alter the character and structure of New York in the half-century following 1820, with the population explosion again serving as the catalyst for change. By 1870 nearly a million people lived in New York, newcomers being largely responsible for the city's swelling ranks. Unlike the earlier period when Americans in general and New Englanders in particular constituted the largest contingent of new arrivals in the city, the majority after 1820 were from abroad. Starting in the second quarter of the nineteenth century New York shifted from a city populated mainly by Americans to one populated mainly by foreigners: by 1870 roughly four out of every nine New Yorkers were foreign-born, nearly half of them Irish and another third of German extraction. A clearer indication of the foreign influence in the city was the fact that only slightly more than one in six New Yorkers could claim two native-born parents.[31] During the antebellum period tensions between Americans and foreigners would color much of New York life and its institutions, and on several occasions would explode in nativistic outbursts.[32]

The numerical growth of Manhattan only partially revealed the urbanization of the city. By the Civil War decade New York had become the dynamic center of a loosely knit metropolitan area. More than half a million people resided in the four other boroughs that are now part of New York City, with the overwhelming majority living in Brooklyn, then the nation's third largest city. In addition, significant increments occurred across the river in New Jersey. By 1870 Newark was the fourteenth largest American city, with a population in excess of 100,000, and the number of people residing in Jersey City rose from roughly 29,000 in 1860 to 82,000 a decade later.[33]

New York's economic growth continued to coincide with the urbanization of the city and the surrounding area. By the mid-nineteenth century the entire country, with the exception of New England, became New York's hinterland, with rival cities competing with each other for business New York could not handle. By 1860 two-thirds of America's imports and one-third of its exports passed through Manhattan, which stood firmly as America's premier port and was ranked worldwide behind only London and Liverpool. New York also emerged as the nation's leading city in manufacturing by 1830; forty years later the value of goods produced in the city exceeded $300 million. Despite the growth of industry, however, New York could not be described as a manufacturing city. In 1870 only one-tenth of the city's work force engaged in manufacturing. Commerce, finance, and land remained the major economic areas of New York's wealthiest residents, and the city continued to build on its reputation as America's credit and banking center. In addition to the growth of highly speculative commercial banks, New Yorkers created more conservative insurance and trust companies, as well as mutual saving banks. By 1870 deposits in New York banks reached almost $250 million.[34]

The benefits of the city's economic growth were hardly distributed equally, and increasingly New York was viewed as a society divided into rich and poor. The ability of merchant-capitalists to take greater advantage of the changing economic universe resulted in an ever-increasing concentration of wealth in the hands of the few. By 1845 a mere 1 percent of New York's residents held nearly half of the city's wealth, and the leading 4 percent possessed almost four-fifths of the total financial resources. The proportion of wealth held by New York's elite no doubt rose over the next few decades, and in 1861 one writer estimated that 115 millionaires resided in New York. The 1863 tax roll also indicates the fabulous wealth of some New Yorkers: seventy-nine residents earned more than $100,000 that year, and retailer Alexander T. Stewart made over a million dollars.[35] Even as the rich became richer, the economic expansion of New York permitted newcomers to climb high on the financial ladder. More than half of New York's most affluent residents just prior to the Civil War represented either first- or second-generation wealth, and five-eighths of them had been born outside of New York.[36]

During the antebellum period the Knickerbockers established numerous social clubs as a way of proclaiming their status and identifying it to peers and inferiors. From their base in business the nouveaux riches infiltrated the charitable, social, and cultural institutions of the established elite. Despite its presence and its growing ostentation, New York high society by mid-century had retained some of its tradition of graciousness and modesty. The lavishness that would later mark New York's "smart set" was already evident, however, even more so by 1870. As early as the 1840s older elites quietly berated the life-style of the nouveaux riches, and criticism of first- and second-generation arrivistes intensified after the Civil War.[37]

While members of the new elite began to exert considerable influence on business and to a lesser extent cultural and charitable activities, professional politicians replaced businessmen as the city's elected officials. The political dominance of the Tweed Ring in post–Civil War New York symbolized this trend and marked the emergence of the urban political machine. More than a quarter-century earlier, men of plebian background began serving as city councilmen, a change that in part was due to the interaction of politics with the city's evolving social, demographic, and economic institutions. The older upper and middle classes, who never presented any effective competition, failed to adjust to the changing urban conditions that spawned these new politicians, who in turn were adept at exploiting the growing complexities and chaotic conditions of middle- and lower-class urban life. The success of these men also rested on their willingness to trade jobs for immigrant votes and special favors for businessmen's bribes and support, as well as their ability to act as middlemen in bridging the widening gap between social and business interest and obsolete and ineffective political institutions.[38]

New York's middle class fell far behind the upper class in terms of wealth. While one observer of the city noted that the 1860 tax roll reflected the paucity of men of moderate means, this group in fact constituted nearly 40 percent of the city's population by the mid-nineteenth century. Made up of small businessmen, professionals, clerks, salespeople, and the most highly paid, skilled artisans, the middle class was an important component of commercial New York.[39]

The tremendous increase in the number of poor New Yorkers was one result of the city's changing population and economy. By 1870 more than five of every eight residents were worth less than $100, with immigrants overwhelmingly clinging to the lowest rung of the economic ladder. Aided by transportation developments, the upper and middle classes moved north, while the pauper class continued to crowd into the city's lower wards. With 163.5 people per acre living in Manhattan's seven lower wards by 1850, New York had become the most densely populated city in the world. A decade later, about 500,000 people were crowded into 18,000 tenement houses, and more than 5 percent resided in squalid cellar dwellings.[40] New York "had never been a model of civic order and virtue," as one scholar notes, "but the situation seemed to significantly worsen during the generally depressed and depressing decade after 1837." While each of the growing number of problems had a unique origin and solution, common themes were evident in the various ills that beset New Yorkers. The city's less formal institutions of the pre-1820 period were unable to cope with problems of overcrowding, poverty, crime, fires, and so on. The erosion of the old community under the pressures of modernization necessitated that New Yorkers begin their own "search for order."[41]

Reformers, motivated by a collage of reasons, were primarily, if not always, concerned with the social order. Social problems were generally considered a product of individual moral defects, which were believed to be especially prevalent among foreigners; hence, the early reformers focused their efforts on religious and educational instruction through benevolent voluntary associations, which did little to ameliorate the city's diverse social ills. The magnitude of the problem was largely responsible for their failure; however, their efforts also were limited by the inability of their leaders to grasp the depth and nature of the urban crisis, by their lack of sympathy and understanding for the people they professed to help, and by their greater concern for social control.[42]

The inadequacies of the voluntary association approach became increasingly evident by the 1840s. While reform throughout the antebellum period remained closely allied with religion, reformers increasingly couched their rhetoric in secular terms and expressed the need to create more pragmatic solutions to social problems. Voluntary associations and city missions thus began to cater as much to the physical as to the spiritual well-being of the downtrodden. This new orientation was dramatically illustrated in the expanding role of municipal government, as New Yorkers came to believe that city officials should assume responsiblility for promoting and controlling many of the institutions designed to provide social stability and preserve private property. Consequently, the municipal government played an ever-expanding role in the major social institutions of the city. By 1870 New Yorkers had established permanent governing bodies in several critical areas of urban life, such as education, law enforcement, fire protection, and sanitation.[43]

While urban growth produced a host of social problems, economic expansion enhanced New York's cosmopolitan reputation and continued to stimulate the growing entertainment industry. In the mid-1850s one newspaper stated that it had "never heard of anybody so unreasonable as to complain of a dearth of amusements in New York, or the absence of a variety in their character." By the post–Civil War years New York had at least twenty theaters and offered a broad spectrum of entertainment, from opera to burlesque. Box office receipts soon averaged three million dollars a year, and the New York *Herald* viewed this as an indicator of the city's prosperity and commercial status. Club life began in earnest in the 1830s with the establishment of a number of influential, elite organizations; forty years later a leading observer noted that approximately 100 clubs, with not less than 5,000 members, existed in New York. While social clubs became the domain of the upper and, to a lesser extent, middle classes, the tavern remained the center of lower-class amusements. Nearly 6,000 such businesses existed in New York by the 1850s. Although respectable New Yorkers viewed the tavern and other lower-class hangouts as the breeding grounds for most of the city's social ills, they perceived the creation of Central Park as an expression of New York's civilized and cosmopolitan character. Many park supporters felt that this new recreational area would foster a democratic community, uplifting the downtrodden and integrating them into the mainstream of middle-class values.[44]

The transformation of New York from a preindustrial city to an emerging modern city ushered in a new era in sports. Already the beneficiaries of a rich sports heritage by the standards of the day, between 1820 and 1870 sports participants in New York would markedly increase and athletics would assume a modern structure and ideology. Similar to the modernization of other New York institutions, the revolutionary changes in sport would not be completed by 1870; nevertheless, the essential framework in terms of an institutional structure and ideological sanctions would be firmly established.

SECTION I

SPORTS OF THE TURF:
THOROUGHBREDS AND TROTTERS

May 27, 1823, was a beautiful spring day in New York. The city bubbled with anticipation, for on this day the North and the South would do battle on the turf for $20,000 per side. Ever since the sectional contest had been announced the previous November, excitement had been mounting throughout the country, and at least a week prior to the big event spectators began to find their way into the city. By the morning of the race an estimated 20,000 visitors were taxing the resources of hotels, boardinghouses, inns, and taverns in the metropolitan area. Local newspapers concurred that never before had such a strain been placed on the city.[1]

For several days prior to the match people made preparations for the trip to the Union Course in Jamaica, on Long Island. Every public vehicle and many private ones were readied. Ferry companies advertised the best and quickest way to make the crossover from the city, and newspapers advised the public to purchase tickets in advance and leave the city early. Beginning at dawn on the appointed day the roads to the track were jammed with carriages of all kinds, interspersed with men on horseback and on foot. By mid-afternoon the city appeared to have been evacuated. At post time about 50,000 spectators reportedly packed the relatively new course.[2] With the stands unable to accommodate the crowd, many people spilled onto the track, forming a solid line for a quarter of a mile to the right and left of the judges' box. With some difficulty racing officials partially cleared the running area, and at 1:10 P.M., ten minutes after the designated starting time, Eclipse and Henry, representing the North and South respectively, went off to the taps of the drums.[3]

Given the reputations of these two horses, the large amount of money

27

staked, and the tremendous sectional and state pride riding on the outcome, the general public was aware that this was the most important horse race ever run in America. They also recognized that the match would rekindle interest in the sport throughout the North in general and New York in particular. However, the huge throng of spectators and those who impatiently awaited the results throughout the nation could not foresee that this intersectional race would come to symbolize the birth of a new era in American sport.

Although the Eclipse-Henry race marked the beginning of a new athletic period, organized horse racing in America began in the seventeenth century. Richard Nicholls, the first English governor of New York, established the institution of racing in 1665 by offering a silver cup to be run for each spring and fall. In the eighteenth century organized racing emerged throughout most of colonial America. By the 1760s the local character of horse racing, in common with other phases of colonial life, began to dissolve as leading sportsmen raced their horses on different tracks throughout the colonies. By the outbreak of the Revolution horse racing had assumed a more coherent, organized pattern, yet it lacked uniform rules, well-kept tracks, and a means for the dissemination of racing knowledge and statistics. Another half-century passed before horse racing took on the characteristics of a modern sport.[4]

During the 1700s horse racing was popular among New York's gentry, and annual races were run regularly for purses ranging from ten to fifty pounds. By the Revolutionary period only Charlestonians could compete with New Yorkers in their enthusiastic support for horse racing. While the struggle for independence had serious repercussions for horse racing in most colonies, it had virtually no effect on the fortunes of the sport in New York. In 1774 the Continental Congress banned horse racing, but British occupation of New York guaranteed its continuation. With races often run for the diversion of British officers and troops, New York became "the center of racing until the war was over."[5]

Organized racing continued in New York for more than a decade following the evacuation of the British army. However, difficulties in the breeding industry, the absence of local leadership, and the increasing strength of an antiracing crusade in the North made it impossible to resurrect the glory days of colonial racing. By the start of the nineteenth century those opposed to racing took command, and in 1802 New York became the first of several northern states to abolish horse racing. The Act to Prevent Horseracing ended legalized racing in New York for nearly twenty years,[6] although it failed to totally curtail the sport in the metropolitan area. Enforcement was lax, and a handful of owners continued to breed and race their horses. In 1804 a group of Long Island agriculturists began sponsoring races, but after a few campaigns their organization collapsed. Another racing club was created in 1819, but it too proved unsuccessful. Despite the persistence of racing, critics of the legislation claimed that it severely hindered the improvement of the breed in New York and New Jersey,[7] and by 1821 they succeeded in having the bill modified. The first state to abolish horse racing became the first to reconsider its position.

Drawing heavily on a rich racing heritage, those who revived the sport in New York also sparked the emergence of a new era in racing. In the next half-century horse racing would undergo revolutionary change. By 1870 the style of thoroughbred races would be radically altered and the sport would adopt some modern structures. Harness racing, by contrast, would modernize more rapidly. A popular, though informal and unorganized, pastime during the first quarter of the nineteenth century, trotting would become America's first truly modern sport.

The racehorse American Eclipse. From a drawing by Edward Troye.

The 1845 intersectional race between Fashion and Peytonia, at the Union Course, on Long Island. From a drawing by Currier and Ives.

2

The Early Modernization of
Horse Racing, 1820–45

In 1820 horse racing was still a premodern sport. It had achieved some degree of organization during the colonial period, but by 1820 it was organized only on a local level. Rules continued to vary widely among the many local jockey clubs, and no means existed for the dissemination of racing knowledge and statistics. The style of racing conformed to the traditional pattern, with its emphasis on long-distance contests and heat races. The sport was still conducted on a limited basis, with small fields and few spectators. By 1845, however, thoroughbred racing had begun to assume a modern structure due to the growth of the sport nationally. Sports journals and stud books surfaced, national racing schedules were publicized, and efforts were made to standardize the rules. The appearance of track promoters and enclosed racing grounds illustrated the growing commercialization of the sport.

A return to legalized racing in New York in 1821 played an important part in the sport's modernization. During the next twenty-five years New York would be the center of horse racing: it offered the biggest purses, the largest crowds, and the most important races, including all five major intersectional contests. The creation in 1831 of the *Spirit of the Times,* the first weekly sports journal, further enhanced New York's leadership role. Despite its preeminent position, however, racing in New York followed a cyclical pattern and by 1845 was in a virtual state of collapse. Numerous factors would contribute to the vicissitudes of the sport, including the interaction between economic factors, both internal and external, and the extent to which wealthy New Yorkers were willing to sponsor horse racing. The tension created between the traditional racing world and the emerging modern one was the major reason for the waning popularity of the sport. Unable to survive within the traditional framework, yet unwilling to commit to the modern one, New York horsemen temporarily gave up on the sport. With the decline of racing in New York, the early modernization of thoroughbred racing reached an impasse.

Horse racing in New York began to prosper in the years following the revival of the sport in 1821. The establishment of a jockey club, the creation of a new racetrack, the encouragement by the press, and two intersectional contests in the early 1820s all contributed to the growing popularity of the sport. The exploits of Eclipse were the major reason for this renewed interest. By the end of the decade, however, the sport entered a down cycle and it appeared that horse racing might be discontinued.

Legalized racing resumed in New York State in 1821 when legislators passed a bill to modify the 1802 antiracing law. Dwight Akers, a turf historian, viewed the move as an indicator that New Yorkers were tired of their "noble experiment." Closer scrutiny of the situation does not substantiate this perspective. The bill, introduced by John Alsop King at the end of the 1821 legislative session, attracted little attention or debate, and the closeness of the final vote, 53–50, indicates that overwhelming sentiment did not exist for reviving the sport. Quite the contrary, even while passing the bill legislators continued to express a distrust of the demoralizing concomitants of horse racing. Thus, they not only limited racing to twice a year in Queens County, on Long Island, but overwhelmingly defeated a proposal to also permit racing in nearby Kings County. The legislators took steps to further safeguard the public by making it mandatory that the sheriff be present on racing days to preserve order and remove all the gaming tables.[1]

Support for the bill rested on the time-honored justification for horse racing—that it would stimulate improvement of the breed. In addition, proponents asserted that the antiracing legislation had been ineffective and only served to place "sharps" in control of the sport. By sanctioning trials of speed, respectable citizens could reassert their influence and give the proper tone to horse racing.[2] It is impossible to determine precisely who were the chief proponents of the 1821 bill, although they probably were influential gentlemen, turfmen, and breeders, some of whom illegally raced their horses on Long Island tracks during the years the sport was banned. One fact is clear, however: New York City and the surrounding area played a crucial role in the bill's passage. City assemblymen voted seven to one for the bill, and those from nearby Suffolk and Queens counties provided four positive and no negative votes. Given the slim victory, this eleven-to-one vote in favor of the legislation was critical to its adoption.[3]

To encourage horse racing in New York prominent residents of the city and the surrounding area established a new jockey club, the New York Association for the Improvement of the Breed (NYAIB). Through liberal purses they sought to stimulate the sport and, more specifically, entice southern owners to bring their horses north to race. A new racetrack, the Union Course, was constructed on Long Island, and when it opened in October 1821, it quickly became the center of racing in New York and throughout the North, a position it maintained for the next quarter-century.[4] The efforts of the NYAIB to rejuvenate horse racing won the unconditional support of a large segment of the New York press. They pointed with pride to the jockey club's ability to preserve order and prevent gambling. During each of the early meetings they notified their readers that good sport would take place, claiming that each was the best racing card ever seen in New York. The *Post* noted in 1823 that the NYAIB had "spared no pain, nor expense" in making horse racing fashionable, enjoyable, and comfortable.[5]

The style of racing remained as it had been during the colonial period. In the fall and spring New Yorkers held three-day racing meetings. Since horsemen considered "bottom" (endurance) as well as speed to be essential for a premier horse, races were run in heats at distances from one to four miles. With one contest occurring daily, only a limited number of horses were present for each session. The prize money the NYAIB offered throughout the 1820s ranged from $1,000 to $1,900 per meeting; purses varied for each race, with the biggest share going to the winner of the prestigious four-mile race. The size of the stakes also depended on the number of horses starting and whether any southern-owned horses were in the field. While small by today's standard, the purses exceeded amounts offered at southern tracks. Clearly, a variety of factors helped to generate tremendous excitement in the renewed races, but the key was the performers who attracted the crowds. Given the deterioration of horse racing in New York since the Revolution, something more was necessary than just good horses or interesting contests. What was needed was a superstar, and Eclipse filled the bill.

Foaled in 1814, Eclipse was owned and bred by Gen. Nathaniel Coles of Long Island. As was the custom of the day, the colt was not put into training for three years. In 1818 Coles entered Eclipse in a race on Long Island, a contest he easily won, and the following year he sold the horse to Cornelius Van Ranst of New York City for $3,000. Entered in two Long Island races that year, the horse emerged victorious on both occasions.[6] By 1820 Eclipse was ready to be put to stud, but the response to Van Ranst's advertisement brought the owner little satisfaction. In an attempt to stimulate business Van Ranst took out another ad: "The subscriber, the owner of the celebrated horse, American Eclipse, have concluded to put him to mares for the ensuing season, but desiring to remove all doubts to his being the greatest *racer* in the United States, hereby offers to match him against any horse, mare or gelding, that can be named within one month from this date." Van Ranst was willing to race for not less than $2,000 but found no takers. Placed into stud, Eclipse did not race in 1820. Given his age and the condition of horse racing in new York, his racing career appeared to be over.[7]

With the relaxation of antiracing legislation in 1821, Van Ranst brought Eclipse out of retirement both to encourage the sport and to stimulate interest in his horse. During the first three racing sessions at the Union Course Eclipse's contests against the best horses from the South drew large crowds, and each time he emerged triumphant. By 1822 most New Yorkers shared the *Post*'s opinion that Eclipse "was the greatest horse for bottom and speed in America."[8] Then, just prior to the fall 1822 racing meeting in New York, James J. Harrison of Virginia proposed a race between Eclipse and his own horse Sir Charles, to take place in mid-November at the Washington Course for a stake of $5,000–$10,000. Harrison declared that if Eclipse emerged victorious he could retire as the undisputed champion. Van Ranst accepted, choosing to wager the larger sum so that the "objective of [the] contest may correspond with the fame of the horses."[9]

The Eclipse–Sir Charles match, wrote one New York newspaper, caused "great anxiety among the sportsmen of the city, in fact we may say among those who are not sportsmen, for the interest in the great National Race seemed to be universal." The largest crowd ever at the Washington Course had come out to see the race, but at the last moment it was cancelled due to an injury Sir Charles had sustained during a workout a few days earlier. The backers of Eclipse refused an offer of $1,000 to postpone the race for ten days; instead, the forfeiture of $5,000 was paid. Then, in lieu of the original contest (four miles, best two out of three heats), Harrison suggested one four-mile race between the two horses for $1,500. The proposal was immediately accepted, and Eclipse was an easy victor. It was rumored that Harrison had not expected his horse to win but had made the offer to ease the disappointment of the crowd. Members of New York's jockey club attending the match denied this claim, noting that the backers of Sir Charles believed he could go at least one heat; they further pointed out that some southerners had wagered heavily on the horse to win.[10]

New York sportsmen felt that the events on the Washington turf had conclusively demonstrated the superiority of Eclipse. Southerners disagreed, arguing that the qualities of northern and southern horses had not been tested fairly. Another race was inevitable. William R. Johnson, of Virginia, nicknamed the "Napoleon of the Turf," immediately proposed another contest. He agreed to come up with a southern horse to race against Eclipse at the Union Course the following spring for $20,000 per side, with a $3,000 forfeiture. The challenge was quickly accepted, and John C. Stevens, of Hoboken, New Jersey, posted the forfeit money on behalf of a group of New York turfmen.[11]

The action of these New Yorkers illustrates the supreme confidence they had in Eclipse. The horse had already been used for stud and would be nine years old by the time of the scheduled contest. Furthermore, the southerners would not have to name their horse until a half-hour before the race, while any kind of accident could befall the star of New York racing between November 1822 and May 1823. Johnson was given full responsibility for the southern strategy and could command the services of any southern thoroughbred. He decided to prepare no less than five horses for the race. As the day of the race approached, the North-South battle was the major topic of conversation in New York. The *American* stated that Eclipse "is in every mouth and hopes and fears hang upon the issue, such as in this country at least never waited upon brute beast (we mean no disrespect to the noble champion) before." Most New Yorkers were confident of their hero's ability, yet there were those who expressed concern. John Pintard confessed that since Eclipse's power was known, "it is presumed that the South would not attempt to match him unless in full confidence of success."[12]

At roughly 12:30 P.M. on May 27, 1823, the southern challenger, the four-year-old Henry, made his appearance on the track at the Union Course. When Eclipse entered his northern supporters were dismayed by the fact that Samuel Purdy, his regular jockey, was not aboard; instead, William Crafts took the reins. By lot Eclipse drew the inside pole for the first four-mile heat. Henry's trainer placed his horse well out on the track, approximately twenty-five feet from his adversary, and at the taps of the drums Henry sprinted out to a three-length lead by the first quarter of a mile. The position of the horses remained unchanged until the homestretch, when Eclipse cut the lead to a length and a half. He could not make up any more ground, however, and Henry emerged victorious in the record-setting time of 7:37 minutes.[13]

Eclipse's supporters were shocked by his defeat, the first time in his racing career that he had lost a heat. Many northerners felt that Crafts could not handle Eclipse and that a replacement was necessary. (It was not uncommon during this period to change riders between heats.) Precisely what occurred at this juncture is shrouded in the numerous tales and anecdotes connected with the race, but it is clear that Samuel Purdy was aboard Eclipse for the second heat.[14]

Henry again took an early lead and his rider set a quick pace in the hope of wearing down the older horse. For about two and three-quarter miles the southern horse held a two-length lead. At this point Purdy began to take Eclipse to the outside, but then he gambled and pushed his horse to the inside to pass. Amid the roar of the crowd, John Randolph of Roanoke, a leading backer of Henry, was heard to shout in his high-pitched voice, "You can't do it Mr. Purdy! You can't do it Mr. Purdy!" The veteran rider did do it, however, and as the horses entered the backstretch of the final mile, Eclipse overtook his adversary. Despite Henry's late rush, Eclipse won, setting a record for the fastest second heat, 7:49 minutes.

The momentum had shifted and southern forces felt compelled to change their jockey. In the third and deciding heat Eclipse quickly gained the lead and under Purdy's constant prodding was able to maintain it for three and three-quarter miles. Henry tried to come from behind, but his charge at the New York horse proved to no avail. The winning time of 8:24 minutes indicates the horses' state of exhaustion.[15]

Those who had not attended the contest waited anxiously for the results. The *Post* came out with a special edition, probably the first sporting extra in American journalism, while the *American* did not go to press until informed of the winner. The coverage of the race in subsequent days was extraordinary, especially given the four-sheet format of local newspapers and the limited space allocated to news. The picture drawn by the New York newspapers was generally favorable. They noted that numerous men of wealth and taste were present and that the ladies' stands were nicely filled. Although the match attracted a large crowd, perfect decorum was evident among a gathering of good losers and subdued winners.[16]

Several newspapers expressed certain reservations about the contest, however. The *Statesmen* admitted sectional partisanship had been restrained but objected to intersectional races because they might eventually lead to deep-rooted hostility. The severest criticism of the contest stemmed from the heavy wagering on the outcome. The *Niles Register* (Baltimore) estimated that over a million dollars had changed hands and insisted that "few have gained much by it—but many have lost what should have went to the payment of their just debts, and are ruined." The *Post* denied that heavy betting had taken place, given the significance of the contest, but that contention appears to be as invalid as the figures of the *Register*. There seems to be no doubt that extensive wagering occurred, especially in view of the strong state and sectional pride riding on the outcome of the race and the fact that several of the horsemen involved had reputations as heavy gamblers.[17]

In contrast to the picture of gracious losers presented by New York newspapers, many southerners were openly disgruntled. For a year following the match they continued to insist that they had the superior horse, and they offered a variety of excuses for Henry's defeat.[18] At one time or another several southerners proposed a rematch. The first offer came just one day after the race, when Johnson suggested a confrontation between Eclipse and an unnamed southern contender, for $20,000–$50,000, to take place at the upcoming fall meeting in Washington. This time Stevens rejected the challenge on behalf of the northern syndicate, stating that the "bet just decided was made under circumstances of excitement, which might in some measure apologize for its rashness but would scarcely justify it as an example; and I trust that the part I took in it, will not be considered proof of my intention to become a patron of sporting on so extensive a scale." He claimed that the supporters of Eclipse remained supremely confident in the horse's ability to win, but they felt that because of Eclipse's age nothing should be done "to risk the life or reputation of the noble animal whose generous, and almost incredible exertions, have gained for the North so signal a victory, and for himself such well earned and never failing renown." Despite numerous speculations that Eclipse would return to the turf one more time, Van Ranst resolutely decided to retire the horse undefeated, a position the New York press supported.[19]

Coming at a time when sectional tensions were intensifying—following the Missouri Comprise and preceding the presidential election of 1824— the race, like many international sporting contests today, took on symbolic meaning. For some observers Eclipse's victory was a fortuitous omen for the northern candidate, John Q. Adams. The political symbolism associated with the contest helps in part to explain the angry rhetoric that followed the race. The *American* noted that northerners were being warned to bear "their triumph submissively, and . . . the safety of the union depends on our moderation." Critical of southern sensitivity, it claimed that the Union did not depend on the outcome of a horse race and that the results would not aid the cause of the northern candidate. Yet northerners viewed Eclipse's success as more than a vindication of their training methods. They identified with the horse's courage, confidence, and success and felt they had demonstrated their own manliness by supporting the aged but tested hero against considerable odds. Moreover, they realized that they had defeated the South at its own game, just a few years after the revival of the sport in the North. The meaning of the race was not lost on southerners, either, and helps to clarify why they were so desirous of a rematch and so adamant in their refusal to accept Eclipse's superiority despite his constant triumphs. The account of Josiah Quincy, son of a prominent Boston minister and a spectator on that fateful day, illustrates the race's lasting symbolic significance: "It seems to have foreshadowed the sterner conflict that occurred forty years afterwards. The victory resulted in both cases from the same cause—the power of endurance."[20]

Eclipse's success brought with it a dramatic rise in his stud fee, which was what Van Ranst had hoped for when he brought the horse out of retirement. From $12.50 per mare in 1820 the price jumped to $50 immediately following the race with Henry, and by the mid-1830s Eclipse commanded the fantastic sum of $100 for each mare he served.[21] He remained the property of Van Ranst until 1825, when Stevens and his brother-in-law, Walter Livingston, bought the horse for $10,000, to prevent his sale to southerners. The *Post* insisted, "That is as it should be. Eclipse would have been a loss to the State of New York and New Jersey that could have been difficult, if not impossible, to repair." When the Stevens-Livingston partnership dissolved two years later, Livingston acquired the horse at public auction for $8,050. In 1832 Eclipse was moved to Virginia, ironically coming under the charge of James J. Harrison and later Col. Johnson. After several seasons in the Old Dominion, the horse went on to Kentucky, where he remained for the rest of his life, although he was leased on occasion to breeders in Alabama and Tennessee. On July 11, 1847, the great horse died in Shelby, Kentucky, at the age of thirty-three.[22]

Horse racing in New York continued to prosper after Eclipse's retirement. Although no superstar emerged, the quality of racehorses was high and the number of horses lining up for every race increased.[23] The climax of the early years of racing in New York came in 1825 when the long-desired North-South rematch took place. The battle between Ariel of New York and Flirtilla of Virginia created excitement among the city's sportsmen, although it did not stir the imagination of the populace, either in New York or nationally, as the Eclipse-Henry confrontation had. The race proved to be an exact reversal of the original match, with Ariel winning the first heat and Flirtilla the next two. The South thereby achieved the revenge it so urgently sought. While races between northern and southern horses continued in New York, eleven years passed before another intersectional match took place.[24]

By the mid-1820s New York's newspapers contended that the revival of horse racing had been an unqualified success, and they pointed to the utilitarian benefits derived from the sport. The *Post* stated that the NYAIB had effectively stimulated interest among farmers in the breeding of horses, the result being an extremely profitable pursuit as well as a stock "which could bid defiance to the whole United States." The *American* noted that objections to racing may be raised because of its association with gambling, but it justified the sport on utilitarian grounds: "The improvement of our horses is indeed manifest; and reciprocal benefits to the raiser and consumer of this article of luxury and use, ought to be a sufficient balance to the objections which questionably exist to a certain degree against racing." In addition, the newspaper offered a new argument in favor of horse racing, one that quite possibly emerged from the Eclipse-Henry experience:

it pointed out that the sport attracted visitors who spent their money in the city.[25]

Horse racing in New York experienced several lean years following the Ariel-Flirtilla race, with several interacting problems contributing to the decline of the sport, among them the deterioration of the Union Course. The track there was in poor condition, the clubhouse needed repairs, the stands were decaying, and the police force was inadequate. The NYAIB's financial plight also aggravated matters. The club was in debt to the owners of the racetrack, and, more significantly, the purses it offered were insufficient to attract good horses, particularly from the South. As interest waned and attendance dropped it appeared that the NYAIB might dissolve.

To rectify the problems of horse racing, Cadwallader R. Colden, an NYAIB member, attempted to put the sport on a firmer economic foundation. He proposed that the club sell $10,000 worth of stock, in shares ranging from $500 to $1,000. Although he found several supporters, most NYAIB members were unwilling to invest such a large amount of money in horse racing. Colden then offered a second, more acceptable plan: he would assume full responsibility for the management of the Union Course if the club resigned its interest in the track.[26] Thus, in 1829 Colden took over the racetrack and introduced two innovations to stimulate the sport and make his investment profitable. With the racing schedule already extended from three to five days at each meeting, Colden believed that the practice of offering only one race each day did not create sufficient excitement to attract even the most ardent spectators for so many consecutive days; hence, he decided to reduce the number of racing days and generally offer two races each day. To compensate for the lost days Colden offered a second racing card, two weeks after the first meeting, thus making it economically feasible for good horses to be brought to the New York tracks. His second innovation was to enclose the entire course and charge an admission fee to the track. Although charging admission to a horse race was not new, in the past such fees were either for choice locations or a place in the grandstand. Now everybody who wanted to see the race had to pay a price, ranging from three dollars for a four-horse carriage to a quarter for general admission. Colden recognized that there would be some resistance to his plan, but he felt that the fee was necessary "to promote racing upon a scale, as would induce gentlemen to encounter the expense of training horses."[27]

Colden's endeavors to revive horse racing at the Union Course, which included $5,000 yearly in prize money, proved to be a dismal failure. On October 20, 1830, a riot broke out at the Long Island track when the four-mile race was cancelled because the proprietor lacked the funds to make up the purse. The *Post* hoped that the disturbance would not undermine the sport and felt that the incident should convince Colden of his "utter inability to manage the course hereafter."[28] He was subsequently forced to resign his rights as the proprietor of the Union Course, even though he personally blamed the collapse of his project on a small clique which he claimed controlled the club and was responsible for bringing the sport to its low ebb in 1828. He further asserted that the NYAIB had required a smaller subscription fee from its members than he requested; had assumed money for themselves which rightfully belonged to him; and had failed to contribute its share of the purses. As a result he was forced to bear an excessive financial burden.[29] The NYAIB saw no reason to reply to Colden's allegations, which did not appear in print for nearly a year. Moreover, the press made it clear that the majority of the city's turfmen accepted the NYAIB's contention that Colden's incompetence had led to the difficulties at the Union Course.[30]

Certainly, Colden was not totally responsible for the condition of racing in New York; the sport had experienced difficulties even prior to his assumption of control of the Union Course, and the NYAIB probably did renege on some of the money it owed him. However, he definitely erred in trying to rejuvenate racing on such a grandiose scale. His personality alienated many of the city's leading horsemen and further aggravated the situation. Yet most of his problems were intimately tied to the new kind of management gradually emerging in American horse racing, techniques he applied in New York. Previously, jockey clubs or owners of horses, motivated by their own personal interest in the sport, governed the various courses. Under the new system financial profit was the promoter's major concern. He leased or owned the course, provided for the upkeep of the track and stands, made arrangements for the horses that would run there, and scheduled the meeting days. With the jockey club supposedly paying at least part of the purses, the promoter's profit was expected to come from gate receipts and "donations" by interested groups that benefited from the sport. Colden's experience illustrates that this type of management often did not work; as a financial venture New York's racetracks proved far from profitable.[31]

Other promoters of horse racing confronted many of the same problems Colden did in his attempt to make his enterprise successful. A small but vocal minority of horsemen opposed the new management system, viewing the promoter as an interloper, not an assistant, who injected the principles of business and profit onto the track. A more significant dilemma stemmed from the promoter's continued dependence on jockey clubs and horse owners to whom they were forced to be subservient. The aggressive Colden, a member of one of New York's oldest and most respected families, was incapable of such behavior. Yet personality alone cannot fully explain Colden's failure since other promoters of racing in antebellum New York proved only slightly more successful. Undermining all their efforts were the economics of the sport, combined with their inability and unwillingness to commercialize thoroughbred racing beyond primitive stages, points to be elaborated on later in this chapter.[32]

Horse racing in New York began another upward surge following the Colden fiasco. This time growth of the sport was linked to the tremendous national expansion of horse racing and the proliferation of the breeding industry. During the 1830s there was a marked resurgence in the importation of foreign stock, and the new arrivals, many of outstanding quality, stimulated an exciting new racing era.[33] The resurgence of racing in New York proved fleeting, however. With the onset of an economic depression in 1837 many of the old racing problems reappeared. Despite two intersectional contests before large crowds, horse racing was again on the verge of collapse by the mid-1840s.

The NYAIB reassumed control of racing in New York for two years after the Colden incident. In 1833 Alexander L. Botts of Virginia became the proprietor of the Union Course and another Virginian, David H. Branch, became his partner a year or two later. Both Botts and Branch had already established their reputations as proprietors of racecourses in their native state, and New Yorkers expected that the Virginians' connection with southern sportsmen would facilitate their bringing southern horses to the city. Furthermore, supporters hoped that the backgrounds of the two men would lend to the New York turf the fashionable air that horse racing had achieved in the South. Their policies did not vary extensively from those of their predecessor. They, too, subscribed to the theory that generous financial support of racing would attract large crowds, and during the nine years Botts and Branch supervised the Union Course, 107 purse races were run for a total of $54,000. The Virginians also introduced "Produce Stakes" to the New York turf, and the 83 match and sweepstakes races that were run on the Long Island track helped to fill the coffers of the nation's horsemen.[34]

Under the management of the Virginians horse racing in antebellum New York reached its peak between 1833 and 1837. Membership in the jockey club markedly rose, and the increase in prize money brought more and better quality horses to the Union Course. Even on good days in the 1820s five horses rarely started a contest, but by the next decade this was a common occurrence—at times as many as eight or nine horses went off to the taps of the drums. The high point of horse racing during the 1830s was the revival of the intersectional contest at the spring 1836 meeting, when the South again emerged victorious.[35]

The prosperous state of horse racing in New York and the faith turfmen had in its future in the mid-1830s were exemplified by the establishment of the aptly named Beacon Course in Hoboken, New Jersey. The long and expensive journey to the Long Island track had for some time made the city's sportsmen cognizant of the benefits to be derived from an easily accessible racecourse directly across the Hudson River. However, New Jersey's antiracing legislation thwarted attempts to take advantage of the better locale. With the modification of that state's racing law in 1834 the door was opened for the construction of a new track.

Cadwallader R. Colden was the major force behind the Beacon Course. He had been seeking a new place of business ever since he lost possession of the Union Course. Coming to a verbal agreement with Cyrus S. Browning, owner of the land, to lease the grounds at an annual rate of $6,000, Colden spent six months supervising the building of the racecourse. At the last moment, however, Browning received better leasing terms from Botts and Branch and backed out of his agreement with Colden. The Virginians' partnership with Browning thus enabled them to maintain their monopoly over racing in the New York area.[36]

The Beacon Course was the most lavish undertaking of its kind, with an estimated price tag of more than $60,000. Opened in November 1837 amid great expectations and support from the local press, the luxurious and convenient New Jersey track failed to entice the followers of the sport. While horse racing continued there until 1845, the Beacon Course was turned over primarily to trotting matches and other sports activities. The beacon of the future became, in reality, the symbol of the demise of horse racing in antebellum New York.[37]

As in the past, the decline of racing in New York during this period was gradual. The depression of 1837 had severe repercussions on the city's economy, as numerous mercantile houses succumbed to the economic crisis. The effect of this financial debacle on horse racing was immediate. Attendance at the fall 1837 meeting was visibly down, and within a year the problems of the turf had become acute. Given the poor economic circumstances evident throughout the city, it is surprising that observers of the sport viewed its problems as purely local, internal ones. The complaints were familiar: the rundown condition of the Union Course; mismanagement by the proprietors; and the lack of leadership provided by the New York Jockey Club. The only new charge was that the admission fee to the track and the expensive toll extracted by ferry and railroad companies discouraged interested fans from attending the races.[38]

William T. Porter, the *Spirit*'s influential editor, echoed Colden's complaints of a decade earlier. He, too, insisted that the crux of horse racing's difficulties was the inadequate financial support provided by the jockey club, without which proprietors could not attract quality horses and still realize a profit. Porter's solution was similarly unoriginal: he restated Colden's concept of a club financed by the leading and wealthiest New York turfmen, who would provide an economic base by contributing

$5,000 annually, in shares ranging from $200 to $500. Furthermore, he proposed that any individual could become an honorary member of the jockey club, with full privileges of the course, for an annual fee of $20.[39] Jockey club members conceded that steps had to be taken to improve the lot of racing, but they rejected sponsoring the sport on such a grandiose scale. In 1839 the club took more moderate steps, establishing an association for three years with an annual subscription rate ranging from $20 to $50.[40] The membership fee was quite steep for this era, especially considering the limited number of racing days each year. While it is not known how many members joined the reorganized club, it is perfectly clear that the club did little to alter the direction of the sport.

As horse racing in New York deteriorated, with no prospect for improvement, the Virginians bailed out. Branch sold his racing interests in 1840, claiming that his family was ill suited for the northern climate. Botts held out for another year, then he returned to Virginia as well. Their management of both the Union and Beacon courses reflected the unsettled condition of horse racing in New York during the 1820s and 1830s. Yet in spite of the failure of early promoters and the dismal state of horse racing throughout the North, during the two decades prior to the Civil War there were men who continued to believe that money could be made from racing in the nation's most populated city.

One of these was Henry K. Toler, a New Jersey resident and a former steward of the New York Jockey Club, who took over the Union Course in 1842. In his brief tenure he proved no more successful than his predecessors, although he got off to a propitious start when another intersectional contest was arranged. On November 5, 1841, James Long of Virginia, owner of Boston, and his turf advisor, none other than Col. Johnson, proposed a $20,000 match race against Fashion, the leading northern thoroughbred, to take place at the next spring meeting at the Union Course. Their objective was to revenge the ignominious defeat Fashion had handed their horse in a purse race a week earlier at a Camden, New Jersey, course. Acceptance of the challenge initially appeared unlikely, since Fashion's owner, William H. Gibbon, did not believe in personal wagers on his horse. The *Spirit,* hopeful of having the contest take place, recommended that a party of northern sportsmen purchase the filly. At the last moment, however, Gibbon acquiesced and loaned the horse to Toler, who sponsored Fashion, along with a group of twenty to thirty sportsmen. Gibbon's gesture was in part a response to overwhelming public sentiment for the contest, but it may have been due as well to a request by his friend Toler, who needed such a race to rejuvenate the ailing sport and make his enterprise successful.[41]

The Fashion-Boston match received tremendous publicity from the day the race was announced in December 1841. The *Spirit* regularly carried reports about the contestants, and letters dealing with all facets of the race were published in its weekly columns. Not since the first North-South confrontation in 1823 had such universal interest been manifested in a horse race. With the vast improvements in communications over the years the 1842 battle surpassed any other contest in the magnitude of excitement it generated nationally. Lovers of horse racing in New York understandably came to view the Fashion-Boston race as the catalyst necessary to revive the glory days of the turf.[42]

Visitors from all parts of the country flocked to New York City to watch the race (the crowd was estimated at between 50,000 and 70,000). Boston was made a slight favorite; but the *Spirit* reported that it had never seen so little money wagered on the outcome of such an important contest. The first heat was an exciting one, with Fashion winning by a little more than a length. Coming home in 7:32½ minutes for the four miles, the filly broke the world's record by two and a half seconds. The second heat was close for three miles, but on the final lap the nine-year-old Boston tired and Fashion crossed the finish line sixty yards ahead of her opponent to win the match.[43]

Numerous incidents marred the contest and tempered northern jubilation over Fashion's victory. Porter severely criticized the entire enterprise, saving his sharpest rebuke for the proprietor whose incompetence was responsible for most of the difficulties. Toler's most heinous crime, according to Porter, was the sin of avarice: the ten-dollar admission fee was nothing less than extortion. The fact that the ticket holder would have access to the track for the remainder of the year was of little consolation to the many racing fans who had traveled long distances solely to watch the intersectional battle. Porter argued that this inexcusable act placed the New York turf in a bad light as far as the nation's sports community was concerned.[44]

The entire affair was a grave disappointment to those who had predicted that the match would reawaken the dormant spirit of horse racing in New York. Even if all had gone well, it is doubtful that the intersectional contest could have stimulated any lasting revival of the sport, given the deteriorating condition of racing throughout the North and the decline of the breeding industry. When the North-South race turned into a public relations fiasco, the enthusiasm it had generated quickly dissipated. The sport declined rapidly over the next several years. Attendance at races dropped sharply, as even turf regulars stayed away.[45] When another North-South race was announced in 1845, horse racing had deteriorated to the point that no one really believed the excitement over an intersectional contest could generate any permanent interest in the sport.

Although New Yorkers remained apathetic to regular races, they continued to be intrigued by intersectional confrontations. The press estimated that 70,000–100,000 people, the largest crowd ever to witness a horse race at the Union Course, were present to see Peytonia challenge Fashion. The entire affair, under Porter's supervision, was relatively free from the incidents that had marred the previous contest. The race was exceedingly close, but in both heats the heavy underdog Peytonia crossed the finish line first.[46] Thus ended a horse racing era in New York. While Fashion avenged the setback with an easy victory over Peytonia fifteen days later in a purse race at Camden, her triumph was a shallow one for New York racing.[47] For some time the popularity of the sport had lingered exclusively on the excitement created by the North-South contests. But the 1845 match would be the last, and therefore the deciding race, in the series between the two regions, as North and South moved closer toward a far more serious confrontation. Fashion's defeat in the final contest brought the era to a fitting close.

The instability of horse racing in New York originated in the problems and changes within the breeding industry. The return of legalized racing in 1821 did, to a certain extent, revitalize the breeding of racehorses in the metropolitan area, but the industry remained smaller than, if not inferior to, its southern counterparts. Fewer northern stables resulted in the continual dependence of the New York turf on southern horses, which accentuated the uncertainty of racing in New York. Fortunately, the money offered from purses, sweepstakes, and match races in America's wealthiest city proved sufficient to attract horses from most of the leading southern stables, except during the late 1820s. Since races occurred on a limited basis, the combination of northern and southern horses was of sufficient quality and quantity to ensure exciting contests.[48]

During the early 1830s the prosperity of both racing and the breeding industry fostered among breeders a mentality that foresaw unending riches. Indicative of this expansive mood was the widespread and expensive importation of English stallions and mares, which quickly created a top-heavy, inflated industry. To recoup the cost of imported horses owners demanded correspondingly higher stud fees, with the result that the price of a new foal was driven up. By the end of the decade an almost impossible rate of success by breeders was necessary to make their enterprises profitable.[49]

The depression of 1837 intensified the problems of an already over-expanded industry. Prices paid for horses fell sharply, often below the cost of breeding them, and the industry declined at a rate even more rapid than its upward thrust in the previous decade.[50] The frail northern industry was particularly hard hit by the economic upheaval, and those who invested in racehorses divested themselves of their stock. The depressed economy also had dire consequences for racing and breeding in Virginia and throughout the Old South (with the exception of South Carolina), the region from which the New York track heavily drew its horses. By the 1840s the center of racing had shifted to the newer regions of the South, with Kentucky as the breeding capital and New Orleans as the racing capital. With the increased distance from the center of the breeding industry to the New York tracks, the money being offered to induce southern horsemen to bring their thoroughbreds to Manhattan was no longer sufficient. Racing would not be truly revived in New York until the immediate post–Civil War years, when southern horsemen once again became dependent on the revenues of northern tracks.[51]

The problems breeders confronted by the end of the 1830s occurred within, and were partially caused by, an industry taking its first steps toward modernization. The growth of racing in the 1820s and 1830s had stimulated the breakdown of the regional character of breeding, as evidenced by the relocation of Eclipse, after his racing career ended, from New York to Virginia to Kentucky. In fact, while intersectional contests continued into the 1840s and generated considerable interest, often taking on symbolic meaning, the horses competing in these races increasingly shared a common lineage.[52] Further indicative of the emerging national scope of breeding was the appearance of national sports journals and the publication in 1833 of the first American stud book. While the need for such a reference book had long been recognized, it is no coincidence that horsemen first seriously discussed the project at the start of intersectional racing.[53]

The growth of racing led to breeding as an increasingly specialized industry. Prior to 1820 even the swiftest thoroughbreds were frequently bred to horses within the common stock. However, as the amount of available prize money rose there was a simultaneous increase in the number of horses being placed in training for the track and in the stud fees owners demanded for the services of leading thoroughbreds. These rising costs put such horses outside the price range of breeders of common stock and facilitated the emergence of thoroughbred breeding as a self-contained industry: thoroughbreds were now being bred for the sole purpose of producing other thoroughbreds for racing and breeding. This symbiotic relationship between breeding and racing complicated the ability of northern horsemen to adjust to the impact of an economic depression on both industries. However, the underlying problem with breeding and racing in New York was the absence of sufficient financial backing. Both Cadwallader Colden and William Porter felt that while the sport labored under a variety of problems, the lack of economic support from the jockey club was the key weakness. Each man proposed the creation of a "super jockey club," to be sponsored by the wealthiest turfmen in the New York area; each man's proposal was rejected.

Frequent references to the importance of economics and the constant discussion in the press of the need to provide larger purses raise questions about the traditional perception of antebellum horsemen as wealthy men who were interested in the sport for the "glory rather than the money." The *Spirit* claimed that no northern turfmen pursued racing as a profession, that most of them "are deeply engaged in business, or are the head of large corporations . . .; their connection with the Turf is a sort of recreation, and the only attention paid to their horses is during occasional relaxations from other pursuits."[54] Between 1821 and 1845 New York horsemen were clearly wealthy. Four of the twelve identifiable New York turfmen were among the wealthiest 200 New Yorkers in 1828, while another was the son of a member of this select group; of the remaining seven, there were four prosperous merchants, a doctor, and the editor of the *American,* all of whom belonged to prominent New York families. Cornelius Van Ranst, the one-time owner of Eclipse, was listed as a breeder in the city directory; he came from a well-established New York family. The wealth of residents from the surrounding area who raced horses seemed to conform to the pattern found for the city's horsemen. For example, Nathaniel and Butler Coles of Long Island were prosperous millowners; James Bathgate owned a large estate in Westchester County; and the Stevens brothers (John Cox and Robert Livingston) of Hoboken were among the wealthiest residents of the metropolitan area.[55]

Although these horsemen were all wealthy, their racing behavior cannot be explained solely by reference to "status theory."[56] It is undeniable that status played a critical part in their turf involvement: rich New Yorkers were attracted to horse racing because it dramatically identified and confirmed their high status to both peers and inferiors; moreover, horse racing brought them into contact with the upper class from other areas, thereby permitting them to proclaim their position beyond local boundaries. However, it would be erroneous to perceive wealthy New Yorkers as engaged in "conspicuous consumption" or "conspicuous leisure," for to minimize the importance of financial consideration would result in misunderstanding the character of the New York horseman.

New York horsemen embraced both the business and sporting sides of horse racing, an integration that was vital to the sanctioning of the sport and to legitimating their involvement in it. They never felt uncomfortable with amusements in general, viewing them as an integral part of a somewhat genteel social life. Nevertheless, the extensive expenditure required to sustain their stables, purely for sport, was inconsistent with their class values. They firmly accepted the justification of racing as resting with its utilitarian benefits. Nor should it be misconstrued that such a position was a mere rationale for their action. City turfmen expressed no psychic tension or doubt over their activity on the track. As the leaders of the sport and influential men in their community, they genuinely believed that racing served a useful societal function by encouraging the breeding industry and stimulating the betterment of the blood horse. While they were willing to invest their money in good horses, they neither perceived themselves as extensive patrons of the sport nor condoned their endeavors when they entailed a large financial burden. They expected a just compensation for their investment; at worst, they calculated that their expenses should be covered. Furthermore, they did not view this position as inconsistent with their status as sportsmen. The *Spirit* firmly recognized the connection between the business and sporting sides of horse racing when it noted that "gentlemen must be induced *to* COME UPON *the turf* by a prospect of realizing something like a remuneration instead of paying dearly not only for their sport, but for that of other people." When horsemen could no longer profit from the sport, the justification of their involvement in horse racing no longer existed. Although after the depression in 1837 wealthy New York horsemen still possessed the means to sustain their stables, their business instincts clearly dominated their sporting habits: as the value of their horses fell, they began to divest themselves of their stock.[57]

Members of New York's various jockey clubs also revealed no inclination to become extensive patrons of racing. Unfortunately, there are no records of the membership of these clubs, although newspaper accounts reveal the names of officers and committee members of the New York Jockey Club for the years 1839–45. It is noteworthy that horse owners did not dominate the leadership of this racing association—only six of the nineteen officers sponsored a horse on the New York track. Nevertheless, both groups appear to have been drawn from similar socioeconomic backgrounds, although the owners probably possessed a greater degree of wealth. For example, only two of seven non-horse-owning officers living in New York, Peter A. Jay and N. Gouveneur Kortright, appeared on the list of the wealthiest New Yorkers in either 1828 or 1845; the remainder, men such as the eminent lawyer J. Prescott Hall, were quite well-to-do. The only exception was William Porter, whose financial position was always shaky. Non-horse-owning officers from the surrounding area were also from well-established families: John A. King of Queens County, an active supporter of racing, was the son of Rufus King; Denning Duer, a New York banker but a New Jersey resident, was the grandson of wealthy New York merchant James Gore King.

The amount Colden and Porter recommended for membership in the proposed "super jockey club," somewhere between $500 and $1,000, was prohibitive even for these well-to-do officials. Among the officers who could have afforded it, their conservative bent probably explains why they never seriously considered the suggestion. The call for wealthy men to finance racing illustrates that leading observers believed that jockey clubs could not amass the needed capital simply through the collection of regular membership dues, an assessment that was, by and large, accurate. The amount of the dues was not the problem, for the usual $20 fee was easily affordable by wealthy New Yorkers. The more serious dilemma was the number of club members. Even at the height of racing's prosperity, the New York Jockey Club probably attracted somewhere between 150 and 200 members, which strongly indicates that racing never won the support of New York's upper class to the extent that it did among the planter class in the South.

The opposition to horse racing on religious grounds and because of its association with gambling further aggravated the problems of the sport and contributed to its weak economic foundation. While these objections could not destroy the sport they did play an inhibiting role. Both issues placed racing on the defensive and alienated a segment of New York's population who could have afforded to become jockey club members. It is clear from what little data are available that wealthy New Yorkers of New England descent, an increasing component of the city's elite, were conspicuous by their absence. As a result, horse racing in New York remained almost exclusively in the hands of the older, dwindling Knickerbocker group, who alone could not provide a sufficient number of members to sustain the sport financially.[58]

Just as the unwillingness of wealthy New York sportsmen to become patrons of racing contributed to its demise, so too did the failure of racing leaders to adopt more progressive means of financing the sport. As early as 1836 John C. Stevens recommended that purses be divided proportionally, rather than all the prize money going to the winner. This procedure, he claimed, "would induce many a man to train and enter a horse that would not think of doing so under the present rules" and "render racing less of a monopoly, by dividing among a number that which is now given (and often unjustly) to one." Stevens's proposal evoked considerable comment and criticism, but his leadership role in New York racing led the jockey club and the proprietors of the Union Course to accede to his suggestion. After a brief trial, however, the experiment was abandoned.[59]

Even prior to 1830 Cadwallader Colden had recognized that the successful survival of racing in New York required that the sport generate revenues from gate receipts. While enclosed courses and admission fees became common practice in the 1830s, the commercialization of horse racing did not advance beyond a primitive stage. Several factors limited the development of this phase of the sport. From the outset racing was elitist, and the emergence of racing promoters did little to alter this situation. Even if the promoter had wanted to reach out to a more broadly based clientele, and there is no evidence for this in New York, his strong dependence on wealthy sportsmen would have inhibited any significant movement in this direction.

The problems and cost of reaching and entering the course served as a greater deterrent to the commercialization of the sport. The difficulty of merely getting to the Long Island tracks had been noted as early as the colonial period. While transportation conditions improved by the 1820s, the hardship of reaching the track from the city continued to restrict attendance, and those who managed the journey found that it was not cheap. By the 1830s the *Spirit* estimated that the combined cost of arriving at the Union Course by ferry and railroad was one dollar, and that the service was "so bad that whoever could went by private conveyance, which cost nearer to five dollars than one."[60] The price of admission to the track is difficult to pinpoint since it fluctuated widely. The minimum charge for entering the course and standing on the field was at least a quarter and usually fifty cents; the average price of a ticket was generally between one and two dollars. Thus, it would appear that the cost of reaching, entering, and returning from the racetrack was at least three and probably closer to five dollars, an amount that deterred the sport from attracting a mass audience. In all likelihood spectators at New York races generally came from no further down the social ladder than the prosperous middle class.

The small scale on which horse racing was run also inhibited the successful commercialization of the sport. By the 1840s New York's racing season consisted of one week of races in both the spring and fall, which allowed a promoter little flexibility and made him unable to adjust to adverse conditions, such as one or more days of inclement weather. The style of racing further complicated the process by limiting the amount of sport and the opportunities to gamble to at most two races per day. Given the difficulties and expense of reaching the racecourse, this system placed a premium on the promoter being able to provide exciting contests and horses with good reputations, something that was frequently beyond his capability. By the late 1830s there was some consideration to introducing the "modern" dash system of racing already in use in England. While this newer system would facilitate more races, the traditionalism of northern and southern horsemen stifled such a change.[61]

The limited commercialization of horse racing and the precarious financial condition of the sport in antebellum New York strongly suggest that crowd sizes were much smaller than reported by the press. While data on the economics of racing are virtually nonexistent, Colden provided an invaluable, albeit limited, account of the financial workings of horse racing during his brief tenure as the proprietor of the Union Course. His figures suggest that running the track cost no more than $20,000 yearly.

Assuming he received no financial support from the jockey club or other sources, to break even he would have had to take in an average of $2,000 per day, based on an annual racing calendar of ten days. If the average price of admission was only fifty cents, it would have taken 4,000 spectators daily to cover his expenses, and neither he nor other promoters achieved that in the long run.[62]

The capacity of the Union Course further substantiates the claim of small crowds. Colden insisted that the seating capacity of the track was roughly 2,000 and that another 3,000 people could find standing room; he said he was willing to expand the course to accommodate 6,000 spectators.[63] Hence, it is difficult to accept published reports of crowds of 50,000 or more at intersectional contests. In fact, it would not be surprising if the North-South confrontations attracted only half the number of people reported, and probably less. If promoters were men who understood a profit-and-loss sheet, a large crowd at one match would have changed the structure and number of intersectional contests. Rather than having the horses' owners or a syndicate put up the prize money, a promoter could have offered $5,000 and still have covered his costs for an entire year if he attracted 25,000 fans at $1 each. The fact that this never occurred, even during the crisis years, strongly indicates that crowd sizes were far less than reported.

By 1845 horse racing still had a basically premodern sports pattern, yet during the previous quarter-century it had begun to assume a somewhat modern form as a result of the growth of racing nationally. By the end of the colonial period the sport had achieved some organizational structure, although the extent to which it became organized in New York and elsewhere in the years after 1821 far exceeded earlier developments. By the 1830s the significant increase in the number of jockey clubs and racetracks nationwide also necessitated coordination of the various racing schedules. While no formal racing calendar emerged, a systematic schedule developed through the efforts of the national sports journals, one that permitted horses to run in the winter and early spring in the South and in the late spring and fall in the North.

The extent to which the various jockey clubs sought to standardize the rules of horse racing further reflects the nascent modernization of the sport. In the early nineteenth century, racing rules lacked precision, enforcement was whimsical, and favoritism "was by no means unknown, partisanship being the rule rather than the exception."[64] With the continual breakdown of the local character of racing, the need for definitive rules and consistent interpretations became mandatory to the success of the sport. Consequently, local jockey clubs, such as the New York Jockey Club, regularly published their rules in the national sports journals.

Throughout the 1830s there were recommendations for a central racing organization to establish uniform rules and to create a court of appeals to rule on doubtful interpretations. Initially proposed by John Stuart Skinner, the influential editor of the Baltimore-based *American Turf Register*, the idea won the strong backing of the editor of the *Spirit*. Despite its advocacy by these two leading sports journals, the powers and prerogatives of the local jockey clubs were too entrenched to bring this desired reform to fruition.[65] While progress was made, national uniformity was still not evident by the mid-1840s.

Horse racing made significant and more permanent advances in terms of the amount of written material disseminated about the sport. The growth of sports journalism and other forms of racing literature were directly related to the expansion and increasing organization of racing. While reports could be found in the colonial press they were sporadic and often inaccurate. But as racing expanded beyond local boundaries horsemen required more authentic accounts of the performances and pedigrees of thoroughbreds, as well as a medium for the exchange of news and ideas. The result was the creation of the first American stud book and, more crucial to the development of horse racing in particular and athletics in general, the beginning of the sports press.

Skinner founded the *American Turf Register and Sporting Magazine,* the first significant American sports periodical, in 1829. This monthly magazine had the dual objective of providing summaries of all races in America and Canada and of documenting and authenticating the history of racing and the breeding history of American horses. With the 1831 publication of the *Spirit of the Times,* by William T. Porter, the center of sports journalism shifted to New York. Although the objectives of the *Spirit* were similar to those of the *Turf Register,* by the mid-1830s it had clearly gained the upper hand over its rival. As a weekly it provided the public with earlier reports of races. The *Spirit*'s style was crisper and more readable than its formal, stodgy competitor. And the *Turf Register* suffered from the withdrawal of Skinner as editor. Once the *Spirit* placed New York at the center of sports journalism the city never relinquished its leadership position. In fact, New York's dominant role in American sports derived largely from its position as the nation's sports communication center.[66]

With the temporary collapse of horse racing in New York and the North in the mid-1840s the limited early modernization of the sport reached an impasse. The turf once again became largely a regional sport. Although only minor advances were made between 1821 and 1845, the growth of racing and breeding had placed severe strains on its traditional pattern. During the next twenty years that pattern survived, albeit in a weakened condition, until New York horsemen adopted a modern racing system in the post–Civil War years.

Fast trotters on Harlem Lane, in New York City. From a drawing by J. Beard.

3

Harness Racing as the First
Modern Sport

The decline of horse racing in New York City by 1845 did not spell the
end of all forms of racing. As the fortunes of the running horse crumbled
the press took increasing note of the activities of the trotting horse. By
the early 1840s sports journalists suggested that the "ugly duckling" had
become the legitimate rival of the thoroughbred for the hearts of racing
fans. In 1847 the *Herald* pointed out that "for several years past, trotting
has been gradually taking the precedence of running in this part of the
country; while one specie of amusements has been going into decay the
other has risen to heights never before attained."[1]

Harness racing emerged as a popular pastime in the first quarter of the
nineteenth century and in 1820 was still a premodern sport.[2] It consisted
primarily of informal road contests, generally run in the northeastern
region of the country. The sport was unorganized, lacked standardized
rules, attracted limited public attention, and kept no permanent records.
By 1870 harness racing had become a modern sport, signaled by the
creation of the National Trotting Association. Not only had it developed
into a highly organized sport, with fairly uniform rules and contests taking
place throughout the nation, but the coverage it received in the daily and
sporting press, the systematic recording of statistics, and the appearance
in 1871 of the first stud book devoted exclusively to trotting, showed
that it had evolved into a modern sport. Harness racing proved to be the
first successfully commercialized sport, emerging as the number one

This chapter originally appeared as "The First Modern Sport in America: Harness Racing
in New York City, 1825–70," *Journal of Sport History* 8 (Spring 1981): 5–32. It has since
been revised for inclusion in this volume.

spectator sport by the mid-nineteenth century. Not until after the Civil War did baseball challenge the supreme position of trotting in America.

Whereas horse racing was rooted in the agrarian past, harness racing was an urban product. Trotting first emerged on urban roads and developed its most salient modern characteristics in the city, with New York playing a more critical role than any other urban area. As early as 1832 the *Spirit* recognized that New York City was preeminent in the breeding and training of trotters. Nearly a quarter of a century later a frequent correspondent to that sports journal maintained that trotting was indigenous to Manhattan and that there were "more fine horses here than can be found any where else in the world."[3] The importance of New York to the growth of the sport did not derive solely from its concentration of the best stock in the region, however. There also were more trotting tracks, more races, and more prize money in New York than anywhere else in the country. Because the sport was first organized and commercialized there, New York set the pattern that was followed on a national scale.

Sport historians have suggested that antiracing legislation passed by several northern states, including New York, stimulated the growth of trotting in the first quarter of the nineteenth century. Denied the racecourse, lovers of fast horses took to a more natural track — the roadways. While ill suited for the feet of the running horse, the hard roads were ideal for the trotter. "It is no accident," one historian concluded, "that the racing of trotters began in regions where horses could be 'raced' only in defiance of law."[4] However, since enforcement was lax, at least in New York, horsemen did not take to the road as a substitute for the prohibited racecourse. Rather, trotting emerged when it did in New York and other sections of the Northeast because improvements in the roads made the sport possible. John Hervey argued that "it was only natural that the speed of the harness horse found its first testing grounds upon the smooth hard roads whose networks radiated from the northeastern cities . . . especially those of the Boston–New York–Philadelphia region."[5]

Sportsmen began racing their "roadsters," as street trotters came to be called, because it provided them with a convenient, participatory, and relatively inexpensive amusement. Third Avenue quickly became New York's major trotting site, a five-mile length of roadway that began outside the residential portion of the city. It was perfectly suited for informal trials of speed and in close proximity to the homes of horsemen. Races generally commenced when the day's work had been completed and usually lasted until dusk. Numerous taverns dotted the highway, where reinsmen could relax, arrange races, and discuss the latest sports developments.[6]

These spontaneous contests appealed to the city's horsemen because they allowed for personal participation. Unlike thoroughbred racing, where the owner and rider had long been separated, trotting permitted the sportsman to demonstrate the prowess of his horse as well as his own skill as a reinsman. In addition, trotting did not require the capital outlay of thoroughbred racing. The trotter was not a pure breed but rather a horse drawn from the common stock with the ability to trot. The plebian horses used in these races were almost always used by their owners for day-to-day activities.[7]

Trotting in the early nineteenth century consisted almost exclusively of impromptu contests, although a permanent structure began to emerge. The first trotting tracks in the metropolitan area were extensions of the racecourses used for thoroughbreds, the most significant of which was located in Harlem, where the first recorded performance by an American trotter took place in 1806. Several years later the first track exclusively for harness racing was built in Harlem next to the Red House Tavern. The course became the major site for the Third Avenue racing crowd, and it appears that the track was constructed for their benefit. While horse racing took place on both Harlem courses, the tracks were essentially training grounds for the city's roadsters.[8]

More formal matches, either on city roads or tracks, were a natural outgrowth of the spontaneous races, or "brushes," which took place on New York City streets. Since the press paid scant attention to these matches information exists on only a handful of them. Probably the most important of the early contests occurred in 1818 when William Jones, a prominent Long Island horseman, wagered Col. Bond of Maryland that he could produce a horse that could trot a mile in less than three minutes. The race, for a $1,000 stake, caused great excitement among the city's sporting circle. With the odds against success, Boston Pony accomplished the feat in a fraction less than the required time.[9]

The formation of the New York Trotting Club in the winter of 1824–25 marked the first critical step in the modernization of the sport. While there is no information on the members of the first organized trotting club in America, most of them were probably men who raced their roadsters on Third Avenue and elsewhere in the metropolitan area. The creators of the club were inspired by the success of the New York Association for the Improvement of the Breed (NYAIB), established three years earlier. In terms of both its objectives and methods, the trotting club drew heavily on the experiences of horse racing. Similar to their NYAIB counterparts, trotting club members justified their association on utilitarian grounds, instituted twice yearly meetings, and constructed a racecourse (in Centerville, on Long Island) to facilitate the growth of the sport.[10]

Trotting in New York made significant advances as both a participatory and a spectator sport in the two decades following the formation of the trotting club. In 1835 the *Spirit* noted that the "number of fast horses for which our city is so celebrated is steadily accumulating." With some exaggeration one observer claimed that "there was scarce a gentleman in New York, who did not own one or two fast [trotting] horses." The rising cost of good trotters further indicated the increasing appeal of the sport.[11] In addition, races on the city's tracks, especially the major ones, generated considerable excitement among the New York sports crowd. In 1838 the *Herald* reported that the contest between Dutchman and Ratner created "as much interest in our city and neighborhood" as the recent intersectional contest between John Bascombe and Post Boy.[12]

The emerging commercialization of trotting most accurately dramatizes the growth of the sport. By the mid-1830s entrepreneurs began to tap the public interest in harness racing on New York's streets and tracks. After the Beacon Course failed as a thoroughbred racecourse, the proprietors began sponsoring trotting contests solely for the purpose of reaping financial reward from the gate receipts. By the early 1840s businessmen had replaced the original sponsors of trotting as the major promoters of the sport.[13]

Like their counterparts in horse racing, trotting men valued a horse with both speed and endurance. Early contests were held in heats ranging from one to five miles; by the 1840s, however, most contests were one-mile heats with the winner required to win three heats. Occasionally trotters engaged in long-distance contests, from 20 to 100 miles, usually run against time but in several cases against other horses. These contests remained in vogue until the mid-nineteenth century, when they came under attack for their cruelty to the horses. (When one trotter died in 1853, after successfully completing a 100-mile race in less than nine hours, two newspapers severely criticized this type of contest.[14]) By the outbreak of the Civil War long-distance races had become a thing of the past, although the complaints of the press had little to do with their decline. Rather, as the price of good trotting horses rose, such races were no longer economically feasible given the greater potential for injury to the horses involved.

Organized trotting made important progress in its first twenty years, but it continued to take a back seat to horse racing. The press coverage harness racing received indicates the secondary status of this turf sport. While it won the polite endorsement of New York newspapers, reports of races, even important ones, remained limited. Although John S. Skinner and Cadwallader R. Colden approved of the sport, the monthly journals they edited were devoted almost exclusively to thoroughbred racing, providing the barest summaries and details of developments on trotting tracks. Only William T. Porter's *Spirit* paid any significant attention to trotting, and even then the extent of coverage did not correspond to the growth of the sport. Along with his contemporaries Porter probably believed that thoroughbred racing was the one truly legitimate turf sport.

As thoroughbred racing declined in popularity throughout the North in the decade following the 1837 depression, harness racing surged to new heights. Observers of both sports claimed that their corresponding fates were closely linked to the characteristics associated with the two different types of horses. In contrast to the aristocratic and foreign thoroughbred, the trotter was perceived as the democratic, utilitarian, and, by logical extension, American horse. Implicit was the belief that harness racing surpassed horse racing as the leading turf sport because it more accurately captured the spirit of America. Henry W. Herbert (better known as Frank Forester), the first significant historian of the American turf, recognized the close connection between the nature of the horses and the popularity of the respective sports. Since cost restricted the ownership of thoroughbreds to wealthy men, Herbert believed that horse racing could never truly become a popular sport. By contrast, the trotter was common to all and the "most truly characteristic and national type of horse" in America. In this country, the transplanted Englishman concluded, trotting "is the people's sport, the people's pastime, and, consequently, is, and will be, supported by the people."[15]

Herbert's perspective provides a starting point for understanding the maturation of trotting only if such terms as democratic, utilitarian, and even American are broadly conceived. While he and his contemporaries grossly exaggerated the extent to which the masses owned these plebian and relatively inexpensive horses, ownership was far more widespread than for thoroughbreds.[16] Precise data are nonexistent, but the available information permits a logically deduced profile. Apparently, only a small number of trotting men came from the upper class, yet the cost of buying and keeping trotters was still sufficiently high to all but exclude those individuals below the middle class. It appears that most owners came from the more prosperous segments of the middle class, men who enjoyed a comfortable, but hardly opulent, life-style. Individuals of more moderate means could still own a roadster because of its limited price and utilitarian nature. This was particularly the case for those men who worked in New York's various food markets. Their involvement in harness racing gave credence to the adage "a butcher rides a trotter," often used to illustrate the democratic nature of such horses.[17]

The *Herald* repeatedly insisted that the decline of horse racing stemmed from the fact that the thoroughbred had little practical value. Conceding that trotting "may not be attended with all the high zest and excitement" of thoroughbred racing, the newspaper emphasized that "it is a more useful sport, as the qualities in the horse which it is calculated to develop are more valuable and more intimately connected with the daily business of life."[18] The growth of harness racing also reflected shifting patterns of travel. With the improvement of roads and wagons, the driving horse increasingly replaced the saddle horse as the basic means of convoy in the Northeast and the Middle Atlantic states. As Peter Welsh pointed out, there was "a direct correlation between the improved modes of transportation and their popular manifestation on the trotting track."[19]

Since Americans believed that the true nature of the trotter, both democratic and utilitarian, could only be developed in this country, they perceived the trotter as a native product, although they were familiar with its English antecedents. In 1853 the *Herald* wrote, "We are the first who have attached particular importance to the breeding of trotting horses, and in this respect . . . have shown the practical nature of our character."[20] Such assumptions may be passed off as American chauvinism, but the contention that both the sport and the horse were indigenous products does contain merit. Harness racing had been a popular pastime in England, but its emergence as a sport first occurred in the United States.[21] Similarly, the establishment of a distinct breed of trotting horses was undeniably American, although the process was not completed until the late nineteenth century.

However, it was the perception, more than the reality, of the trotter as an American horse that was critical to the growth of the sport. While harness racing never wrapped itself in the Stars and Stripes to the extent that baseball did, nationalistic overtones served to sanction trotting as it had not sanctioned horse racing. Oliver Wendell Holmes, Sr., captured these sentiments in noting that the running horse was a gambling toy while the trotting horse was a useful animal. "Horse racing is not a republican institution; horse-trotting is."[22] Although this sort of explanation has some merit, other critical factors must be examined to construct a more comprehensive view of the maturation of harness racing. Trotting's supreme position in the turf world can be understood in terms of three interacting forces: the increased potential for commercialized amusements made possible by urban and economic expansion; the greater susceptibility of this sport to commercialization than any of its counterparts; and the more innovative nature of trotting.

The absence of surplus wealth and concentrated populations traditionally restricted the development of commercialized amusements. During the antebellum period these two major barriers began to give way under the impact of urban and economic growth. The expanding economy not only led to a significant increase in wealth but, more importantly, broadened the availability of discretionary income among a wider segment of the population. The higher concentration of people in one area facilitated the creation of a greater number of permanent institutions devoted to commercialized amusements, all of which shared three essential features: they were cheaper; their success depended on volume; and they appealed to a broad segment of the populace. Present in New York City even before the 1840s, these newer forms of popular entertainment mushroomed under the impact of rapid urban and economic growth. As one scholar points out, commercialized amusements underwent "an expansion of new proportions" during a lengthy era of general prosperity between 1843 and 1860.[23]

The plebian character of the trotter and its relatively inexpensive price tag made the sport prone to commercialization. Since the trotting horse cost less than the thoroughbred, the prize money track proprietors offered did not have to be as great in order that the owners of trotters might recoup their expenses and realize a profit. As late as 1860 purses in New York rarely exceeded $250, and at the smaller tracks contests were run for as little as $10. Naturally, the stakes were higher in match races—by 1850 a few trotting contests were run for as much as $5,000 per side— but in general the amounts fell below those that existed for similar kinds of thoroughbred races. Also, because purses were lower and trotters were more durable, more races were possible each year. Whereas a good thoroughbred might race only six or seven times a year, trotters usually started at least twice as many races annually and their careers lasted longer, many racing into their teens. More importantly, trotting horses came from the common stock, so there were more of them to race, the impact of which can be seen in terms of the respective racing seasons in New York. There were at most a total of four weeks of thoroughbred racing, but hardly a week would pass, except during the winter, without a trotting match taking place somewhere in the metropolitan area. Finally, harness racing was not bogged down in the aristocratic trappings that characterized horse racing. In 1843 the *Spirit* recognized that trotting men were more innovative and aggressive than their horse racing coun- terparts and predicted that as a result of their greater "enterprise, industry and go *aheadiveness*," trotting would soon be "a most formidable rival of thoroughbred racing in the North." Nearly a quarter of a century later *Turf, Field and Farm,* essentially a thoroughbred journal, gave the same basic reason, using exactly the same words, to explain the greater popularity of harness racing.[24]

Trotting also proved to be more innovative than horse racing in two critical ways. First, the different social backgrounds of those involved affected the tone of the two turf sports. Wealthy men and/or those from established families engaged in thoroughbred racing, while most of the owners of trotting horses were middle class in origin. While thoroughbreds were run for and by the upper class, harness racing enticed a broader segment of the populace, with the commercially minded proprietors of trotting tracks catering more readily to all ticket holders. Complaints of exclusiveness, aristocracy, and snobbishness leveled by the press against the various New York jockey clubs were not leveled against trotting. A leading sports journal noted in 1856 that horse racing "will never succeed in New York until it and its attended arrangements are put on a more democratic basis—something approaching the order of the first class trotting races. Then, like the trots, it will get the support of the people."[25] Second, trotting was a comparatively new sport and thus was not inhibited by tradition, unlike horse racing. This absence of institutional confinements made it easier for trotting to adjust to commercialization. While races were still long by today's standards, the sport adopted a modified dash system much earlier than horse racing did, with the result that still more races were possible. These contests also took place in a wide variety of styles, providing greater diversity and more interest.

Harness racing surged to the forefront of the turf world and athletics in general because it captured the flow of the American experience more than any other sport of its day. In common with other forms of popular entertainment the emergence of trotting as a spectator sport was the result of the two dynamic forces, urbanization and economic expansion, which were transforming and modernizing American life. These agents of change would have had far less impact on trotting had it not been predisposed toward commercialization. While the nature of the horse played a critical role, of equal significance was the fact that those who governed trotting, at least from the standpoint of sport, internalized the values of modern society. As such, they placed a greater premium on innovation rather than tradition, on cash rather than class.

In the two decades preceding the Civil War harness racing progressed rapidly as the most popular spectator sport in New York and the nation. While changes in social and economic conditions created the setting for the growth of the sport, the performers attracted the crowds. During the early years of organized trotting many horses left their mark on the history of the sport, but it was Lady Suffolk who set the standard of excellence. Her fifteen-year career, from 1838 to 1853, illustrated the changing nature of trotting.[26]

Foaled in 1833, Lady Suffolk was bred by Leonard Lawrence of Suffolk County, Long Island, from which she drew her name. Lady was a descendant of imported Messanger, whose impact on the American thoroughbred and trotter was profound.[27] Although Lady Suffolk came from good racing stock, she was not being prepared for a trotting career. As a weanling she was sold for $60, then resold as a two-year-old for

$90. At age four she was pulling a butcher or oyster cart when David Bryan purchased her for $112.50 for use in his livery stable. There her prowess went undiscovered until William Porter rented her for a tour of the Long Island tracks. Lady's speed and good gait impressed the editor of the *Spirit,* and he told Bryan that she had too much potential as a racer to be wasted in his livery. In the spring of 1838 Bryan entered Lady in her first race, and the "Old Grey Mare," as she was later affectionately described, completed the mile contest in three minutes flat, winning the less than fabulous sum of $11.

Bryan, of Celtic (possibly Irish) origin, was the embodiment of the professional ethic that came to dominate harness racing. To him Lady Suffolk was not "first and foremost, a sporting animal" but "a mint of money, a nugget of rich metal to be melted by him in the heat of competition and struck off into dollars." He raced the grey mare mainly in the New York area because that was where he lived and, more importantly, because the city's tracks provided the best financial opportunities. However, like other professional trotting men of his day, Bryan also campaigned with Lady Suffolk on the growing number of tracks throughout the country, going as far west as St. Louis and as far south as New Orleans.[28] He had the reputation of being a poor reinsman, one who placed excessive demands on his trotter. Nevertheless, he was an unqualified success by the new professional standard. He entered Lady in 162 races and won between $35,000 and $60,000. Lady's ability to achieve victory, despite the clumsy and inept driving of her owner, clearly derived from her saintly demeanor, an unbreakable spirit, and her remarkable endurance. At age nineteen, her last full year on the track, the Old Grey Mare demonstrated tremendous stamina by coming to the start twelve times.[29]

Harness racing had emerged as America's leading spectator sport by the time Lady Suffolk was retired in 1853. During the 1850s the sport became an integral part of the county fair, and the public's desire to see harness races resulted in the construction of a number of trotting tracks nationwide—by 1858 one sports journal estimated that over seventy such tracks existed in America.[30] Expanding press coverage of harness racing corresponded to its growth. In New York the daily newspapers naturally focused on contests within the metropolitan area, but New York–based sports journals reported on races throughout the country and soon began publishing statistics.

New York City continued to dominate the development of harness racing even though the sport expanded nationally. At least seven trotting tracks existed in the metropolitan area, and three of them—Union, Fashion, and Centerville—hosted first-class contests. More significantly, with the increasing importance of gate receipts, harness racing in New

York drew the largest crowds. Between 6,000 and 8,000 spectators were usually present at each of the four to six leading matches held annually, and attendance would jump into double figures whenever Flora Temple, who followed Lady Suffolk as the "princess of the turf," was racing. Within a period of seventeen days in 1859 her contests with Ethan Allen and then Princess drew crowds of 12,000 and 20,000, respectively.[31]

The growth of harness racing as a spectacle did not occur without problems, however. As the commercial and professional ethic came to dominate the sport, suspicions of irregularities on the trotting track markedly increased. The question of the integrity of harness racing produced the first extensive discussion about the honesty of professional-commercial sport. Cries of foul play on New York tracks were heard as early as the 1830s. In 1837 the *Spirit* claimed that the public was beginning to express concern about the improprieties on the trotting track and insisted that men of character must immediately bar from the track those who disgrace the sport, or else the "trotting course and everything pertaining to them must 'go to pot.' "[32] While complaints persisted it was not until the 1850s that the New York press vociferously repeated the charges. Fundamentally, these statements did not vary from the theme, solution, or dire prediction the *Spirit* had offered more than a decade earlier. In 1857 the *Times* adamantly asserted that many owners of fast trotters simply would not allow their horses to compete in races since the courses had "fallen under the control of men who made use of them to subserve their own private interests and pecuniary gains."[33]

While it would be naive to assume that no races in New York were fixed, the frequent charges that contests were rigged appear to have been grossly exaggerated. Evidence and exposés of these "clandestine arrangements" are significantly lacking, and it is not surprising that the arguments developed a predictable rhythm. Many of the assertions could even be cast aside as sensational journalism. From time to time, moreover, statements in the press not only challenged the prevailing view but contradicted previous reports.[34] Hence the rise of the "manipulative theory," which derived from three interrelated factors: the nonexistence of investigative commissions; a limited concept of upset; and the nature of professional sport and the attitudes toward professional athletics. In the absence of an effective investigating body charges of irregularities were rarely examined. The lack of a critical institutional structure for the governance of sport served to fuel rumor and innuendo and thus made personal judgment the sole criteria for deciding the honesty of a race.[35] While nineteenth-century journalists were conscious that luck could play a part in the outcome of an athletic contest, when the favorite lost they generally offered some excuse. The present-day concept of upset — based on the realization that on certain occasions a competitor can achieve a level of performance above the usual standard and quite possibly never achieve it again—so critical to the integrity of professional sport today, did not exist in the mid-nineteenth century, and any unexpected occurrence frequently was translated as a fix.

The nature of professional athletics made creditable the assertion that races were fixed. Since the major purpose of the contest was to make money, there were no guarantees that the event would not be manipulated to maximize the profit. A certain class bias against the professional athlete accentuated the suspicion inherent in the professional system. The prevailing attitude was that the public was assured of honest contests only when the "better classes" governed sport.[36]

The strong temptation that confronted the professional athlete goes far in explaining why the press so vehemently opposed "hippodroming," or the making of contests for the sole purpose of splitting the gate receipts, in contrast to racing for stakes and purses. With no money depending on the outcome, and therefore no incentive to win, these "concocted affairs" were perfect races to rig. As the *Clipper* pointed out, "Many matches advertised for heavy stakes are merely for 'gate money' and so arranged that the winners are known to the 'initiated' before the event ever took place."[37] The suspicion of wrongdoing was justifiably heightened by the less than candid policy of track promoters who billed what was essentially an "exhibition" as a match race for large stakes, although this shady practice did not prove that contests were fixed. In 1860 the *Spirit* conceded that hippodroming had become an established method of scheduling races, yet it doubted "if there is one-tenth part of the rascality on a trotting track that many people suppose."[38]

Hippodroming was a legitimate response to the financial considerations of both horse owners and track proprietors. Hiram Woodruff claimed that Flora Temple caused the new system because the horse was in a class by herself, and "could not get a match on even terms, and was excluded from all purses." It is unlikely that Flora Temple or any other horse fostered hippodroming. Instead, the method emerged from the inadequacy of the prevalent winner-take-all system. The new arrangement made it possible for an owner to recover part of his costs and possibly emerge with a profit even though his horse was defeated. As such it facilitated an expansion in the number of trotters and the number of races. Equally important for the proprietors, it guaranteed the presence of the super horses, which in turn meant huge crowds. "No matter how these 'little arrangements' are concocted," the *Clipper* was forced to conclude, "it is but fair to say that they generally made interesting races, and in that way the spectators are pleased."[39]

Serious doubts must be raised about the view that widespread manipulation of races followed on the heels of the growth of professional-commercial harness racing. While dishonest contests occurred in New York they were the exception rather than the rule. Nevertheless, professionalization did significantly alter the character of trotting races. The emphasis of amateur turfmen on style and sportsmanship yielded to the sole objective of success, as jockeys adopted tricks and tactics that if not outright violations of the rules at least permitted them to bend the rules to their advantage. Such practices were often criticized and indeed contributed to the belief that there was a lack of propriety on the trotting track; they also foreshadowed what was to come in all professional sports. As Harold Seymour points out, these techniques were consistent with the dominant American values "in that it was results that counted, not how hard you tried or how sporting you behaved."[40]

While commercialization became harness racing's leading characteristic by the 1850s, informal trials of speed persisted on New York's streets. As the city grew, however, severe restrictions were placed on the roadster. By the 1860s the road runners had moved from Third Avenue to Harlem Lane in upper Manhattan, but that location also succumbed to the forces of progress. Dismayed by the imminent loss of the city's last good driving area, the editor of *Wilkes' Spirit* wrote that it was "incumbent upon the city's authorities to supply the vacancy created by the occupation of Harlem Lane." Since New York was the headquarters of the fast trotter, anything less "would be a national loss, as well as a municipal sham and disgrace."[41]

The call for any sort of government intervention might have been considered too far-sighted; instead, trotting men took steps more typical of the period, organizing private associations that bought or rented their own tracks. The first of these clubs was the Elm Park Pleasure Grounds Association, established in the late 1850s. The majority of its approximately 400 members were prosperous businessmen, although a few were men of considerable wealth, most notably Cornelius Vanderbilt and Robert Bonner.[42] Of all New York's road drivers, none had a more dramatic impact on the development of harness racing than Bonner. Born in Londonderry, Ireland, in 1824, he amassed a fortune by the time he was thirty as owner of the *New York Ledger,* a weekly family journal. In 1856 his physician advised him to seek outdoor recreation for health reasons, so Bonner bought a trotter and began driving on the New York roadways. He had a few brushes with Vanderbilt, and what emerged was a friendly rivalry between the two for ownership of the best trotters. Dwight Akers, a leading turf historian, insisted that the Bonner-Vanderbilt duel "marked the beginning of a change that provided the sport not only with strong financial backing but an efficient leadership." The confrontation between the steamship magnate and the newspaper tycoon did not initiate a new era, but it symbolized and gave impetus to an already existing process.[43]

Bonner's attitude toward racing complicated the confrontation yet indirectly heightened the excitement. A strict Presbyterian, he refused to allow his horses to take part in public races—he strongly opposed races for stakes because of the intimate connection between racing and gambling. Seemingly, the question of who had the fastest horses could not be settled. The issue came to a head in 1862 when Vanderbilt, with an eye toward Bonner, announced that he would race his team of Plow Boy and Post Boy against any other team, driven by the owner, for $10,000. He doubtless "chuckled at the discomfiture of his rival," wrote one of Vanderbilt's biographers. On May 13, 1862, Bonner drove his team of Lady Palmer and Flatbush Maid to the races at the Fashion Course, and at the request of the editor of *Wilkes' Spirit,* he agreed to display the speed of his famous mares for a handful of friends when the day's racing program had ended. Word leaked out and much of the crowd, including Vanderbilt, remained. Undaunted, Bonner took to the track, promising to lower the day's best time for the mile, 2:31¼ minutes. His team ran a fast 2:32½, but since he had expected to do better he decided to go for a second mile. The applause for a fine performance stopped instantly. As the team passed the back stretch the second time, George Wilkes reported, they "seemed to be absolutely flying, or as if flying swiftly without apparent effort along a line of railway. Each stroke of both grand animals fell together with exactitude of clock work." Bonner's mares finished in an incredible 2:28 minutes. Moving to checkmate his opponent, he told the crowd that while he opposed gambling, he would present a $10,000 gift to any gentleman who could drive his team faster. Vanderbilt had clearly been beaten at his own game. As good as his horses were, they were no match for Bonner's.[44]

While Bonner disapproved of track racing, he was clearly king of the road races. He spent lavishly, purchasing some of the best trotters of his era. Between 1859 and 1870 Bonner bought thirteen horses at a total cost of $162,000. His prize purchase, Dexter, was the number one trotter of his day. By the time Bonner retired in 1890 he had spent nearly half a million dollars to buy horses, including $40,000 each for Maud S. and Pocahantas.[45]

His reputation as a horseman did not derive solely from his ownership of probably the largest and best stable, however. As the *Tribune* pointed out he did more than any other man to elevate the trotting horse to a position of respectability. Prior to Bonner's involvement acceptable society viewed the owners of trotting horses as fast men "who spent their afternoons trotting from tavern to tavern . . . [and] had too much money in their pockets." Bonner was crucial in altering this negative impression.

A man of impeccable character, a staunch churchman, he neither smoked, drank, nor swore. As such he brought a dignity to the sport that other parvenu, such as the salty Vanderbilt, never could. With his influence the ownership of trotting horses became acceptable, so much so that "men of affairs, men of money, men of social position began to buy trotters, drive them on the roads and even enter them for races on the public tracks. From New York, the vogue spread to other cities."[46]

It is undeniable, indeed almost inevitable, that the possession of trotting horses gradually brought greater respectability in New York society when wealthy men became involved in the sport. This development did not emerge from a shift in attitude on the part of the city's "upper crust" but rather from a shift in composition. As the old-line elite gave way to the onslaught of new wealth, they also lost their position as arbiters of culture. Those on the rise, from whom trotting men were overwhelmingly drawn, dictated new standards based on their own views of acceptability. Thus, the increasing involvement of affluent New Yorkers in trotting must be understood against the backdrop of the plutocratic nature of the city. Since high society was easily accessible to those with new money, and since these newcomers were unsure of the traditions and prerogatives they were now privy to, they chose to dictate a new elite structure, one that encouraged publicity and fostered a fashionable style of conspicuous luxury. Although such traits did not emerge as dominant in New York society until the 1870s, they were already present to some extent among the city's elite prior to the Civil War.[47]

As they would in other sports, the nouveaux riches became involved in trotting in New York as a means of status confirmation. Interesting differences existed, however, between their role in trotting and in other sports activities. The new elite asserted its position by patronizing those sports with an upper-class heritage or those sports only wealthy men could afford. In the early years harness racing had none of these characteristics, so to function as other upper-class sports did its exclusiveness had to be created. Two interrelated processes accomplished this transformation: the purchasing of the best trotters by wealthy men, and the rationalization of the breeding industry.

By the 1860s the affluent were willing to pay premium prices for trotters, resulting in their monopoly of the best horses.[48] The soaring costs were in part a product of the growing popularity of the sport and in part a result of the increasing number of bidders in a relatively fixed market— there could be only a few champions each period. The law of supply and demand, important though it was, did not fully explain the price structure. For example, Bonner bought Dexter in 1867 for the incredible sum of $33,000, even though the seller, George Trussle of Chicago, had paid just $14,000 for him two years earlier. The fabulous sums were a critical part of the status game: to have obtained the best horses for anything less would not have satisfied the need of these men to demonstrate their wealth and status.

The rationalization of the breeding industry further encouraged the concentration of good trotting horses in the hands of wealthy men. In the mid-nineteenth century breeding required little capital, organization, or promotion. While some attention was paid to pedigree, lineage was usually a matter of guesswork if not outright falsification. The small scale on which business was run was not conducive to very selective breeding, yet its random nature had the valuable result of widely diffusing the bloodlines of the best animals. This haphazard method "contributed to the sport a delightful element of uncertainty, discovery and surprise, the satisfaction of making something out of nothing." It also enabled David Bryan and William M. Rysdyk, a former farmhand, to find fame and fortune with Lady Suffolk and Hambletonian, at a cost of less than $250 for the two horses.[49]

Within two or three decades small-time breeders yielded to the wealthy owners of larger stables, men who kept horses for pleasure, profit, or both. These well-capitalized stock farms gathered up the best trotters, a concentration of talent and money that permitted the breeding of trotting horses to become a more rationalized process. At the smaller stables the swift trotter was essentially a sideline, albeit an important one, to the general stud services being provided; the major objective was procreation and the overall improvement of a particular breed. In the larger stables speed was the sole objective. Using innovative techniques the big farms became "laboratories of speed," and as one turf historian concluded, "a system of breeding that had diffused the qualities of the best sires so widely through the common horse stock was replaced by a system more narrowly concentrated but for that reason more likely to produce exceptional results."[50]

Four critical steps were taken during the 1870s to further rationalize the breeding industry: (1) the creation of the first turf register devoted exclusively to the trotting horse (1871); (2) the appearance of the first sports journal, *Wallace's Monthly Magazine,* concerned primarily with trotting affairs (1875); (3) the formation of the National Association of Trotting Horse Breeders (1876); and (4) the establishment of a standard breed of trotting horse (1879).[51] By the end of the decade the rationalization of the breeding industry had solidified the ownership of the leading trotters in the hands of the wealthy. Unable to compete with the big farms, smaller breeders found their horses restricted to tracks at county fairs. The idea that a horse could be unhitched from a butcher's cart and made into a racing champion was relegated to dime novels and serials in popular magazines.

Neither the shift in the social composition of the owners of trotting horses nor changes in the breeding industry undermined the popularity of harness racing. Since the initial growth of the sport was strongly linked to the inexpensive cost of the trotter and its broadly based ownership, why did the sport continue to enjoy widespread popular appeal in the aftermath of these profound alterations? Surely the persistent perception of the trotter as a democratic and utilitarian animal played a contributing role. As late as 1884 one newspaper insisted that the "millionaire horsemen with their mammoth establishments and invested thousands, represent but a small fraction of the money employed in this special industry."[52] While the contention that the average farmer represented the backbone of the sport was inaccurate, the tremendous growth of harness racing at the county fair, with its rural connotations, did give the sport a democratic aura.[53]

The link between the growth of harness racing, changes in the breeding industry, and the commercialization of the sport made it virtually impossible for wealthy owners to claim trotting exclusively for their own class. While considerations of status contributed to elite involvement, financial concerns were always present for the overwhelming majority of these turfmen. To offset rising costs required a corresponding expansion in the economics of the sport. Consequently, trotting men continued to welcome the general public and their money (from gate receipts and gambling) as a means of defraying their expenses and making a profit. In catering to a broad segment of the population, owners, breeders, and promoters alike perpetuated trotting as the "people's pastime."

In the 1860s harness racing was experiencing tremendous success as a commercialized spectator sport in New York. The outbreak of the Civil War meant a brief pause in the general prosperity of the sport, but racing was back in full swing by the fall of 1862. During the next year trotting in New York appeared to be one continuous stream of match races, symbolized by a series of six races, each for $5,000, between General Butler and George Patchen. These matches attracted large audiences to the various courses, and in 1864 the *Clipper* noted that the previous season was "successful beyond precedent, alike in the quantity and quality of the sport which it had produced."[54] More significant for the overall development of the sport was the increasing size of the purses being offered. For example, the prize money tendered at the Fashion Course more than tripled between 1862 and 1870, from $3,750 to $11,500. By the early 1870s the aggregate sum of the purses offered by New York's three leading tracks during their weekly sessions exceeded $25,000. In addition, proprietors scheduled other purse contests from time to time.[55] Races that would have been run for no more than $250 in the 1850s were run for about $1,000 by the early 1860s and for as much as $5,000 by the end of that decade.

This development was paralleled by an increase in the number of trotters starting a race. Whereas four horses at most might have entered a race in the 1850s, that figure was the norm by the early 1860s, and it was not uncommon to find as many as seven horses in a contest. When there were seventy-eight entries for ten races at the Fashion Course in 1864, *Wilkes' Spirit* called it by far the greatest number ever for a regular meeting. To facilitate matters the track proprietors adopted a policy of sweepstakes racing that had long been used in thoroughbred racing, with nominations to these contests sometimes coming as much as a year in advance.[56]

The continued expansion of harness racing in New York City and throughout the nation in the years following the Civil War led to several problems, the most serious one, according to the press, being the specter of the fix. Calling on the track proprietors to purge trotting of its evil elements, they predicted dire consequences if their advice went unheeded.[57] No significant action was taken until 1869 when the Narragansett (Rhode Island) Trotting Association called for a convention of track operators. Meeting in New York the following February, delegates from forty-six tracks in fifteen states founded the National Trotting Association for the Promotion of the Interest of the Trotting Turf, later simplified to the National Trotting Association (NTA). The stated objectives of the NTA were the creation of uniform governing policies and the prevention and punishment of racing fraud. Members adopted rules that would be used at all the tracks under the association's jurisdiction and created a board of appeals to rule on all kinds of infractions at the local level. To give the board muscle the NTA ruled that suspension of one track was applicable to all tracks within the federation.[58]

Turf historians have accepted the desire to reform the evils of trotting as the major factor behind the creation of the trotting association. They recognized the need for changes in the institutional structure of harness racing but perceived this development as a means to a larger end.[59] Since the charges of race fixing were grossly exaggerated, however, the lofty ideals assigned by these observers must also be questioned. In fact, when the NTA was founded several individuals asked how the track proprietors, who had at least tacitly accepted the fraudulent behavior even though they may not have been responsible for it, were going to lead a reform movement. Interestingly, the right of track operators to represent the "trotting fraternity" at the convention was based on their vested economic interest in the sport.[60]

The formation of the National Trotting Association can be more appropriately examined as a response to the major problems of the sport:

the inefficiency of uncoordinated local organizations, and local rules that failed to meet the needs of track proprietors and owners of horses. As early as 1858 one sports journal noted the growth of harness racing and called for the creation of a national organization to govern the sport.[61] Only with the tremendous expansion of trotting in the post–Civil War years did the extant institutional structures become incapable of meeting the requirements of the sport. Far from being a means to an end, the NTA was an end in itself—to borrow a popular historical phrase, it was part of harness racing's "search for order." While the system of local rules did not prove too unwieldy when harness racing depended mainly on match races or contests with small fields comprised largely of neighborhood horses, it became inoperative with the growth of the sport. In 1862 the Fashion Course rewrote its rules to adjust to the increasing number of starters. Such a simple matter as positioning the horses on the track prior to each heat, once left up to individual drivers, now had to be codified. Moreover, by the 1860s New York tracks were beginning to handicap races to maintain a competitive balance among the rising number of horses on the course. And the number of new tracks throughout America added to the need for uniformity in the rules. Thus, to facilitate the easy movement of horses from course to course, standardized rules and regulations became a necessity.[62]

The NTA drew heavily on the experience of the New York tracks. Since the leading sports journals were located in the city, New York's rules were often published and were in use at a goodly number of courses throughout the country prior to the convention. Isaiah Rynders, the only New Yorker on the nine-man committee selected to draft the NTA's regulations, was chairman of the group. John L. Cassady, a delegate at the convention and a leading commentator on the trotting scene, maintained that Rynders was the busiest and most influential man at the convention.[63] His presence and influence raises an additional question of those who perceived the NTA as a reform group led by men in white hats. A former riverboat gambler, founder of the notorious Empire Club (a major New York gang), influential member of Tammany Hall, and a leading "shoulder hitter," Rynders was reputed to be the man most responsible for the "organized system of terrorism and ruffianism in city politics." Clearly, he was the prototype of the individual the press frequently accused of wielding a negative influence on racing.[64] If a man like Rynders was leading the reform, from whom were they reforming the turf?

In addition to the need for uniform rules, the expansion of harness racing made it imperative that the various track schedules be coordinated. For example, in New York City it was not so much a question of synchronizing the schedules of the major tracks as dealing with increased competition from new tracks outside the metropolitan area. With these courses offering good prize money to attract top-notch horses, even New Yorkers lacked the financial resources to meet the combined competition of these tracks. While the city remained the capital of the sport its former monopoly of the best horses was undermined. In the post–Civil War years track proprietors were forced to abandon their policy of arranging purse races throughout the year and adopt a more compact racing schedule. Thus, to guarantee the presence of the best talent the enlarged racing market needed some form of systematic scheduling to avoid conflicting engagements.[65]

The founding of the National Trotting Association in 1870 symbolized the transformation of harness racing from a premodern to a modern sport. In contrast to the informal road contests that took place in the Northeast half a century earlier, harness racing had evolved into a highly organized, national sport with relatively uniform rules. The emergence of a trotting literature (stud book and *Wallace's Monthly Magazine*) and developments in the breeding industry (the formation of the National Association of Trotting Horse Breeders and the establishment of the standard breed) in the 1870s further demonstrated the centralizing and modernizing forces at work in the sport. One social historian noted that harness racing "had grown to such mammoth proportions and won a greater share of the public attention than any other public pastime which contributed to the enjoyment of the people."[66]

As early as 1820 New York City played a critical role in the development of harness racing, a sport that emerged on urban roads and was first organized and commercialized in urban areas. The urbanization of America as a whole also contributed significantly to the expansion, transformation, and modernization of harness racing. While its popularity at county fairs gave the sport a strong rural base, even there it was a mere extension of the system that had matured in the city. So dominant was New York's position in harness racing that it set the basic tone and direction for the national development of the sport. While its stranglehold was somewhat loosened after the Civil War, it nonetheless retained its preeminent position. In 1870 New York City was what it had been throughout this era — the center of harness racing.

The first meeting at Jerome Park, in Westchester County. From a drawing by George Schlegel.

4

Horse Racing Comes of Age,
1845–70

By 1845 horse racing in New York was in a state of virtual collapse. Northern horsemen withdrew their active support and the breeding industry deteriorated throughout the region. For the next twenty years the sport floundered, although several attempts were made to rejuvenate it. Not until wealthy New Yorkers created the American Jockey Club in 1866 was thoroughbred racing once again established on a firm basis in the nation's leading metropolis. The devastating effects of the Civil War on southern racing also played a role in New York's reemergence as the nation's premier horse racing city. New York horsemen launched a new racing era by adopting the dash system of racing, which did not immediately alter the tone or structure of the sport but was the critical catalyst for the subsequent modernization of racing during the last three decades of the nineteenth century.

Horse racing continued for a few years following the fifth and final intersectional contest in 1845, but only the best horses attracted a crowd. When Passenger defeated Fashion in October 1847 a large gathering was present on the Union Course to provide the last hurrah for a dying sport. In 1849 New York did not hold a spring meeting and the fall session was a dismal failure. Horse racing had stopped completely by 1850, and it would be four years before the thoroughbreds returned to New York.[1]

A handful of New Yorkers were joined by other Americans in believing that under proper supervision horse racing could prosper in the nation's most populous city. Between 1854 and 1864 they made several unsuccessful attempts to revive the sport. Their first attempt was an outgrowth of a movement to establish a national jockey club and racecourse, something the leading sports journals had advocated in the 1830s. The majority of support came from those who lived in areas where racing had declined. Besides the advantages of uniform rules, proponents hoped that the establishment of a national track would enhance the prestige of the sport and thereby rekindle interest in their respective locales. Most advocates thought the track should be in Washington, D.C., but when southerners refused to support the program, for a variety of reasons, nothing came of it.[2]

A coalition of New York and southern turfmen undertook to reinstate racing in the city on a grandiose scale. In late 1853 John I. Snediker advertised races for the following spring at the Union Course, but he dropped the project in early 1854 when the state legislature granted S. J. Carter of New Orleans a charter permitting the construction of a new racecourse in Queens County and the incorporation of a racing association. While Carter became the proprietor of the new track, the major backers of the plan were William W. Boyden of Tennessee and Lovell Purdy, the son of the man who had been aboard Eclipse in the 1820s. For $85,000 this group purchased the 141-acre Willet Farm in Newtown, on Long Island, for the site of the track. A 12,000-seat grandstand was planned and the total capacity for the course was estimated at between 25,000 and 50,000. The spectacular enterprise, named the National Course, cost roughly a quarter of a million dollars for both the land and construction of the racing plant.[3]

Opened in June 1854 the promoters and the newly created National Jockey Club sponsored the most extensive racing card to date. They hosted a series of match and sweepstake races and presented two meetings each year, with each session lasting six days and with two races occurring daily. They offered $6,000 in prize money, more than double the purses awarded during the prosperous period of the mid-1830s. Various New York hotels contributed to the purses and had races named after them. Then, to put the finishing touch on this grand scheme Boyden proposed two international races to take place the following year. The challenge was never accepted, and in any event he lost control of the track before such races could be run.[4]

After the initial session the press was nearly unanimous in declaring that the "success of the National Course is now established beyond a doubt." The huge purses attracted the leading horses, the arrangements, especially for the ladies, proved comfortable, and perfect decorum prevailed during the two weeks of racing. The *Clipper* dissented, however, singling out the cost of admission and insisting that the National Course was "intended altogether for the aristocracy, and the high prices are intended to keep the people out." This policy was not an effective way to reform the sport, warned the *Clipper,* and when the novelty of the new track finally wore off, "better arrangements must be made for the future, otherwise the golden dreams of the proprietors will vanish into thin air."[5]

After the fall meeting it became evident that the owners of the National Course were in deep financial trouble. Although the schedule was good and the prize money remained high, attendance had declined significantly. The failure of the track rested with gross mismanagement by the proprietors, the *Clipper* claimed. Not only was the admission fee still too high, but some of the announced contests never took place. The less critical *Times* pointed out that many good horses were present but only one was from the North; without local horses competing, interest in the sport waned. When the owners failed to pay their mortgage the course was foreclosed in February 1855.[6]

The showman P. T. Barnum and Dr. John Weldon, a Georgia gambler and turfman, briefly flirted with the idea of managing the track. Uncharacteristically, the *Spirit* failed to give the potential sponsors much support, pointing out that Barnum had never been present at the races. Its major objection, however, was Weldon's plan to introduce southern weights onto the northern track, something the *Spirit* viewed as sacrilegious. When litigation over true ownership of the course prevented Barnum from obtaining an undisputed deed, he and his partner dropped the idea of sponsoring racing.[7]

The sport returned to New York in 1856 with the establishment of the Fashion Jockey Club. In all probability many of the people who had been part of the previous club comprised the new association. They renamed the Newtown track the Fashion Course, in honor of the great northern mare; however, that change did nothing to alter the sport's fortune. The *Herald* noted that the racing season sponsored by the new club had been contemptible. When the state legislature granted a new charter to a group headed by Lovell Purdy in the spring of 1857, the revitalized club brought Otway P. Hare of Virginia, one of the nation's leading turf proprietors, to New York to supervise the track. By the summer of 1857 Purdy lost control of the course when John Cassady outbid his group for the track lease. Cassady's single undertaking proved no more successful than his predecessors'.[8] The dismal campaign marked the beginning of the end for thoroughbred racing at the Fashion Course, which only four years earlier had been built to make New York City once again the showcase of racing.

A few diehard New York turfmen, led by Purdy, persisted in their belief that racing could prosper in the metropolitan area. Incensed when the Fashion Jockey Club lost control of the track in Newtown, Purdy portrayed the new manager as an opportunistic interloper and linked his own associates with those revered turfmen who had governed the sport during the previous generation. Purdy's message was a familiar one: only under proper supervision—his, of course—would the glory days of horse racing return to New York. He offered a new approach to financing horse racing: the creation of an association, distinct from a jockey club, with the power to sell bonds to the public (for five years at 7 percent interest, paid semiannually). Purdy sought to raise $75,000 by promoting horse racing as a profitable investment. The new association purchased the old trotting track in Centerville, on Long Island, and renamed it the Eclipse Course. In the spring of 1859 it held its only meeting. Despite progressive financing Purdy and his associates met the same fate as other groups who tried to rejuvenate the sport.[9]

By the outbreak of the Civil War horse racing in New York was no better off than it had been a decade earlier. Several racing meetings were held during the war years but attracted only sparse gatherings. The press paid lip service to the potential of a turf revival, but such pronouncements lacked their earlier gusto and confidence. As the war came to a close the outlook for horse racing in New York was bleak, but forces were already gathering to reestablish the sport in New York on a permanent basis.[10]

Many reasons were offered for the dismal condition of horse racing in New York between 1845 and 1865, but the press most frequently cited mismanagement. While there was general agreement that the governance of the sport left something to be desired, no consensus existed on where the responsibility for the problem lay. Some writers suggested that the management of racing had fallen into "the hands of men devoid of honor and honesty, who prostituted the sport in the advancement of their own selfish and pecuniary gains, and as a legitimate consequence, lost the confidence of the public." Others blamed the ineffective policies of the old guard, especially the high cost of admission, for the failure of the sport to win public support. Several members of the press believed that the absence or the ineffectiveness of jockey clubs was responsible. Without a strong jockey club to provide the necessary leadership, they insisted, no promoter, no matter how "enterprising or well known he may be on the turf," could ever succeed.[11]

While problems of management and leadership contributed to the persistent decline of thoroughbred racing in New York, the deterioration of the breeding industry in the North was the major reason for the sport's grim condition. The breeding industry had never really recovered from the devastating effects of the economic depression of 1837 and was in a state of collapse by the mid-nineteenth century. In 1850 only a single thoroughbred stallion was in service on Long Island, once an active breeding area. Both the *Spirit* and *Porter's Spirit* recognized that the absence of a sufficient number of first-class thoroughbred stallions in the New York region was critical to the failure of the sport.[12]

The collapse of this cornerstone of northern racing gave those who supported the efforts to stimulate the sport in New York little chance to succeed. A paucity of local horses made the proprietors of the city's tracks almost totally dependent on southern thoroughbreds. The prize money offered continued to be among the highest in America, but southerners could no longer be induced to bring their horses to the metropolitan area on a regular basis, given the distance and dangers of transporting their animals, the minor prestige to be gained from victories on the New York tracks, the differences in weights, the intersectional tensions, and the absence of any other northern tracks on which to compete. The lack of a sufficient quality and quantity of thoroughbreds, as well as the growing competition from other spectator sports, made it exceedingly difficult to recreate an interest in horse racing in New York.

The officers of New York's various jockey clubs between 1854 and 1864 were both similar to and different from their counterparts in the previous generation. Not surprisingly, they too resided, on the whole, in New York City and vicinity: of forty-two (out of forty-nine officers listed) individuals for whom residency could be established, thirty-eight (90.5 percent) lived in New York City and vicinity, twenty-one of them in Manhattan. Only three officers—John A. King, William H. Gibbons, and Henry K. Toler—had been actively involved in horse racing a decade or two earlier. While the leaders of the jockey clubs were different, they shared many of the same socioeconomic characteristics of their predecessors. Nearly 75 percent (twenty out of twenty-seven on whom data exist) of the members were engaged in either commerce or finance, three were listed as professional men, and two others were "gentlemen." Only Charles J. Foster, the influential editor of *Wilkes' Spirit,* and Isaiah Rynders, United States marshal and political boss, had less prestigious occupations. Similar to the officers of New York's earlier jockey clubs, most of the men were financially well-to-do, although the extent of their affluence no doubt fluctuated considerably among them. Six officers were direct descendants of the city's wealthiest 300 residents in 1845, and many others came from well-established families in the city and the surrounding area. Where they differed from their predecessors was in the great diversity of their social origins. The majority continued to come from prominent families of the metropolitan area, but an increasing percentage were drawn from families not associated with New York's antebellum elite. In some cases these men were the sons of leading residents of upstate New York or New England; in other cases they were from middle-class backgrounds. This trend became more pronounced in subsequent years.[13]

The resurgence of the northern turf occurred not in the nation's most populous city but rather in Saratoga, New York.[14] A strange coalition of New Yorkers initiated racing in this upstate resort city, led by John Morrissey, the former heavyweight boxing champion and a prominent Tammany Hall figure. Morrissey had made his fortune as a casino operator catering to opulent New Yorkers. To his dismay, although he mingled with the New York elite he never became one of them; consequently, he enlisted the support of two solid New York turfmen, John R. Hunter and William R. Travers, to ensure the respectability of his undertaking. When the inaugural four-day meeting at Saratoga in August 1863 proved successful, the group moved to establish racing there on a permanent basis, building a new track and forming a jockey club. The new association was comprised "entirely of gentlemen of high social position," with the majority of officers coming from New York City and vicinity. Morrissey was conspicuously absent from the list of incorporators of the Saratoga Association for the Improvement of the Breed, but he retained a majority of the stock in the company. With the former pugilist providing most of the cash, and Travers, Hunter, and others providing the class, horse racing at Saratoga proved eminently successful. As early as 1864 the press favorably compared the status, dignity, and fashion of racing there with that of the Royal Ascot in England.[15]

The success of racing at Saratoga encouraged New Yorkers to again make the sport fashionable in their own backyard. The architect and dominant figure of this movement was Leonard Jerome, the American grandfather of Sir Winston Churchill and a prominent Wall Street financier who had become a millionaire by selling short during the panic of 1857. The handsome Jerome gained his greatest notoriety, however, as the leader of the city's social set. A lover of sport, he had been a major backer of racing at Saratoga and was the first vice-president of the jockey club there.[16]

Probably late in 1865 Jerome decided that the nation's leading city needed a racecourse patterned after the elaborate European tracks. In collaboration with other turfmen he formed the American Jockey Club (AJC) and then purchased the 230-acre Bathgate estate in Westchester County, which he leased to the club for the new course. Jerome and others connected with the project were familiar with the land since the Bathgates had been breeding horses there since at least the 1820s. They also selected an area north of the city because New York turfmen had long expressed dissatisfaction wtih the Long Island tracks. Jerome offered up to $25,000 to defray expenses, although he embarked on the adventure convinced that the cost of operating the track could easily be met. Jerome Park, as the racecourse was appropriately named, proved to be an overwhelming success, and not a single penny of Jerome's generous subsidy was ever spent.[17]

The opening of Jerome Park on September 25, 1866, was the gala event of the year. General Ulysses S. Grant was the guest of honor, and the press naturally gave the festive occasion extensive coverage, focusing almost as much attention on who was there as what races were held. They noted that everyone who was anyone in the metropolitan area was present, including Josie Wood, the young and lovely owner of New York's most renowned sporting establishment, who arrived in her "luxurious victoria, escorted by liveried footmen." Among those of the city's prosperous but seamier side, only millionaire abortionist Madame Restall was absent, to the relief of many.[18]

From its inception few doubted the eventual success of the American Jockey Club. Prior to the inaugural meeting, one newspaper even claimed that the AJC was destined to "become the arbiter of [the] sport in this country." While the publicity was similar to the build-up given to previous racing associations in New York, this time the rhetoric exuded a new confidence. Developments during the AJC's first five years did not disappoint the prognosticators, for the press unanimously declared that both the quality and quantity of thoroughbreds at Jerome Park were outstanding. Under the sponsorship of the new club, moreover, racing had achieved a degree of fashion and respectability heretofore unknown in New York, even during the era of Eclipse. The significant increase in the number of women present at the track was also a radical departure from former days when the *Spirit* complained that their absence was a contributory factor to the failure of the sport in New York. Under the guidance of the AJC racing became more than a sporting event — it was a social outing, an arena for the "beautiful people" to see and be seen. By 1870 the *Herald* wrote that the jockey club had "speedily attained the exalted position of the exemplar of the turf. As a sporting organization it has no superior in the world."[19]

Observers agreed that the major reason for the resurgence of horse racing in New York was that men of wealth and integrity had once again taken control of the sport. Their leadership weeded out those nefarious influences that had been responsible for earlier mismanagement and racing's declining popularity. Having thus cleansed the sport of its corrupting influences, the American Jockey Club succeeded because it made the racetrack an attractive place for fashionable and respectable citizens.[20] The argument that the takeover of the tracks in 1845–65 by self-seeking individuals had been responsible for the collapse of the sport now hardened into the singular explanation of racing's earlier demise. The rapid success of the AJC, guided by prominent New Yorkers, gave credence to the argument and served the interest of the club, naturally glorifying the new racing association as a reformer of the turf. The propaganda that the jockey club and its allies in the press promoted was more than self-adulation, however; it also provided a critical underpinning of its elitist policies. The lessons to be drawn had a familiar ring: not only must the "better class" govern racing if it was to prosper, but as custodians of the sport the elite must be accorded the freedom and power to ensure that outside negative forces would not corrupt it once more.[21]

The reform thesis distorts the cause of racing's revival in post–Civil War New York and the unique contribution of AJC turfmen to the modern development of the sport. The problems with horse racing had been economic, not managerial, and it was the changing financial climate that encouraged New Yorkers to again invest in horses. Indeed, the rebirth of northern racing followed from the destruction of southern racing. As early as 1863 the *Herald* pointed out that "the war now raging in the South, and extending to some regions of the Western states has deprived owners of racing stock there of their usual fields of turf operation, and consequently induces them to come North." To maintain their investment, southern breeders began racing their horses at Saratoga and at Paterson, New Jersey; and they became even more dependent on the revitalized northern turf in the postwar years. While racing eventually returned to several southern cities it was but a vain attempt to revive an earlier glory. By 1872 the Metarie Course in New Orleans, once the symbol of elegance and excellence in southern racing, was in disrepair and had been turned into a cemetery. Control of the sport shifted firmly to the North, with New York as its capital.[22]

While the dependency of southern turfmen on northern tracks provided the initial thrust for racing's return to Manhattan and vicinity, the AJC probably would have gone the way of other jockey clubs if it had relied solely on southern horses. Even during the antebellum period southerners could not supply the city's tracks with a sufficient number of horses to generate continued interest in the sport. Now that the Civil War had undermined much of the financial base of the southern breeding industry, not to mention the destruction of many fine thoroughbreds, it would have been impossible for them to provide all the horses needed on northern tracks. Experience had demonstrated that some degree of local ownership was necessary to stimulate elite interest and support.[23]

Although a handful of thoroughbreds remained in the metropolitan area during the dark days of racing, affluent residents of New York and vicinity again began purchasing and breeding thoroughbreds in the 1860s. By the end of the decade there were fifteen owners in and around the city. These men, like their predecessors, were wealthy, but they no longer came from the antebellum upper class. Six of eleven owners on whom data exist originally were from outside the metropolitan area; only John F. Purdy and John G. Hecksher were native New Yorkers. The majority of these horsemen came from upper-class backgrounds, but only four were related to the city's antebellum leaders.[24] The wealth of thoroughbred owners in the 1860s continued to derive from traditional sources—commerce, finance, and real estate; not one man had made his fortune in manufacturing or industry. While the majority of them were not native New Yorkers, by the mid-1860s they had infiltrated the city's elite social institutions: eight were members of the prestigious Union Club and ten belonged to the New York Yacht Club. Only William H. Gibbon and T. B. Read, both New Jersey residents, were not members of either club. While New York's racing enclave became part of the upper echelon, the outgoing life-style of these horsemen, especially their leaders—August Belmont, Leonard Jerome, and William Travers—shared more in common with the New York elite of the Gilded Age than with their predecessors during the Jacksonian era.

The creation of racing stables by wealthy New Yorkers in the 1860s was a product of personal and social factors. Many of these men had cultivated an active interest in the turf even prior to the Civil War.[25] While their involvement was rooted in individual tastes, like turfmen both previously and subsequently, status considerations also motivated this group. The ownership of thoroughbreds continued to serve as a vehicle for proclaiming, buttressing, and integrating the horsemen's elite status.[26]

Although personal satisfaction and status theory explain the motivation of New York horsemen, they do not explain the timing. The reemergence of the northern breeding industry, like the sport, occurred as the South released its stranglehold. Just as the center of racing and breeding shifted to the South in the two decades prior to the Civil War, when northern tracks failed in their attempts to attract southern horses and northern breeders could no longer cover their expenses, so did racing and breeding shift northward again after the war. As northern tracks reopened and prospered, New York horsemen could meet their expenses and thus were able to revive the breeding industry in the North.[27]

The move from New Orleans back to New York was more than just a change in the center of racing; it also marked the beginning of a new era. John B. Irving, secretary of the American Jockey Club, in a promotional pamphlet written prior to the inaugural meeting, stated that a new period was about to commence with the formation of the new jockey club. This propaganda piece and similar articles by club allies in the press identified the emergence of a new era with elite sponsorship of racing and the general reform thesis, although they never clarified precisely what would be novel about racing under the new club's direction.[28] Indeed, they contributed to the development of horse racing not as reformers but as innovators.[29] Under their leadership an entirely different system of racing emerged, one that eventually produced results that some members of the jockey club would have abhorred but nonetheless gradually transformed and modernized horse racing in America.

The abandonment of the old system of heat racing was at the crux of the change.[30] In its place New Yorkers adopted the model already prevalent in England — the dash system, with its fractional distances and greater emphasis on speed. This change had been foreshadowed even in America for some time, for turf statistics indicate the decline of the long-distance thoroughbred race for two decades prior to the Civil War.[31] Yet it was not until New Yorkers once again became the leaders of the sport that the dash system became the dominant mode of racing. It must be noted that heat racing did not die out right away. The Inaugural Stakes at Jerome Park remained a traditional four-mile heat race, but by 1868 the *Herald* conceded that dashes had become the prevalent form of racing, even though the editors vehemently disapproved of this system.[32] The *Times* responded to the charge that the imported racing form resulted in the "decadence of the American turf and the deterioration of the American race-horse" by claiming that the current thoroughbreds could not only go faster but had as much stamina as their predecessors. Furthermore, the basic advantage of the dash system was that it facilitated an expansion of the sport: the newer form, with its shorter distances, did not break down thoroughbreds as rapidly as the older one had, and at the same time it permitted more races to take place daily.[33] The introduction of other changes, such as handicapping, claiming races, and races for two-year-olds, also augmented the amount of sport.

The impact of the dash system on New York's racing card was evident in the American Jockey Club's first full year. The club broke with the long-held tradition of spring and fall meetings and added a third one during the summer. For the first five years the number of racing days per meeting remained the same, but spectators now saw four and sometimes six contests per day at Jerome Park. The number of entries and starters obviously increased, so that by 1869 approximately 140 thoroughbreds entered the fall meeting, with as many as 8 horses starting a race.

Other important racing changes took place. Match races, the foundation of the sport until the 1830s, declined prior to the Civil War and almost totally disappeared afterward. Contests open only to jockey club members, similarly on the wane since the 1840s, were removed from the racing card. Hence, in the years following the war, racing consisted of "programs of which most if not all events were really, if not formally, public ones."[34] Permanent stakes races soon began in New York, the most famous eventually becoming part of racing's Triple Crown for three-year-olds: the Belmont Stakes, inaugurated in 1867 and named after August Belmont, the American Jockey Club's first president.

The expanded racing program brought a corresponding increase in the amount of prize money. Exact figures often depended on the number of subscribers and the eventual number of entries; however, the premiums offered outright or added to the purses by the AJC demonstrate the financial growth of the sport. At the initial meeting in 1866 the club gave $11,750; by the spring of 1870 the figure had climbed to $13,650. Whereas the NYAIB had offered the modest sum of $2,500 in prize money during the first year of the Union Course, half a century later the premiums given annually at Jerome Park were between $35,000 and $40,000.[35]

The connection between the emergence of the dash system as the dominant mode of racing and the reemergence of New Yorkers as the sport's leaders is hardly coincidental. As long as southerners set the tone and direction for the sport, heat racing remained the prevalent form because it worked for them. Dale Somers notes that had the Civil War not intervened, New Orleans's status as the racing capital "would have probably continued indefinitely. . . . Whatever the shortcomings of the region's planter class, the quality of their thoroughbreds was beyond dispute." Whereas success provided no incentive for change among southerners, failure was the impetus among northerners. The sport could not have been successfully revived in New York if the city's horsemen had continued to rely on the traditional system. It is doubtful that the prize money generated from the traditional style of racing could have offset the increased cost of thoroughbreds as well as the rise in other racing expenses.[36]

The adoption of the dash system not only contributed to the rejuvenation of racing in New York, it also institutionalized the city's leadership position. Financial considerations had always played a vital part in the development of horse racing. With an increased number of races and a corresponding rise in the amount of prize money, economics became an overriding factor. The increasing importance of money in racing gave the wealthiest and most populous urban area a distinct advantage over its rivals. By offering the largest purses New York came to dominate the racing scene yet again. From there the dash system rapidly spread to racing associations throughout the country. Its success in New York no doubt encouraged this development, but the universal acceptance of the new system resulted mainly because the major sports interests—track promoters, purse-conscious owners and breeders, and track gamblers—preferred it and benefited from the expanded programs.[37]

Institutional change rooted in pragmatism produced more than a shift in the style of racing; it gradually stimulated a complete alteration in the tone of the sport. "To support these stepped-up programs, which required more and bigger purses," William Robertson noted, "it became necessary to depend on public patronage. The pure concept of sport for sport's sake had to be tempered with the realities of economic necessity, and gambling exchanged its stool in the corner for a seat at the main table."[38] While the dash system eventually encouraged the commercialization of horse racing, with its more diverse class attendance, during the last third of the nineteenth century, in 1870 this development was not evident on New York tracks. In fact, the press frequently criticized the AJC during its first five years for its "aristocratic" and exclusive admission policy. Echoing their earlier complaints, a majority of the press claimed that entrance fees prohibited many respectable individuals from attending races and called for a more equitable rate. The *Herald* went one step further and campaigned to reinstitute the English system of free admission to the course, with the exception of the grandstand. *Wilkes' Spirit* agreed that the plan would help popularize the sport and conceded that it was "eminently successful in England," but it insisted that the plan was not applicable for the conditions of the American turf. Here the track did not attract a sufficient number of spectators "as to make the admittance to the stands, and rents of the booths, sufficient to defray all expenses, and to give liberal purses and costly plates, as in England." In 1869 Sir Roderick W. Cameron, an Englishman by birth, proposed the *Herald's* plan at an AJC meeting on the grounds that the objective of the club "ought to be the encouragement and promotion of the sport among the people," but it never even came to a vote.[39]

Although gate receipts, which came to a minimum of $3,000 daily, clearly played an important part in meeting the expenses of the sport in New York, the unwillingness of the AJC to sanction free entry or even reduce the cost of admission went beyond monetary considerations. What differentiated horse racing in America and England was a product of social, not financial, considerations. While the upper class governed horse racing in both countries, differences in class structure, obviously a matter of degree, but important nonetheless, affected their sporting behaviors. In England the class lines were more rigidly drawn and the upper class was also more firmly entrenched; by contrast, the American upper class, especially as it existed in post–Civil War New York, was generally more open yet also less secure about its status and prerogatives. Furthermore, the sporting behaviors of the two elite groups were not solely a product of class; each reflected the extent to which traditional elements remained embedded in their respective societies. The upper class in England retained to a far greater extent the behavioral patterns of a rural and traditional aristocracy, which had long nurtured its paternalism, and continued to do so. The more secure position of the elites, combined with their paternalistic heritage and an entrenched system of deference, at times enabled them to mingle at and even participate in sports events with other social groups, albeit never on equal terms. Since the elements that nurtured interclass involvement in sport in England did not exist here to the same degree and/or in the same combination, the American upper class was always a bit reluctant to participate in sports activities with individuals from other social ranks.[40]

Even as the press clamored for a more liberal admission fee and disapproved of the jockey club's disdain for the public, the central focus of their criticism revolved around the policy of restricting the main section of the grandstand to club members. The *Herald* argued that compelling the paying public "to take such inferior positions as may be assigned them . . . [especially] when the spot allocated to the club is not more than half occupied" was an "obnoxious feature." The *Times,* in the past a strong supporter of the AJC, joined the chorus of critics, pointing out in 1867 that a cautious policy had been necessary to ensure the respectability of the course, but such severe restrictions were no longer required.[41] It was uniformly agreed, however, that Leonard Jerome was not responsible for the "exclusive, illiberal and aristocratic" management of Jerome Park. The press also carefully pointed out that such undemocratic practices did not represent the sentiments of the majority of club members. One sports journal maintained that these men were "in general no better off than the public, but are the victims of the governing clique." At a time when consensus was rare in the press, there was general agreement that the club's ruling oligarchy, a group of fifty life members, was responsible for the inegalitarian management of the racetrack. Noted one publication, these men, these "sticklers for exclusiveness," are "the *parvenus* of New York society and form its 'codfish aristocracy.' "[42] The press also repeatedly charged that this oligarchical structure was inconsistent with American values and traditions. Since the membership at large greatly outnumbered this "House of Lords," it was downright despotic that fifty life members "should possess a monopoly over the management of the affairs of the club." The New York press called for a complete revision of the jockey club's constitution and the creation of a more democratic governing body.[43]

The recently established *Turf, Field and Farm* rushed to the defense of the AJC. It criticized the jealous custodians of the rights of the people for denouncing "the gentleman's idea of racing, as an element at war with free republican institutions," especially given the national benefit that accrued from wealthy men's support of the sport. The publication went on to repeat the familiar theme that racing could only succeed when governed by gentlemanly principles and when wealthy men were given the freedom necessary to guarantee the sport's respectability. It asserted that since racing was dependent on the "liberality of wealthy gentlemen," the AJC had the right to decide who may enter the course and to take any steps it deemed proper to ensure the prosperity of its amusements.[44]

By 1869 the public had become so vocal on the issue of the club's right to exclusive control of racing that a meeting of the AJC governing committee was called. Despite proposals that admission be free to all and that the club section of the grandstand be opened to the public, only one minor change took place: the AJC would now permit nonmembers to enter the club section when introduced by a member, who would be "responsible for the respectability of the parties." All the new policy accomplished, *Wilkes' Spirit* concluded, was to make anyone sitting anywhere else appear less than respectable.[45] While the tremendous expansion of horse racing would eventually contribute to the breakdown of class barriers at the track, none of this was evident to those who attended Jerome Park in the late 1860s. "Racing is for the rich," August Belmont is quoted as saying, an accurate assessment of the condition of horse racing in New York in 1870.[46]

The ability of the American Jockey Club to succeed without relying on mass support was due to the willingness of wealthy New Yorkers to promote horse racing, the gate receipts provided by the well-to-do sporting fraternity and the "beautiful people," and the money the club received from its concessions of the rights to sell gambling pools at Jerome Park. Since the 1850s American tracks had been using the pool system of wagering, whereby the pool-seller paid the racing association a flat fee. Such arrangements made tracks like Jerome Park partners in the gambling business.[47]

Although opposition to horse racing persisted on the grounds that it fostered and encouraged gambling, New York newspapers had long since countered that argument by pointing to the benefits derived from the sport. Slight but important shifts in the attitude toward the relationship between racing and gambling began to emerge in the 1860s. Journalists continued to point out the public's proclivity to gamble and stated that there was little difference between wagering on sports contests and other, more acceptable forms of speculation. While they spoke of gambling in distrustful terms, they nonetheless came to see it as a necessary evil as far as horse racing was concerned. One correspondent in *Wilkes' Spirit* accurately noted, "Were it not for betting, co-relative with racing, racing would very soon die out."[48]

The increasing financial requirements of the sport were behind the shifting attitude of the press toward gambling. Even as the press came to condone gambling they never fully accepted the pool-seller, those men from lower-class origins who were engaged in "cunning machinations." Many viewed the boisterous spectacle of the pool-sellers' transactions as vulgar and abhorrent,[49] but the crux of the matter, once again, was largely economic. With pool-sellers making a net profit of $6,000–$7,000 per meeting, and at times as much as $12,000–$15,000, and with prize money and other expenses constantly on the rise, both *Turf, Farm and Field* and

Wilkes' Spirit advocated the abolition of the pool-seller and the takeover of gambling at the track by a racing association. This, they argued, would ensure the integrity of the activity and provide the jockey club and thoroughbred owners with much-needed revenue.[50] Despite the proposal the AJC continued to rely on the pool-seller, raising further doubt as to the perception of the club as a turf reformer. It no doubt attempted to eliminate the worst abuses associated with gambling, but it was more than willing to cooperate with gamblers when doing so served its own self-interest.

The changing style of horse racing did not in any way undermine the utilitarian justification of the sport. The press still declared that improvement of the breed was the fundamental objective of racing. However, they never examined how the practical benefits would be derived, although they surely realized that such expensive thoroughbreds were not going to be bred to common horses. Possibly they believed that breeding for the racecourse would have "spin-off" benefits for other aspects of the industry as well as common-stock breeders.[51]

The utilitarian thesis was not restricted solely to the betterment of the breed. The press noted that racing produced direct and indirect economic benefits for New York City by attracting visitors to the area who spent their money at the races and at other businesses. The sport's recreational value was also a popular theme, for horse racing provided spectators with a legitimate excuse to escape the congestion and pollution of the city. The drive to Jerome Park and its rustic setting were of sufficient benefit in themselves to encourage people to attend the contests. As a diversion, some papers insisted, racing had a civilizing effect. "When conducted by gentlemen on honorable principles," racing was "an avenue for the development of public spirit in a manly arena, whereby all classes of society may be benefitted."[52]

Such arguments were not new, but their increasing usage to sanction the sport reflected, in part, a growing insecurity with the older justification for improvement of the breed. The press continued to pay lip service to this rationale, but their statements lacked the confidence and certainty of antebellum observers. While it was once easy to believe that trials of speed led to improved thoroughbreds, the recent changes in the nature of horse racing made it exceedingly difficult to suppose that these noble animals had any practical benefit except for sport. The newer justifications were thus a product of the maturing view of the role of sport in an urban community.[53]

SECTION II

BALL GAMES IN THE CITY: CRICKET AND BASEBALL

A variety of simple bat, base, and ball games had been played throughout the colonial period, but not until the first four decades of the nineteenth century did they take hold as popular pastimes, especially in the more settled regions of New England and the Middle Atlantic states. By 1840 these structurally similar games, played under several names—rounders, town ball, and the most popular, baseball—were premodern in character. Informal and unorganized, ball games were played purely on a local level; they rarely attracted spectators, and no information about them was included in local newspapers. Rules and regulations varied from community to community, and the game usually had no prescribed number of players. These simple ball games were well suited for essentially rural America, where space was readily available, equipment was cheap—balls and bats could be constructed from easily available materials—and the only preparation needed was laying out bases or goals.[1]

In contrast to premodern baseball, cricket began to assume a somewhat modern character in America by 1840. The sport already had achieved a modicum of organization, as evidenced by the sporadic appearance of cricket clubs in New York and other cities. Modernization of the sport in England also meant that standardized rules were available. But in other ways American cricket remained premodern in character. Similar to baseball, cricket was played solely on a local level, received little public attention, and was not subject to recordkeeping. By 1870 both cricket and baseball had become modern sports, but the two had taken divergent paths. While baseball was being described as the national pastime, cricket as a popular sport had passed into oblivion.

For more than a century, popular observers of cricket and baseball have asserted that national characteristics and national origins determined the destinies of these two sports. This explanation emerged in the late 1850s and early 1860s when journalists began to juxtapose baseball and cricket as representative of the national character of Americans and Englishmen, respectively. By the turn of the twentieth century the national pastime's well-developed ideology maintained that baseball was America's preeminent sport because it embodied America's experiences, virtues, and values.[2] These nationalistic overtones climaxed when professional baseball, led by Albert G. Spalding, former major league pitcher and sporting goods magnate, sought to prove beyond a doubt that baseball truly was an American sport. Drawing on flimsy evidence Spalding's self-appointed commission concluded that Abner Doubleday had created baseball in 1839 in Cooperstown, New York. The report allowed Spalding and others to unequivocally state that baseball was an indigenous sport untainted by any relationship to a foreign game.[3] Given the universal acceptance of baseball's popular mythology, the reason for cricket's fate was self-evident. As a foreign sport with aristocratic overtones it had little in common with democratic America.

Sport historians have not altered the basic contours of the popular explanation of baseball's success and cricket's failure even though their research not only shows that baseball evolved from the English game of rounders but exposes many of the fallacies of baseball's popular mythology. Harold Seymour maintains that baseball emerged as the dominant bat-and-ball game in the Civil War period because it was faster, more action-packed, and better suited for the rapidly changing American environment than cricket, and because at a time of intense nativism there was an intrinsic aversion to cricket simply because it was English.[4]

Australian historian Ian Tyrrell is the lone dissenter from the majority view that national characteristics and nationalistic sentiments explain the fates of baseball and cricket. He maintains that scholars have too readily imposed subsequent societal and sports developments in discussing the destinies of these two ball games and have failed to examine closely the character of both sports when they were first introduced in America. He insists that "it is important not to assume that the rise of baseball was inevitable," or "that baseball was uniquely and ideally suited to the American environment." For Tyrrell, the destinies of baseball and cricket derived from their emergence between 1850 and 1880 as sports of distinct social clases: cricket became an upper-class sport, while artisan groups dominated baseball.[5]

Tyrrell's article contains several perceptive insights and his criticism of the accepted interpretation of baseball's rise and cricket's demise is quite accurate.[6] There are several problems with the effort to link the course of the two ball games to national characteristics. Tyrrell has already shown that the pace of the two games, a central component of this thesis, was initially not as different as it would later become.[7] More significantly, the multitude of statements on how baseball and cricket represented different national characters contain much rhetoric but little substance, and in fact are predicated on the acceptance of an unchanging, yet vague and undefined, American character.[8] The result of all this has been the creation of an analysis that is both deterministic and ahistorical.

Reliance on nationalistic sentiments to explain the fates of the two ball games is also fraught with drawbacks. For example, if the English origin of cricket was responsible for its failure to establish itself in America, then why were almost all the major sports being played in America at that time English in origin, or at least had been brought to this country via England? And if anti-English sentiment produced such an aversion to cricket, why did Americans at the same time import croquet and adopt the English dash system in horse racing? While various problems exist with the view that Americans rejected cricket because it was English, it is true that baseball in the years before and after the Civil War benefited from nationalistic sentiments. Recognition of that fact does not require acceptance of nationalism as a determining factor in the fates of the two ball games. It does, however, necessitate that greater attention be paid to the issue of timing. In examining these two ball games historians, including Tyrrell, have begun their analyses with the rise of baseball in the 1850s, and in doing so they fail to explain why the older sport of cricket did not emerge as a popular pastime prior to that. If cricket had solidified its position in America before baseball became so popular, the destinies of both sports might have been different. As Allen Guttmann recently noted, chronological priority can become cultural preference.[9]

The current status of the scholarly literature on cricket and baseball contributes to the erroneous view of the causes of their divergent fates. Historical studies of cricket in America are virtually nonexistent; as a result, most conclusions concerning the sport derive from studies of baseball and surveys of other American sports. Cricket is examined merely as an antecedent to and/or a foil for the more important success story of baseball, an approach that hardly lends itself to a detailed and accurate examination of the forces that shaped the game of cricket in America.[10] Similarly, while numerous popular and a growing number of scholarly histories of baseball exist, scant attention is paid to the sport's early development; instead, writers concentrate on professional baseball, starting with the formation of the National League in 1876. Baseball prior to 1870 is examined cursorily at best, and even then mainly as a backdrop to subsequent developments.[11] While several writers devote more space to the early years of baseball, their works, typical of the genre, are narrative, anecdotal, and do not explore the broader relationship between sports and society.[12] Scholarly examinations of the national pastime also focus overwhelmingly on the evolution of professional baseball. Moreover, when they have examined baseball prior to 1870 their works suffer from a limited appreciation of the social and sporting environment of the times. They impose later standards of social class and more recent sports concepts and standards on antebellum New Yorkers, with distortion the inevitable outcome.[13]

In the next three chapters, then, I shall examine the modernization of cricket and baseball in Manhattan and Brooklyn between 1840 and 1870 as a means of clarifying the reasons for the divergence of the two sports.[14] These neighboring areas constituted the center of baseball and cricket during their critical years of maturation and played a vital role in shaping both the development and destinies of these games nationally.

An international cricket match between the St. George and the Canadian clubs. From a drawing in *The Atlas,* September 29, 1844.

A cricket match between the St. George and the New England clubs. From a drawing in *Gleason's Pictorial,* October 4, 1851.

5

The Failure of Cricket
as an American Sport

Between 1840 and 1870 cricket in America evolved from a premodern to a modern sport. For the first fifteen years it was the leading ball game in the country and in fact received more attention in the press than any other sport, with the exception of horse and harness racing. By the end of this period, however, baseball had not only replaced cricket as America's leading ball game, but cricket disappeared from the mainstream of American sports.

The failure of cricket derived from the nature and structure of American society and their influence on the country's ball-playing tradition; the host of social and cultural changes that occurred between 1840 and 1860; and the impact of the institutionalization, modernization, and maturation of cricket in England and their relationship to the transplanting of the sport in this country. These influences will be examined in four stages: the factors that inhibited growth of the sport prior to 1840; the development of cricket in Manhattan and Brooklyn in 1840–60; the challenges presented by baseball and the linked fates of the two ball games in 1855–65; and the failure of cricket in terms of skill, sponsorship, structure, and stage of development. The chapter ends with a brief discussion of the changes in cricket during its decline.

Cricket had been introduced into the colonies by the start of the eighteenth century, but participation was sporadic until the decades following the Revolution. The formation of cricket clubs in New York and other cities illustrates the growth of the sport. Clubs probably existed in Manhattan during the war, since a 1786 advertisement for bats and balls was addressed "To The Cricket Club." However, there is almost no information about these clubs, or even how many existed. Most of them were probably short-lived and may have lacked the formal organizational structure of later cricket associations.[1] In any event, the game was played largely on an informal basis, and cricketers probably played as much single wicket as the eleven-man game. The contests that did take place were mainly between club members, although a rare interclub match might be held (New York newspapers recorded only one such match between 1820 and 1838).[2]

By 1840 cricket in America remained a novelty sport, played almost exclusively by English immigrants; by comparison, it had been popular in England for nearly a century, particularly in the southern region. Since English practices strongly influenced sports developments in this country, why didn't Americans take up cricket?[3] The answer can be found in a variety of interrelated factors, but the primary one was the respective ball-playing traditions of the two countries. Whereas the English had a long heritage of ball playing by young men and adult males, such activity became popular in America only at the start of the nineteenth century, and even then it was basically an amusement for children and young boys.

Differences in the extent of ball playing in England and America were a product of several varying societal conditions. Before examining these differences it is necessary to briefly discuss the origin of ball games and their emergence in Christian culture. Unlike other sports which sprang from day-to-day activities, ball games originated in religious and magical functions and were closely associated with fertility rites. The Church adopted these ritualistic ball games and used them for Christian purposes, with some modification in their meaning. In Europe various ball games became part of the Easter observance and other springtime customs. Robert Henderson maintains that "the subsequent development of the bat and ball games so familiar to us" hinged on the "adoption of the pagan ball rites into the Easter Christian ceremonies."[4]

By medieval times ball games were tightly interwoven with life in rural England, being associated with Christian holidays, parish feasts, and other religious activities. Some opposition always existed to these games, as well as to other forms of traditional recreations, but not until the beginning of the early modern period did a vigorous reform movement, led by dissident Puritans, "present a powerful challenge to the customary practices of popular recreations." Their emphasis on a strict Sabbath and their fears that amusements distracted people from their basic religious and social duties both shaped the Puritan view of sport. They also objected strongly to traditional recreations because they were rooted in pagan and popish practices and "were rich in the sort of ceremony and ritual which poorly suited the Protestant consciousness." Their influence in curtailing the pastimes of the populace proved fleeting, however, because of the persistence of a traditional social structure and its continuing role in providing the dominant English symbols and values. As a result, there remained a "widespread need for the sort of ceremonial values which the traditional recreations embodied and sustained," and which continued to be "reinforced by the rituals of community and the ties of paternalism." As late as the mid-eighteenth century, Robert Malcolmson has pointed out, traditional recreations in England were still "thriving, deeply rooted and widely practiced."[5]

In contrast to the English experience, various factors mitigated against the proliferation of ball games in America. Scholars generally look to the rural-agricultural nature of early American society, with its strains of individualism, as well as to religious opposition to sport in general, to explain the paucity of ball playing in this country.[6] These elements were important, but they do not provide a sufficient explanation, especially since ball games existed in agricultural England and since Americans actively engaged in other sports. A more adequate perspective for understanding the relative absence of ball playing is the comparative weakness in America of the kind of ritualistic, traditional, and communal society that nurtured and provided the context for these games in England. Clearly, prior to 1800 American society was predominantly traditional, yet to a much different extent and in different ways than English society. Richard Brown has noted that by the end of the seventeenth century the entire process of colonial settlement—with its profound impact on economics, politics, religion, and social relations—had delivered "shattering blows to basic traditional structures." While the "traditional social edifices did not come tumbling down," cracks developed, and America's traditional society survived in "a weakened, vitiated condition." Both the rate and extent to which American society moved away from the traditional mode were probably insufficient, in and of themselves, to preclude the development of ball games. Nevertheless, the slow erosion of traditional society clearly had some effect, for even in England communal ball games, most notably football, had declined in popularity by the end of the eighteenth century.[7]

Other influences meshed with the decline of traditional society to inhibit ball games from taking root in this country. The degree to which Americans were less ritualistic and deferential than their English counterparts played a contributory role, as did the more critical absence of a landed gentry and a feudal shire system, elements that alone or in combination were vital in providing structure and meaning for team ball games in England.[8] By contrast, other sports that took root in America derived from and were supported by a different tradition, connected as they were with utilitarian, day-to-day activities and overwhelmingly individual or dual in nature. They did not require the elaborate setting of team games and thus could be more easily transplanted to this country. Also, since ball playing here lacked the social meaning and setting it had in England, it was not considered an acceptable manly activity. The majority of participants were from an age group in which physical skills were lacking. Hence, ball playing in America did not advance for some time beyond the simple forms, such as rounders, played by English schoolboys.

During the first four decades of the nineteenth century Americans began to participate increasingly in ball games, but cricket made little headway. The reasons for its limited growth can be understood by briefly examining the character and historical development of the sport in England.[9] By the start of the Victorian period four factors characterized English cricket. First, cricket had evolved from a simple batting game into a highly skilled, complex, competitive sport. The emergence of a distinct class of professional cricketers indicates the maturation of the sport. Second, cricket had assumed the basic characteristics of a modern sport — it was organized, with standardized rules, and governed by a central authority, the Marylebone Cricket Club. Its close and occasionally tainted association with gambling was a third factor: from the outset wagering had been critical to the popularity of the sport, and matches were often played for large stakes. While gambling spurred the growth of cricket it also painted an unfavorable picture of an era when matches were bought and sold and the sport "smelled of the pub and the betting ring."[10] Finally, the "gentlemen's game" in England was one in which all social classes participated; it was not unusual for commoners to compete against and with aristocrats. This class interaction caused some concern at first, but by the nineteenth century it was perceived as one of the sport's major virtues. The long heritage of paternalistic sporting practices among the upper class and the maintenance of class distinctions by the division of cricketers into gentlemen and players facilitated an outward egalitarianism on the cricket field.[11] Because members of the upper class bet heavily on these contests, they hired the best players regardless of class standing. In fact, the sheer number of men required for this team sport would have made the maturation of cricket in still largely rural England exceedingly difficult had the English social structure not permitted participation between plebians and patricians.

The continued American belief that ball playing was a pastime for children and young boys was the first and foremost reason why cricket could not establish roots here between 1800 and 1840. Since the majority of the participants were from an age group which lacked the physical characteristics to play a highly skilled sport, they continued to engage in the schoolboy game of baseball. Similarly, young men and adults had no reason or motivation to seek out the complex, skillful sport of cricket even on those occasions when they played ball since ball playing still had no "manly" virtues and values.

The attitude of the upper class toward gambling and interclass participation in sport militated against the growth of cricket in America. Gambling among the upper class never reached the same proportions nor achieved the same degree of social acceptance that it had among the English aristocracy. And, as I discuss in chapter 4, America's elite chose not to participate in sports activities with other social classes. Hence, cricket players in America were different from their English counterparts. Here, the majority of participants were emigrants from the emerging industrial centers of northern England; as such, the sport was "closely bound up with steak and ale," the working class, and gambling. Young children and adolescent boys rarely participated, probably because their anxious American parents viewed the sport "as one of the brightest on the primrose paths to the everlasting bonfire." Clearly, cricket was a far cry from the innocent ball games children played.[12]

By 1840, when cricket had emerged as a modern, mature sport in England and when baseball in America was still considered child's play, the game of bat, ball, and wicket played a very minor role in American sport. It had failed to establish a position as America's leading ball game and could do little to meet the challenge of baseball in the coming decades.

Between 1840 and 1860 the dawning of modern America, resulting from increasing urbanization, economic growth, and societal change, stimulated the creation of this country's ball-playing heritage. These forces established a setting conducive to the growth of ball games and were influential in shaping new attitudes toward ball playing. Cricket, as the more mature, advanced game, responded first, becoming an organized sport. The increasing number of cricket clubs encouraged formal matches, and the contests, long played by uniform rules, were no longer confined to city, state, or even national boundaries. The growing amount of press coverage, the keeping of statistics and records, and the beginning of an American cricket literature further indicate the modernization of the sport.

Although cricket clubs had existed in New York since the Revolution, the formation of that city's St. George Cricket Club in 1839–40 marked the beginning of organized cricket in America. In contrast to earlier clubs, this club survived for an extended period, during the next thirty years becoming the most influential club in New York City and throughout the nation. It had its origins in two 1838 cricket contests,[13] the first a match for $100 between former English residents of Sheffield and Nottingham. Prior to the contest Long Island cricketers challenged those in Manhattan and vicinity to a game for $500. Several weeks after the first contest the *Spirit* announced that the New York Cricket Club had accepted the Long Islanders' challenge. In all likelihood the New York team, of which six members were from the Sheffield squad, was put together solely for the purpose of this game.[14] There was considerable interest in the Long Island–New York contest, a match that the *Spirit* noted "will doubtless prove the forerunner of the great effort to procure permanent footing here for this favorite game." In 1839 members of both squads decided to band together and organize a new cricket club. On April 23, 1840 — St. George's Day — the club was duly named.[15]

In its first action the St. George Club announced that it was willing to play a friendly home-and-home match with any club from no further south than Philadelphia or no further north than the Albany-Troy area, for between $100 and $500. The proposal confirms that the club members, all Englishmen, still accepted as proper the custom of playing for side bets. Their willingness to participate in contests beyond local boundaries was an important break with cricket's premodern pattern, and their challenge indicated that the function of the club was not merely to promote a recreational activity but also to provide a competitive situation for its more highly skilled players.[16]

The club's first contest took them far beyond the boundaries set by their initial challenge. In August 1840 the Dragon Slayers left for Canada, having made arrangements for a contest with the Toronto Cricket Club through a man who identified himself as Mr. Phillpots, an officer of that club. When they reached their destination they learned that an imposter had acted on behalf of the Toronto Club, whose members now graciously offered to play them for $250. The New Yorkers easily won against the unprepared Toronto team,[17] but the unscheduled game served to mark the beginning of a series of matches between the two clubs. In 1839 the *Spirit* had suggested that a contest with a Canadian team would be an effective means of popularizing the sport in America, and that recommendation now proved generally accurate. While cricket never achieved overwhelming popularity in this country, these international games did bring attention to the sport in general and to the St. George Club in particular.[18]

Interest in the contests grew from their international flavor as well as the controversy surrounding various incidents that marred the competition. In 1844 the Toronto cricketers refused to play when the New York team arrived in Canada with three professional players from the Union Cricket Club of Philadelphia. The *Spirit* provided extensive coverage concerning the players' eligibility, although it clearly felt that the Canadians were justified in their complaint. A letter to the *Herald* claimed that the Toronto Club had backed out of the contest only because it feared defeat, a position the paper apparently endorsed in view of its reprinting of an article from the *Kingston British Whig* that severely chastized the Canadian cricketers. While there were the usual statements in the press that the incident was bad for the game, the controversy merely heightened interest in the sport. Indeed, when the two clubs met in Hoboken, New Jersey, later that year, approximately 5,000 spectators were present, and it was reported that $50,000 in bets rode on the outcome.[19] In 1845 the Dragon Slayers challenged Canadian cricketers, under the auspices of the Montreal Cricket Club, to a home-and-home series for the best players from America and Canada. The contest marked the first time in any sport that representatives of different countries competed on the athletic field. These international matches ended abruptly the following year when the Canadian squad walked off the field after a fight broke out between opposing players, and it would be seven years before international competition resumed.[20]

As of 1848 the St. George Club had sixty-seven members and six playing professionals.[21] Almost all Englishmen by birth, these cricketers were primarily merchants and agents of English import houses, although skilled craftsmen made up slightly more than 20 percent of the membership.[22] While data as to their economic standing are limited, the majority appear to have come from the comfortable middle class, although some were no doubt well-to-do and influential members of New York's English community. While the activities of the Dragon Slayers in the 1840s helped publicize the sport, and the club remained the most influential cricket organization in New York during the next two decades, it was not especially popular with the city's sports crowd. Henry Chadwick, the era's leading sportswriter, noted that "the exclusiveness of its members, drawn wholly from a distinctive class, and foreign at that, and the slightest inducement they held for the propagation of the game among native born citizens particularly, had alienated all respect and esteem from them on the part of the general public to which cricket was a novelty."[23]

In 1844 the New York Cricket Club was established in response to the illiberal policies of the St. George Club and as a result of growing interest in the sport. The major force behind the new club was John Richards, English-born owner of the nation's leading sports journal. Many of its early members, including William T. Porter, the club's first president, also were associated with the *Spirit*. The club lacked pretentiousness and sought to encourage membership by keeping the admission fee low. There are no complete records of the New York Cricket Club's membership, although it appears that the majority were also Englishmen, with Americans playing a small but active role in the organization. Club members probably did not come from the commercial class and were not as well-to-do as the St. George cricketers.[24]

During the late 1840s there was an increase in the number of cricket clubs in New York and nationally. At least six clubs were formed in the metropolitan area alone, but with the exception of a club in Newark, New Jersey, they survived for only a few years. Cricket clubs were also formed throughout America. George Kirsch maintains that by 1850 at least twenty cricket clubs, enrolling perhaps 500 active players, existed in more than a dozen American communities.[25]

This growth was minor compared to the advances the sport made in the 1850s. The revival of international contests in 1853 stimulated further interest in cricket. "For weeks, we may say months," the *Spirit* noted, the American-Canadian match "has been the all-absorbing topic in sporting circles." The annual contest, alternating between New York and Montreal, drew huge crowds in the American city. *Porter's Spirit* claimed that between 8,000 and 10,000 spectators attended the two-day match in 1856, and the *Spirit* noted that many people from Canada and the Northeast witnessed that same contest.[26]

The more careful selection of players illustrates the importance of these international contests. The *Spirit* noted in 1853 that to muster the best eleven cricketers the selection committee was holding tryouts, and it recommended that clubs from outside the New York metropolitan area send their "crack" players. In June 1857 two all-star games were held in New York, the first matching the best cricketers from the city against those from other parts of the country, and the second pairing an English-born eleven and sixteen American-born players. These matches had the dual purpose of gathering the country's best players prior to selection of eleven Americans who would play against Canada and publicizing the sport, giving it "a character and importance . . . not yet attained in this country."[27]

During this period the number of clubs, players, and games played continued to increase. Kirsch estimates that by 1860 there were possibly as many as 400 clubs, with 10,000 players.[28] By 1859 there were 10 cricket clubs in Brooklyn and Manhattan and at least 5 more teams in the surrounding area, which meant a corresponding rise in the number of cricketers participating in contests. In 1850, for example, only 46 cricketers played the game for the New York and St. George clubs; but by 1859 nearly 300 players were competing in games for the 10 Brooklyn and Manhattan clubs. The number of contests also increased, from seven at the start of the decade to fifty by its end. The majority of these games were, quite naturally, against teams from within the metropolitan area, but clubs from upstate New York, Connecticut, Massachusetts, and Pennsylvania would often travel to Brooklyn and Manhattan to compete against the local favorites. These intercity contests did not carry the symbolic meaning of the international contests, or measure up to the urban rivalries that would later take hold in baseball, but the *Brooklyn Eagle* was proud nonetheless when a Brooklyn club succeeded against a New York rival.[29]

The organizational development of cricket in antebellum America reached a climax when delegates from ten clubs met in New York City in May 1857. William Lacy and Thomas Falcon of the Albany and Philadelphia clubs had called the meeting, the first in a series of annual conventions. The remaining eight clubs were from the metropolitan area, although the Union Club of Cincinnati, the squad from Lowell, Massachusetts, and a team from Cleveland all sent letters of support. The purpose of the meeting was to coordinate the activities of the increasing number of teams, discuss common problems, and in general centralize the game and give it a national character. The *Clipper* viewed the national association as the "first important step towards placing the noble game on a sure and permanent basis in America." It felt that the obstacles to success were gradually being overcome and that Americans could look forward to the day when cricket "shall be adopted as one of our *national sports* [emphasis mine] and form one of the connecting links of that bond of brotherhood which ought to exist between the sons of old England and young America."[30]

The increasing press coverage the game received coincided with its growth. Since the formation of the St. George Cricket Club, New York's sports journals, and to a lesser extent the daily newspapers, provided reports and box scores for most of the cricket contests in the city and in Brooklyn. As early as 1847 one writer recommended that clubs from the United States and Canada send reports of their contests to the *Spirit* so that an annual statistical profile might be constructed as a means of assessing the performance of the various cricketers. Another decade passed before the journal began to regularly publish these statistical summaries, and even then it confined such reports mainly, although not exclusively, to players from teams in the immediate vicinity. Several cricket manuals appeared, the first published in 1847, which were essentially Americanized versions of English manuals. They included information on how to play the game, what the rules were, and sometimes what benefits derived from participation in cricket.[31]

The press not only chronicled the growth of the sport but commented favorably on it. The *Spirit,* with its close association to cricket in general and the New York Cricket Club in particular, was the game's biggest booster. Positive statements also appeared in all the city's dailies. The *Herald* noted, for example, that the increasing popularity of cricket "speaks well for the growing taste of the people." When students at the Free Academy in New York City began playing cricket, the *Tribune* wrote: "Whoever started these boys to practice the game deserves great credit—

it is manly, healthy and invigorating exercise and ought to be attended more or less at all schools." The *Times* stated that cricket was "innocent in its tendency, admirable for the confirmation of vigorous health and should come into habitual use in every city and village."[32]

This media support was based on the newer attitudes toward and justification of sport in general (see the conclusion), which rested on the role of athletics in promoting better health, high morals, and good character. Such an outlook was particularly useful for the growth of ball games, as it no longer sought a direct relationship between sport and utilitarian, day-to-day activities. For example, the press most frequently emphasized the healthful benefits to be derived from participation in cricket, particularly the value of playing "in the open sunlight, on the green turf, and in the pure air, under all the circumstances most favorable to the reinvigorating of those who engage in it." The outdoor benefits accrued to participants and spectators alike, who were encouraged to attend the contests for it would "let them breathe for once the pure breath of Nature."[33]

Several sportswriters noted that cricket was "not mere exercise of the muscles, nor merely play," but a sport that "educates or brings out what education has, or ought to have, for its objective, it educates the character." Henry Chadwick justified cricket on the grounds that it instilled character values, and he would frequently point out that cricket "calls into play most of the cardinal virtues": a player must be sober and temperate; and success on the field requires fortitude, self-denial, and obedience. In Chadwick's words, cricket "teaches a love of order, discipline, and fair play."[34]

The character value argument had profound importance for the development of ball games in general, and it was especially critical to the acceptance of ball playing as a manly activity. Claims that ball playing promoted healthful exercise were important but did little if anything to overcome the charge that ball playing was for children; hence, statements that cricket and baseball were manly often accompanied claims that they were healthy activities.[35] While it was rarely explained what constituted a manly sport, the idea probably related to the skills involved. The character value argument then took manliness beyond a mere demonstration of physical prowess and linked it to virtues such as courage, fortitude, discipline, and so on. The argument concluded that if ball games called these virtues into play—and in fact they were critical to doing well at such sports—then ball playing was obviously one way of demonstrating manhood.[36]

Given the assertion that baseball's success stemmed from the fact that it embodied American values, it is necessary to take note of one final critical point. The characteristics used to illustrate this relationship were initially articulated in the justification of cricket, a connection that is not surprising since Chadwick was the leading spokesman for both sports.[37]

Between 1855 and 1865 the position of cricket vis-à-vis baseball changed dramatically. While several baseball clubs already existed in Brooklyn and Manhattan by 1855, cricket was clearly the leading ball game. It attracted more attention in the New York press than any other sport, with the exception of horse and harness racing, but it is striking to note the total absence of any discussion of cricket in terms that would be used later to explain the status of the sport. Clearly, there was no opposition to the sport because it was English. The *Times* recognized that few Americans understood the sport completely but suggested that it was something that Yankees "may be proud to play well." The press hailed the increasing American participation in the sport. When native-born cricketers from the New York and Newark cricket clubs met in 1854 in the first match made up exclusively of American players, the press praised the contest. As late as 1857 the *Clipper* denied that only Englishmen played cricket: "Even if this was the case why should it deter Americans from enjoying and participating in this sport, we cannot imagine. But it is not so. Americans are, and have been for some time past, taking a most active interest in the game—many of them are really good players, whilst others give promise of future excellence."[38]

Cricket's prospects thus appeared quite bright as a result of slow but steady advances. In 1855 there was every reason to believe, as the *Clipper* later noted, that cricket was "rapidly making its way into popular favor as one of our national games" and would soon be a game of the masses.[39] However, the growth of cricket between 1855 and 1861 was minor compared to the advances made by baseball. The *Spirit* summarized the general attitude of the press in 1859 when it wrote that "cricket has its admirers, but it is evident that it will never have the universality that baseball will."[40] As baseball surged to the forefront of America's bat-and-ball games, sportswriters sought ways to explain its greater popularity. Initially, they focused not on national characteristics but almost exclusively on the national origins of the two games, proclaiming baseball an American game, one that was long familiar to American schoolboys.[41]

Simultaneous with the rise of baseball the press began to criticize the management of cricket. The *Times* claimed that the prejudices of Englishmen and their domination of the sport stifled American participation. When Yankees "fairly attempted a share of the honors on the field, they stood no chance," as English cricketers "by fair means or foul, always conspired to seize the victory" and even "hired professional players to conduct the game for them when the odds were on Jonathan's side." Consequently, the newspaper concluded, "it came to be believed that no man who did not drop his 'H's' could possibly win honors at bowling or wicket keeping." Others pointed to the ineffectiveness of the national cricket association, and the *Clipper* claimed that at the first two conferences "so little was achieved to result in any permanent good for the game."[42]

Despite the press's change of heart, baseball and cricket remained competitors for public attention. The steady growth of cricket received a positive boost in 1859 when the All-England Eleven, a group of professional cricketers, toured North America. The *Spirit* had touted such a visit as early as 1849, but it was not seriously discussed until 1856 when Henry Sharpe, a New York Cricket Club officer, and a man named Pickering from the Montreal Cricket Club wrote to a group in England to ascertain the possibility of a tour of North America by the All-England Eleven. When the English players demanded $6,500, the New York Club dropped the plan, claiming there was insufficient interest to warrant the expense. Robert Waller of the St. George Club picked up on the idea the following year, but the project was held in abeyance until his club could find a suitable field. Then, in 1859 Edwin A. Stevens, a leading New York sportsman and Commodore of the New York Yacht Club, offered part of his estate in Hoboken, New Jersey, as a site for the matches, and the St. George and Montreal clubs promptly finalized plans for the arrival of the English cricketers.[43]

The day before the contest the *Times* reported that many visitors had arrived in the metropolitan area and it expected that thousands of New Yorkers would cross the North River to watch the match, despite the high admission fee. Its forecast proved accurate, as an estimated 25,000 spectators showed up during the two-day match, a crowd "made up mostly of those who were curious as to the manner of cricket, and who desired to see men who had become so famous as cricket players in England."[44] Only an eternal optimist would have expected an American victory, but the ease with which the Englishmen crushed the Americans, even though the latter were permitted to use twenty-two players, came as somewhat of a surprise and an embarrassment. In an effort to save national pride the *Herald* and the *Clipper* both pointed out that the "ignominious defeat" could not be interpreted as an "American defeat." They noted that the international contest had been inaccurately billed as an English-American contest: only three members of the American squad were native-born, and of the remaining nineteen English-born cricketers at least half were "not even American citizens, *never have been naturalized,* and probably have not the remotest idea of renouncing their allegiance to the British crown."[45]

Despite the outcome the international contest stimulated considerable interest in cricket, and in 1860 three more clubs were established in Manhattan and Brooklyn, bringing the total number of teams to thirteen, the highwater mark prior to 1870. Of these, the American Cricket Club generated considerable comment because it restricted membership to native-born players, or at least to individuals who had been residents of the country since age five and were naturalized citizens. The press hoped that the new club would provide indigenous leadership to the sport and thereby ease the growing dissatisfaction with the English domination of cricket. Optimism also stemmed from the presence in the American Club of many of Brooklyn's leading baseball players, including James Creighton, the sport's first superstar. There was a feeling among sportswriters, never coherently articulated, that these Americans would soon be able to beat the English at their own game.[46]

The growing number of baseball players participating in cricket did not derive from nationalistic sentiments or from media recommendations that ball players engage in the more skillful sport of cricket as a means of improving their baseball-playing ability. Rather, their involvement was directly linked to the arrival of the touring English professionals, for they not only got to see how the sport should be played, but they were probably quite impressed with the skill of these paid performers. As athletes, the Americans had to be intrigued by the complexity of the sport and challenged by its difficulty.[47]

The outbreak of the Civil War had a dramatic and immediate impact on cricket, as it did on all other sports. While the number of cricket contests markedly declined in 1861, the *Clipper* optimistically noted "the fact that we have any proves that the game has that favorable hold on public opinion calculated to make it a permanent and popular institution." However, as normalcy returned to other segments of the New York sporting scene by late 1862, it became evident that the problems of cricket went beyond the negative impact of civil strife. The prospect for the 1863 season was not very promising, one sports journal noted, "not on account of the war . . . but simply for the want of clubs to play matches with." By 1864 the number of cricket clubs in Manhattan and Brooklyn had dropped to slightly less than half what it had been four years earlier. The American Cricket Club had disbanded and the New York Cricket Club was a mere shadow of what it had been during the Richards-Porter era.[48] The national association stopped meeting after the 1862 season, and the *Clipper* now maintained that it had failed to provide leadership in the sport. With each succeeding year the convention had "diminished alike in the number of delegates as in its influence over the several clubs that were represented."[49] Press coverage was severely limited and little hope was held out for the future of cricket. By the time peace returned to America in 1865 the fate of cricket in this country had been sealed.

Just as baseball and cricket took divergent paths during the Civil War, explanations for the rise of one sport and the demise of the other took on decidedly nationalistic tones. In 1862 the *Eagle* wrote that as cricket "is not an American game, but purely an English game, it will never be much in vogue with Americans, especially New Yorkers, who are for fast and not slow things." Several weeks later the paper elaborated on this point, maintaining that "a game in such favor with the English cannot well have much attraction for the American, the disposition of both people being as different as baseball is from cricket. One game is full of excitement and activity, while the other is interesting but tardy." Cricket was a "bore to an American, who could not think of playing a match for two consecutive days."[50]

These sentiments were not totally novel. Since 1855 the popularity of baseball and cricket had been discussed in terms of American and English games, and the press had noted before the pace of the two ball games. The *Eagle*'s analysis differed from earlier ones, however, in that it made an effort to synthesize the various points of views into a single explanation for the fates of the two sports. Furthermore, none of the earlier articles had so strongly linked the pace of the ball games with national characteristics. Thus, the *Eagle*'s assessment was the first to contain the strong suggestion that cricket's destiny was inevitable.

In the immediate post–Civil War period the explanation that the fates of baseball and cricket were tied to national characteristics emerged as the major interpretation for the status of the two sports. In 1866 the *Herald* proclaimed that the "national game of America is now, *par excellence,* baseball." In contrast to the slow and serious pace of cricket, Americans want "constant life and motion in sport," and hence "our game chimes with our national character."[51]

Analysis of the interaction between changing cultural and social conditions and the historical development of baseball and cricket leads to a more insightful understanding of the respective success and failure of these two sports. The destinies of the two ball games originated in those factors that caused the absence of a manly ball-playing tradition in pre-1840 America. The greater familiarity of Americans with the child's game of baseball provided it with an early advantage over cricket, but this was not an insurmountable obstacle. In the early years participation in baseball remained limited and informal, and the game received little public attention. As a more mature, modern sport, cricket responded first to changing social conditions and a new attitude toward adult participation in ball games; however, it was precisely these characteristics that limited the growth of cricket at a time when it held center stage. In essence, cricket failed because it was too advanced and too institutionalized for a society that lacked a manly ball-playing tradition. Americans drew from the only heritage they had—that of a child's game—and gradually transformed baseball as they knew it into a modern, mature sport.

The decline of cricket can be assessed in terms of the interacting elements of skill, sponsorship, structure, and stage of development. Henry Chadwick claimed that cricket "is unquestionably the most scientific game of ball," and the press universally acknowledged that view. *Porter's Spirit* noted that there "are many fine points in cricket which base-ball has not, and for real science it is preferable." The *Herald* argued that a cricketer would have no trouble with baseball, but a baseball player, "no matter how excellent he is, cannot play cricket."[52] Since a strong relationship exists between the ability to execute a sports skill and involvement in that sport, it seems clear that Americans did not turn to cricket initially because they did not have the necessary ball-playing skills to engage in such a complex sport.

In spite of the fact that Americans had plenty of time between the formation of the St. George Cricket Club in 1840 and the rise of baseball in the mid-1850s to adequately hone their skills, they did not do so. The major reason for this failure to develop ball-playing prowess was that for the overwhelming majority of participants ball games were recreational rather than competitive.[53] The challenges of cricket were no doubt an impetus for several of the leading baseball players to join cricket clubs, particularly after the touring English professionals demonstrated how the sport should be played. But most ball players were not serious athletes; for them the attraction of ball games was not the degree of difficulty but rather the sheer enjoyment of playing, the social interaction, and the healthful exercise. The complexity of cricket consequently was a major drawback. In fact, the simplicity of baseball and the ease with which it could be learned won the praise of the press and provided an explanation for its popularity.[54]

The fate of cricket was not influenced by the fact that it was an English game but that the sport was run for and by Englishmen. The problems created by English control was one of the initial explanations the press offered for cricket's difficulties in America. Nor did this point of view immediately die out when references to national characteristics became the accepted interpretation in the years following the Civil War. "If the same effort had been made to popularize cricket as have been made in behalf of Base Ball," the *Clipper* wrote in 1868, "the game would have been more in favor than it is, but the snobbish exclusiveness of the parties who owned and controlled English cricket in this country exerted a baneful influence upon the game, and made it very unpopular."[55] Cricket clubs were formed to promote the sport, but just as important they functioned as a means of preserving English identity. For example, as the first cricket club in New York, the St. George Club could have been more aptly named the New York Cricket Club, or something to identify it with the city. Instead, the Dragon Slayers chose a name that clearly would be associated with their homeland. Although the press viewed this influential club as the symbol of English exclusiveness, such practices no doubt existed, if to a lesser extent, among other area clubs as well.

English leadership was certainly a result of their greater familiarity with the sport and the absence of a manly ball-playing tradition in America, yet they sustained their position largely by default. The American upper class could have easily usurped control of the sport, given the foreign background of its major supporters, but they generally refrained from doing so. One exception was in Philadelphia, where cricket was firmly in the hands of the upper class by the outbreak of the Civil War. As a result the Quaker City was one of the few places where the sport actually flourished in the years following the sectional struggle.[56] Of course, this raises the question of why New York's elite did not become involved in cricket and leads to speculation as to what might have been the fate of that sport if they had. The answer rests at least partly in the fact that by the time cricket gained public notice in the mid-1840s the more active New Yorkers had already committed themselves to several other sports, including the bat-and-ball game of racquets, which, although different in some ways, provided its players with manly and healthful exercise. New York's upper class thus had little incentive to become involved in cricket.[57]

The impact that upper-class New Yorkers might have had on the development of cricket is impossible to assess with any degree of certainty. However, it is safe to say that the sport's chances of succeeding would have been better if the city's social and economic leaders had lent it their support as well as an American stamp of approval. Other social groups, notably members of the respectable middle class who were instrumental in the rise of baseball, might have—but did not—become involved in cricket in an effort to emulate the sports practices of the upper class.[58] Upper-class support also would have made it easier for proponents of cricket to pass off baseball as a simple game unworthy of manly attention.[59] Be that as it may, New York's elite chose not to support cricket in America, and Philadelphia's gentleman class simply lacked sufficient influence to alter the fate of the sport. Organized baseball had its origins in New York City and that was where any challenge to the sport had to be met. Also, as the center of sports communication, sporting practices in New York were more likely to shape sporting practices throughout the country.

The press, in their examinations of the nature of baseball and cricket and their repeated efforts to link them to national characteristics, could point out only two ways in which the sports differed: the length of time it took to complete a contest in both sports; and, in contrast to the more skillful sport of cricket, baseball was faster and more action-packed. While these elements undoubtedly contributed to the success of baseball and the failure of cricket, neither offers an entirely satisfactory explanation.

The problem with the claim that cricket contests took too long to be popular with Americans is that it focused on the relationship between the availability of free time and the popularity of cricket solely in terms of the sport as competition rather than recreation, in effect placing the cart before the horse. The question should have been to what extent the availability of free time served to inhibit participation in the sport. That most cricket (and baseball) clubs met two afternoons a week illustrates that the rhythm and hours of business in antebellum New York provided the commercial class sufficient time to engage in the sport. Similarly, the fact that artisans played cricket here and in England indicates that time was not a critical factor.[60] Of course, the two days required to complete a cricket contest may have been a deterrent, although the need to play two full innings (a complete match), while mandatory in high-level competition, was less necessary in a recreational setting. In fact, a goodly number of the friendly contests between cricket clubs in Manhattan and Brooklyn were limited to one inning, or restricted to one day of play.[61]

Despite constant repetition of the claim that baseball became more popular because it was a faster and more action-packed game, no one has explained what made it that way. Structural differences in the two ball games are obvious. Whereas a cricket inning lasts until all eleven offensive players are retired, a baseball inning lasts for only three outs. And in contrast to baseball's rotation system of batting, each batter in cricket continues to hit until he is retired. These distinguishing elements help illustrate what made baseball a more action-packed game. The structural differences influenced the two ball games as spectator sports and, more importantly, had a profound impact on them as participatory sports.

The concept of action has been focal in explaining much about America's sports trends, but it lacks clarity and precision. Popular usage implies rapid movement and, more recently, sanctioned violence (as in football). The problem is that this approach strips drama—the process by which the contest unfolds and reaches its climax—from the concept. Action in sport can be more productively analyzed as the movement of the participants within the context of the drama. And since drama can exist at times without movement, in fact can be heightened by nonmovement, action as a framework for understanding American sports patterns cannot be restricted to its current usage. Viewed in this way baseball is clearly a livelier sport, for the more rapid interchange between offense and defense provides the sport with an ebb and flow that is lacking in cricket. As the fortunes of the two teams alternate with each shift from offense to defense, the structure of the baseball inning produces a more rapidly changing tension. These vicissitudes serve to heighten the drama of the contest and thereby create a sport which Americans interpret as more action-packed.[62] As a more exciting drama baseball was considered a better spectator sport, a factor that, while influential, played a secondary role in the fates of the two ball games.

By the early 1860s, when baseball emerged as a sports spectacle, it had already surpassed cricket in terms of participant involvement as a direct result of the structural differences between the two games. The batting system in cricket provides the batter with more opportunities to hit, but once he is retired his involvement in the inning ceases. Because of the length of a cricket inning there is an extended period of time when each participant is not, and has no chance of becoming, involved in the contest. By comparison, baseball allows the player fewer chances to hit, but because of the frequent alternations between offense and defense and the nature of the rotation system of batting there is no long period of time when any one participant is out of the action.[63]

The differing extent of the participant's involvement with the action of cricket and baseball contests had important ramifications for the two ball games as participatory sports. Individual sporting tastes and habits are influenced by a variety of factors, but whatever one's personal preferences, the basic objective of a participant, simple as it may sound, is to play. By removing players from the contest for an extended period of time, cricket violates one of the cardinal principles of a good partici-patory sport—maximum playing time. Americans thus turned to a ball game whose basic structure made it a better participatory sport.

Finally, the stage of development of the two sports affected the success of baseball and the failure of cricket. No one asked—hence no one explained—why cricket was not modified to meet American needs and values. Since baseball derived from the English game of rounders (and football, the other dominant American sport, from rugby), such alteration would have been consistent with this nation's sporting patterns. In fact, several observers did call for the reform of cricket and the need to Americanize the sport, but to no avail. Perhaps, since for the majority of cricketers the sport functioned as a means of identifying with their native land, there simply was no motivation to Americanize the sport. This was clearly an important factor, but if the problem derived solely from English control, why didn't Americans reform the game when they governed the sport in this country in the latter part of the nineteenth century? While the human dimension is the agent of the historical process, human behavior is rooted in cultural and institutional developments.[64]

The emergence of cricket as a modern and mature sport in England provides a basis for understanding the absence of change in America. But first we must examine the changing structure of sport during premodern, early modern, and modern stages.[65] During the premodern stage, rules, norms, and sanctions are generally simple, unwritten, and legitimated by local tradition. Changes occur over a long period of time, almost as an imperceptible drift from the participant's point of view. With the onset of modernization, structural innovations occur more rapidly as competition moves beyond local boundaries. The expansion of the sport causes new rules and regulations to replace the older, local ones. The codification of rules marks the beginning of the institutionalization of the newer structures, and the creation of a central authority produces a mechanism to administer and facilitate rational change. The early institutional developments do not stifle the process of change. Continued innovation results from the fact that the maturation of any sport as a skillful, competitive activity takes place at a different rate than its modernization. As a result, the structure of the sport continues to be altered to meet the demands of new situations, including a growing complexity. At a certain point the structural blueprint of the sport—its fundamental rules, norms and sanctions—becomes firmly established. With the institutionalization of this structure the second stage ends and the third one begins. During the modern stage structural innovation continues although it is less frequent and usually occurs at the periphery of the structure of the sport.

Cricket had a well-defined structure by the start of the Victorian period. The tremendous growth of the sport during the first half of the nineteenth century produced, amid considerable controversy, cricket's last major innovation—the shift from underhand to overhand bowling.[66] Far from illustrating a structural system still open to innovation, the heated debate and resistance to the newer style indicates that the structure of cricket was firmly established, thus making change virtually impossible in America. When a delegate to the first national conference proposed that new rules be established or that they at least revise the rules of the Marylebone Cricket Club as a means of popularizing the sport and removing its foreign taint, two delegates objected, saying that the game would cease to be cricket.[67] The opposition to innovation, influenced by the desire of Englishmen to preserve national identity, derived from the acceptance of cricket's structure as *the* way to play the sport. Even Americans accepted cricket's structure as proper. In response to the proposal, *Porter's Spirit* claimed that "we cannot, for the life of us, see how a convention can form a better set of Laws of Cricket, than those of the Marylebone Cricket Club." Other advocates of change, notably the *Clipper*, focused more on what it considered the long, unnecessary delays between innings and the amount of time it took to complete a contest than on the structure of the sport.[68]

In contrast to cricket, baseball arrived in America at a much earlier stage in its development. There was, therefore, nothing sacrosanct in its rules, norms, and sanctions, and the structure of the sport was easily changed by trial and error. Roughly sixty years elapsed from the time the Knickerbockers established their own rules in the 1840s until baseball was fully institutionalized, and by then it occupied a preeminent position in American athletics and held a special place in American life.

The divergent patterns of modernization of cricket and baseball had a profound effect on the organization of the respective sports on a national level. The failure of the national cricket conference was rooted in an acceptance of the rules as written and, although not actually articulated, in the authority of the Marylebone Cricket Club. This self-defeating action stripped the conference of the essential aspect of a national governing body: the ability to create and administer the rules. As the *Clipper* came to realize by 1859, there was simply no need for a national cricket association. Baseball's national association, by comparison, played a vital role in the structure of the sport. Consequently, its annual meeting drew considerable public attention and a large number of delegates. The importance of the national association went beyond its influence on the development of baseball, however. The ultimate authority over the new national pastime rested with a native population, giving testimony to the fact that baseball had become an American sport even if it had originally been an English game. Cricket could never achieve this type of national identification in America.[69]

While the fate of cricket in America had been sealed by 1865, the sport survived in the clubs of men of wealth and status, as well as at several leading eastern prep schools and universities. Under the sponsorship of the well-to-do the number of cricket clubs throughout the country actually increased in the last quarter of the nineteenth century. By the beginning of the new century, however, the sport entered an era of permanent decline and almost totally disappeared from the American sporting scene by the 1920s.[70]

The stamina of cricket clubs was evident in New York in the immediate post–Civil War period, although the press agreed that the St. George Club was the only viable organization in the metropolitan area.[71] The club remained among America's most important cricket clubs even though the sport's capital had shifted from New York to Philadelphia after 1865. The St. George Club had 143 members, some of them the best cricketers in America, and was financially sound, as evidenced by the construction of a new cricket grounds at Bergen Hills, New Jersey, in 1866 at a cost of $20,000–$40,000.[72] The majority of club members were still Englishmen by birth, but Americans had increasingly joined them.

The social composition of the St. George Cricket Club had been changing for about a decade prior to the end of the Civil War. Henry Chadwick claimed that the club underwent radical transformation after it moved in 1854 from grounds next to the Red House in Harlem to a new course in Hoboken.[73] Table 2 indicates that the metamorphosis was more gradual. The identifiable occupations of more than half of the club members did not change much between 1848 and 1859, although there was a marked increase in the number and proportion of members engaged in finance. Between 1859 and 1865, despite the virtual collapse of the sport throughout the area, membership nearly doubled, with the most significant changes occurring among merchants and financiers.

The birthplaces of the cricketers reflected a considerable change between 1848 and 1859, due in part to rapid turnover in the club's membership. Only one-seventh of the Dragon Slayers on the 1848 roster were still in the club eleven years later. Biographical data on the 1859 squad are limited, but it is evident that the number of American-born cricketers increased, although they continued to represent only a small fraction of the membership. There was only one identifiable American member in 1848, but at least seven (9.3 percent) of the seventy-five cricketers on the 1859 roster were American-born, and they came mainly from the city's upper-middle and upper classes. The financial status of the English-born cricketers is more difficult to assess, but in all probability they were slightly better off than earlier members, with most of them coming from the prosperous middle class.[74]

The percentage of American-born St. George Club members increased only slightly between 1859 and 1865. Of the club's 143 cricketers in 1865, at least 16 (11.3 percent) were Americans, possibly more. In general,

TABLE 2. Occupations of St. George Cricket Club Members, 1848–65

	1848		1859		1865	
	N	%	N	%	N	%
Merchant	20	57.1	23	51.1	52	59.5
Financier	0	—	7	15.5	13	14.8
Professional	5	14.3	6	13.3	9	10.2
Skilled Craftsman	8	22.9	7	15.5	5	5.7
Manufacturer	1	2.9	0	—	2	2.3
Clerk	1	2.9	1	2.9	2	2.3
Consul	0	—	1	2.2	1	1.2
Executive	0	—	0	—	3	3.4
Gentleman	0	—	0	—	1	1.1
Total	35		45		88	

these men came from the city's upper-middle class, although some were from fabulously wealthy families, including William Douglass, Lloyd Aspinwall, and Franklin Allen. The economic status of the Englishmen in the club is difficult to assess, but the occupations of most of the members, the excellent financial condition of the club, and their connections with wealthy American businessmen all strongly suggest that at least the majority of the Englishmen were well-to-do.

As the social composition of the Dragon Slayers changed, so did the function of the club: after 1865 it served mainly to unite the members of New York City's Anglo and American financial and commercial communities.[75] Wealthy Americans increasingly viewed the aristocracy as "a proper mode of maintaining social distinctions" and perceived the Anglo-Saxon inheritance as the "joint possession of the two countries."[76] By participating in some of the same sporting activities as the English upper class, they not only sought to demonstrate their status in this country but confirm their growing importance within the international community as well.

While many of the earlier barriers to American participation in ball games dissipated, cricket still did not become a major sport among New York's upper class. They continued to express a preference for more expensive sports, such as yachting and horse racing; although several individuals from New York's leading families did join the St. George Cricket Club, it was probably because their affiliation provided a link to the English aristocracy as well as to other urban elites. Other sports clubs performed a similar function yet carried greater prestige among New York elites, so it is probably safe to assume that economics—in the form of establishing ties with the Anglo financial and commercial communities— had as much to do with American involvement in cricket clubs as the sport itself did. Having already lost the popular battle to baseball, the inability of cricket to win the support of the urban upper class, except in Philadelphia and to a lesser extent in Boston, contributed significantly to its ultimate demise. With the growth of other wealthy sports cricket rapidly disappeared from the American sports scene after 1900, even in Philadelphia.

Even though cricket failed to establish American roots, its impact on sport exceeded the extent to which it was played here. David Voigt has recognized baseball's debt to cricket, noting that the umpire was common to both, the language of early baseball writers drew heavily from cricket, and the cricket experiences of baseball pioneers like Henry Chadwick and Harry Wright were responsible for many of the early baseball innovations.[77] The influence of cricket went beyond these overt connections, however, in that the justification for baseball was drawn almost entirely from the rhetoric used to sanction cricket. More significant still is the fact that as the first major ball game in America, and as a major English sport, cricket served as a model by which baseball measured its own growth and maturity.

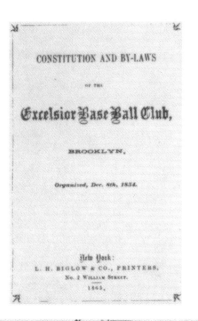

CONSTITUTION AND BY-LAWS

OF THE

Excelsior Base Ball Club,

BROOKLYN.

Organized, Dec. 8th, 1854.

New York:
L. H. BIGLOW & CO., PRINTERS,
No. 2 WILLIAM STREET.
1863.

---

20   CONSTITUTION.

the complainant be furnished by them, unless ordered to do so by the Club. A member shall be entitled to submit a written defense.

ARTICLE XV.

SEC. 1. All Special Committees shall report at the next meeting after their appointment, unless an extension of time be granted them by the President; if they do not then comply they shall be discharged.

SEC. 2. All books, papers. money, or other property, belonging to the Club, in the possession of any officer, shall be delivered up to his successor in office forthwith

ARTICLE XVI.

There shall be adopted a code of By-Laws which, in connection with this Constitution, shall govern the Club.

ARTICLE XVII.

Every proposed alteration, amendment, or addition to this Constitution or to the By-Laws, must be submitted, in writing, at least one month before action thereon can be taken, when, if two-thirds of the members present concur, the said proposition may be adopted.

BY-LAWS.

FOR

FIELD EXERCISE.

ARTICLE I.

SEC. 1. When assembled for field exercise, the presiding officer shall designate two members to act as Captains, who shall select the players for each side, carefully arranging them in such manner that each side shall be as nearly equal in merit, as players, as possible; the choice of sides shall then be tossed for by the Captains, and the first side in hand shall be decided in like manner.

SEC. 2. The Captains shall have absolute direction of the game, appoint a Scorer, designate the position each player shall have in the field; *giving preference in each position to members*, which position cannot be changed without the Captain's consent.

SEC. 3. When assembled for field exercise, the presiding officer shall appoint an Umpire, who shall

6

The Early Years of Baseball, 1845–60

Between 1845 and the outbreak of the Civil War, baseball evolved from a simple, informal child's game into an organized sport with standardized rules. The formation of the National Association of Base Ball Players in 1857, the increasing press coverage of baseball, the rising spectator interest, the emergence of statistics, and the appearance of baseball's first guidebook in 1860 further exemplified the modernization and growing popularity of the sport during these years.

Baseball propagandists have long sought to give the sport a pastoral image, but from the outset organized baseball was an urban product.[1] In the pre–Civil War years New York City and Brooklyn virtually dominated the development of baseball, even though numerous northeastern cities boasted their own teams, as did a handful of midwestern and southern cities. In fact, by 1860 a baseball club had been established as far west as San Francisco, although the "New York game" triumphed over all other styles of play.

The emergence of baseball as an organized sport can be traced to a dozen clubs that sprang up in Manhattan and Brooklyn between 1845 and 1855, beginning with the Knickerbocker Base Ball Club. In 1842 several gentlemen in search of outdoor exercise and social enjoyment had gathered at a vacant lot at the corner of Twenty-seventh Street and Madison Avenue in Manhattan to play a child's ball game. The growth of the city's residential and commercial community eventually forced them to seek another playing field further north, and after three years of unorganized play Alexander J. Cartwright, Jr., recommended the establishment of a permanent club and promised to recruit more members.

The team accepted Cartwright's proposal, drew up a constitution, devised rules for the game, and secured a permanent site at Elysian Fields in Hoboken, New Jersey, for a fee of seventy-five dollars per year for both the field and the dressing room.[2]

Historians universally accept the Knickerbockers as baseball's pioneer club, even as many of them recognize the existence of earlier teams. Those teams, they are quick to note, were either unorganized, in existence for only a few years, or played some other variation of baseball, such as town ball. One of the pre-Knickerbocker teams, known as the New York Club, did attract more interest than the others, but as Henry Chadwick wrote in 1861 the Knickerbockers deserved "the honor of being the pioneer of the present game of Base Ball." Interest in the New York Club derived mainly from its one-sided, 23–1 victory in 1846 over the Knickerbockers, in what was once believed to be baseball's first match. The New York Club's crushing victory indicates that their players were not novices; in fact, Duncan F. Curry, the first president of the Knickerbockers, later claimed that several of the opposing players were experienced cricketers.[3]

Several references in the *New York Herald* late in 1845, unnoticed by other historians, provide further insights into the New York Club and the early history of organized baseball. On October 21 the *Herald* noted an upcoming match between the New York Club and a team known as the Brooklyn Club. The newspaper did not report the outcome of what must now be considered the first interclub contest, but four days later it indicated that in a rematch the New Yorkers had defeated the Brooklyn squad, 37–19.[4] In a more revealing statement the *Herald* reported on November 11 that members of the New York Club were gathered on its diamond at Elysian Fields to mark the team's second anniversary, making it clear that they had been meeting regularly since 1843. The fact that they played at Elysian Fields and probably paid a rental fee suggests that they were organized, although not, in all likelihood, to the same degree as the Knickerbockers with their formal constitution.[5]

As the sport's first important and long-term club, existing until 1882, the Knickerbockers served as the organizational model for the multitude of baseball teams that emerged in the 1850s. Its major contribution was the establishment of the basic patterns and rules of baseball. A far cry from the rules that now govern the sport, these early rules were certainly more sophisticated than the ones used in the child's game of baseball. Today's fans would find the Knickerbocker game both crude and amusing, yet they would recognize it as baseball.[6]

The Knickerbocker Base Ball Club generally has been portrayed in the literature as a group of urban gentlemen with a certain standing in the community who sought to restrict the game of baseball to their own kind. More a social club than a sports team, congeniality on the field and postgame dinners supposedly were as important to the Knickerbockers as winning. In spirit and tone they were more akin to upper-class sportsmen, such as cricketers and tennis players, than later ball players with their win-at-all-cost philosophy. Many writers also believed that the Knickerbockers sought to establish themselves as the social arbiters of baseball, following the example set by the Marylebone Cricket Club.[7]

This popular portrayal contains some grain of truth, but it is marked by inconsistencies and is based on limited evidence that suffers from serious gaps in the literature. Available biographical information and economic data on New York ball players, while scarce, do permit a profile of the social class of the Knickerbockers if we examine their known occupations and extrapolate from what they were not. The majority between 1845 and 1850 had white-collar jobs, yet only slightly more than one-third of the forty-four ballplayers whose occupations could be identified were involved in commerce and finance, a far lower percentage than among members of the St. George Cricket Club, for example. Doctors and lawyers constituted one-fourth of the club members, and the remaining two-fifths engaged in nonmanual, but less financially rewarding, occupations, with clerks and similar lower-level white-collar workers making up slightly less than one-sixth of baseball's first organized team.

The occupational structure of the Knickerbockers indicates that the members were drawn at least from the middle class, but there is no evidence to support the contention that on the whole they were from the city's upper class or were wealthy urban gentlemen. Certainly, some men in the club were financially well-to-do, such as Benjamin C. Lee, whose father, James, was an honorary member and worth an estimated $20,000 in 1845. Another member, J. Paige Mumford, was the son of a well-known merchant; however, his father was worth only $3,000 in 1845, enough for a comfortable, but hardly an opulent, life-style.[8] Thus, while some of the Knickerbockers may have come from the upper-middle class, the majority appear to have been prosperous middle-class New Yorkers, much like Alexander Cartwright, at whose suggestion the club was formed. A few years prior to leaving the city in 1849, Cartwright, who had been a clerk, and his elder brother had opened a bookstore.[9]

In terms of social class, then, the Knickerbockers hardly conformed to the typical image of status-seekers. Nor did the intent of the club or its initial action reveal a desire to limit baseball to the upper-middle class. Rather, the sole purpose seems to have been engaging in an activity that promoted health, recreation, and social enjoyment among the members. The most striking feature of the Knickerbocker Club during its early years is the almost total absence of outside competition, suggesting that these men attached limited importance to baseball per se. After the game

against the New York Club in 1846, the Knickerbockers did not engage
in contests with any other clubs until 1851. They neither emulated the
semiorganized New York Club, which played several games against a
group of Brooklyn cricketers, nor did they follow the lead of New York's
first cricket club in challenging teams outside the city. While the Knickerbockers adopted their own rules, they must have been aware that
numerous variations of baseball had long been played in the Northeast.
Yet club records reveal no effort to find out if gentlemen elsewhere had
organized baseball clubs. In an important but unpublished piece of research,
Robert Henderson helps us understand why the Knickerbocker Club
made no apparent effort to engage in friendly contests with other teams:
the club was itself on the verge of collapse during the early years because
many of its members often failed to show up for scheduled practices.[10]
The club's condition and the casual attitude of its members contrasted
sharply with the popular contention that the Knickerbockers sought to
become the social arbiters of the sport.

Another problem with the prevalent view is that it does not explain
why there was no mention of baseball in the press until 1853, with the
exception of a few references to the New York Club in 1845. The absence
of information cannot, however, be interpreted as any one group's desire
for exclusivity, since status confirmation involves not the absence of
publicity but quite the opposite, its demonstration. This was clearly the
pattern in all upper-class sports.[11] The failure of the Knickerbockers to
ensure public recognition of their organization probably indicated a
defensive posture toward involvement in baseball. Given their social status
and the prevailing attitude toward ball playing, their reaction is not
surprising; after all, they were grown men of some stature playing a child's
game. They could rationalize their participation by pointing to the health
and recreational benefits of baseball, but their social insecurities and their
personal doubts concerning the manliness of the game inhibited them
from openly announcing the organization.

A rash of baseball clubs came into existence in the New York City
area between 1850 and 1855, probably in response to the increasing
encouragement of many forms of outdoor recreation and with the example
of organized cricket already a decade old. The Washington Club, later
renamed the Gotham Club, began playing around 1850 on the field of
the St. George Cricket Club in Harlem. Several members had played on
the New York Club in 1846, indicating that they were not novices and
strongly suggesting that prior to 1850 other adult men besides the
Knickerbockers played baseball, if only informally and on an irregular
basis.[12] In 1851 the Washington squad challenged the Knickerbockers to
a home-and-home series. The annual contests between the two clubs
attracted some public interest, and in 1853 both the *Spirit* and the *New*

York Mercury reported briefly on one of the games.[13] Three more clubs—the Eagle, the Empire, and the Baltic—were organized in Manhattan during 1854 and 1855, while seven teams were formed in Brooklyn. The Excelsiors, Brooklyn's first baseball club, was organized in December 1854 by John H. Suydam and several of his friends, who had witnessed a contest between the Knickerbockers and Eagles that fall.

The Eckford Club was the second organized squad in Brooklyn. Historians maintain that the club, comprised of shipwrights and mechanics who could keep practice only once a week (in contrast to other teams which met twice weekly), marked the first break with the Knickerbockers' notion of baseball as a gentlemen's game.[14] While formation of this club undeniably symbolized a change in the economic and social composition of baseball players in the early years, the extent of that change has been grossly exaggerated. For example, individuals who worked in New York's shipyards, the center for such construction in the United States and, at times, the world, were the best-paid craftsmen in the city. These shipwrights had been able to insulate themselves from the kinds of social and economic changes that undermined the pay and prestige of artisans in other crafts, in general earning a sufficient annual income to allow them to live within reach of the middle class. It is also significant that between 20 and 25 percent of the Eckford members were employed in nonmanual occupations.[15] Thus, there does not appear to have been radical economic differences between members of the Eckford and Knickerbocker clubs, although clearly there were social differences. But did these translate into varying behavioral patterns?

While we can never be sure, several interrelated factors suggest that members of the Eckford Club belonged to the segment of the working class that held many middle-class values. The presence of white-collar workers on this largely manual-skilled team was in part an extension of the paternalistic relationship between master shipbuilders and their workers, but it was also an indicator of shared beliefs, as was the selection of the club's name. Henry Eckford, a Scotch-Irish immigrant, was New York's richest and most successful shipbuilder in the antebellum period. By identifying with him, these craftsmen gave testimony to their faith in middle-class values, especially upward mobility. One final point: when the issue of professional baseball first emerged in the late 1850s, Francis Pidgeon, president of the Eckford Club, opposed compensation for players, maintaining that the game was for pleasure, not profit.[16]

To ascertain more precisely the social class of Brooklyn and New York ball players we must examine in some detail their types of occupations during different time periods.[17] Between 1850 and 1855 most ball players engaged mainly in nonmanual forms of employment (see Table 3). No unskilled workers were on baseball teams in either city; but skilled

TABLE 3. Occupational Structure of Area Baseball Players, 1850–55

	New York City		Brooklyn		Combined	
	N	%	N	%	N	%
Professional–High White-Collar	26	41.9	9	28.1	35	37.2
Low White-Collar–Proprietor	28	45.2	9	28.1	37	39.4
Skilled Craftsman	8	12.9	14	43.8	22	23.4
Total	62		32		94	

craftsmen comprised about one-fourth of the players, a fact that indicates widespread knowledge of the game at this early stage and further confirms the absence of an effort to restrict baseball to the "better class." However, there were striking occupational differences between ball players of the two cities. There is no clear-cut reason for this, since both groups had access to the same kinds of jobs.[18] Indeed, it may have been only a temporary development, because the differences were less evident during the next fifteen years. Brooklyn players still came from more plebian backgrounds, a trend that no doubt persisted as a result of the greater availability of open space on which to play. Even more critical, perhaps, was the fact that Brooklyn's economic growth did not keep pace with its population, which increased from about 7,000 in 1820 to slightly less than 100,000 three decades later. Moreover, in contrast to the cosmopolitan nature of New York City, Brooklyn retained much of its small-city, plebian atmosphere; hence, its ball players were more likely to be drawn from middle-level occupations.[19]

Baseball's growth in the mid-1850s corresponded with, and was stimulated by, the coverage it was receiving in the Spirit and some daily newspapers. Beginning in 1853 the press provided brief reports of contests, usually no more than three or four lines, often accompanied by a crude box score; they also noted the formation of new clubs. In response to the increasing number of baseball clubs in the metropolitan area, the Spirit published the Knickerbockers' rules in 1855, along with a diagram of the playing field.[20] The Herald, impressed with the rising number of clubs, maintained that baseball "bids fair to soon be as popular as the favorite game of cricket," an opinion that was shared by the Spirit, despite its close ties with cricket: "The interest in the game of Base Ball appears to be on the rise, and it bids fair to become our most popular game." That prediction proved absolutely correct.[21]

Baseball grew tremendously in the five years prior to the Civil War, replacing cricket as the nation's leading ball game. From only a dozen clubs in Brooklyn and New York in 1855, the number of organized teams increased eightfold in just three years, to 71 in Brooklyn and 25 in Manhattan. Counting ball clubs already formed in nearby New Jersey, Westchester County, and on Long Island, there were over 125 teams in the metropolitan area. It is impossible to say exactly how many people played base ball in the neighboring cities. The *Herald* claimed in 1859 that there were more members in Brooklyn and New York City baseball clubs than in all the other clubs combined. The statement is no doubt inaccurate, but it reflects the extent to which the press was awed by the surging popularity of baseball.[22]

The rapid increase in the number of clubs and contests created the need to clarify and codify the various rules of the game. At the end of the 1855 season the *Herald* reported that a preliminary meeting was held as the first step toward creating a central governing body for baseball, but the absence of a follow-up story indicates that nothing apparently came of it. *Porter's Spirit* noted in October 1856 that a convention of baseball clubs to amend the rules seemed imminent. In December of that year the Knickerbockers, in an effort to "promote additional interest in baseball," and quite possibly because they were prodded by other clubs, called for a convention of teams from New York City and vicinity. Delegates from fourteen clubs, all from Manhattan and Brooklyn, met in 1857 and elected Dr. Daniel D. Adams of the Knickerbockers as president. They reconfirmed the rules of baseball's pioneer club with one major change: adoption of the nine-inning game (instead of ending a contest when a team scored twenty-one runs, or aces). The most significant debate, however, revolved around the Knickerbockers' proposal that to retire the batter the ball be caught on the fly instead of on the first bounce. The delegates rejected such a change and continued to do so every year until 1863, despite wide support in the press.[23]

The presidents of New York's four oldest clubs—Knickerbocker, Gotham, Eagle, and Empire—called another meeting in 1858, and the number of clubs represented increased to twenty-six. The convention adopted the name National Association of Base Ball Players (NABBP), even though all the teams represented came from what is currently New York City, with the exception of one team from New Brunswick, New Jersey.[24] The association basically reconfirmed the rules established the previous year and elected new officers. The Knickerbockers were conspicuous by their absence from the executive council, leading baseball historians to erroneously interpret this as a blunt rejection of the club and its effort to be the social arbiter of the sport.[25]

Again, the events simply do not support the contention that the Knickerbockers were trying to become baseball's equivalent to the Marylebone Cricket Club. In 1857 they decided to restrict their contests to those clubs who practiced on their grounds at Elysian Fields, a policy chastised in a letter to *Porter's Spirit*.[26] I contend that the Knickerbockers' desire for the company of their own kind when playing baseball illustrates that for them the game continued to perform mainly a social rather than a competitive function. In fact, they showed no desire to govern baseball, even though as the oldest club and the sport's earliest rule maker, new teams and the press looked to them for leadership. Instead of consolidating these advantages into a position of power, the Knickerbockers shied away from asserting any leadership role whatsoever.

While some disenchantment existed with the Knickerbockers' lack of leadership, their failure to be elected to any "national" office in 1858 was not the product of a revolt from below by "democratic" delegates disenchanted with their supposed aristocratic policies. The new association officers all came from clubs with occupational structures similar to the Knickerbockers'. Of the NABBP's six executives, there were three lawyers, a doctor, a merchant, and one whose occupation could not be ascertained. William H. Van Cott was a deserving choice as president of the NABBP, having been a member of the Gotham Club since at least 1851 and its president since 1856; he also wrote the first letter to the press about baseball in 1854.[27] Contrary to charges by later scholars, the press did not comment on the absence of the Knickerbockers from the executive council, and baseball's pioneer club articulated no displeasure with the outcome of the election. Moreover, they were not totally eliminated from a position of influence: from 1858 to 1862 Dr. Adams served as the head of the important NABBP rules committee.

Popular opinion aside, the Knickerbockers' attitude toward other clubs was clearly revealed in a debate over the admission of junior clubs.[28] When the convention overwhelmingly rejected the credentials of these young men, by a 34-to-8 vote, the press unanimously disapproved. *Porter's Spirit* blamed the outcome on "a clique of men" who have "plenty of money, and a proportionate lack of strength of body and energy of spirit . . . [and who] wish to make the game a means of showing off their figures in fancy dress, and their wealth in fancy dinners." The paper recommended that the junior clubs call their own convention, and in 1860 thirty squads established the National Association of Junior Baseball Clubs.[29] Not only was Adams among the handful of men who supported junior clubs, but he wrote the minority report favoring admission of all teams. While the Knickerbockers preferred to participate in sports with their own social peers, they clearly did not want to restrict the growth of baseball in any way, nor emerge as the equivalent of the Marylebone Cricket Club.[30]

The formation of the NABBP was pivotal in the history of the sport, "marking the close of one baseball era and the beginning of another, in which the players and their representatives would meet annually in convention to revise the rules, settle disputes and control their own game."[31] Although often weak and ineffective, baseball's first centralized organization governed the sport for the next thirteen years. By the eve of the Civil War membership in the NABBP had increased to over sixty clubs, the majority still being from New York and vicinity, again illustrating that organized baseball was concentrated in this region. As the sport's popularity spread rapidly in the 1850s, clubs were established in most northeastern cities and in other parts of the country. While the NABBP did not reflect baseball's growing national character until after the Civil War, the 1859 election of Henry Schrivner of Baltimore's Excelsior Club as the association's second vice-president symbolized the growing presence of non–New York teams.[32]

Although one of the functions of the NABBP was to centralize the rules of baseball, the *Spirit* noted in 1859 that differences still existed in how the game was played in the East. Within several years, however, the New York–style game emerged triumphant. The earlier organization of the sport in New York City and the establishment there of the NABBP naturally contributed to this development, but the major reason that this particular style dominated was that it was used in America's sports communication center, where all the national sports journals were located.[33] This centralization of the rules did little to alter the style of play, however. Prior to the Civil War baseball remained essentially a hitter's game, as demonstrated by the number of runs scored (frequently at least twenty per team).

Despite the primitive play, a fair degree of sophistication began to emerge in terms of the execution of the game. One correspondent to *Porter's Spirit* noted that during a run-down infielders should throw the ball as seldom as possible and the pitcher should occupy the uncovered base; and in case a runner attempted to steal third base, the shortstop should back up the third baseman to safeguard against an errant throw by the catcher. There were no called balls and strikes, but the same writer pointed out that "many think that a ball that will curve as it approaches the striker is much more difficult to bat than one that takes a straight course."[34] There were numerous other suggestions as to how to make baseball a more "scientific" sport, such as a recommendation in the press that ball players specialize at one position.[35] Yet the change most frequently advocated—and the one most hotly contested—was the adoption of the fly rule. Universally endorsed by sports journalists, their rhetoric and sharp denunciation of the NABBP for failing to act suggests that the controversy went beyond merely refining the game. Underlying their advocacy of a more skillful sport were the inevitable comparison with cricket and the question of the manliness of baseball.

The Knickerbocker Club first proposed the fly rule, quite possibly the brainchild of James Whyte Davis, at the 1857 convention.[36] Opponents maintained that catching a fly ball hurt the player's hands and would make baseball too much like cricket. *Porter's Spirit* denied that such catches were injurious and countered that many ball players were former cricketers anyway. It urged that the fly rule not be rejected merely because it was used in cricket and then based its support of the rule on nationalistic considerations: "what an Englishman can do, an American is capable of improving upon."[37] This invocation of patriotism is not surprising since baseball was already being described as the national pastime and its supporters were painfully aware of the fact that it required less skill than the English game of cricket. However, the need to make baseball a more skillful sport went beyond nationalism. A more important motivation for support of the fly rule was to remove from baseball the vestiges of its heritage as an unmanly, child's game.[38] One journalist commented that an important improvement in the match he watched was "several fine catches being made on the fly, instead of the child's play, 'from the bound.' " The change proved "not only more manly, but adds very much to the quickness of perception, and nerve and determination, which makes up the necessary qualifications of a complete fieldsman, either at Base Ball or Cricket."[39]

Baseball propagandists pointed to the healthful benefits to be derived from their brand of outdoor recreation, and even more than cricketers they emphasized the moral benefits as well. One sports journal went so far as to suggest that baseball clubs were an "important and valuable adjunct to the church, inasmuch as a healthy bodily condition is undoubtedly essential to the enjoyment of a peaceful and religious state of mind."[40] However, virtually absent from the discussion of baseball's positive social contributions were references to its role in instilling character values, an argument that was used to confirm the manliness of cricket. The fact that the press ignored the same theme indicates that they were unsure of the manliness of baseball despite repeated claims to the contrary.

Rule changes, especially in the early stages of a developing sport, derive from an effort to meet the contingency of new and changing situations. Yet arguments in support of the fly rule ran counter to the basic direction of change in baseball—to create a balance between offense and defense. "What is more annoying to an admirer of good fielding," *Porter's Spirit* wrote in advocating adoption of the fly rule, "than to see a splendid hit to the center field, such as would merit a home run, entirely nullified by the puny effort of waiting until the force of the ball is spent on the ground and then taking it on the bound."[41] The idea of penalizing a good hit by allowing an easier catch was justification enough for changing the rule, but the focus here and elsewhere was always on fielding and the improvement of this phase of the game, not really on the disadvantages to the hitter. This approach is surprising, but since baseball was already overwhelmingly a hitter's game supporters adopted this argument.

Besides the absence of any structural reason for the fly rule, there is another perplexing problem with the press' support of this innovation. In their analyses of the popularity of baseball and cricket they conceded that cricket was the more complex and scientific sport but that baseball was more popular because it was "more simple in its rules, and a knowledge of it is more easily acquired."[42] Then why tamper with a good thing, especially since the stated objective of ball playing was to beckon the city dweller into the outdoors for healthful exercise? This desire to make the national pastime more difficult further demonstrated the need to make it a more manly sport.

In 1859 the Knickerbocker Club decided to use the fly rule during its contests. The press noted that the experiment clearly proved the superiority of the rule and its positive influence on the sport, and they fully expected it to be passed at the next convention. Although Van Cott, the NABBP president and a long-time opponent of the fly rule, shifted his position "out of courtesy to those gentlemen who seem so earnestly to believe that it would be a desirable improvement," efforts to approve the change failed again and continued to fail for another three years.[43] Henry Chadwick and other sportswriters repeatedly chastised the delegates for failing to adopt the innovative rule, insisting that the players themselves desired a more skillful game. Whether true or not, the momentum was clearly swinging in favor of change. Other clubs began experimenting with the fly rule as players became more proficient fielders, in part through concurrent participation in cricket. The NABBP finally passed the fly rule prior to the 1864 season, by which time organized baseball had changed dramatically.[44]

Symbolic of the growing participant and spectator interest in baseball in the late 1850s was the arrangement of an all-star match in 1858 between players from New York City and Brooklyn clubs. Besides attempting to discover which area had the better players, the series served to show off the sport (as is still the case in the annual confrontation between the National and American leagues). The Fashion Course was rented for the best-two-out-of-three series because it was a neutral site and, more important, because it could accommodate thousands of spectators. To cover expenses an admission fee was charged, making it the first time Americans paid to see a baseball game.[45]

The first game was scheduled for July 13 but was postponed on account of rain, even though nearly 2,000 spectators were on hand. Rescheduled for a week later the initial game in the series drew an "immense concourse" and was a closely contested event, with the play on both sides of the "very highest order." Brooklyn jumped to a 7–1 lead in the third inning, but the New Yorkers rallied to tie the score in the fourth and then outscored their opponents 7–4 in the fifth. Each team scored two runs in the sixth and one in the seventh, then Brooklyn pushed across four runs in the top of the eighth to lead, 18–17. New York countered with five runs, and when they held their opponents scoreless in the ninth they took a one-game lead in the series. The second game, played a month later, attracted a somewhat smaller crowd. Both squads made changes in their lineups. Brooklyn jumped to a 17–3 lead after four innings and coasted home to an easy 29–8 win. They entered the deciding game as a slight favorite, although none of the contests attracted heavy betting. The teams changed lineups once again, with the Brooklyn players coming solely from the Atlantic (six players) and the Eckford (three players) clubs. The Brooklynites scored twice in the top of the first inning, but the New Yorkers countered with seven runs and never relinquished their lead, winning 29–18.[46]

The press agreed that the all-star games had been a huge success and were "extremely favorable to the progress and popularity of the game of Base-Ball." While the New York City players drew first blood in the battle, Brooklyn teams would dominate the sport in the decade that followed, revenging the 1858 defeat in 1861 and winning baseball's unofficial championship from its inception in 1861 until 1867.[47] In a display of boosterism and civic pride, long an integral part of American sport, the Brooklyn *Eagle* proudly told its readers, "Nowhere has the National game of Baseball taken a firmer hold than in Brooklyn and nowhere are there better ballplayers." Given the area's inferiority complex, overshadowed as it was by the giant across the river, it is not surprising that the newspaper was especially pleased when a team from Brooklyn was victorious over a New York City club. "If we are ahead of the big city in nothing else," the *Eagle* wrote, "we can beat her in baseball."[48]

By the end of the 1850s the national pastime had made significant advances both in the New York metropolitan area and throughout the country, although baseball contests remained purely local affairs. The Excelsior Club of Brooklyn broke with this policy prior to the start of the 1860 season when it announced a two-week tour to play teams in the western part of the state. The *Eagle* responded favorably to the idea, noting that "the excursion would not only be an exceedingly pleasant and enjoyable one but it would add greatly to the advances of the popularity of the game in every locality visited." Baseball's first extended road trip proved to be successful as the visitors easily won all six games against less experienced teams. Returning to Brooklyn the Excelsiors took on the Atlantics in a match described as a battle to decide the best baseball team in America. The expected classic confrontation between two equally matched teams turned into a rout, with the Excelsiors manhandling the Atlantics, 23–4, before a huge crowd estimated at 6,000–8,000. The next day the *Eagle* reported that the Atlantics never looked worse and the Excelsiors never looked better. Fresh from victory the Excelsiors went on another tour, going as far south as Baltimore and continuing to attract considerable interest despite one-sided victories over hometown heroes.[49]

The impact of the Excelsior Club on baseball went beyond the interest its tours generated or its success on the field. The club represented changes that were already underway in baseball as a result of the growth of the sport and the increasing competitiveness of the game. Initially composed of the merchants and clerks who formed the club for the benefits to be derived from healthful exercise, the team was totally revamped between 1857 and 1860 as winning took on greater importance and symbolic meaning. Newer and better players were added in a merger with another Brooklyn club, by the decision of two members of the New York Cricket Club to join the baseball team, and with the recruitment of four players from the Star Club, a leading Brooklyn junior squad.[50] Yet with all these changes the Excelsior Club was still considered a club for gentlemen. Many of the new recruits came from respectable families, although the starting nine included players whose economic and social standings placed them below other members. While talent was by no means the sole criteria for membership, it was clearly a major factor in the recruitment of some players.

Of the new Excelsior players none was more important as both a ball player and a symbol of baseball's future than James Creighton, the sport's first superstar, whose arrival in 1860 turned a good team into a powerful one. A reporter for the *Eagle* heard so much about Creighton's prowess as a pitcher that he felt compelled to go see him perform. He noted that the nineteen-year-old threw a "speed ball," but as speed alone was not difficult to hit, he also curved the ball. The reporter claimed that Creighton delivered his pitches "within a few inches of the ground and they rose up about the batsman's hip, and when thus delivered, the result of hitting at the ball is either to miss it or send it high in the air."[51]

Creighton was not only the sport's first premier player, he was, more significantly, baseball's first professional player. How the Excelsior Club compensated him, whether in money or a job, is unknown, but why they chose to violate the NABBP ban against paid players is easier to comprehend. Apparently the young man was from a respectable middle-class family, and considering that his father was only a clerk at city hall, his social standing was probably higher than his economic one. The Creightons were most likely down on their luck, and the Excelsiors agreed to compensate their star pitcher because he lost time at work when on tour and because they had no fear that he would succumb to the evils often associated with professional athletes. While Creighton is the only known baseball professional in the pre–Civil War years, other players probably received gifts or at least had their dues paid by grateful club patrons.[52]

After returning from their southern trip the Excelsiors played the Atlantics again, this time losing in a close game, 15–14. The third, tie-breaking game drew a record crowd of 14,000–20,000, but the contest never reached a conclusion. With the Excelsiors leading 8-6 in the sixth inning their captain pulled the team off the field to protest the unruly behavior of the Atlantic fans after several close calls.[53] While the press absolved both teams of the incident, the deportment of the crowd was symptomatic of the growing rowdyism, excessive questioning of umpire's decisions, and especially gambling and partisanship.[54] "If admirers of this manly pastime desire its future welfare," the *Eagle* pointed out, "they should at once proceed to adopt stringent rules among the various clubs, *against betting on the results of matches played,* for it is unquestionably a regard for their pockets alone that led the majority of those pecuniary interested in the affair to act in the background manner that they did." The *Clipper* saw the problem of gambling as part of "the *spirit of faction* that characterises a large proportion of the community, and in which the foreign element of our immense metropolitan population, and their native offspring especially, delights to indulge."[55] Such problems would continue to plague not only baseball but all highly competitive (especially team and spectator) sports. These problems derive from the shift in the intent of the activity from play to sport, where the seriousness of the process yields to the seriousness of outcome. This shift becomes especially charged when victory takes on communal significance and importance.

Despite these difficulties the press insisted that the 1860 baseball season "may justly rank as the most brilliant one in the brief annals of our national game."[56] The rapid and continuing growth of the sport naturally led observers to seek out its cause, which they attributed to the inexpensiveness and simplicity of the game; the health and moral benefits derived from the activity; and the familiarity of many Americans with the game from their childhood and its association with boyhood frolics. By the outbreak of the Civil War the press had also adopted a fourth, and eventually dominant, explanation for baseball's popularity—namely, that baseball expressed and was suited for the American character and temperament.[57] Ever since then writers have sought to explain baseball's special place in American life. Most have relied on the nebulous idea of baseball's relationship to the national character, although several have focused on other, more interesting interpretations. For example, Allen Guttmann maintains that the major reason for baseball's preeminent position among American sport is its place in the cycle of seasons and its tendency toward extreme quantification.[58] While such explanations contain some validity, they do not provide, even collectively, a satisfying framework for understanding why baseball has long been America's number one sport.

The most important factor in explaining baseball's leadership role is its emergence as a popular pastime at a critical juncture in the history of American athletics. Baseball was not the first organized sport, the first successful spectator sport, nor the first sport to enjoy widespread popularity. However, it was the first sport to take advantage of the changing attitude toward athletics. More than any other sport of its day baseball fulfilled the requirements of the new sporting universe created by the changing social and urban environment of the antebellum period. The rapid spread of baseball clubs illustrated "a great popular want" for outdoor recreation,[59] and while other sports could have served this need, few had baseball's advantages. Not only was it inexpensive, but it combined individual play within a team setting. It is no coincidence that there was an increasing emphasis on team, at the expense of individual, sports with the shift from premodern to modern sport. While several factors shaped this development, one contributory reason was that team sports more readily served the character value argument so important to the justification of athletics.[60]

The unquestioned acceptance of baseball as the national pastime contributed greatly to its preeminent position in the sports world. Both the absence of an entrenched competitor and timing played a vital role here. As early as 1857 the *Spirit* claimed that baseball "must be regarded as a national pastime," yet organized baseball at that time was confined to the New York metropolitan area, although various children's forms of the game were well known throughout the country. This premature description might have reflected a certain parochialism on the part of the New York–based sports journal, but the desire to promote an American sport was probably the real reason for this contention. In an article entitled "National Sport and Their Uses" the *Times* argued that strenuous athletic activity was necessary to combat the physical degeneracy of urban residents and that the more extensive participation in sport in England was responsible for their longer lifespan. "To reproduce the tastes and habits of English sporting life in this country is neither possible nor desirable," the newspaper maintained, but "to develop analogous tendencies of an original and specific character appropriate to our national trials and opportunities is both very possible and desirable." A statement in *Porter's Spirit* clearly suggested that baseball "ought to be looked upon in this country with the same national enthusiasm" as cricket in England because "there should be some game peculiar to the citizens of the United

States." Its advocacy of baseball was not based on the fact that the sport
was manly, healthful, or a pleasure to the young, since that would "say
nothing specifically in its praise, because all movements of the body in
the open air are so." Instead, *Porter's Spirit* rested its support for baseball
on the belief that the time had come "that some attempt was made to
set up a game that could be termed a 'Native American Sport.' "[61]

The search for a national pastime grew out of the sporting revolution
of the antebellum period. As with other cultural forms, the maturation
of sport in this country led to the desire on the part of Americans to
emancipate their games from foreign patterns. Such nationalistic overtones
were already present in harness racing, but this nonparticipatory sport
could not emerge as a symbol of an athletic movement with healthful
exercise as its major rationale. Since baseball filled the bill, the press
prematurely dubbed the game the national pastime, a symbol of, and spur
to, America's athletic changes.

The erroneous popular belief that baseball was indigenous to America
facilitated the contention that baseball was indeed the national pastime.
Robin Carver had delineated the relationship between baseball and the
English game of rounders as early as 1839 in his *Book of Sport*. While
the children's book was quite popular, many adults were probably
unfamiliar with its content, while others no doubt forgot or ignored the
relationship. Many Americans innocently presumed that the game was
native to this country since they had been playing it for so long and since
rounders attracted no public attention in England.[62] As baseball gained
in popularity, however, a letter to the *Herald* in 1859 pointed out that
English schoolboys had played baseball under the name of rounders for
more than a century, and the following year Henry Chadwick, an English-
born sportswriter living in America, also noted baseball's English origins.
Given Chadwick's authoritative position and the presence of Englishmen
on the baseball diamond, the reassertion that baseball evolved from
rounders went virtually unchallenged until years later, when Albert G.
Spalding and his self-appointed commission sought to purify the game
through the propagation of the Abner Doubleday Myth.[63]

Having raised doubts as to just how American the national pastime
was, Chadwick immediately reassured his adopted countrymen that "this
invigorating exercise and manly pastime may be now justly termed the
American game of Ball, for though of English origin, it has been so
modified and improved of late years in this country, as almost to deprive
it of any of its original features beyond the mere groundwork of the
game." Significant changes in baseball had already taken place, but that
any Englishman could easily recognize the game as a variation of rounders
indicates that such a claim was a bit premature. Chadwick clearly felt
that Americans needed a sport they could call their own and that baseball

was well suited as the national pastime because it was peculiarly adapted to the American character. He never insisted, however, as many writers did, that baseball was an inherently better game than cricket—it was simply an excellent way to popularize physical education and a healthy outdoor sport.[64] His argument, adopted by other writers, contained elements of the truth for a radical change in the character of the sport had taken place, if not by 1860 then clearly by 1870. As a "game" form baseball was not a native product but had evolved from earlier ball games of which rounders was its most direct ancestor. As a "sport" form baseball was indigenous to America, for it was in this country that baseball was organized and the rules standardized. In essence, while baseball originated as an English game it became an American sport.

The acceptance of baseball as the national pastime and the perception of it as the embodiment of the American temperament was critical to its long-lasting preeminent position. While criticism of baseball was evident even after 1870, it mostly concerned the professional game. By 1900, when college football first came out from behind ivy-covered walls, criticism of baseball had not only abated but the sport was unquestionably accepted as one of America's finest democratic institutions. In 1919 the eminent philosopher Morris Cohen claimed that baseball was the American religion. Indeed, thanks to a pervasive and popular ideology and mythology, baseball had an incalculable head start over any of its serious sports rivals.[65]

Through all this the press never hesitated to point out its contribution to the growth of baseball as a national sport. Although that view was self-serving and slightly exaggerated it was not entirely without merit. Increasing coverage of the sport in the 1850s corresponded with the growing number of clubs and contests and the public desire for such news. The press, especially sports journals such as *Porter's Spirit* and the *Clipper,* disseminated information on how to play the game, how the clubs were organized, what the various teams in New York City and vicinity, and the country as well, were doing—in other words, they publicized the game. Baseball reporting made only minor advances during this period as newspapers continued to provide only brief summaries of contests and crude box scores that merely detailed the runs and outs made by each player. By the end of the 1850s, however, sports journals began to compile annual statistics of players and teams, as they did for cricket, as a means of assessing performances.[66] The pre–Civil War period also saw the rudimentary beginnings of a baseball literature. In 1857 a frequent correspondent to *Porter's Spirit* noted that many cricket books existed and that one was needed for baseball, too. *Beadle's Dime Base Ball Player,* edited by Henry Chadwick and published in 1860, was the first annual guidebook for the sport; approximately 50,000 copies were sold. Essentially a rehash of Chadwick's newspaper articles, the guidebook discussed the origins of baseball, published the NABBP rules, provided statistics from the previous year, and offered a brief statement as to the physical and moral benefits of baseball.[67]

The occupational structure of New York City and Brooklyn ball players changed significantly with the rising popularity of the sport. Baseball shifted from an upper-middle–middle-class game to one dominated by men from the middle–lower-middle classes. While professional–high white-collar and low white-collar–proprietor workers made up slightly more than three-quarters of the ball players of these neighboring cities between 1850 and 1855 (see Table 3), the latter group, along with skilled craftsmen, comprised roughly the same proportion during the next five-year interval (see Table 4). This change was almost directly related to the increasing percentage of skilled craftsmen and the declining proportion of professional–high white-collar workers. The evidence clearly indicates that baseball in Brooklyn and New York City had become a broadly based sport by the outbreak of the Civil War, although unskilled workers, roughly one-third of the work force of each city, remained virtually absent from the diamond. It should be further noted that roughly half of the skilled craftsmen were connected with crafts that were able to minimize the negative impact "metropolitan industrialization" had on a large section of New York's skilled craftsmen. Besides those in the shipping industry, discussed earlier, ball players in both cities worked in the printing, construction, and especially the food industries (one-sixth of all New York ball players were in the food industry, while one-tenth of all Brooklyn players engaged in food-related occupations, including ten men from the Atlantic Club). While many of the skilled workers came from the more prosperous crafts, the fact that one-sixth of all New York and Brooklyn ball players worked at jobs where they barely earned a living wage testifies to the broad appeal of the national pastime.[68]

The general membership of New York City and Brooklyn baseball clubs

TABLE 4. Occupational Structure of Area Baseball Players, 1856–60

	New York City		Brooklyn		Combined	
	N	%	N	%	N	%
Professional–High White-Collar	41	21.9	31	18.2	72	20.2
Low White-Collar–Proprietor	83	44.4	73	42.9	156	43.7
Skilled Craftsman	61	32.6	63	37.1	124	34.7
Unskilled Worker	2	1.1	3	1.8	5	1.4
Total	187		170		357	

was from the middling ranks, but middle- to upper-middle-class men were elected officers of these clubs: over three-quarters of them were from the two higher-status occupational groups (see Table 5). The 12.9 percent difference between baseball officers and total club membership resulted almost exclusively from the shifting proportion of professionals and skilled craftsmen. This change was evident in both cities, although Brooklyn officers, like Brooklyn ball players, had more plebian backgrounds. NABBP delegates between 1857 and 1860 held even more lucrative jobs (see Table 6). Since officers and delegates were a more visible group, they were more easily identifiable — constituting probably no more than one-fourth of the membership, they accounted for 41.5 percent of the known ball players. When baseball's nonofficer membership is examined, the sport's middle-class character emerges even more clearly (see Table 7). Between 1856 and 1860 only one-eighth of the nonofficers were drawn from the more prestigious and lucrative occupations; the remaining players were divided roughly equally between the next two groups, with only a minute percentage being unskilled workers.

Although variations existed between officers and nonofficers there were no differences between members who participated in ball games and those who did not. The occupational structure of ball players who engaged in at least one game (on the first team of their respective clubs) during this five-year interval was remarkably similar to the total membership (compare Tables 8 and 4). Active participants — those who participated

TABLE 5. Occupational Structure of Area Baseball Club Officers, 1856–60

	New York City		Brooklyn		Combined	
	N	%	N	%	N	%
Professional–High White-Collar	23	33.8	21	30.0	44	31.9
Low White-Collar–Proprietor	34	50.0	28	40.0	62	44.9
Skilled Craftsman	11	16.2	21	30.0	32	23.2
Total	68		70		138	

TABLE 6. Occupational Structure of Area NABBP Delegates, 1857–60

	New York City		Brooklyn		Combined	
	N	%	N	%	N	%
Professional–High White-Collar	14	43.8	6	35.3	20	40.8
Low White-Collar–Proprietor	12	37.5	7	41.2	19	38.8
Skilled Craftsman	6	18.8	4	23.5	10	20.4
Total	32		17		49	

TABLE 7. Occupational Structure of Nonofficer Members of Area Baseball Clubs, 1856–60

	New York City		Brooklyn		Combined	
	N	%	N	%	N	%
Professional–High White-Collar	16	14.4	10	10.2	26	12.4
Low White-Collar–Proprietor	45	40.5	43	43.9	88	42.1
Skilled Craftsman	48	43.2	42	42.9	90	43.1
Unskilled Worker	2	1.8	3	3.1	5	2.4
Total	111		98		209	

TABLE 8. Occupational Structure of Area Baseball Players, 1856–60

	New York City		Brooklyn		Combined	
	N	%	N	%	N	%
Professional–High White-Collar	21	11.9	13	18.1	34	20.2
Low White-Collar–Proprietor	40	41.7	28	38.9	68	40.5
Skilled Craftsman	33	34.3	29	40.3	62	36.9
Unskilled Worker	2	2.1	2	2.8	4	2.4
Total	96		72		168	

TABLE 9. Occupational Structure of Active Area Baseball Players, 1856–60

	New York City		Brooklyn		Combined	
	N	%	N	%	N	%
Professional–High White-Collar	8	17.8	3	7.9	11	13.3
Low White-Collar–Proprietor	18	40.0	12	31.6	30	36.1
Skilled Craftsman	18	40.0	22	57.9	40	48.2
Unskilled Worker	1	2.2	1	2.6	2	2.4
Total	45		38		83	

in four first-team games during any one year, or ten games in five years—varied significantly from the general membership (see Table 9). Skilled craftsmen comprised nearly half the ball players of the two cities who engaged frequently in baseball contests, with 40 percent of these men employed in the food industry. The next higher occupational group comprised another 36.1 percent of the active participants, with clerks (and similar workers) accounting for 40 percent of this group. Thus, clerks and food-industry workers together made up one-third of the active participants, while those engaged in the most and least lucrative occupations together made up less than one-sixth of the city's leading ball players.

By the mid-1850s baseball in New York City and Brooklyn began to slip from the polite hands of the urban gentlemen, becoming a sport for all social classes, with the notable exception of unskilled workers. On the playing field, clerks, a select group of proprietors, and skilled craftsmen in particular dominated the sport. The high percentage of craftsmen among baseball's active participants, especially in Brooklyn and even before the commercialization and professionalization of the sport, indicates that they were not lured to baseball by these later developments; instead, their presence in large numbers was vital to the emergence of this later stage.

Several factors contributed to the involvement of skilled craftsmen in baseball. The inexpensiveness of the sport and the fact that they could easily engage in it without disturbing their work schedules (or in the case of ball players who worked in the food industry, had occupations that were completed by midday) facilitated participation. A high percentage of baseball's craftsmen, most notably those in the shipping and food industries, engaged in occupations where the relationship between master craftsmen and their employees was generally good. In fact, one possible reason for the considerable number of ball-playing members from the butcher community is that master craftsmen in this industry may have promoted and sponsored clubs. Clearly, these men were frequently the officers and NABBP delegates of clubs comprised of butchers.[69]

Most important of all, craftsmen had a rich sporting heritage in general, especially among those artisans who belonged to the group Bruce Laurie described as "traditionalist." New York butchers were typical of this group, known as lusty chaps who glorified in their stamina and physical prowess. While they engaged in a variety of sports, baseball held a special attraction for them and for other artisans. Unlike other sports they participated in, such as boxing and animal sports, which were illegal, publicly castigated, and usually conducted surreptitiously, baseball was socially respectable and favorably reported on in the press. Participation in baseball thereby provided butchers with an arena to demonstrate that they were part of the respectable community at a time when they had an unrivaled reputation for forming gangs and for drunken carousing. One reason master craftsmen in this industry, who were regarded as respectable, sober, and substantial, may have promoted baseball clubs among their employees was to counterbalance this negative image and to provide an alternative recreation to those frequently engaged in.[70] Finally, baseball offered artisans a vehicle for enhancing their prestige and influence within their own communities, which had long appreciated and rewarded physical prowess and sporting success. With the growing popularity of baseball, artisans also could win prestige within the larger community of players and fans, thereby further enhancing their standing in their own communities. Thus, it was a search for fame rather than fortune that initially attracted these workers to baseball.

The game of baseball made significant advances in the fifteen years after the Knickerbockers organized the first club. Now a popular participant and spectator sport, baseball was well on its way toward modernization by the outbreak of the Civil War. The growth of the game and the rapid advances it made, especially between 1855 and 1860, set the stage for the tremendous changes that would occur during the next decade.

The second game of the championship match between the Atlantics of Brooklyn and th Athletics of Philadelphia, 1866. From *America's National Game*, by A. G. Spaulding.

7

Baseball Matures and Turns Professional, 1860–70

In the 1860s the maturation and modernization of baseball made significant advances. By the end of the decade baseball emerged as a highly competitive, commercialized spectator sport dominated by a small group of professional players. The formation of baseball's first professional league, the National Association of Professional Base Ball Players, in March 1871, symbolized the changing character of the sport. Brooklyn and New York City continued to share the distinction of being the baseball capital as their ball clubs reigned supreme on the playing field throughout most of the 1860s and, more importantly, set the tone and direction of the sport. Immediately following the Civil War, however, as numerous ball clubs were organized throughout the country and as these teams increasingly raided Brooklyn and New York squads of many of their better ball players, the teams in the New York area had less impact on the sport. The era of dominance symbolically ended when the Cincinnati Red Stockings went undefeated and won baseball's championship in 1869. By 1870 the national scope of baseball made it impossible for any city to manage a stranglehold on the sport.

During the winter of 1861 two Brooklyn ball clubs, not satisfied with a season that only lasted from early spring to late fall, agreed to play a baseball game on ice skates. "The baulks [sic] and other mishaps," the *Spirit* wrote, "were a source of infinite merriment to some ten thousand spectators during the progress of the game, and if lots of fun be a desideratum in public amusements, let the new idea be encouraged by all means." The fact that such an unusual contest took place, and that such a huge crowd turned out to witness it, testifies to baseball's popularity.

A few months later the *Brooklyn Eagle* predicted that the upcoming baseball season promised to be one of great interest. Before the campaign could get underway, however, shots were fired on Fort Sumter and many ball players traded their bats for rifles.[1]

Baseball existed throughout the Civil War years in Brooklyn and Manhattan, but in a weakened condition. The number of clubs decreased by more than 60 percent during the first three years of the war. Junior clubs were particularly hard hit and several senior squads existed in name only. While the sharp decline produced a corresponding reduction in the number of contests, most clubs managed to play some games, usually when a sufficient number of veterans had returned from the war. The better organized and more competitive teams were able to play more frequently than their recreational counterparts.[2] Yet in spite of the problems created by the war, baseball's popularity continued unabated among fans in the metropolitan area, with the better contests attracting crowds of no less than 5,000 spectators. When the Atlantic and Eckford clubs battled for the championship in 1862, some 15,000 people reportedly were at the game. "First class ball matches," the *Clipper* wrote in 1863, "seem to attract greater crowds of spectators, this season, than any other class of out-door sports."[3]

By 1864 baseball in New York City and vicinity began to return slowly to prewar conditions. The number of clubs increased to more than double the 1863 total, although there still were fewer than in 1860. By the end of the war the pace picked up, however, and in June 1865 the *Herald* pointed out that the sport had "received an immense impetus since the close of the war." The return of "hundreds of players" from the South "has materially strengthened the various clubs . . . and thus far the season has opened more auspiciously than any other since 1860." On any given day except Sunday fans could find a game going on somewhere in the metropolitan area. The press continued to remark on the huge crowds, and when the Atlantics battled the Mutuals before 15,000–20,000 spectators in August 1865, the *Times* was convinced that local residents had baseball on the brain.[4]

At the end of the 1865 baseball campaign Henry Chadwick claimed that never before had there been so brilliant a season: more first-class matches had been played, more clubs had competed in contests, more clubs had been organized, and larger crowds had been present than during any previous season since baseball was inaugurated.[5] He was optimistically referring to baseball on a national level, but his impressions were generally accurate for Brooklyn and New York City as well. Despite the hardships of war, certain developments in the sport were evident by mid-1865: the emergence of a championship system, and the commercialization and professionalization of the sport. The future direction of baseball in Brooklyn and New York City clearly had been established.

The emergence of a championship system contributed to the ongoing popularity of baseball and flowed naturally from the increasing competitiveness of the teams.[6] The National Association of Base Ball Players (NABBP) never established formal rules to determine baseball's champion, so the ball clubs, the press, and the public created their own. The accepted standard was that the championship club retained its title until the same challenger defeated them twice, in a best-of-three series, in the same year. Between 1861 and 1865 sportswriters did not comment on the inequities of such a simplistic system, possibly because of its newness. A more likely reason was that the system proved adequate during the Civil War: there were only a few challengers for the title, the championship was confined to the metropolitan area (although the Athletics of Philadelphia entered the competition in 1863), and each winner from 1863 to 1865 had an undefeated season.

The press did not ignore the impact of the championship on the sport, however. In 1863 the *Eagle* perceptively pointed out that the "bitter rivalry that ensues, the objectionable effects that are likely to be made to increasing the player strength of the contending clubs, and the general discord that is thereby introduced, to say nothing of the evils arising from the encouragement that is also given to the gambling spirit by the opportunity afforded for betting in large amounts by the means of these contests, afford sufficient proof of the injurious effect they have on the welfare of the game." The Brooklyn newspaper did not oppose competition but rather differentiated between creditable, manly rivalries and spirited, cowardly ones: the former "admits of every fair to excel" but "gracefully yields to the creditable success of an opposing club"; the latter does not hesitate in depriving adversaries "of anticipated triumphs, exalts in every petty annoyance their opposition may be subjected to, [and] denies them every credit they may be entitled to."[7]

Also at issue was the rowdyism that accompanied championship contests. The *Clipper* noted that these games attracted an "objectionable influence" among the many spectators, which "seriously conflicts with the best interest of baseball . . . [and] if permitted to continue, would soon bring the game down to a very low level." The newspaper recommended at one time that championship contests might best be played only at enclosed ballfields. In another vein the *Clipper* pointed out that the championship system had led to a monopoly of the top-notch players by just a few teams. In depriving other clubs of such players these teams in effect reduced the number of serious challengers and consequently diminished interest in the sport.[8]

The commercialization of baseball was tied closely to the increasing competitiveness of ball games and the number of fans who witnessed them. In 1862 William H. Cammeyer opened the Union Grounds in Brooklyn's eastern district, providing the playing field (which he had successfully used as a skating ring the previous winter) rent free to three ball clubs in exchange for the right to charge a ten-cent admission fee to their contests.[9] Such fees had long been part of sports events in New York City, but until the 1860s ball games, whether cricket or baseball, had been free to the public, with the exception of the 1858 all-star baseball game and the 1859 international cricket contest—in these special cases the tariff was justified (or accepted) as necessary to help defray the expenses of arranging the contest—and the benefits that cricket clubs held for their professional players. (The *Spirit* did not object to the admission fee, usually fifty cents, to these benefits but expressed dislike of the system because it reduced the player to the level of a beggar.) Such postseason exhibitions often drew small crowds.[10]

In 1860 the St. George Cricket Club announced that it was going to charge a fee for its regular matches in an attempt to defray the cost of its new grounds. Sportswriters castigated the club policy, insisting that the new policy was "entirely unnecessary in a financial sense, and one calculated to be detrimental to the future progress of the game." They claimed that money should be collected only for special matches, especially since cricket did not attract many spectators even when the contests were free.[11]

In contrast to its attitude toward the St. George Club, the *Clipper* did not protest Cammeyer's admission fee. It approved the tariff because it would help keep better order at the ball games and because the objective was "merely to defray contingent expenses, as the director looks only to the receipts from the skating pond for any profitable return for the money invested." Henry Chadwick did not view Cammeyer's endeavor in such ennobling terms, but neither did he protest it. He objectively noted that the considerable expense of the proprietor, estimated at $12,000, required that he either charge a rental fee to the clubs or an admission fee to the fans. Since the grounds could accommodate only three ball clubs, a rental fee would not permit him to meet his expenses. Chadwick further insisted that a tariff was only improper when leveled by a ball club, but "in regards to grounds laid out by outside parties for pecuniary profit, the matter assumes an entirely different aspect."[12]

The right of sports entrepreneurs to charge a fee and make a profit had long been accepted. In the final analysis, however, the introduction of business into baseball did not rest on the distinction between private clubs or private ownership, or on other theoretical questions, but on the willingness of the public to pay the price. The success of Cammeyer's venture spurred others to follow suit, and in 1864 Messrs. Weed and Decker converted their skating grounds in Brooklyn's western district into a ballfield. The Capitoline Grounds, the *Herald* wrote, was the "most extensive and complete ball grounds in the United States, and in every respect is suited for important contests."[13]

More than any other sport in America baseball came to symbolize the increasing tendency of Americans to watch athletic contests. Scholars universally recognize that commercialized spectator sports are an urban product, and they advance a "substitution theory" to explain the relationship between spectator sports and the city. According to this thesis, increasing urbanization undermined traditional recreation patterns. Restrictions of time and space, limitations imposed on people crowded into small living areas without parks or open land, low productivity of labor, and an underdeveloped transportation system—all this served to cut off the urban masses from the leisure activities in which they participated in their former rural environment. The rise of spectator sports permitted onlookers to enjoy "vicariously what they would have liked to do themselves, and the excitement which they worked up released emotions pent-up by the drabness of their lives."[14] The substitution theory, rooted in an antiurban view, is premised on the belief that individuals from all social and economic ranks attended sports events and that participation in sport is natural while spectatorship is artificial (something less than "true" sport). The participant-spectator dichotomy fits neatly into the traditional American perception of rural and urban and makes it clear that the artificial city produced artificial sport.[15]

There is, however, little evidence to support the substitution theory. While changes in New York City placed strains on the sports practices of its residents, especially among the poor, the groups that suffered the most from shifting social conditions did not attend sports events. At the same time that an underdeveloped transportation system inhibited the physical recreations of urban dwellers, it also prevented them from witnessing sports events, since racetracks, the scene of most of the antebellum spectator sports, were located outside the city. Far from attracting fans from all social ranks, spectators at New York sports events prior to the Civil War came from no further down the social ladder than the more prosperous members of the middle class.[16] By the time baseball emerged as a commercialized spectator sport, New Yorkers had for some time been paying to watch other sports events. The national pastime differed from most antebellum spectator sports in that the ballparks were located in the city and the admission fee was much lower. As a result, attendance at baseball games was more broadly based than at other spectator sports, but even here the substitution theory does not apply, for the lower class neither played nor attended baseball games.

The rise of spectator sports did not derive from the urban masses seeking a vicarious substitute for the "real thing" but was rooted in the urban and economic expansion of the period. Spectator sports emerged in nineteenth-century urban areas because that was where a sufficient number of people lived with sufficient income to sustain these sports on a permanent basis. Yet, while this explains the potential for commercialized amusements, it does not explain the motivation for attending them, a complex issue for which there are varying interpretations.[17] It may be suggested that while spectator sports performed a variety of individual and communal functions, attendance at them was not a manifestation of, or response to, the antinatural urban environment. However, the character of the modern city, notably its rational economic order and greater division of labor, did facilitate the consumption of sport by nineteenth-century urban dwellers. Dale Somers, for example, accurately notes, "Suppliers of commercialized amusements, led by P. T. Barnum, realized that people who bought food instead of growing their own; purchased clothing instead of making it; who rented or bought homes instead of building them would purchase pleasure if they were attractively packaged and cleverly sold."[18]

The sports entrepreneur was an American phenomenon, one that probably should have occurred first in England since commercialism in sport is a product of modernization and many sports modernized earlier in England. However, the ongoing strength of the English aristocracy and its dominance of the sporting life of that country inhibited anything more than early commercialization. Not until the later part of the nineteenth century, when industrialization had eroded the sporting bond between commoner and gentry, did commercialized sport begin to any significant degree in England.[19]

The upper class in America sponsored sport for its peers but refused to become patrons of sport to the extent that its English counterparts had. Consequently, even a traditional upper-class sport such as horse racing began to assume commercial form as early as the 1830s. This attitude of the upper class was particularly evident as regards sponsorship of sport for other social classes. Since they did not practice the paternalism of England's aristocracy, sports entrepreneurs stepped in to fill the void. By 1870 America's two leading spectator sports—harness racing and baseball—had become commercialized, with the pattern being the same for both: middle-class businessmen became financially involved in sports that appealed to their own social class, providing services for and catering to a specific group; and these new entrepreneurs further stimulated the growth and popularity of harness racing and baseball. It is no coincidence that the maturation and modernization of both of these sports far exceeded similar developments in all other sports in America.

The professionalization of baseball coincided with the emergence of the championship system and the commercialization of the sport. Before the Civil War James Creighton, the game's leading player, and possibly several others received some form of compensation from their clubs, even though the NABBP prohibited payments to players. With the increasing public demand for victorious teams during the early 1860s, clubs actively sought better ball players. In 1863 several teams offered money to Al Reach, baseball's leading player following Creighton's death, to lure him from the Eckford Club. The highest bid came from Arthur P. Gorman of Baltimore, a future NABBP president and United States Senator, but Reach chose to play with the Philadelphia Athletics because he could commute more easily to his home in Flushing, on Long Island. Although Reach is the only known player prior to 1865 to receive a flat fee for playing baseball, Brooklyn and Manhattan teams provided other inducements, such as gifts or jobs, to attract talented recruits. Postseason benefit games, similar to those in cricket, were played as early as 1861 to financially reward ball players. These annual benefits lasted throughout the war years but then quickly became passé when players demanded a regular share of the gate receipts. Although precisely when this practice began is unclear, but there is evidence that William Cammeyer initially refused the players' demands on the grounds that he assumed the financial risk while providing the club free use of the ballpark. He nevertheless capitulated, in part because he needed the players in order to keep his business going and quite possibly because of the competition from the Capitoline Grounds.[20]

Public awareness of the professionalization of baseball emerged slowly since payments to players were made in secret. In 1863 the *Eagle* reported that "ball matches have of late years got to be quite serious affairs, and some have even intimated that ballplaying has become quite a money making business, many finding it to pay well to play well." The following year the newspaper acknowledged that there existed three categories of ball players — professionals, amateurs, and muffins — a distinction it insisted was based on skill level, not economics. By this reasoning professional ball players, unlike professional cricketers, were simply the most proficient, not those that were being paid. By contrast, Chadwick claimed in 1864 that "the system of professional ballplaying began to manifest itself," for although previously practiced to some extent, "it became common knowledge in baseball circles that some ballplayers received compensation." The following year the *Eagle,* while recognizing the growth of the play-for-pay movement, admitted that it was uncertain how prevalent the practice had become among local teams.[21]

Seymour notes that during the 1860s baseball passed through a "twilight stage from amateurism to professionalism under the very nose of the amateur Association." While scholars have examined the reasons for the professionalization of baseball, they have not explained why the NABBP would pass a rule prohibiting the use of professional players, instead assuming that such a rule was a logical extension of the view that baseball was a gentlemen's game.[22] This assumption erroneously injects later sports concepts and developments—the division of athletics into amateur and professional, with the accompanying class overtones—into the discussion. Clearly, antebellum New Yorkers recognized that differences existed between men who participated in sport as a business and those who participated for recreational purposes. Similarly, it can be conceded that a certain antiprofessional bias already existed. Nevertheless, the key point is not the presence of these sentiments but the striking absence of any debate about professionalism prior to the mid-1850s, even though professional athletes already participated in several sports. While various factors contributed to the professionalization of baseball, the rapid growth of the play-for-pay movement could not have occurred if a strong and entrenched antiprofessional sentiment had truly existed.[23]

It is significant that the NABBP waited two years after its formation to pass the rule prohibiting professional players. The delay suggests that the rule was a response to an existing or a perceived problem. Since the press did not give the slightest hint that any ball players were being compensated, the NABBP action was more likely a response to the growing problem in professional cricket.[24]

The criticism of professional cricket was different than the later objections to professional athletes or professional athletics in general. Disapproval here was confined solely to nonprofessionals playing professionals in club matches, as no objection was voiced with regard to paying someone for teaching a skill. Moreover, opposition to playing salaried athletes did not entail a criticism of professional cricketers. Quite the contrary, the character and integrity of these cricketers were unimpeachable, and the press always held them in high regard.[25] The objections Americans had to professional cricketers were quite possibly motivated by their own inability to compete financially with the wealthier English clubs, particularly the St. George Cricket Club. In 1858 the *Times* articulated the growing sentiment that the hiring of professionals was one of the ploys English-born cricketers used to prevent Americans from fairly sharing the honors on the playing field. It must be noted, however, that Philadelphia cricket clubs, comprised of wealthy members of that city's upper class, had hired professional cricketers and allowed them to play in their contests since the 1840s.[26]

In the late 1860s two newspapers maintained that the initial opposition to professional baseball stemmed from the fear that trained athletes would be an obstacle to equitable competition. However, Frank Pidgeon, the author of the NABBP bill against professionalism, stated his objection in economic terms; namely, baseball should be played for pleasure, not profit.[27] After passage of the bill the *Clipper* charged that it had "something of an aristocratic odor" and exhibited "a rather uncharitable disposition towards poor players." *Porter's Spirit* also favored compensating players, claiming it was democratic and would level class distinctions. Pidgeon, the Eckford Club delegate and a dockbuilder by profession, responded that his objection was not based on "snobbish inclinations" but the fact that paying players would give the wealthier clubs an undue advantage. The rule prohibiting compensation would provide " 'honest poverty' a fair chance, and in a struggle for supremacy between clubs [would] let skill, courage and endurance decide who shall be the victors." More importantly, he saw in professionalization a loss of personal independence, a significant and repeated artisan fear during the antebellum period. Quite simply, he did not want to see ball players bought and sold like cattle.[28]

Pidgeon's position on this issue lends credence to the argument that the initial opposition to paying athletes derived from a desire to ensure competitive balance. To what extent other artisans shared Pidgeon's view of professionalism is difficult to say. Regardless of their perspective, this occupational group always comprised a minority of the NABBP delegates. Moreover, the skilled workers who represented their clubs at the annual convention generally came from the more prosperous segment of this occupational group. So in another sense Pidgeon's argument did contain an element of the "gentlemen's" position.

The absence of a monolithic attitude toward compensation, even among gentlemen, further complicates our understanding the reasons for passage of the NABBP rule. The majority of gentlemen players were opposed on principle to paying athletes, but the example of the Philadelphia cricket clubs illustrates that there were some who, even if they would not take money for playing, did not object to rewarding skilled performers. In fact, many of the early known violators of the NABBP's prohibition were from teams that were considered gentlemen's clubs. Their actions cannot be seen simply as hypocritical; some form of self-justification for their behavior was necessary. *Porter's Spirit* maintained, "If from any circumstance, personal or pecuniary, a lover of the sport cannot afford a day to travel from his home to play a match of cricket and baseball, and his brother members of the club are able and willing to remunerate him for his time and expenses, why should they not be permitted to do so?" This argument offered gentlemen a palatable defense for compensation because it did not present ball playing as a career. Further complicating the issue was the uncertainty of what constituted a professional player. As late as 1865 a correspondent to the *Clipper* asked if a benefit held for the Atlantics made them professionals. The writer was expressing a widely held opinion that monetary assistance should be permitted only if the player needed the money to overcome some financial handicap.[29]

While diverse reasons led to the NABBP prohibition, the belief that baseball should be a recreational and not a business activity unified the opponents of professionalism, but it did not automatically entail a rejection of compensation—no one disapproved of an individual making money by teaching sports skills. The criticism of the business of baseball derived from the fact that professionalism was seen by many as the dramatic and inevitable result of taking the activity too seriously. On the few occasions prior to 1865 when professional baseball was discussed, the arguments revolved around the no-nonsense approach to ball contests and the undue emphasis on victory.[30]

What was really at the heart of the objection to professional baseball was the ideological justification of sport. Ball games were sanctioned initially on the grounds that they provided urban dwellers with innocent amusement and necessary healthful outdoor exercise. Within this frame-work trials of skill served as a means of heightening the enjoyment and thus further stimulating participation in this beneficial activity. When the search for victory became the essence of competition, the country's Puritan legacy, with its suspicion of sport, reared its head: since Americans should find no redeeming social value in a baseball victory, painstaking efforts to achieve this goal were not only a waste of time but counter-productive to the ideal objective of the activity. Such a view sheds new light on the discrepancy between theory and action. Although the NABBP's antiprofessional legislation obviously meant that payments would have to be made secretly, the ball clubs or individual members who compensated new recruits never openly questioned the rule or sought to reform it. Any call for change would require a public admission that they took the game seriously, that they were concerned with and attached importance to winning—and they were not prepared to admit that.

In combination with other factors the justification of sport produced an undercurrent of antiprofessionalism in American athletics. This pre–Civil War sentiment had not yet hardened into the amateur ideology that would emerge in the last decades of the nineteenth century. Moreover, there were important differences between the ante- and postbellum objections to professional sports: whereas the latter were premised on the belief that money destroyed true sport, the former were based on the feeling that excess destroyed true sport.

During the Civil War the occupational structure of New York City and Brooklyn ball players was remarkably similar to what it had been in 1855–60 (see Table 10). The middle and lower-middle classes continued to dominate baseball, with nearly 80 percent of the players coming from

TABLE 10. Occupational Structure of Area Baseball Players, 1861–65

	New York City		Brooklyn		Combined	
	N	%	N	%	N	%
Professional–High White-Collar	48	22.4	12	11.4	60	18.8
Low White-Collar–Proprietor	91	42.5	54	51.4	145	45.5
Skilled Craftsman	70	32.7	37	35.2	107	33.5
Unskilled Worker	5	2.3	2	1.9	7	2.2
Total	214		105		319	

TABLE 11. Occupational Structure of Area Baseball Club Officers, 1861–65

	New York City		Brooklyn		Combined	
	N	%	N	%	N	%
Professional–High White-Collar	18	22.8	6	13.6	24	19.5
Low White-Collar–Proprietor	41	51.9	27	61.4	68	55.3
Skilled Craftsman	20	25.3	11	25.0	31	25.2
Total	79		44		123	

TABLE 12. Occupational Structure of Area NABBP Delegates, 1861–65

	New York City		Brooklyn		Combined	
	N	%	N	%	N	%
Professional–High White-Collar	10	31.3	3	15.8	13	25.5
Low White-Collar–Proprietor	16	50.0	13	68.4	29	56.9
Skilled Craftsman	6	18.8	3	15.8	9	17.6
Total	32		19		51	

the low white-collar–proprietor and skilled craftsman groups. The occupational structure of the club officers and NABBP delegates differed significantly, however, as men from the middle ranks began to govern the sport (see Tables 11 and 12). Nonmanual workers continued to comprise roughly three-fourths of the club officers in the two cities, but the proportion of professional–high white-collar workers and those from the low white-collar–proprietor group changed considerably, the former declining 10 percent and the later increasing roughly 12 percent. Middle-class leadership was especially pronounced in Brooklyn, where slightly more than three out of every five officers were employed in low white-collar–proprietor positions. Changes in the occupational structure of NABBP delegates followed the same pattern, with the higher group declining 15.3 percent and the middle group increasing 18.1 percent. The percentage of skilled craftsmen in positions of leadership was still less than it was for club membership alone. Clearly, while most of baseball's policymakers no longer represented the lucrative occupations, they did not represent the lower-middle class ones either.

The breakdown by occupational level of ball players who participated in at least one game between 1861 and 1865 closely resembles that for club membership in general.[31] Active participants — those who participated in at least seven games in any one year or twenty-five games in a five-year period — still varied from the general membership (see Table 13), although the difference was not as great as it had been in the immediate prewar years. Significant changes occurred in the composition of active participants, however. Nearly half of this group now were middle-rank employees rather than skilled craftsmen, as in 1856–60. Since the latter group reemerged as the most active participants during the next five-year period, the shifting ratio in 1861–65 appears to have been a product of the war. Changes in the composition of active participants occurred mainly in New York City, making the differences between that city and Brooklyn even more pronounced. Nearly one-fifth of the active players in New York held high-level jobs while not a single one of Brooklyn's active participants had a lucrative occupation. Conversely, skilled craftsmen comprised 15.6 percent of New York's active participants and 56 percent of Brooklyn's.

The growth of baseball, slowed by the Civil War, took off at a dizzying rate in the five years after Lee's surrender at Appomattox. By 1867 there were more than a hundred clubs in Brooklyn and Manhattan. Employees and their employers often formed company teams, and ball clubs also were organized at New York University, Columbia College, and City College. The press even occasionally reported the scores of public and high school games.[32]

While the sport made steady progress in the Northeast, its most rapid advances occurred in those parts of the country, notably the Midwest,

TABLE 13. Occupational Structure of Active Area Baseball Players, 1861–65

	New York City		Brooklyn		Combined	
	N	%	N	%	N	%
Professional–High White-Collar	6	19.4	0	—	6	10.7
Low White-Collar–Proprietor	16	51.6	10	40.0	26	46.4
Skilled Craftsman	8	25.8	14	56.0	22	39.3
Unskilled Worker	1	3.2	1	4.0	2	3.6
Total	31		25		56	

where only a small number of clubs had existed prior to 1860. *Wilkes'*
Spirit claimed that there were 2,000 organized baseball clubs in America
in 1867, and that year the NABBP had over 300 members, more than
three times its prewar number, with delegates coming from seventeen
states and the District of Columbia. This surge was similarly reflected in
attendance figures at ball games. Clearly, baseball had emerged from the
war as an extremely popular sports spectacle for urban dwellers across
the country. In 1869 the *Times* maintained that the leading matches
nationwide attracted some 200,000 onlookers annually.[33] Each baseball
season the press insisted that that season had been better than the previous
one. Baseball "has attained a higher position in the present season," the
Eagle wrote in 1866, "than it ever before held." Three years later the
Times claimed that the "game had been played more in the present season
than any other. It also has been played better." In 1870 *Wilkes' Spirit*
maintained, "There never was greater activity in baseball circles than the
present season. From every part of the country there comes reports of
games played." The tremendous expansion of baseball as both a participant
and spectator sport solidified it as America's national pastime.[34]

While roughly 100,000 Americans participated in organized baseball, a
small number of professional players and a handful of professional teams
came to dominate the sport in the immediate post–Civil War years. The
baseball capital had three professional teams, the Atlantics and Eckfords
in Brooklyn and the Mutuals in New York City. Professional players also
constituted the majority of, and possibly the entire, Union squad in nearby
Morrisiana (now part of the Bronx). Several other teams in the area
compensated some of their players When professional players made up
both squads in several 1868 all-star games between Manhattan and
Brooklyn clubs, it became clear that they held a preeminent position in
the baseball world of the two cities.[35]

The championship system and commercialism remained at the heart of
the movement to professionalize baseball. During the antebellum period
teams rarely scheduled more than a dozen contests annually, but by 1865
several competitive New York City and Brooklyn clubs were playing
twenty games a year; three years later all three professional clubs in the
area participated in more than fifty contests annually. With the growth
of the sport the practice of taking teams on the road markedly increased.
Professional squads toured the country in search of glory and gate receipts.
Although the Atlantics, Eckfords, and Mutuals regularly participated in
contests outside the metropolitan area, these tours were not as important
for them as they were for other professional squads. With well-established
reputations the three clubs from New York City and Brooklyn had little
to gain by victories over mainly amateur nines. More importantly, they
could make more money by playing contests in the nation's leading

metropolis, where the competition was better, the rivalries stronger, and the crowds larger. In fact, the battles between the Atlantics and the Mutuals foreshadowed the later rivalry between the Brooklyn Dodgers and the New York Giants. *Wilkes' Spirit* captured the essence of these confrontations: "no other game throughout the year arouses the same amount of excitement that the Atlantic-Mutual games do. . . . there is a certain amount of party feeling imparted to the game which appears to make the spectators feel as if they themselves were engaged in the strife and not merely lookers-on; and it is this feeling that gives such a genuine hearty ring to the shouts of applause from either side."[36]

The *Eagle* claimed in 1868 that for the previous two years the public had only attended the matches of first-class clubs. The vast throngs witnessing these contests certainly testified to baseball's tremendous popularity.[37] Nevertheless, criticism of the championship matches increased throughout the 1860s. The *Times* insisted that the system was "anything but productive of the good of the game," while the *Chronicle* claimed that the major objection to all championship matches lay in "the quarrels, bickering and general ill-will which they have invariably engendered."[38] Almost all newspapers commented on the unruly behavior that at times accompanied these games, and several newspapers advocated that ball clubs "encourage the patronage of the fair sex" to combat the problem and ensure the respectability of the sport. Taking a common Victorian theme and applying it to a sports setting, the *Chronicle* commented that the "presence of an assemblage of ladies purifies the moral atmosphere of a baseball gathering repressing as it does, all the outbursts of intemperate language which the excitement of a contest so frequently induces." On a similar note, Henry Chadwick welcomed the proposed increase in the admission fee from a dime to a quarter, insisting that the masses would not relish this practice but that the respectable portion of the community regarded it "as a desirable improvement" since it kept out the blackguards and ruffians.[39]

Despite the mounting criticism of the championship matches the press unanimously agreed that such a system was inevitable. Even the *Times,* the sharpest critic, pointed out that "all sports have their championship contests . . . [and] custom seems to sanction the effort of a baseball club to become the championship organization of the country." The *Chronicle* wished for the day when championship contests would become a thing of the past but acknowledged that it had "little hope of seeing the result achieved very soon." In an 1868 editorial the *Eagle* placed the championship system in a more positive light: "If anything is worth doing, it is worth doing well; it is an honor to excel in any legitimate pursuit."[40]

In the immediate post–Civil War years the structural weaknesses of the championship system became evident with the continued growth of the sport and the emergence of talented teams outside the metropolitan area. In 1867 the *Chronicle* claimed that the baseball title had become less meaningful every year. Certainly, there was merit to the argument that the system was absurd since any fourth-rate club could accidently win two games and declare itself the champion; just as it was obvious that several clubs were ducking serious challengers. The *Clipper* declared that the system discriminated against clubs from outside the metropolitan area, and in 1868 its owner, Frank Queen, in an apparent attempt to encourage outside challengers, offered a "Gold Ball" to the winner of the championship. The title went undecided, however, when the Atlantics and the Mutuals failed to play the tie-breaking game. Disappointed by the events, Queen said that had he anticipated the "present complicated state of affairs," he would have presented the ball to the winner of the most games.[41]

The press clearly recognized that the rules governing the championship system should be changed, but they continued their ambivalence toward the efforts to define baseball's best, believing that the competing teams should establish their own code. In early 1870, however, the *Eagle* suggested that the professional clubs meet in a tournament in September to determine the champion. It was not until the formation of baseball's first professional league the following year that some type of systematic scheduling was effected to annually define baseball's best.[42]

While the demand for victory stimulated professionalism, the commercialization of baseball paid for it. In 1867 the price of admission to Brooklyn's enclosed ballfields rose from a dime to a quarter, although promoters had charged the higher amount for important contests the previous year. Proprietors justified the increase with lofty statements about attracting better-behaved crowds, and so on, although one sports journal pointed out that the public was coerced into the higher fee "simply because the proprietors of the grounds have had to share the gate receipts" with the ball players. Nevertheless, the fee for watching a ball game was still the "smallest . . . demanded for any kind of amusement." Within three years proprietors and professional teams in New York City and Brooklyn began experimenting with a fifty-cent tariff, charging that amount for the most important contests, such as between the Atlantics and the Cincinnati Red Stockings or the Mutuals and the Philadelphia Athletics.[43]

Both professional clubs in Brooklyn had for some time played for a share of the gate receipts. By 1867 the Atlantics were paying William Cammeyer 40 percent of the receipts plus expenses for the use of the Union Grounds. What was left was probably divided equally among the players, although some veteran or star players possibly received larger shares. The Mutuals, who were controlled in the 1860s by a group of local politicians closely associated with "Boss" Tweed, did things differently. Initially, young recruits were given patronage jobs, often in the coroner's office, a practice that continued after the war. Although some players probably began sharing in the gate receipts when the ball club moved to the Union Grounds in 1867, there is strong evidence that by the following year many of the Mutuals were being paid salaries outright; within two years the entire nine was on the payroll.[44]

This policy of regular cash payments to professional players was more common among clubs outside the metropolitan area—which is not surprising, considering that to compete against teams in the more established areas required greater financial incentives to attract experienced players. New York City and vicinity was the major market for recruiting professional athletes, and the press frequently reported on the many local boys playing for clubs outside the metropolitan area. The Cincinnati Red Stockings, who were undefeated in 1869, included five members—Harry and George Wright, Fred Waterson, Asa Brainard, and Charles Sweasy—who had received their early baseball experience in the New York City area. The following year Chicago recruited seven players originally from baseball's capital in its quest to emulate Cincinnati.[45]

By the late 1860s observers of the national pastime recognized that baseball had become a business. Unfortunately, data on the economics of early professional baseball are limited to a few public statements, such as the *Times* report in 1868 that the seven or eight leading clubs in the nation divided $100,000 in gate receipts that year. Statistics from that period are notoriously unreliable, but in all likelihood each of the three professional clubs in New York City and Brooklyn took in $10,000–$15,000, with the Atlantic Club receiving the most money in admission fees and the Eckford Club the least. If such figures are at all accurate, then professional ball players on those two teams earned $600–$900 a year, and area players often received larger sums when they joined outside teams. In 1869 the *Times* claimed that the salaries of all ball players ranged from $1,000 to $2,500. Although these figures were inflated by as much as $500, by the end of the Civil War decade baseball clearly had become a lucrative occupation for young men.[46]

The emergence of professional baseball led to a unique problem in sport: "revolving" (when a player jumps from one team to another). Brooklyn and New York City ball players frequently changed teams, usually at the end of the season but sometimes during it. In the 1850s the NABBP had adopted a policy to protect against the use of ringers and, to a lesser extent, deter one club from raiding another for players.[47] Although such incidents occurred from time to time, revolving remained a minor baseball problem until the post–Civil War period when the increased demand for victory led to players jumping from team to team for pecuniary gain. In the middle of the 1866 season the *Eagle* noted that "so many changes have been made among the players that it is now a difficult matter to know where to place some." Three years later the *Clipper* pointed out that revolving was going on "full blast" and was being "carried on in a shameless and open manner." To illustrate the growing problem the *Eagle* told of one Brooklyn player who had been with six different teams during the previous three seasons.[48]

The press condemned revolvers, insisting that they brought "contempt upon themselves and upon the game." Although they disapproved of the players' lack of loyalty, their major objection was legalistic. The *Times* acknowledged the right of professional ball players to better their position at the end of a season but complained that revolvers "break regular engagements and written contracts without hesitation and impugnity" when offered more lucrative financial rewards elsewhere. Henry Chadwick insisted that he knew of several players from northern cities engaged by western clubs "who after having been the recipient of pecuniary favors as well as cordial greetings and kindly welcomes, have gone off to other clubs without so much as by your leave." While metropolitan players were involved in several cases of revolving, the three professional clubs in Manhattan and Brooklyn did not raid each other's teams and only the Mutuals accepted or enticed revolvers (in both cases players originally from the area).[49]

In 1867 the NABBP expanded its transfer rule from thirty to sixty days to discourage these fraudulent practices. The change had little impact, however, in part because most of the revolving took place either before the season began (but after players had signed their contracts) or during the early part of the year. By the end of the decade the need for more stringent rules was obvious and prompted the *Clipper* to call for the blackballing of frequent revolvers, while the *Times* proposed that clubs boycott teams with players who "had broken a written engagement of any club." The appeal to ball clubs to patrol themselves did little to alter the situation, for revolving obviously could not have occurred without the tacit consent of management, "who dangled the bait before the star players."[50]

The specter of gambling and a possible fix also coincided with the changing commercial and professional character of the sport. In 1866 the *Clipper* claimed that championship contests "resemble very much those hippodrome affairs our turfmen are in the habit of indulging in for money making purposes." A year later the *Chronicle* maintained that "the greatest evil connected with those championship games, and one which culminated this season in bringing the game into greater disrepute than we ever imagined . . . is the betting of thousands of dollars upon the results of championship contests, and the arrangements of leading matches with the sole view of increasing the receipts at the gates of enclosed ballgrounds."[51] The right of the entrepreneur to charge a tariff and thereby profit from the gate receipts remained unchallenged, and opposition even waned with regard to private clubs charging admission to their contests (several clubs, including nonprofessional teams, adopted this policy as a means of defraying expenses). However, Henry Chadwick insisted that proprietors of ballparks made a serious mistake when they consented to share their legitimate profits with the clubs playing on their grounds. His objection stemmed from the "tendency to evil habits, which is associated with the system." Since large amounts of money were taken in at these important contests, the sportswriter asked, what was to prevent the winner of the first game of a best-of-three series from intentionally losing the second game to force a third game and another payday? Rumors that the second game was a hippodrome were not uncommon when clubs split the first two games of a championship series. Hence, the press advocated paying straight salaries to players rather than a share of the gate receipts.[52]

In discussing the relationship between betting and baseball, the press repeated the same arguments they had used in examining the influence of gambling on turf sports (see chap. 4). The *Times* warned that wagering was destroying the intrinsic value of baseball and eventually would lead to the demise of the sport. The *Herald* countered that the sport should not be condemned because people bet on the outcome, noting that horse racing had "not depreciated; and yet it is and always has been a medium for gambling." *Wilkes' Spirit* went one step further, claiming that gambling heightened the spectator's enjoyment of the contest.[53] By the late 1860s most of the press tacitly accepted the practice of betting on sports events although they did not condone it. They took every opportunity to point out that gambling was not a product of sport but a reflection of the American proclivity to speculate on almost anything. Moralistic homilies would not stop people from placing wagers on athletic events, but the press continued to emphasize the potential danger to the integrity of baseball when large amounts of money were tied up in the outcome of any contest. The professionalization of sport, for reasons discussed in chapter 2, accentuated the fear of fraudulent practices. In 1868 the *Eagle* articulated this fear when it charged that gamblers had taken control of some of the most noted baseball clubs.[54]

An earlier scandal, in 1865, involving three members of the Mutuals, Thomas B. Devyr, Ed Duffy, and William Wansley, who sold a game against the Eckford Club, heightened public concern over the damaging influence of gambling and gamblers. In a letter confessing his wrongdoing Devyr claimed that Wansley, knowing he was nearly penniless, offered him $300 (of which he received only $30) to dump the game, although he was not required to do anything specific to earn the money. The Mutuals expelled the three men, but two years later reinstated Devyr based on what they considered were mitigating circumstances—the fact that the player had openly confessed, and because they felt that his two-year expulsion from the sport had been sufficient punishment. The *Eagle* disapproved of the decision but the *Clipper* could "not condemn the club for their action." The *Chronicle* provided a detailed examination of the Devyr case in an article probably written by Henry Chadwick, an outspoken critic of gambling. The baseball journal favored leniency since the crime had been committed two years earlier and since the player had already been severely dealt with by being barred from playing and from the social recognition that accrued to ball players. Any punishment should "prevent a repetition of an offense, not indulge in the spirit of revenge," Chadwick cautioned. The NABBP's judiciary committee sanctioned the Mutuals' action in 1867 when it dismissed all current complaints against the New York club (for playing Devyr) on the grounds that it lacked proof of his collusion with Wansley.[55]

Rumors of corruption persisted throughout the late 1860s, although the scandal of 1865 is the only known case of a fixed ball game during this period. Talk of wrongdoing on the diamond did not occur with the same frequency or certainty found in harness racing, however. While this may have reflected genuine contemporary observations, it is likely that the press, having already declared baseball the national pastime and embodied it with nationalistic overtones, sought intentionally or not to protect the image of the sport. The same newspapers that reported rumors of questionable practices on the ballfield were quick to deny those charges on other occasions. The *Herald* noted that prior to an Atlantic defeat the game was rumored to be a hippodrome, but its reporter insisted that the Brooklyn club's loss was a simple case of being outplayed. *Wilkes' Spirit* noted that the character of some of the Atlantic players was unimpeachable, but it conceded that the reputations of other members were questionable. The sports journal pointed out, however, that no fraudulent behavior had been proven and, more importantly, admitted that it was difficult to tell if a game had been sold. The latter statement is noteworthy since *Wilkes' Spirit* leveled charges of fixed harness races more frequently than any other publication. If it was difficult to ascertain when a baseball game was dumped, one wonders what made fraud easier to detect in harness racing.[56]

A more important reason for the different attitudes toward the possibility of corruption in the two sports was what Jim Brosnan, author and retired baseball pitcher, described as the "long season." With professional baseball clubs playing fifty or more games a year by 1868, the press began to recognize that the cyclical character of the season—extended road trips, slumps, and the general drudgery of numerous contests—was a likely cause for the unlikely results of some contests. The *Clipper* rejected as simplistic the public notion that "any defeat of a first class club by a second rate team has to be due to the influence of the gambling element." The paper noted, "It cannot be expected that a club can win *every* game; and if it *should* lose a game or two when the odds are biggest in their favor, it does not *always* follow that the 'thing was fixed.' " Spectators simply demanded too much of the players: "If the public believes that their favorites are in the habit of 'chucking' games, let the public go in and see if they can do any better."[57]

To what extent corruption was part of the game in the 1860s is impossible to say with any accuracy. While it would be naive to assume that the 1865 scandal was the only case of a contest being fixed, charges that gambling interests had taken control of the sport were grossly exaggerated.[58] Guilt by association had a lot to do with the scandalous reputation of the Mutuals, for example, although the 1865 incident, the subsequent reinstatement of one player, and the club's implication in several cases of revolving certainly tarnished their image. However, most of the damage resulted from the ball club's close ties to Tammany Hall in general and "Boss" Tweed in particular. Henry Chadwick noted in 1869 that the aldermen lackies of "Boss" Tweed had authorized $1,500 in city funds to assist the Mutuals, which he considered a corrupt professional organization. And when an NABBP delegate learned the following year that Tweed had given the Mutuals $7,500 of his own money, he was certain the "Boss" would "get his money back somehow."[59] The argument was that men who used politics for personal gain would not hesitate to do the same with baseball. But would men who stole thousands of dollars from the city have a need to fix ball games, especially since the amount of money wagered was never that great and the task itself was exceedingly difficult?

The Mutuals, even by professional standards of the day, had many talented ball players and long possessed a reputation as the strongest hitting team in New York City or Brooklyn. Yet as the press frequently pointed out, the Mutuals were ineffectively managed and the players lacked the necessary discipline and *esprit de corps* critical to victory; the ball club also suffered from a rapid turnover of players. Thus, Mutual defeats could have been as much a product of these baseball factors as of the influence of gambling or crooked politicians.[60]

The connection of Tweed and other politicos with a baseball team was not unique. Since the 1840s New York politicians increasingly had come to share the same social backgrounds as members of ball clubs, so it was not surprising to find a goodly number of elected officials on the ballfield. The press often took note of ball games between New York aldermen and supervisors, reporting these "muffin" contests, played by rotund men, in a humorous light. City Hall politicians also joined baseball clubs, and sometimes even started their own. Their enjoyment of the sport was no doubt the primary reason for their association with these clubs, but their involvement also provided political opportunities and advantages, given the tremendous popularity of the sport. As early as 1863, the *Eagle* noted that politicians had "begun to see that the baseball community are sufficiently numerous and influential to be looked after." Two years later the *Clipper* articulated the same theme: since baseball "has undoubtedly become an institution of the country . . . politicians are commencing to curry the favor with the fraternity of ballplayers, as a class of our 'fellow citizens' worthy of the attention of 'our influential men.' " Henry Chadwick also noted that both political parties courted ball players because of their tremendous popularity. All these observers disapproved of the connection between politicos and baseball, fearing that these men would corrupt the national pastime as they did everything else.[61]

Politicians realized that they had much to gain by affiliating with certain players and clubs, especially in terms of solidifying their own leadership positions in the wards. For example, they could win local support by helping to finance ball clubs. In 1870 former alderman Henry Hughes gave $300 to the Social Club for equipment and other expenses,[62] and other ward leaders gave smaller amounts to sustain favorite teams and players. Politicians also benefited indirectly by their association with men who were less socially and economically mobile, although they all shared similar backgrounds. In effect, by rubbing shoulders with ball players they demonstrated that they were still "one of the people."

"Boss" Tweed's association with baseball also derived from personal and political reasons, not the desire to profit from gambling on games. Since 1866 he had been a member of the Mutual's board of trustees, although he was not actively involved in the club's day-to-day operations. It was well known that he was the major figure behind New York's leading club, however, and he was visible at several of the team's contests. For Tweed baseball served as symbolic politics, providing a forum in which to demonstrate his affinity with the masses.[63]

As the play-for-pay movement gained momentum there was extensive and often heated public debate on the nature of professional athletics. The most frequent and serious charge was that the introduction of the business element brought the game of baseball into disrepute. One delegate to the national convention insisted that the "custom of publically hiring men to play the game of Base Ball [is] reprehensible and injurious to the best interest of the game." Sportswriters disapproved of professional baseball because they felt the majority of the players "were not men of moral habits or integrity of character." A letter to one newspaper stated, "You know very well that a man who makes a *business of playing ball* is not a man to be relied upon in a match where great interests are centered, or on which a large amount of money is pending." The *Times,* the most severe critic of professional baseball, claimed that the national pastime, "worthy of encouragement" as a recreation, "as a business calls upon us to revise our notions of its usefulness." The morality of professional baseball was particularly questionable: "At best it is an excuse for gambling; at worst, a viller device for 'jockeying' and swindling than ever disgraced the turf." An 1870 editorial in the *Times* concluded that a healthy and energetic young man could find "many ways of earning a livelihood more creditable to himself and more profitable to his country than by playing in baseball matches."[64]

Professional baseball also had its defenders. A letter to the *Eagle* argued that it was a legitimate way to earn a living. The *Herald* favorably compared ball players to other entertainers: "No person thinks ill of an actor or acrobat who receives a regular salary for his performance, and certainly a professional ballplayer should be honored and as honorable as any other performer." In 1869 the *Eagle* pointed out that the professionalization of baseball seemingly had not interfered with its popularity or made it a mere vehicle for gambling.[65]

As early as 1866 Henry Chadwick wisely maintained that the entire debate was nonproductive since professional baseball was a fait accompli. In his view it was a legitimate occupation, there being no reason why a man cannot "honestly devote his time and labor to the service of a baseball club as an employed professional." He recognized the problems that accompanied professionalism but insisted that any evils associated with money and sport derived from the heavy wagering and the corrupting influence of the gambling class, not from compensating the players. The NABBP's rule banning professional players merely aggravated the situation by forcing players and clubs into deceptive, dishonest practices. More stringent rules would not curtail professionalism since "whenever money is to be made, legitimate or otherwise, men will be found to make it." Given current developments and future possibilities, Chadwick asserted, the key question facing the baseball fraternity was, "Shall money making be allowed to follow the dirty avenue of fraud and dishonesty . . . or shall it be guided into a path of legitimate occupation, which any man can engage in without discredit to himself"? In true Victorian form the English-born sportswriter argued that reform would result only by effective regulation of paid players; and to this end he recommended that the NABBP recognize and endorse professional baseball.[66]

The majority of the New York press concurred with Chadwick. They also accepted the idea that ball players should be divided into amateurs and professionals, a division that would be consistent with the realities of the baseball world. One newspaper favored the split because it would help to eradicate the corrupting influence of professionalism on amateur players. The NABBP was persuaded in 1868 to endorse the division of players into two classes, a move the *Times* insisted was one of the most important ever made. The change had little impact on the sport, however, and the NABBP rescinded the rule within a year. Chadwick argued that the experience of the past few seasons had "conclusively shown how badly many of our professional clubs have been managed," but he objected to the NABBP's rescission, pointing out that everything that had been done "to place professional ball playing upon a reputable footing has been nullified." The *Clipper* claimed that the NABBP's action necessitated either the voluntary withdrawal of the amateurs from the national association or the expulsion of the professionals.[67] Tensions between the two groups mounted during the 1870 season as the press argued over which group was in control. One journal insisted that roughly twenty professional clubs had managed to gain control of the NABBP during the past few years; another paper maintained that such a premise was absurd since amateur oganizations vastly outnumbered professional squads.[68] Before the annual convention in December two newspapers accurately predicted the demise of the existing association unless action was taken to preserve the amateur interest. The final blow came when the Mutuals persuaded the NABBP's judiciary committee to reinstate William Wansley, the man convicted of fixing a game five years earlier.[69]

In response to developments at the annual convention Dr. Joseph B. Jones led a movement to create a baseball association comprised solely of amateur clubs. Jones, a long-time member of the Excelsiors and former head of the NABBP's rules committee, was supported by the Knicker-bockers, who had dropped out of the association in 1869. The proposal was also well received by the press, which claimed that an amateur association would redeem the national pastime "from the odium attached to it by the evils introduced under the abuses of the worst phases of professional ball playing." The *Clipper* called it the most important amateur development since the 1857 convention, while the *Eagle* declared that "every ballplayer who desires the status of things restored, such as prevailed in the early years of our national Game, will do his utmost to aid in making the coming convention a success."[70]

In March 1871 twenty-six clubs, fourteen from Brooklyn and New York City, established the National Association of Amateur Base Ball Players (NAABBP) at a meeting in the baseball capital. The new association adopted the basic rules of the parent organization. While they obviously prohibited professional involvement, the question of what to do with gate receipts led to heated debate. The *Eagle* noted that the NAABBP was splintered into two groups: the "simon pure," such as the Knickerbockers, and the "half breeds," who collected an admission fee to their games. The leadership of the new organization probably came from the "simon pure" group, but the "half breeds" appear to have constituted the majority of the membership. When the Stars, an old Brooklyn club, threatened to withdraw from the association if they were not permitted to extract a tariff, a compromise was struck that allowed teams to collect money when they were on tour and under certain other unusual circumstances.[71]

Ten professional clubs from the East and Midwest were meeting in New York at about the same time as guests of the Mutuals, the end result being the creation of the National Association of Professional Base Ball Players (NAPBBP). The idea that professional clubs should create their own organization had been bantered about for some time, but only after the amateur clubs withdrew from the NABBP were steps taken to form a new association for professionals. Despite the earlier reservations of the press, the first professional league was well received, the *Times* maintaining that professional players would find their own association the "best means of conducting their system of ballplaying so as to make it pecuniary profitable, and at the same time more reputable than it is at present."[72]

The formation of a professional players' association was critical in the history of organized baseball, although as baseball historian David Q. Voigt correctly notes, the steps taken to deal with the problems of the professional game, such as championships, scheduling, revolving, and the amount and distribution of the admission fee, "were hardly revolution- ary."[73] The significance of baseball's first professional league derived from the fact that it institutionalized the changes in baseball, especially in the aftermath of the sport's rapid growth in the post–Civil War period. The NAPBBP provided the play-for-pay movement with a legitimate structure and thus endowed professional baseball with a sense of greater stability. By contrast, little is known about the amateur association that was formed, except that it never really got off the ground and ceased to exist after 1874. With the formation of the National League in 1876, professionals came to dominate organized baseball and would continue to dictate major changes in the rules and styles of play.

Baseball made significant advances during the 1860s, its first decade as a professional sport. The press frequently pointed out that ball players had never been more skillful. The *Eagle* claimed that even second-class clubs played a better game than the best clubs during the halcyon days of nonprofessionals and no gate receipts. While players were becoming more proficient at all levels, the most rapid advances obviously occurred among the professionals, who embodied the new ethic—victory by any possible means. As Harold Seymour correctly points out, "Ingenuity, trickery and tactics hitherto considered unsportsmanlike were not only accepted but acclaimed in the new passion for victory." Dicky Pearce, the star shortstop of the Atlantics, was the first player to employ the bunt as a successful offensive weapon. Another shortstop, George Wright, intentionally dropped pop flies with runners on first and second base so he could make a double play.[74]

It was difficult to refute the assessment of the *Times* that championship clubs had made baseball into a science. The sport increasingly was compared to cricket in terms of skill, with the *Herald* proclaiming that the earlier objection, "that compared to cricket, it [baseball] was child's play, can no longer be raised." When a group of professional cricketers arrived in New York in 1868, the *Eagle* informed them that if they went to the ballpark they would see a "manly game." The Union Club of Morrisiana easily beat the Englishmen in a game of baseball, solidifying the confidence of the press that our national pastime was as demanding as cricket.[75]

In contrasting baseball in the immediate pre- and post–Civil War periods, Henry Chadwick noted that once it was possible for men aged forty or more to excel at the sport and that with only a few weeks of practice any player could make a creditable showing. "What a change has taken place in ten short years!" he concluded. It was obvious that baseball, at least at a highly competitive level, now required specialization, training, and discipline. Moreover, a natural concomitant of professionalism in baseball, as with the other sports, was the growing domination of the game by young men.[76] For example, the average age of the twenty-nine players on the three professional clubs in Brooklyn and New York City was only slightly more than twenty-four (ages ranged from nineteen to thirty-four, with twenty-three competitors being twenty-five or under and only two being over thirty). Despite their relatively tender ages and the newness of organized baseball, these players had amassed considerable baseball experience. The ten members of the Atlantics had been with that team for an average of just less than six years, which no doubt contributed to their success, and almost everyone on the team had played for several seasons with at least one of the many junior clubs in the metropolitan area. By the post–Civil War period a young man had to participate in organized competitive baseball by the age of sixteen or he had little, if any, chance of becoming a professional ball player.[77]

Competitive baseball could "no longer be regarded as a simple recreation." To excel required not only experience but rigorous training both on and off the field. The *Eagle* insisted that professional clubs and players owed it to the public, whose money supported the teams and athletes, to train hard. Because baseball fans had become knowledgeable about the finer points of the game, the newspapers warned ball players that if they did not "put themselves in that condition to win the applause of the public and its favor then their occupation is gone, for, in theatrical parlance, they will fail to 'draw' and their revenues will be shut off."[78] The press further advised professional players on the need for a proper diet, the need to curtail late hours, and the problems of drinking. They urged professional clubs to establish a system whereby each player specialized at one position and individual excellence was subordinated to the workings of the team as a whole. Throughout the Civil War years the press had noted that the success of the 1860 Excelsior Club derived from its players promptly obeying the commands of their captain, a point that the overwhelming majority of clubs chose to ignore. In 1869 the well-trained, well-disciplined Cincinnati Red Stockings, led by manager Harry Wright—who applied his experience as a professional cricketer to baseball—came to New York City and Brooklyn and swept the leading clubs there en route to an undefeated season. In unison the press insisted that the Cincinnati club had taught the home-town heroes what should have been obvious—that "steady, temperate habits and constant training are all conditions precedent to all first class professional organizations." The Reds' success, one newspaper concluded, had ushered in a new era in baseball, one in which nine men would be trained to perfection.[79]

The Cincinnati victories over New York's and Brooklyn's finest teams, and its eventual championship, signaled the end of the latter's domination of baseball. Earlier, there had been signs that the neighboring cities might be relinquishing their preeminent position. In 1867 the NABBP convention was held outside of New York for the first time, and the following year Henry Chadwick claimed that "New York has no longer the exclusive right of being considered the center of the baseball republic, although, without doubt, the *locale* of the strongest clubs." No one on a Brooklyn or New York city team received in 1868 the recently initiated "Gold Ball" offered to the best player at each position. Yet New Yorkers remained convinced that baseball was their game. If reminded that local clubs occasionally lost to squads from outside the metropolitan area, they pointed out that those clubs were always able to redeem themselves, giving credence to the contention that their initial defeat was a hippodrome affair; they could also point out that a Brooklyn club had always been the champion. In 1868 the *Eagle* asserted that no first-class clubs existed outside the city, a seemingly parochial statement unless we consider the fact that there was sufficient evidence to nurture—if not entirely support—this perspective.[80]

Obviously, then, the Reds' victories took New Yorkers by surprise, although many fans knew of the visitors' skills since five of the players had come from New York. To save face, some disgruntled observers pointed out that the Reds' triumph could not be construed as a Cincinnati victory since so many of the players were New Yorkers. The press uniformly rejected this argument: "To say that several of the Cincinnati nine belong to New York has nothing whatsoever to do with the question, for to Cincinnati all the honor is due for organizing such a splendid team, and of training them up to their present standard of excellence." Henry Chadwick saw it as an unfortunate detraction, since he felt that all professional teams were "eclectic." While professional clubs were rarely comprised solely of players from their own cities, sharp differences existed between the Reds and the New York and Brooklyn teams. With only one exception players from the metropolitan area were on the three professional teams in New York City and Brooklyn in the post–Civil War years; by contrast, the Reds had only one Ohio player on their squad. Nevertheless, the press sanctioned a critical underpinning of professional athletics when they accepted the principle that professional athletes were the legitimate representatives of the city in which they were employed.[81]

When the Reds returned to New York in 1870 they were still undefeated, a disputed tie with the Troy Haymakers being the only blemish on their record. Opening with an easy 16–3 victory over the Mutuals, they met the Atlantics the next day at Capitoline Grounds before a crowd of slightly more than 9,000 spectators (more people might have attended if the price of admission had not been raised to fifty cents). With Asa Brainard pitching for the Reds and George Zettlein for the Atlantics, the visitors broke on top with two runs in the first inning and one in the third. The Atlantics battled back with two runs in both the fourth and sixth innings, but the Reds managed to score twice in the seventh to regain the lead. The Atlantics tied the score in the bottom of the eighth, and the ninth inning "was contested with a stubborness beyond telling" that resulted in neither team scoring. Assuming the game had ended in a tie the Atlantics prepared to leave as the crowd spilled out onto the field. The Cincinnati manager protested, however, saying that extra innings were required, and after consulting with Henry Chadwick the umpire correctly ruled in the Reds' favor.

When the game resumed the visitors were held scoreless in the tenth inning. The Atlantics managed to place runners on first and second with only one out, but their threat ended when George Wright, the Reds' shortstop, intentionally dropped a fly ball and turned it into a double play. Bouyed by Wright's outstanding defensive play, his teammates scored two runs in the top of the eleventh inning, causing many dejected Atlantic fans to leave for home. The Brooklyn club rallied with a lead-off single, then Joe Start, "Old Reliable," hit a long fly ball to right, which might have been caught were it not for the overflow crowd. When the outfielder failed to reach the ball, Start made it to third base, then scored the tying run when Robert Ferguson followed with a clean single. Amid the ensuing pandemonium Zettlein hit a hard ground ball that was bobbled by the first baseman, who then threw wildly to third in an attempt to cut off the runner. Ferguson raced across home plate and the Atlantics registered a thrilling come-from-behind 8–7 victory.[82] In an editorial, the sentiments of which would be repeated at other times, in other cities, for other clubs, the *Eagle* informed its readers that the Atlantics represented all that was good in Brooklyn: "The deep chord with which the victory vibrated in the city's heart, more than anything we know demonstrated the depth and keenness of the sentiment of local pride, pride in Brooklyn, which is so distinguishing a characteristic of this people. . . . It is a Brooklyn victory won by Brooklyn boys and Brooklyn salutes them."[83]

The Cincinnati team's loss marked the beginning of the end for one of baseball's model clubs. They dropped games to the Philadelphia Athletics and Chicago White Stockings later that year, and for a variety of reasons disbanded after the 1870 season. Nevertheless, the Atlantics' victory did little to restore its prestige or the preeminence of New York and Brooklyn baseball. In fact, the Atlantics lost their next game and eventually succumbed to internal strife. Since 1867 several members had voiced objections to the professionalization of the club and others complained that the starting nine had become their "own masters." With membership dwindling the club finally decided to reorganize after the 1870 season. The result was the departure of six of the Atlantics starting players for other professional teams.[84]

Although New York no longer dominated the sport, the fact that professional baseball first took hold in the metropolitan area meant that its influence would continue to be felt during the NAPBBP's five-year existence. Of the 319 individuals who played in baseball's first professional league, slightly more than 20 percent were born in New York City and vicinity (see Table 14); another 17 players who were born elsewhere or

TABLE 14. Birthplace of NAPBBP Players and Managers, 1871–75

	Players		Managers	
	N	%	N	%
Brooklyn	38	11.9	6	20.0
New York City	20	6.3	4	13.3
Metropolitan Area	8	2.5	2	6.7
Non–Metropolitan Area	184	57.7	11	36.7
Unknown	69	21.6	7	23.3
Total	319		30	

Source: *The Baseball Encyclopedia* (New York: Macmillan, 1973).

whose birthplaces are not known received their initial training in the New York metropolitan region. Closer scrutiny reveals that the longer a player stayed in the league, the more likely it was that he was from New York City and vicinity (see Table 15). Moreover, 40 percent of the managers in the NAPBBP were born in the metropolitan area, and three others— Harry Wright, Al Reach, and Richard Higham—Englishmen by birth and sons of cricketers, initially played organized baseball in New York.

The emergence of baseball as a skillful, competitive sport requiring physical training and discipline affected the arguments used to support and encourage the sport. Baseball propagandists continued to point to its health and recreational benefits, but they also began to comment on its value as a counterbalance to the evils of the city. The *Eagle* claimed that participation in junior clubs kept boys out of mischief, that the recreations of the ballfield prevented the young from visiting the "haunts of dissipation." Henry Chadwick argued, "As a remedy for the many evils resulting from the immoral association boys and young men of our cities are apt to become connected with, the game merits the endorsement of every clergyman in the country."[85] The idea that the national pastime developed character was also part of the rhetoric of baseball's supporters. Again, Chadwick declared, "Nothing in the form of a recreative exercise has been introduced into the educational institutions of the country so well calculated to promote . . . the development of the manly attributes of courage, nerve, pluck and endurances, as the game of baseball."[86]

The connection between sport and developing character values was critical since it legitimated baseball as a highly competitive sport, something the ideological justifications noted earlier could not do. Those who

TABLE 15. Birthplace of Long-Term NAPBBP Players, 1871–75, Based on Longevity

	At Least Ten Games		Two Years		Five Years	
	N	%	N	%	N	%
Brooklyn	31	14.7	26	18.2	10	21.7
New York City	20	9.5	14	9.8	4	8.7
Metropolitan Area	7	3.3	7	4.8	4	8.7
Total	58	27.5	47	32.8	18	39.1
Non–Metropolitan Area	129	61.1	81	56.6	27	58.7
Unknown	24	11.4	15	10.5	1	2.2
Total	153	72.5	96	67.1	28	60.9
Combined	211		143		46	

Source: *The Baseball Encyclopedia* (New York: Macmillan, 1973).

continued to subscribe to the belief that baseball was simply recreational, as the *Times* did, naturally rejected the newer argument.[87] The claim that sport promoted moral behavior added little to the argument; however, the contention that the ballfield could serve as a laboratory for certain learning experiences facilitated the acceptance of baseball as something more than a simple diversion. To achieve the objective of the contest — victory — required not only practice in certain sports skills but also practice in behavior skills — specifically, discipline, self-control, and teamwork. The contest became a test of how well a player learned both nonutilitarian sports skills and skills that had practical value and were strongly identified with manhood. As a teacher and tester of manhood, baseball was not merely a game but a valuable educational tool.

For those who accepted this argument, a major objection to the professionalization of sport was eliminated, in addition to providing the professional athlete with a new task — setting an example for youth. As early as 1861 the *Clipper* described the model ball player as a combination athlete and Christian gentleman. Antiprofessional sentiments and class bias restricted the full emergence of the professional athlete as a role model until the start of the twentieth century, although the ingredients — a new ideology that sanctioned a highly competitive sport, identified it with manly character traits, and glorified its heroes — were present by 1870.[88]

The dramatic increase in the media coverage baseball received during the 1860s corresponded with, and in turn was stimulated by, the surging popularity of the sport. The press, particularly the dailies, gave baseball more newspaper space than any other sport. While New York City and Brooklyn papers covered the overall development of baseball, they increasingly focused on the professional and top-notch amateur clubs. Two or three columns were devoted to major contests, and sometimes the press provided an inning-by-inning account of a particularly important game. "Hot stove" reports appeared as early as February — preseason reports that informed the public which players had joined new clubs since the end of the previous season, what the latest baseball rumors were, which teams merited a close look, and how fans should prepare for the upcoming season. Only between late November and mid-February was there limited baseball news, although the events that transpired at the annual convention provided an opportunity to keep baseball in the public eye.

The introduction of the *Chronicle* in 1867, the first journal devoted mainly to baseball, pointed to the growing desire for information on the national pastime. Henry Chadwick was the editor of this baseball weekly, often described as the "Organ of the Fraternity." He also edited the annual guidebook, which by the mid-1860s had a circulation of over

65,000, and many other baseball manuals. Such publications "widened the scope of leisure pastimes by enabling fans to keep abreast of changing rules and franchises and follow by statistics and articles the latest deeds of their diamond heroes."[89] Chadwick's two major contributions to baseball reporting, however, were the development of the box score and the calculation of batting averages. By the early 1860s the reader could look at the box score, modified from the one used in cricket, and find the at-bats, runs, hits, putouts, and assists of each player. And because Chadwick recognized that the former method—reporting the runs a player scored—did not adequately measure his performance, he devised a system of hits per at-bats as the best indicator of a player's offensive skills.

More than any other team sport baseball is naturally suited to quantification. Allen Guttmann has noted the important contribution of statistics to the popularity of baseball,[90] but several additional points should be made. During the 1860s, despite significant advances in compiling and reporting baseball statistics, there still was no weekly composite of a player's performance, as now appears in the Sunday paper. Sports journals and baseball guidebooks only printed postseason compilations. Finally, the growing importance of statistics was closely linked to the emergence of professional clubs nationwide. Since teams might travel to a certain city only once a year, accurate statistics provided fans with a way of comparing ball players in the absence of repeated direct observation.

Between 1866 and 1870 the occupational structure of New York City and Brooklyn ball players did not change much over the previous ten years (see Table 16). Over 75 percent of the players still came from the two middle categories, although the percentage was higher in Brooklyn than in New York City. About one out of every five players held more prestigious and lucrative positions, yet only a handful of this group were from the upper echelons of New York society. While the elite turned to racquets and, to a lesser extent, cricket, their sons joined junior baseball clubs such as the Mohicans.[91] The lower class remained all but absent from organized baseball.

TABLE 16. Occupational Structure of Area Initial Baseball Players, 1866–70

	New York City		Brooklyn		Combined	
	N	%	N	%	N	%
Professional–High White-Collar	51	25.5	13	14.0	64	21.8
Low White-Collar–Proprietor	92	46.0	47	50.5	139	47.4
Skilled Craftsman	54	27.0	33	35.5	87	29.7
Unskilled Worker	3	1.5	0	—	3	1.0
Total	200		93		293	

Just as economics kept the poor from participating, racial discrimination kept blacks out of the mainstream of organized baseball. The first report of black participation in baseball occurred in 1862, when the contest between the Unknown and Monitor clubs of Brooklyn was reported in the *Eagle* under the contemptible headline, "A New Sensation in Baseball Circles—Sambo as Ballplayer and Dinah as an Emulator." Five years passed before the press again mentioned black teams in the metropolitan area.[92]

In 1867 the NABBP's nominating committee unanimously opposed the admission of any club "composed of one or more colored persons." Harold Seymour notes that the committee's reasoning was an "ingenious bit of casuistry and evasion." It decided that "if colored clubs were admitted there would be in all probability some division of feelings, whereas, by excluding them no injury could result to anybody, and the possibility of any rupture being created on political grounds would be avoided." The press took a stand that followed traditional political lines: the Democratic *Eagle* opposed admission (its arguments were virtually the same as the NABBP's) and the Republican *Times* maintained that right-minded delegates must thoroughly condemn this prohibition as inconsistent with the events of the last decade. The nonpartisan *Wilkes' Spirit* noted that only in America did color bar players from participating in sport and that it was not "a lessening of dignity nor in the least disparaging" for white men to compete with blacks. Although black players continued to form their own clubs and occasionally compete against whites, they would remain outside the mainstream of organized baseball for the next seventy-five years. If the national pastime was the embodiment of the American way, it was just as clearly the embodiment of America's racial attitudes.[93]

The occupational structure of club officers from New York City and Brooklyn varied only slightly from the pattern established during the Civil War. Men from the middle level continued to comprise more than half the officials (see Table 17). This pattern hides the significant changes that occurred in each of the respective cities, however. In Manhattan the

TABLE 17. Occupational Structure of Area Baseball Club Officers, 1866–70

	New York City		Brooklyn		Combined	
	N	%	N	%	N	%
Professional–High White-Collar	14	21.2	8	21.1	22	21.2
Low White-Collar–Proprietor	41	62.1	19	50.0	60	57.7
Skilled Craftsman	11	16.7	11	28.9	22	21.2
Total	66		38		104	

percentage for the middle level rose ten points, mainly at the expense of skilled craftsmen; in Brooklyn the middle level declined more than 10 percent as the upper and lower levels increased by 7.5 and 3.9 percent respectively.

The occupational structure of NABBP delegates between 1866 and 1870 presents a curious pattern[94] (see Table 18): for the first time the structures of the delegates and the general club membership were similar; and the percentage of higher-level occupations was the same as the percentage for skilled craftsmen in both New York City and Brooklyn. The majority of the delegates who were skilled craftsmen still came from the various food industries, and almost all of them had been members of their respective clubs since prior to 1860.

The occupations of ball players participating in at least one game again closely paralleled the structure of the total membership,[95] but radical changes occurred in the occupational structure of active participants (those who played in at least twenty games in one year or seventy-five games in five years) compared to the previous five-year interval (see Table 19). Over 90 percent of these players held middle and lower-middle jobs, a pattern more closely resembling that for active participants in the pre–Civil War years. The percentage of unskilled workers among active players remained the same as for 1861–65, and there were only one-third as many players from the upper level as during the previous five-year interval.

Twenty-four of the twenty-eight active participants went on to play in

TABLE 18. Occupational Structure of Area NABBP Delegates, 1866–70

	New York City		Brooklyn		Combined	
	N	%	N	%	N	%
Professional–High White-Collar	6	20.7	5	35.7	11	25.6
Low White-Collar–Proprietor	17	58.6	4	28.6	21	48.6
Skilled Craftsman	6	20.7	5	35.7	11	25.6
Total	29		14		43	

TABLE 19. Occupational Structure of Active Area Baseball Players, 1866–70

	N	%
Professional–High White-Collar	1	3.6
Low White-Collar–Proprietor	10	35.7
Skilled Craftsman	16	57.1
Unskilled Worker	1	3.6
Total	28	

the NAPBBP. Of the four who did not join, Nathan Jewell, a member of the Excelsiors, was the son of a prominent sugar refiner and merchant and had no economic incentive to become a professional ball player because he was already involved in his father's lucrative business. Age as much as occupation prevented William McMahon and George Flannery from joining the professional league. McMahon, a member of the Mutuals and a theatrical manager, had retired from active competition in 1869 at the age of thirty-six; Flannery was in his late twenties and had a secure government job. Thomas Devyr, the lone unskilled worker, did not catch on with a professional club, but it is not certain whether it was because of his age, ability, or involvement in the 1865 scandal. One point is clear, however: professional ball players did not come from the lower class.[96]

There is evidence to support the contention of the *Times* in 1869 that professional players were generally young mechanics.[97] Fifteen of the twenty-four active players who competed in the NAPBBP were manual workers, as were six of ten other Brooklyn and New York City men who played in the 1860s but were not active participants in 1866–70 (most were already playing for clubs outside the area). Skilled craftsmen provided 61.8 percent of the professional players in that period, and the remainder were from the middle class, mostly clerks or similar middle-level occupations.

Since providing jobs was one method of compensating ball players, it is only natural to wonder whether the occupations of these men accurately reflected their class backgrounds. Biographical material is quite limited, but the existing data tend to confirm middle- and lower-middle-class origins: Asa Brainard, the flaky Cincinnati pitcher, was the son of a small-time New York merchant; George Hall, who was expelled from professional baseball in 1877 for dumping several games, came from a respectable middle-class Brooklyn family; Lipman Pike, the first great Jewish ball player, was the son of a haberdasher; Richard Higham's father was a leading New York cricketer and an officer of the New York Cricket Club; Charlie Smith, the star third baseman of the Atlantics, worked in his father's vegetable store; Sam Wright, the father of Harry and George, was not a man of means, but the cricketer was one of the most respected men in New York sports circles; and Al Reach came from the English artisan class.[98] Two other factors suggest that the occupations of the ball players reflected their actual backgrounds. Before becoming professionals, baseball players had to compete on junior clubs to nurture their skills, and there is no evidence that an appreciable number of lower-class men were involved in organized baseball. In addition, many of those who eventually became professionals had played at some time for clubs with gentlemanly reputations. While these clubs might have actively recruited good players despite class background, it is unlikely that they would have turned to the lower class for talented performers.

By 1870 professional baseball had become a lucrative occupation, with annual salaries ranging from $500 to $2,000, figures that rose further during the NAPBBP years. While the salaries of ball players depended on many factors — talent, age, and other occupational possibilities, for example — their incomes "always compared favorably with middle range incomes in business or in the professions." Yet slightly less than two-thirds (twenty-two) of the initial thirty-four professionals from Brooklyn and New York City (those who played in the 1860s and then in the NAPBBP) joined the professional league in its first year of existence.[99] It is no coincidence that seventeen of them were skilled craftsmen and more than half of the first-year professionals competed for teams outside the city. Three men from the latter group were engaged in nonmanual occupations: Fred Waterman and Asa Brainard, who left the city to play in Cincinnati prior to 1870, and George Zettlein, the Atlantic pitcher, who had earlier refused to sign with the Cincinnati Reds because of his political job but eventually joined the Chicago White Stockings.[100]

The proportion of players from the middle ranks increased when the Atlantic and Eckford clubs joined the NAPBBP in 1872. In all likelihood these players also competed in 1871 for these clubs or other gate-sharing squads. The longevity of a player's career was naturally connected to talent and age, but it was also linked to class status (see Table 20). In the case of John Galvin, who played one game for the Atlantics in 1872 and again in 1874, probably as a replacement for an injured player, his short career was clearly related to his lack of ability. John Gedney, a law student and clerk, was perhaps the best defensive left fielder of his day. But when

TABLE 20. Occupational Structure of Area Professional Baseball Players vs. Longevity

Full Years Played[a]	Low White-Collar–Proprietor	Skilled Craftsman	Combined
Less than one	2	2	4
One	4	4	8
Two	2	1	3
Three	1	3	4
Four	3	2	5
Five	1	9	10
Total	13	21	34

[a] For statistical purposes a full year consists of at least ten games.
Source: *The Baseball Encyclopedia*, 205–29.

his batting average went from .323 in 1874 to .198 the following year, although only twenty-six years old, he decided to quit rather than try to make a comeback.[101] It is also notable that the majority of white-collar workers (nine) played their entire careers for metropolitan area teams.

Although many New York City and Brooklyn ball players were paid to compete throughout the 1860s, the idea of baseball as a career was slow to evolve. Sixteen of the initial thirty-four professionals played their entire careers in the metropolitan area; two other players were with the Atlantics and the Mutuals from 1871 to 1874 before joining teams outside the metropolitan area. The evidence indicates that a baseball career had different meaning for lower-middle- and middle-class youths. In comparison to their white-collar counterparts, skilled craftsmen had longer baseball careers and were more willing to relocate; six of thirteen middle-class players retired before the age of thirty but only five of twenty-one artisans called it quits by that age. Joseph Kett notes that by the 1870s "a sharp difference between the opportunities available to middle and working class youths" was already detectable, although the differences became "much more pronounced as America moved towards the status of a mature industrial society." For lower-middle-class youth, baseball apparently provided an opportunity for social mobility.[102]

While middle-class youths were attracted to professional baseball by high salaries, among other factors, the evidence suggests that they were less likely to view the sport as a career. Star players, such as George Zettlein, stayed in the sport for the big money, but the average white-collar player remained in baseball only briefly due to the uncertainty of paydays, the drudgery of travel, and the low prestige of the profession. If few expected to make baseball a career, then why did they join the NAPBBP in the first place? The lure of money and the thrill of competition obviously played a part, and the chance to prolong their youth may have been a contributing factor as well. By spending a few years in professional baseball these young middle-class men could earn a fairly comfortable living before taking a "real" job. Moreover, playing professional baseball did not place any real strain on familial or occupational ties since most of the players competed for teams in their hometowns.[103]

Sport in general and baseball in particular have long been viewed as an avenue of social mobility, especially for talented, but uneducated, lower-class youth. Scholars like Steven Riess have recently questioned this thesis. He shows that nearly 35 percent of all major league baseball players between 1871 and 1882 slid down into blue-collar jobs after their playing days ended, while many of those who obtained white-collar jobs were employed in relatively low-prestige occupations.[104] The data that are available on the postbaseball careers of twenty-six of the initial thirty-four professionals in Brooklyn and New York City reveal a similar pattern but do not necessarily support Riess's thesis that baseball was not a vehicle for social mobility (see Table 21).[105]

More than 70 percent of the retired Brooklyn and New York City professionals held white-collar jobs when their playing days were over, although fewer than one in six were involved in the more lucrative, prestigious occupations. While the proportion of high white-collar workers was roughly the same for the initial professionals and the 1871–82 major leaguers, the percentage of all white-collar workers among the first professionals was nine points higher. Critical to this difference was the varying percentage of players who became petty proprietors, managers, and officials. Of the ten Brooklyn and New York ball players who worked in these jobs, half were saloon keepers or had similiar jobs, and two others were bookmakers.

In his study of social mobility in Boston, Stephan Thernstrom classifies paid athletes as semiprofessionals.[106] If such categorization accurately depicts the status of athletes, then only 26.9 percent of New York City

TABLE 21. Occupational Structure of Former Baseball Players, 1871–82

	New York City and Brooklyn Initial Professionals		Major Leaguers, 1871–82	
	N	%	N	%
High White-Collar				
Professionals	0	—	4	1.8
Managers, High Officials and				
Major Proprietors	4	15.4	28	12.8
Low White-Collar				
Clerks, Sales, and Kindred Workers	3	11.5	40	18.3
Semiprofessionals	2	7.7	29	13.2
Petty Proprietors, Managers, and				
Low Officials	10	38.5	37	16.9
	19		139	
Farmers	0	—	3	1.4
Blue-Collar				
Skilled	5	19.2	26	11.9
Semiskilled and Service	2	7.7	46	21.0
Unskilled	0	—	6	2.7
	7		78	
Total	26		219	

Sources: Study data; Steven A. Riess, *Touching Base: Professional Baseball in American Culture in the Progressive Era* (Westport, Conn.: Greenwood Press, 1980), 158.

and Brooklyn ball players were occupationally mobile (i.e., moved into the higher white-collar rank, or became clerks and salesmen) after their baseball careers were over. This figure is about four points lower than what Riess found. However, a much smaller percentage of the first professionals fell back on the blue-collar ranks than the 1871–82 group did. Finally, while a small fraction of the 1871–82 players returned to the farm, not one of the city-born players became farmers.

Only a little more than one-fourth of the initial professionals made advances from their playing days to their postcareer occupations, but this fact does not automatically prove that baseball was not a vehicle of social mobility. An examination of the pre- and postbaseball occupations of New York and Brooklyn professionals presents a somewhat more supportive case for the claims that baseball fostered mobility. Eleven of the twenty-six ball players did have more lucrative and prestigious occupations after their playing days ended. Of this group, the Wright brothers and Al Reach personified Horatio Alger success stories. The sons of Englishmen, all three used their baseball careers and connections to make a small fortune in the sporting goods business. Marty Swandell, who played briefly for the Eckford Club in 1872 and the Elizabeth Resolutes in 1873, also made significant advances. The son of a confectioner, Swandell became a wealthy Brooklyn baker by the 1880s.[107] The remaining seven players made minor advances, with five moving from skilled craftsmen to the lower ranks of white-collar workers. Half of the players remained in their initial status, and the positions of Fred Waterman and Asa Brainard declined.

The data on social mobility must be approached cautiously because of the small number of players investigated, the fact that postbaseball careers were often volatile, and most importantly because it is not clear whether a change from skilled craftsman to the lowest rank of white-collar worker meant an improved economic position or reflected the shifting composition of America's economic universe.[108] Nevertheless, a tentative relationship between baseball and social mobility may be supportable. Clearly, a professional baseball career was hardly a guarantee of ongoing riches. However, a significant minority of the players were socially mobile, more so than among the population as a whole. While only a handful of players parlayed their baseball careers into lucrative occupations, a substantial number did make minor advances, typical for most native-born Americans during the nineteenth century. For at least half the ball players, moreover, baseball served as a way of retaining their initial class position during an era of rapid and significant economic change.

Since the early professionals discussed in this study and the ball players from Riess's study were drawn from roughly the same time period, it is natural to speculate on what caused the difference in rates of social mobility. First, a large percentage of the initial professionals played in their hometowns for either all or a good part of their careers; hence, they could more easily retain their communal ties and use their professional fame to economic advantage when their careers ended. Second, it is possible that as natives of the New York metropolitan area, these players were able to partake of the greater economic opportunities available in the nation's leading city.

The maturation and modernization of baseball made rapid strides in the 1860s. The formation of the National Association of Professional Base Ball Players in 1871 symbolized that baseball had become a highly competitive, commercialized spectator sport dominated by a small group of professional players. The nationwide growth of baseball undermined the domination of the sport by New York City and Brooklyn while solidifying baseball's claim to be the national pastime. The creation of baseball's first professional league did not bring a halt to the maturation or modernization of the sport, which continued throughout the last three decades of the nineteenth century. Nevertheless, the subsequent changes in baseball occurred within the framework created during the Civil War decade.

SECTION III

THE DIVERSITY OF SPORT IN THE CITY

In addition to horse and harness racing, cricket and baseball, New Yorkers engaged in a variety of other sports, most of which existed on an informal, unorganized basis prior to 1820, although a handful initially appeared much later. Some of these activities remained essentially leisure sports, such as ice skating, while others became highly competitive spectator sports, such as boxing.[1] Many followed a cyclical pattern of growth, while some hovered on the verge of collapse. By 1870 New Yorkers were participating more frequently in almost all of these sports than they had a half-century earlier.

Blessed with outstanding harbors and rivers, New York City and vicinity played a dominant role in the evolution of such water sports as rowing and yachting. Rowing, which began as a utilitarian display of speed and endurance, later took on most of its modern characteristics as an amateur sport. Trans-Atlantic races and two challenges for the America's Cup created a tremendous interest in yachting; in fact, between 1866 and 1871 the sport received more press coverage than it had in all the previous years combined. By 1871 yachting had become an organized, wealthy man's sport, and in the next decade and a half the number of yachts and yacht clubs in America would increase dramatically. The growth of the sport nationally did not undermine the New York Yacht Club's influence, however, as their "authority held sway with few serious challengers from the outside" for the remainder of the nineteenth century.[2]

Pedestrianism, billiards, boxing, and animal sports emerged as popular spectator sports especially after 1840. While these events appealed to a wide segment of the population in varying degrees, the bachelor subculture formed the nucleus of support for billiards, boxing, and animal sports.

185

Paid athletes, primarily foreign-born members of the manual class, dominated these sports. And with the exception of pedestrianism, each of these sports grew despite moral opposition because of their association with gambling and, in the case of boxing and animal sports, their brutality. By 1870 all four sports had taken on certain modern characteristics, but none of them could be classified as modern. Although the professional element was present, commercialism was still in the early stages, as was the extent to which these sports were organized. With the exception of animal sports, that would come in the next quarter-century.

Between 1820 and 1870 New Yorkers also participated in twenty-one different leisure sports, ranging from fox hunting to ice skating, from fencing to croquet. Some of these activities had a limited following among all classes; others were confined to a particular class or ethnic group. Participation in certain sports, such as bowling, declined during this period, but in others, such as skating, it markedly increased. Many were new to America as late as the 1860s, and all of them achieved only a limited degree of modernization by 1870. Although each of these leisure sports followed a diverse developmental path, collectively they pointed to the overall growth that occurred in New York's sporting institutions.

By 1870 local clubs had been formed for almost all sports, although comparable national associations were virtually absent. Intercity and even international contests were held in several sports. Uniform rules and regulations generally evolved slowly, and statistical data and records emerged at a gradual pace as well. Public interest and a desire for information grew in direct proportion to the increasing coverage athletics received in the daily press and to the emergence of several sports journals. Guidebooks on most sports and the rudiments of a sports literature also began to develop by the 1860s.

Class and ethnicity factors strongly shaped the pattern and structures of these various sports between 1820 and 1870. New Yorkers from all social ranks participated in physical recreations of one form or another, but involvement in organized sport was less broadly based. The lower class was generally excluded from this trend, although individuals from this social and economic group did engage in certain professional sports, most notably boxing. While participation in organized sport generally went no further down the social ladder than the artisan class, sport in New York City was marked nonetheless by class differences. Some sports were the sole prerogative of the upper class, although participation in most sports was not restricted to any single class. The nature and structure of a particular sport was in part determined by which and how many social classes engaged in the same athletic endeavor. Interclass participation was virtually nonexistent. Although class differences in sport existed during the antebellum period, they had not yet hardened into the rigid class distinctions that characterized American sports developments during the last few decades of the nineteenth century, as New Yorkers and others made an effort to separate amateur and professional athletes.

Given the historical development of sport and the nature of immigration during this period, it is not surprising that some sports, with the notable exception of gymnastics, were linked to people from English-speaking countries. Ethnic-based sports clubs helped to preserve national identity in a foreign land as much as they promoted athletic activity.

New York City clearly played an important, at times dominant, role in the evolution of a diverse collection of professional and leisure sports. In the next three chapters I shall explore a myriad of sporting experiences in the city between 1820 and 1870, focusing first on water sports, then on an eclectic group of four professionalized sports, and finally on a host of leisure sports. My aim is to demonstrate the increasing modernization of American sport in general.

The yacht *America*. From a drawing by Currier and Ives.

8

Water Sports: Rowing and Yachting

Between 1820 and 1870 rowing and yachting attracted a considerable amount of attention in New York, although the number of participants was never that high. The growing popularity of these water sports was not surprising, given the increased enthusiasm for all sports during these years, the geography of the area, and the role the city's harbors played in its preeminent economic position. Both sports originated in utilitarian activities but vastly differed in their respective rates of growth, structural patterns, participants, and, ultimately, their fates.

ROWING

In the early nineteenth century rowing races were simply informal, unorganized contests between harbormen; by the end of the century rowing had assumed a modern structure as evidenced by the formation of the National Association of Amateur Oarsmen in 1872. From the outset New Yorkers played a critical role in the development and evolution of the sport, which followed a cyclical pattern and was marked by a significant shift in leadership and focus. Rowing was initially dominated by professionals and quasi professionals, but by the post–Civil War period amateur oarsmen had assumed control of the sport.

Rowing contests in America sprang up among the laborers of the rivers and harbors. During the colonial period salesmen and pilots often sought out the fastest oarsmen in an effort to be the first to reach incoming ships with news and supplies. Such practices led oarsmen, who were proud of their physical prowess, to enter contests for wagers. While these were generally arranged by the rowers themselves, outsiders occasionally

189

donated the purse, hoping to profit from side bets on their favorites. In 1756 the *New York Mercury* made note of a race for twenty dollars, the earliest known report of a rowing contest. Similar races occurred throughout the eighteenth century but attracted little or no public attention.[1]

During the first decade of the nineteenth century rowing races became more popularized. In 1807 John Baptist's boat triumphed over one built by John Chambers; four years later the *Knickerbocker* and the *Invincible*, built by Baptist and Chambers, respectively, met in a confrontation between New York City and Long Island crews, with the former emerging victorious. The tremendous interest in the race prompted Scudder's Museum to buy the winning *Knickerbocker*, where it remained on exhibition until transferred to Barnum's Museum. At that point the *Knickerbocker* was erroneously dubbed the winner of the first American rowing race.[2]

Competitive rowing in seaboard cities increased in the years following the War of 1812. The leading matches in New York, particularly between Baptist and Chambers, attracted many onlookers. When the two rivals met in 1820 for $800 per side, the *Gazette* noted that the race was witnessed by an immense crowd; the *Post* insisted that side bets on the contest ranged from $8,000 to $10,000.[3] The Whitehallers, organized around 1810 and by far the best known and most successful of New York's early crews, challenged their London counterparts to a race for $1,000 in 1824. Their proposal was that they could row 125 miles up the Hudson River in less time than it would take the Englishmen to go 118 miles up the Thames. Nothing came of the challenge, but by the end of the year the Whitehallers competed against English oarsmen in one of the most famous antebellum rowing races.[4]

Captain George Harris docked the English frigate *Hussar* at New York in the late fall of 1824 and quickly became a hero when the locals learned that his crew had saved a New York boat from pirates off the coast of Cuba. A racing devotee, Harris had on board his ship a very fast rowing boat as well as a crew of Thames watermen. When he heard about rowing exploits in New York City, he wrote the *American* that his crew would accept all challengers. The Whitehallers quickly accepted in the *American Star*, a boat built by Chambers. The international contest, for $1,000 per side, created considerable excitement and for several days replaced the upcoming presidential election as the major topic of conversation. The press estimated that 20,000–50,000 spectators lined the wharves to see the four-mile race. The Whitehallers' victory was a source of national pride and convinced Americans of the superiority of their rowers; still, there was high regard for Harris, and the gracious way he accepted defeat tempered nationalistic rhetoric. Several newspapers recommended that the *American Star* be presented to Harris as a gesture of friendship and sportsmanship, but when the owners of the boat made the offer the English captain politely refused.[5]

Interest in rowing remained high for two years. When the Whitehallers challenged a Staten Island crew the entire business community reportedly stopped work and turned out to watch the race. But by the end of the decade reports of rowing matches temporarily disappeared from the pages of New York newspapers. However, the formation of several rowing clubs in the early 1830s indicated a renewed enthusiasm for the sport. In 1834 some of these new clubs established the Castle Garden Amateur Boat Club Association. In sharp contrast to New York watermen, the young men of the Castle Garden Association came from prominent families. These exclusive clubs had such stringent rules that in 1837 they refused to participate in a Poughkeepsie regatta since the association's constitution did not permit them "to row for money, or take part in a Regatta or races with any Club or Clubs independent of those belonging to the Association." The purpose of these clubs was mainly social diversion rather than competitive rowing. Their annual regatta, attended by the New York elite, was as much a display of fashion as of skill. Each club appeared in its own distinct colors and uniforms; and each year the Wave Club, the best crew and quite possibly the wealthiest, came with a new boat constructed by Clarkson Crolius, the leading builder of the day.[6] The Independent Boat Club Association, formed by several other rowing clubs, functioned under much less stringent guidelines. The clubs were more competitive, and while the members probably came from white-collar or professional occupations it was apparent that they were not among the elite.[7]

In 1836 the *Spirit* claimed that there were fifteen to twenty six-oared cutters in New York, while the *Journal of Commerce* reported that forty rowing clubs had been established in the city in the previous two years. The press praised the participants and the sport of rowing, stating that the activity drew young men "away from places where they ruin their morals and health, to pass some of their time in an exercise and amusement which is congenial to virtue and vigor of the body." The *Spirit* contended that "no exercise is so conducive to health as rowing, and no gala so exciting to those who witness or partake in, as a regatta."[8] All the hoopla had little effect on the city's hardworking watermen, particularly the Whitehallers. When their still undefeated crew met the Fulton Meat Market crew in 1837, one newspaper reported that "the *coup d'oui* [sic] from the harbor was magnificent. It appeared as if the city had poured forth all its inhabitants to witness some great contest on which their existence depended." In addition to these quasi-professional races, contests between single scullers became popular. In 1837 and 1838 New Yorkers Stephan Roberts and Sydney Dolan engaged in four important contests and exacted a great deal of attention, providing the impetus for the rise of professional rowing in the next two decades.[9]

New Yorkers' interest in rowing during the 1820s and 1830s was duplicated in other cities. The *Spirit* noted that the rapid rise of the sport required the creation of a distinct department "for the purpose of chronicling the sayings and doings of the different Clubs and Associations throughout the country."[10] The spread of the sport nationwide led to intercity challenges. In 1826 the Whitehallers had proposed a three- to six-mile race against either a Savannah or Charleston crew for $10,000 or more. A decade later a "Southern Coxswain" wrote to the *Spirit* that he hoped a New York club could be persuaded to visit "for a trial with our Georgia clipper for a thousand or two? We cannot carry our oarsmen to New York as they are our slaves, else we might be tempted to visit your city with our boats for a trial on the fair Hudson." Although nothing came of either proposal, New Yorkers had frequent contact with southern oarsmen. The Wave Club always sold their boats to rowers in southern cities, and several New Orleans clubs bought their shells directly from New York boatmakers. While New York rowers did not venture south, they did go up the Hudson to Poughkeepsie and Newburgh, as well as to cities such as Boston. Rowers from these cities reciprocated, coming to New York to compete in rowing races and regattas.[11]

With the exception of horse and harness racing, rowing attracted more press attention during the 1830s than any other sport, which makes it difficult to explain the precipitous decline of rowing in the next decade. Rowing clubs throughout New York were dissolved, and in 1842 the Castle Garden Association held its last regatta. Watermen and professional oarsmen continued to race but attracted little attention. Since similar developments occurred elsewhere, the sudden decline was partially linked to national developments rather than local ones. Dale Somers argues that the stagnation of rowing in New Orleans during this period was a product of the economic difficulties of the early 1840s. Such an argument cannot be applied so readily to explain the status of rowing in New York, however. Rowing prospered there during the worst years of the economic depression of 1837, falling out of favor only when prosperity began to return to the city. Because rowing was not an unduly expensive sport, the economy might have affected young men of moderate means but should have had little impact on the Castle Garden rowers. If financial considerations caused rowing's decline, why is it the sport did not later revive itself, especially since these young men did not substitute another sport for rowing?[12]

While the economic problems of the late 1830s may have been a contributory factor, other influences were more critical to rowing's dismal conditions. As the shifting pattern of commerce and communications gradually undermined the utilitarian value of swift harbormen, interest in their contests also declined. In addition, the surge of rowing, especially in the late 1830s, had been connected largely with elite sponsorship, and after several years these trendsetters lost interest in this sport, although there is no clear-cut reason why.

In the mid-1850s a rowing revival began in New York City. An 1854 *Times* editorial proposed that a rowing regatta be held on the Fourth of July: "We want something to beguile young men from the sedentary relaxation of gaming, or the semi-effeminate skill of the billiard table, and lead them out in God's open air, where health, strength [and] manhood may be earned." The following year the *Spirit* announced that to "more effectively promote sports of this kind, a club has been formed, with the avowed purpose of promoting matches among clubmen." The Empire City Regatta Club was not a rowing club in the sense that its members competed in contests. Rather, it was an organization that sponsored races by offering prize money, usually $400 per regatta. The officials of the club, headed by Stephan Roberts, were mainly boat builders, and although the ten-dollar entrance fee covered part of their costs, their major objective in sponsoring races was to stimulate interest in rowing and consequently in their boats.[13]

The Empire Club's initial regatta was "one of the most successful that has ever taken place in the city," according to the *Herald*. The *Spirit* echoed that sentiment, noting that people from Boston, Toronto, and New Brunswick (Ontario) had come to New York City to watch the races. Buoyed by that club's success, the newly created New York Regatta Club sponsored an Independence Day regatta in 1859, with the city's common council financing the holiday event.[14]

Professional oarsmen were the major attraction for the huge crowds, often estimated at 10,000 people, that turned out to witness the annual events of the Empire and New York clubs. These rowers had been responsible for sustaining at least some interest in the sport in the lean years, and one rowing historian maintained that "it was natural that from the semiprofessional and mixed character of the early regattas ... there should be born a group of professional oarsmen." Professional rowers emerged as leading sports figures and were being challenged for large sums of money in the leading sports journals, in contrast to the privately arranged contests of the 1840s and earlier. Since New York City was the center of professional rowing most of these oarsmen limited their competitions to the metropolitan area, although some did go to Philadelphia to race. As early as 1856, however, a New York crew led by Stephan Roberts was defeated by a St. John's (New Brunswick) squad in a $2,000 per side race on the (neutral) Charles River in Boston. The *Clipper* claimed that over $50,000 changed hands on the outcome of that race alone.[15]

The interest in determining America's leading sculler was indicative of the renewed popularity of professional rowing. In 1859 a championship contest was held off Staten Island, for which Tiffany and Company donated a silver belt plus a $100 prize. Joshua Ward of Newburgh was the winner, a triumph that brought him national acclaim. It also marked the end of New York City's domination of professional rowing in America,[16] although several of the city's crews continued to gain prominence both before and after the Civil War. The *George J. Brown*, manned by the three Biglin brothers and Dennis Leary, was the most successful and famous of New York's four-oared boats. Similar to other professionals, the members of the *Brown* pocketed the money they won at regattas; for match races, however, backers put up the money and kept the winnings, with the crew getting a percentage. In 1865 the *Brown* (renamed the *Samuel Collyer* after its principal backer) competed against the *Floyd T. F. Field* of Poughkeepsie for $3,000 per side, until that time the largest amount ever staked on a rowing race. Each crew showed up in a new shell, and the race "excited more interest throughout the United States than any other affair of the kind ever gotten up in this country or Europe." *Wilkes' Spirit* estimated that $150,000–$200,000 was wagered on the contest, won by the New Yorkers after the judges disallowed a foul claim by the Poughkeepsie crew. The battle was "one of the most exciting and spirited contested acquatic races." The day's event ended in tragedy, however, when a member of the Poughkeepsie crew accidently killed a man who had accused him of throwing the race.[17]

Professional rowing in New York City reached a climax with the 1865 contest. Problems surfaced during the Civil War years when the regattas of the New York and Empire clubs were cancelled in 1861 and 1863 respectively. The rise of professional baseball may have contributed to the decline of professional rowing by deflecting public interest through the creation of new sports heroes. But the major factor was the increasing strength of amateur rowing. The balance of power did not shift from one phase of the sport to the other overnight, however. Professional rowing "steadily decreased in importance with the rise of amateur rowing," and while the leading professional scullers in America were still well known throughout the 1880s, most of the prominent professional oarsmen now came from Canada, England, and Australia.[18]

The seeds for the eventual takeover of the sport by amateurs were sown during 1845–65 when professionals dominated rowing. Collegiate crew and club rowing became the two major directions of the amateur phase of the sport. New York institutions of higher learning played no real part in the rise of collegiate crew, although students at Columbia College formed a rowing organization as early as 1859; fourteen years passed before they entered an intercollegiate regatta, however.[19] By contrast, New York rowing clubs did play a vital role in this phase of amateur rowing. In 1848 the Atalanta Boat Club was established, like its Castle Garden predecessor more of a social organization than a rowing club. Several other clubs were formed during the early 1850s, but virtually all of them disbanded after one or two years. In 1859 six clubs from New York City and vicinity created the Hudson Navy, which held its first regatta the following year; the new association collapsed with the outbreak of the Civil War.[20]

In the five-year period after the intersectional struggle rowing in New York built on the inroads it had made during the late 1850s. While professional contests continued to take place, amateur clubs increasingly became the focus of attention. In 1866 eleven clubs established the Hudson Amateur Rowing Association in an effort to provide a "united organization, with uniform regulations governing them all." The member clubs were almost all from New York City and vicinity, and their assets in boats and boathouses, estimated at over $30,000, indicate that they were made up of wealthy men. A cursory check of the club rosters reveals that New York scions like William P. Douglass, Russell Withers, and Lloyd Aspinwall were oarsmen; many other club members came from the second rank of the city's elite. While the social composition of this rowing organization was similar to most of New York's antebellum rowing clubs, these men were more concerned with competition than their predecessors had been. In 1868 *Wilkes' Spirit* insisted that the Hudson Association was the strongest in the country and "to a great extent holds to its hand the successful future of aquatic sport in America." The *Clipper* agreed: "This association is one of the best and most energetic rowing bodies in the United States and for beauty of equipment, handsome boathouses and unsurpassed boats, they fill a front rank position among the amateur oarsmen of this country."[21]

With roughly fifteen or twenty clubs in New York City and possibly as many in the surrounding area, only Philadelphia came close to challenging the nation's leading metropolis for rowing club supremacy. Several newspapers argued that there should be even more clubs in New York, however, given its aquatic surroundings and the value of the sport. "Its benefits are so great and attainable," the *Times* wrote, "that we shall be glad to see the day when the oar is as familiar to our young men as the bat." The *Herald* contended that "New York in the matter of boating clubs as in everything else, takes the lead of any other city in the Union, not so much because she is the metropolis, but because her position is such surrounded by water, that clubs in the vicinity cannot fail to prosper."[22]

In spite of New York's dominance of the sport, the event that attracted the most attention in the press did not involve New Yorkers, nor did it take place in America. In 1869 New York newspapers anxiously followed the race between crews from Harvard and Oxford universities, on the Thames River in England. The New York *Times* provided extensive coverage of the race and wrote numerous editorials on its significance. The *Herald* devoted nearly two full pages to the contest, even though the Americans lost. In fact, between 1820 and 1870 no other sports event received more press coverage on any one day. Expressing a sentiment that would be repeated later by Baron Pierre de Coubertin and other supporters of the Olympic movement, the *Herald* wrote: "For the time being aquatic sport of an international character are to form the ingredients of popular excitement on both sides of the Atlantic, instead of wars and rumors of war with their grizzly fronts. So much the better. It is part of the progress in modern civilization that we should fight our battles with oars and sails and issue our protocols of victory by electrotelegraphs."[23]

Rowing clubs and associations were formed in every major American city with access to a body of water in the decade following the Civil War. In an editorial entitled "The Golden Era of Aquatic Sports," *Wilkes' Spirit* claimed that "never before has such *furore* been known over an amusement which has heretofore occupied but an indifferent position in general regard." By 1870 roughly 200 rowing clubs existed nationwide, with more forming each year. The sports journal maintained that the increasing number of regattas and the improvement in the skills of the rowers made the past season one of the best and most exciting.[24]

The need to establish order and formulate a definition of amateurism emerged with the rapid proliferation of amateur rowing clubs after the Civil War. In August 1872 twenty-seven clubs, eleven of them from New York City and vicinity, met in Manhattan and established the National Association of Amateur Oarsmen. The new association promulgated uniform rules and created an executive committee to govern the sport, but the effort to define amateurism led to considerable debate. An amateur code was finally drafted and was the basis for the amateur principle in rowing well into the twentieth century. In taking this step oarsmen were the first to clearly separate amateurs from professionals, as had been done in England. The definition of amateurism was widely objected to at the time, and nearly all sportswriters criticized it as harsh and unjust, supporting my contention in chapter 7 that no accepted view of amateurism or professionalism had yet emerged. Eleven of the rowing clubs in attendance at the initial meeting refused to join the new association, but supported by the powerful and wealthy New York and Philadelphia clubs, the National Association of Amateur Oarsmen weathered the storm and gradually extended its influence over the sport throughout the country. Professionals and semiprofessionals nonetheless remained a part of the rowing scene until the last decade of the nineteenth century, despite several efforts to refine and tighten the definition of amateurism.[25]

The triumph of amateurism in rowing contrasted sharply with the success of professionalism in baseball. The most significant factor in the divergent developments of the two sports was the difficulty inherent in rowing which prevented it from emerging as a commercialized endeavor. Since financial supporters could not depend on gate receipts, profit could come only from victory; the drawbacks of the winner-take-all system are obvious. Suffice it to say that without commercial money the days of professional rowing were limited. Amateur rowing continued to evolve, however. And although its glory days had come and gone, the sport achieved by the early 1870s a higher level of modern structure than any other sport in America, with the exception of harness racing and baseball.

YACHTING

Yachting in America quite possibly dates back as far as the Dutch burghers of New Amsterdam.[26] Yacht racing, however, did not begin in America until the mid-1830s, when a small number of wealthy New Yorkers and Bostonians began racing their pleasure boats. In 1835 John Cox Stevens's *Wave* defeated John Cushing's *Sylph* in the first recorded American yacht race, and in the next decade several similar contests took place in and around New York harbor. In early 1844 the *Herald* optimistically wrote, "This country will soon equal England in yachting."[27]

On July 30, 1844, nine yachtsmen met on board the *Gimcrack* and established the New York Yacht Club, marking the beginning of organized yachting in America. While an earlier yacht club had existed in Boston in the 1830s, and there may have been others in New York as well, these clubs survived for only a couple of years and had virtually no impact on the development of the sport. From 1845 to 1870 wealthy urbanites, particularly along the Atlantic coast, formed at least fourteen other yacht clubs. Nevertheless, the history of organized yachting during its first quarter-century was almost totally intertwined with the history of the New York Yacht Club and its members.[28] Created without fanfare or much public notice, it was three days before the *Herald* reported simply that a yacht club, similar to the Royal Yacht Squadron in England, had been established and that its objective was "health and pleasure, combined with a laudable desire to improve our almost perfect naval architecture." In 1846, however, public interest had been piqued enough for the *Spirit* to claim that the club's annual regatta generated more excitement than any other sporting event that year: "Ever since it was announced that a Regatta was to come off . . . the race was looked forward to with the highest possible degree of interest."[29]

The increase in club membership testified to the growing interest in the sport. Two years after its formation the New York Yacht Club had 120 members, although enthusiasm waned a bit after this initial surge. The *Herald* noted in 1847 that there was "a want of taste for yachting among the citizens of New York," evidenced by decreasing press coverage and the club's inability to attract new members.[30] However, yachting received a major boost in 1850 when a syndicate of five New York Yacht Club members, headed by John C. Stevens, commissioned the construction of the yacht *America,* for the express purpose of taking her to England to compete. Stevens's reputation as the leading sportsman in New York— and possibly the country—derived from his early involvement in horse racing. He had always been interested in sailboats, having built his first vessel, the *Diver,* before he was twenty-five. His interest in horse racing began to subside during the mid-1830s, quite possibly because he sensed that the problems of northern racing could not be resolved and/or he had achieved sufficient success and was looking for new adventures. In any case, Stevens began divesting himself of his racehorses in 1838, at the same time stating that he was going to prepare a yacht to take to England to race against the best the British had to offer.[31]

During the next dozen years Stevens continued to think about taking a yacht into English waters. The Great Exhibition of 1851 finally provided the opportunity for him to make good on his claim. As part of the gala event the Royal Yacht Squadron was planning a regatta, and in late 1850 a number of English businessmen wrote to various American merchants suggesting that they send over an American pilot boat to demonstrate its speed. By November a group of men had hired William Brown, New York's leading shipbuilder, to construct a vessel; they chose George Steers, the boating boy wonder, to design it.[32] The *America*'s maiden trial in June 1851 was a resounding flop, as the *Maria* sailed rings around her. Yet Stevens's confidence in the new yacht remained unshaken, and the syndicate remained committed to the project. Other Americans expressed doubts, such as Horace Greeley, the owner of the *Tribune,* who warned Alexander Hamilton's son James: "if you do go, and you are beaten you had better not return to your country."[33]

By the time the *America* departed for England the new yacht and the entire project had revived the public's interest in yachting. The *European Times* warned Englishmen that although the American vessel had already been beaten "her speed should not be considered too lightly by any English vessel entering the list against her." That advice was apparently taken to heart, for Stevens's challenge to race any English yacht for 1,000–10,000 guineas went unanswered, a clear disappointment since he believed the syndicate could profit by wagering heavily on the *America.*[34] On August 16 the *London Times* expressed deep dismay over the failure of English yachtsmen to pick up the gauntlet thrown down by their American counterparts: "If she be permitted to sail back to New York with her challenge unaccepted, . . . there will be some question as to the pith and courage of our men, and yachting must sink immeasurably in public estimation, and must also be deprived of the credit which was wont to be attached to it, of being a nursery of bringing up our national naval spirit to a respectable and well-grown maturity." Responding to the paper's chastisement, Robert Stephenson offered to race his new 100-ton schooner *Titania* for $500 on August 28. Although generally given little chance for victory, he had agreed to the contest to preserve national honor and to set an example for his more cautious countrymen. Stevens was not pleased by the amount of the wager or the general response, and he was prepared to take the *America* home untested. James Hamilton or George Schuyler urged him to enter at least one regatta, and so he entered the *America* in the Royal Yacht Squadron's race around the Isle of Wight; he also accepted Stephenson's challenge, a race the *America* later won easily.[35]

On August 22, 1851, the *America* and seventeen English schooners and cutters took part in the regatta for the 100-guinea cup. A large crowd, including Queen Victoria and Prince Albert, turned out to see the American craft race to victory; although she had been the last to get away, the *America* grabbed a commanding lead by the home stretch and won easily. The triumph was a source of national pride and much rhetoric, both at home and abroad. A letter to the *Spirit,* written from London, compared the outcome to the American Revolution, while another proclaimed that the *America* "bid defiance to a fleet of nearly 700 yachts, whose supposed speed had been a national boast of England." That same writer noted the claims of John Bull that "yacht building was an art in which England was unrivalled and that she was distinguishingly preeminent and alone for the perfection of science in handling them," and remarked that the taste of victory was made that much sweeter. British seadogs quickly discovered that "old England was no match for young America." William Rivers, ambassador to France, felt that national honor had been at stake. Initially opposed to the project, he wrote that there were lessons to be learned from the *America*'s success, although he never elaborated on that point.[36]

For most Americans the meaning of their namesake's success was quite clear. The *Herald* insisted that the victory of the *America* illustrated the country's supremacy at sea. George Templeton Strong, a well-known New York cynic, naturally had a different perspective. He recorded in his diary that "newspapers [are] crowing over the victory of Stevens' yacht . . . ; quite creditable to yacht shipbuilding, but not worthy of the intolerable, vainglorious vaporings that make every newspaper I take up now ridiculous. One would think yacht building were the end of man's existence on earth." More representative of public opinion was the view of John Prescott Hall, who stated at the yacht club reception honoring the conquering heroes, "Their errand was no mission of war . . . , but the contest was to be the strife of art, the science of skill, of manly daring and noble self control." By the end of the speech Hall also pointed out that "national pride, the national character and in some degree, the national honor, was committed to the keeping of our quest. . . . We rejoice in it, not in vainglorious boasting, but in the pride of our descendants, in the fairness and character of our opponents, in the thought that we met every English competitor upon the English seas, and that our flag has never been lowered, except in the graceful courtesies of success."[37]

The *America* victory marked a turning point in the history of yachting, but its significance would have been far less had not the five members of the syndicate offered the newly won cup as a prize for international competition—the America's Cup. At the dinner honoring the syndicate members Stevens announced that the owners of the trophy requested that the club accept it "as a testimony of their gratitude for the interest you have so kindly felt and so often expressed, in our welfare and success," making no specific mention of the eventual use to which the cup would be put. In May 1852 the syndicate established guidelines for an international competition, but for some unknown reason Stevens failed to deliver the drafted letter. For the next five years the trophy remained in the homes of the different owners of the *America*. After Stevens died on June 10, 1857, the letter was probably found among his papers. Redated July 8, 1857, the deed to the cup listed the five original syndicate members, although Hamilton Wilkes had died before the first letter had been drafted (a friend now acted on his behalf).[38]

Copies of the deed were sent to eighteen yacht clubs in seven foreign countries, and at least one sports journal felt that the announcement would be met "with a cordial response from yachtsmen of other nations." However, a dozen years would pass before the first challenge occurred, partly due to the outbreak of the Civil War, but more importantly because interest in international racing had subsided by the mid-1850s. For one thing, English yachtsmen were not willing to venture into American waters (in 1853 the New York Yacht Club had offered a $500 prize for any race in which a foreign vessel competed, yet not a single one came). Then again, British yachtsmen had achieved a measure of revenge in the summer of 1853 when they proved successful against another yacht designed by George Steers, the *Sylvie*. *Bell's Life of London* echoed the sense of British pride: "Nothing could exceed the delight of the owner, her builder and friends, [than] to find that the English yacht had proven victorious, and that the American wonder was defeated."[39]

The earlier victory of the *America* had stimulated tremendous local interest in yachting, as evidenced by increasing membership in the New York Yacht Club—from 157 members in 1850 to three times that many by the outbreak of the Civil War. The social composition of the club appears to have changed during this period, in part the natural by-product of increased membership and in part a result of the changes taking place among the New York elite.[40]

The nine original members of the club were men of inherited wealth, socially prominent men of Knickerbocker descent. Newcomers were also drawn primarily from old New York families, but by the 1850s the nouveaux riches, names like Astor and Vanderbilt, dotted the club's roster. New York City residents from prominent New England families and respectable upstate New York parentage were also affiliated with the yacht club, as were wealthy foreign-born residents of the city, such as August Belmont. Finally, a small contingent were wealthy non–New York City inhabitants, such as Bostonians Robert B. Forbes, William P. Winchester, and David Sears, Jr., George Cadwallader of Philadelphia, and John Carter Brown of Providence, Rhode Island.

The social composition of the New York Yacht Club probably closely paralleled that of the American Jockey Club, although there were differences, mostly a matter of degree. Yacht club members appear to have been wealthier and more socially prominent than their counterparts in horse racing, and they also included more New Yorkers of New England descent (probably since yachting was an accepted sport in that region while horse racing was not). In addition, the yacht club likely catered more to non–New York City residents, although not to politicos such as "Boss" Tweed, Peter Sweeney, and William Brennan, who were jockey club members but were excluded from the yacht club. Horse racing might have been the "Sport of Kings," but in New York City yachting was number one among the wealthy. In fact, with the exception of the Union and Century clubs, the New York Yacht Club probably provided a more accurate gauge of affluence than any other of New York's numerous social organizations.[41]

An increase in the number of yachts in the New York squadron corresponded with the rise in club membership, and by the end of the 1850s roughly fifty vessels were attached to the club, along with a new contingent of yachtsmen, unacquainted with navigation and seamanship. As a result amateur yachting rapidly declined and almost all yachts were turned over to professional skippers. The press and yachtsmen alike accepted this trend as inevitable, given the nautical inexperience of the majority of yacht owners and the tremendous cost of their vessels. Nevertheless, there were those who agreed with the *Times* editorial in 1870: "It would add greatly to the interest in the regatta if the owners acted as their own sailing masters, even if the full capacities of the boats were not fully brought out."[42]

The press had always expressed an ambivalent attitude toward the New York Yacht Club. There was a genuine respect for the members, who were among the city's elite, and more importantly for the club's contribution to the growth of yachting, yet there was also constant criticism of the club's aristocratic policies and practices. In a scathing editorial, "The Snobbish Yacht Club," the *Herald* claimed that no other group in America "bears such an unenviable reputation." It went on to accuse the members of exhibiting "the most narrow-minded selfishness and an affection of refinement and elegance, which to people of judgment and common sense, are supremely absurd."[43]

A perfect example of this tendency toward old-world aristocracy was the failure of the club members to invite or even mention George Steers, the designer of the *America,* at the dinner honoring the yacht's owners. One newspaper charged that the New York Yacht Club refused to share credit for the victory with an outsider, even though Steers represented everything good about America, the land of opportunity. A mechanical genius, Steers was also a hard worker, and at the time of his accidental death in 1856 many Americans believed he was the foremost shipbuilder and designer in the world. Still in his early thirties, the man had achieved financial success, but he was hardly in the economic and social class of most yacht club members. The failure to acknowledge his contribution to a national victory thus was seen as an affront to all he represented and served to emphasize the club's aristocratic, snobbish inclinations. Several prominent New York shipbuilders and other civic leaders held their own dinner to honor Steers, and John Stevens wrote several letters praising Steers and pointing to his important role in the success of the *America.* While both events placated bad feelings, they never eradicated the belief that the yacht club had seriously offended one of the people.[44]

Despite its ambivalence toward the New York Yacht Club, the press never questioned the benefits of yachting. In 1846 the *Herald* maintained that this "exciting sport will be of great advantage to us in a national point of view. It tends to rear a race of hardy, skillful pilots and seamen whose experience and knowledge could be turned to good account in case of war." The newspaper also noted that yachting was a completely innocent, healthful, and invigorating amusement. For the next quarter of a century the practical and recreational arguments remained the major justifications of the sport, although writers offered additional twists from time to time, the most notable being the contribution of yachting to naval architecture.[45]

Of the two rationales, yachting's practical values received more space and attention than did its recreational benefits, as was the case for horse racing. The cost of yachting made the need to demonstrate tangible benefits a critical part of the sanction and rhetoric of the sport. Wealthy New Yorkers became involved in yachting, as they did in horse racing, for personal enjoyment, as a means of conspicuous consumption and a form of status confirmation. In both sports the class values of the wealthy would not permit the tremendous expense unless there was a concomitant belief that something useful — or profitable — would come of it. However, it would be erroneous to assume that the practical argument merely provided a rationale for action. In the age of the clipper ships the connection between yachts and commercial vessels was universally accepted. *Wilkes' Spirit* rejected the assertion that yachting produced skillful sailors or contributed to naval defense but insisted nonetheless that the sport was a valuable means "of advancing the science of building and rigging fast water crafts." Since competition served to test the different yachts, the press encouraged yachtsmen to enter into trials of speed rather than use their vessels merely for pleasure cruises.[46]

The popularity of yachting grew steadily during the 1850s. In 1857 the *Herald* maintained that the "increase of yachts and yachting in this country during the last ten years has been very great and gives promise . . . soon to rival the prominence of this delightful recreation in England." Three years later a prominent yachtsman noted that more people were taking an interest in the affairs of the New York Yacht Club than he had seen for some time. The *Herald* mentioned the improvements in the building of large yachts and the greater activity of yacht owners. However, the growth of the sport came to a rapid halt with the onset of the Civil War. The yacht club called off its annual regatta in 1861, offering their vessels to the Navy "for any purpose compatible with their capacity." They resumed the annual event the following year, but it attracted few entries and limited public interest. A 30.6 percent decline in club membership between 1860 and 1865 further dramatized the general condition of yachting in New York during the war years.[47]

Like many other sports yachting experienced significant growth in the five years following the restoration of peace. Organized clubs were formed in several cities located on suitably large bodies of water, although New York remained far and away the sport's capital. By 1870 there were at least six yacht clubs in New York City and a few others in the immediate vicinity; nevertheless, the New York Yacht Club and its members continued to dominate the development of the sport both locally and nationally.[48]

The New York Yacht Club made up for the losses in club membership suffered during the war and also underwent significant changes in leadership. The group that had governed the club during the antebellum period "had become rather out of touch with the changing times." The new leaders were generally men of more recent wealth and were more active and bolder yachtsmen. James Gordon Bennett, Jr., the spoiled son of the owner of the *Herald,* was representative of this group. Backed by his father's money Bennett used his involvement in sport, particularly his connection with Leonard Jerome, to move within certain segments of New York society. While the prestigious yacht club would never have accepted his father, the younger Bennett became a member in 1858 at the tender age of sixteen. He quickly achieved a reputation as a skilled yachtsman when he won the club's first ocean race in 1858 and further enhanced his status in 1866 when he was the winner of a trans-Atlantic yacht race. In 1867 he was elected a vice-commodore and four years later became commodore.[49]

A major boost to the renewed interest in yachting came late in 1866 with the announcement of a trans-Atlantic yacht race. The contest evolved from a discussion between George A. Osgood, his brother Franklin, and Pierre Lorillard, Jr., concerning the merits of their respective yachts. Having imbibed too much alcohol, they drunkenly proposed that the more than 3,000-mile race be open to anyone willing to put up a $30,000 stake. Besides George Osgood and Lorillard, only Bennett joined in.[50] The December contest, in stormy weather, was a rash undertaking and was marred by the tragic deaths of several of the crew on Lorillard's yacht. The race nevertheless generated considerable discussion and excitement as a result of its innovative nature, the huge amount of money that depended on the outcome, and the stature of the participants. The press, especially Bennett's *Herald,* gave a great deal of space to news of the race, focusing largely on whether the owners should accompany their yachts (only Bennett went with his vessel). The *Times* felt that the contest would be a "pluckier affair" if the owners took charge of their yachts: "They may plead, and doubtless with reason, the claims of business, the discomfort of such a voyage, and the chances of being drowned as reasons why they should not go, but all these hazards and hardships are incidental to the peculiar sport they have seen fit to patronize." *Wilkes' Spirit* disagreed: "It is a test of the speed and staunchness of the vessels, and of the ability of their sailing masters and crews, and that is all that there is about it. The courage and hardihood of the owners are not at all involved."[51]

While the press debated other issues they generally agreed that the trans-Atlantic contest marked a new chapter in the history of yachting. Although a similar race occurred in 1870, blue water ocean racing did not become popular with yachtsmen until the start of the twentieth century.[52] The first such contest did represent certain significant and interrelated yachting developments, however. Schooners had become the standard racing yachts during the 1850s, but the three vessels competing in the 1866 race, all over 200 tons, symbolized the emergence in the post-Civil War years of the "Day of the Great Schooners." The owners of these larger and more expensive yachts also represented a new kind of yachtsman, the common assumption being that they had made their fortunes during the war years and "were of a different class from the Stevens family and the original founders of the club." However, a cursory look at thirty such yachtsmen reveals that while more than half were men of recent wealth, their fortunes were made during the antebellum period. The few yachtsmen of older and more established wealth were not the sons of New York's colonial elite, as were Stevens, Schuyler, and John C. Jay, three of the nine founders of the New York Yacht Club.[53]

Following the daring trans-Atlantic race one newspaper noted that several clubs had sprung up in the metropolitan area and other parts of the country. "In no previous season of American yachting," *Wilkes' Spirit* wrote in 1868, had there been "so great a number of brilliant successes as in that of the present year."[54] The race across the Atlantic also served to rekindle interest in international competition and mark the beginning of a series of events that culminated in the first two challenges for the America's Cup.

When the three yachts from New York arrived in English waters they caused a sensation among that country's sports crowd. The *Herald* noted that the "Atlantic cable dispatches daily continue the record of European ovations of our New York yachtsmen." *Bell's Life of London* described the race as the "greatest sailing feat of modern times." The crossing coincided with a renewed confidence Englishmen had in their own yachts. Earlier that year the English sports journal *Hunt's Yachting Magazine* urged that English yachtsmen challenge for the America's Cup, and further impetus came in 1868 with the arrival of the American schooner *Sappho*. The Poillon brothers, Brooklyn shipwrights, built the 310-ton yacht for the sole purpose of winning whatever wagers could be placed on her and then selling the ship for a handsome profit. The project failed miserably as four English schooners finished ahead of the American vessel. It was that victory over what the British believed was the best example of American yachting that inspired James Ashbury, the owner of the winning *Cambria,* to challenge for the America's Cup.[55]

In many ways Ashbury shared more in common with New York yachtsmen than with the English. Newly rich, his father had established the family fortune as the inventor and largest manufacturer of railway carriages. A bold and aggressive sportsman, Ashbury turned to yachting to enhance his social standing and win popular favor. He hoped that returning the trophy to England would garner him the social acceptance he so strongly desired. Thus, he began a series of correspondences with the New York Yacht Club in 1868, negotiations that, as one writer aptly put it, "resembled commercial treaties by tight fisted businessmen with eyes glued to the main chance." While Ashbury sought to impose his own rules for the competition, the New Yorkers violated the spirit of the cup's deed, and the result was that the first challenge for what is now the oldest international trophy turned into a fiasco.[56]

Besides the personalities involved the deed itself presented problems. Although the document was straightforward it contained a certain elasticity and ambiguity. The "mutual consent" clause provided for the legal machinations that surrounded not only this challenge but many challenges throughout much of the cup's history. The parties engaged in the competition were supposed to make the arrangements for the contest, but if agreement could not be reached then the race would be sailed "over the usual course of the Annual Regatta of the Yacht Club in possession of the Cup, and subject to its Rules of Sailing Regulations." This provision gave the New Yorkers the upper hand in negotiations, and the club used its power to bend Ashbury to its will.[57]

The definition of a "match" race was even more problematic. The yacht club's interpretation required that Ashbury compete against its entire fleet, which was totally unsportsmanlike and in clear violation of the spirit of the deed. However, the *Herald* supported the club's stance: "We are still of the opinion that the America's Cup is a trophy that should only change hands upon the clearest and least questionable demonstration of maritime superiority; that it should be never subjected to narrower terms than those on which the *America* won it when she sailed 'against the world' and beat a fleet of seventeen yachts." An "animated debate" ensued when the definition of "match" came up for final ratification at a meeting of the yacht club in March 1870. Nevertheless, the yacht owners voted overwhelmingly (18–1) to support this position.[58] The press and public generally agreed with the New York club's illiberal policy, partly because of Ashbury's own attempt to dictate the terms of the contest. The nationalistic overtones that had surrounded the *America*'s victory years earlier were more significant in determining public opinion, however, for by the post–Civil War years Americans came to view the cup as a "national trophy," symbolic of their yachting leadership and their maritime supremacy.[59]

In his negotiations with the yacht club Ashbury proposed a trans-Atlantic race as one part of his challenge for the cup. The club refused, but Bennett, who was in England, separately agreed to a westward race across the Atlantic between his yacht *Dauntless* and Ashbury's *Cambria*. After considerable haggling over details, especially on Ashbury's part, the two set sail, arousing considerable excitement. "The uncertainty about the results and impossibility of knowing the precise time when the vessels may be expected," the *Times* maintained, "makes the race of absorbing interest, and the international triumph . . . gives to it widespread and popular attraction." The English yacht arrived first, to the shock and consternation of Americans, and although the press gave Ashbury the credit he deserved, New Yorkers offered a host of excuses. According to popular opinion the outcome was more a case of the *Dauntless* losing than the *Cambria* winning. The *Clipper* decried this attempt to rob Ashbury of his deserved laurels as un-American and unsportsmanlike.[60]

Obviously, New Yorkers were afraid that the *Cambria* might be able to wrest away the America's Cup, but there was little reason for concern since the yacht club had rigged the odds against the challenger. An exceptional yacht might have overcome these obstacles, but the *Cambria* did not fit into this category. When the competition was held on August 8, 1870, she finished tenth among the twenty-four entries. The *Times* felt that American yachtsmen should be "justly congratulated" for "the honorable retention of a testimony to their superiority and management of their vessels." For the *Herald* the significant feature of the race was not that an American yacht had won but that the *Cambria* could not finish ahead of the *America,* which had finished fourth and at the time was owned by the United States Navy.[61]

Although badly beaten Ashbury remained committed to returning the trophy to England. He insisted that he had been treated poorly, a view generally shared by other English yachtsmen, and set about constructing a new yacht, *Livonia*. Once again he entered into negotiations with the New York Yacht Club, which were even more acrimonious than the first time. On both sides of the Atlantic lawyers were brought in to scrutinize the cup's deed. At the recommendation of Dixon Kemp, editor of the *London Field,* Ashbury announced that he would come with challenges from twelve different yacht clubs, thereby permitting him twelve different chances to win. The New Yorkers rejected the absurd plan, pointing out that the deed expressly prohibited such action, but they yielded on the issue of requiring Ashbury to compete against an entire fleet. (The argument that the old interpretation had been unsportsmanlike gained an increasing number of converts, although the majority of the press and public still felt that the club members had acted properly.) At the request of several friends and certain newspapers George L. Schuyler, the sole surviving member of the *America's* syndicate, offered his interpretation in a letter to *Wilkes' Spirit*. He defined a match as competition between two parties and noted, "It seems to me that the present ruling of the club renders the America's trophy useless as 'a Challenge Cup' and . . . I cannot conceive of any yachtsman . . . cross[ing] the ocean for the sole purpose of entering into an almost hopeless contest for this Cup."[62]

The yacht club was not bound by Schuyler's interpretation, and most yachtsmen disagreed with him; however, it was impossible for the club to ignore his opinion, given his role in winning the cup and his position

as one of the original members of the club. The club did reserve for itself
the privilege of selecting any one of the club's yachts on the day of the
race and in addition made the challenge a best-of-seven series. These new
conditions did little to improve Ashbury's chances, and he failed to
triumph against the *Columbia* and *Sappho,* which won four out of five
races. The competition proceeded no more smoothly than the negotiations
had. Ashbury protested his loss in the second race, and several observers
believed that his complaint was sufficient to warrant another race, but
the yacht club overruled the protest. Ashbury claimed victory anyway,
and after the fifth race insisted that the series stood at 3–2. When the
New Yorkers failed to send a representative to the last two races, the
Englishman insisted that he had won the America's Cup by default.[63] The
ludicrous affair did not really end for another two years, with charges
and countercharges crossing the Atlantic. Eventually most Englishmen
tired of Ashbury, although their sports journals and many yachtsmen
continued to believe that the Americans had treated him unfairly. Fourteen
years would pass before another Englishman tried to recapture the trophy.[64]

The challenges for the America's Cup were part of a growing number
of international contests during the last half of the nineteenth century,
particularly between the United States and England. While the Ashbury
challenges were among the most vitriolic of all the international contests,
mainly because of the symbolic meaning of the America's Cup, the
problems associated with those races were not atypical. Tensions in
American-English sporting relations in the 1860s and early 1870s reflected
the political and social tensions between the two countries. However, as
the Anglo-American communities would grow closer together in the last
quarter of the century, the sports contacts between the two nations
became more amiable. The increase in "friendly competition" between
foreign countries coincided with the emergence of the idea that sport
could serve as a means of fostering international understanding and
brotherhood, a movement that climaxed with Baron Pierre de Coubertin
and the creation of the modern Olympics.[65]

The great international boxing match between John C. Heenan and Tom Sayers, in Englan
1860. From a drawing by Currier and Ives.

9

Pedestrianism, Billiards, Boxing, and Animal Sports

Running and walking races, billiards, boxing, and animal sports were all part of life in New York during the colonial period, and city residents increasingly followed these sports between 1820 and 1870, particularly after 1840. The four sports had much in common, including the fact that they were all primarily spectator sports dominated by a small group of professionals who came overwhelmingly from the worker classes and were mostly foreign-born. The growth of each of these sports, with the exception of pedestrianism, was intimately bound up with shifts in the concept of manhood and concomitant changes in male social institutions. Their premodern structures gradually took on certain modern elements, but unlike baseball or harness racing none of them were transformed into truly modern sports despite professional and commercial influences. Their limited modernization raises some questions concerning the assumed relationship between the commercial, professional, and modern aspects of sport.

PEDESTRIANISM

Professional running and walking contests, which I refer to here as pedestrianism, following nineteenth-century terminology, became one of the leading spectator sports in New York City and other parts of America between 1835 and 1860. Interest continued in the post–Civil War period, although to a lesser extent. As was the case with rowing, the tone and

The portion of this chapter on billiards was the basis of an article that originally appeared as "Neglected Sports in American History: The Rise of Billiards in New York City, 1850–71," *Canadian Journal of History of Sport* 12 (Dec. 1981): 1–28.

direction of track and field changed in the last part of the nineteenth century, marked by the formation of the New York Athletic Club in 1868.

Between 1820 and 1835 the New York press noted several local pedestrian races. These were generally arranged privately and always for side bets; on a few occasions they were held in conjunction with horse races, with the track proprietors putting up the purses.[1] The major stimulant to the rise of pedestrianism as a leading spectator sport was a ten-mile race held at the Union Course in April 1835. The contest originated with a sizable wager between John C. Stevens and Samuel L. Gouveneur that Stevens could find a man capable of running ten miles in one hour. He was allowed to start any number of runners, of any nationality or color. To attract competitors Stevens initially offered $1,000 to be divided equally among all those who covered the distance in the required time. By the time of the race, however, it was decided that the first person to cross the finish line in an hour or less would receive the entire $1,000. An extra $100 was offered to the first-, second-, and third-place finishers provided each completed the distance in the allocated time. If only one runner accomplished the feat, he would collect all $300 in bonus money.[2]

The novelty of the experience, the prize money offered, and the sporting reputations of the sponsors produced considerable interest in the contest. Men like Phillip Hone were swept up by the excitement. In his diary he wrote that "without intending it by any means, when I arose this morning I found myself with Robert [his son] . . . on the race course, jostled by every description of people. The crowd on the ground was as great, I think, as at the famous *Eclipse* race, and immense sums were being bet."[3] Nine men, ranging in age from eighteen to thirty-three, started the race. The majority of them were artisans from New York City and vicinity, one was an unskilled laborer, two were foreign-born (Prussia and Ireland), and a couple were farmers from upstate New York and Connecticut. Only three men finished the race, and only Henry Stannard, a 165-pound Connecticut farmer, completed the distance in the required time, finishing in 59:48 minutes. Although Stevens had opened up the race to men of all nationalities and colors, he hoped that an American would win. Thus, Stannard's victory proved doubly rewarding, since the success of this native-born-and-bred farmer was for many confirmation of the superiority of the "true American way," rural living.[4]

The number of pedestrian contests markedly increased in the decade following the "Great Footrace" of 1835, by the mid-1840s emerging behind harness racing as the number two spectator sport in New York. The growing popularity of pedestrianism was linked to the decline of thoroughbred racing, which became unprofitable in the late 1830s (see chap. 2). Proprietors of racetracks, seeking financial alternatives, began sponsoring running contests. The Beacon Course in Hoboken, New Jersey, was the classic example of this shift. Having failed miserably as a thoroughbred track, the course became the scene of many pedestrian races until its demise in 1845.[5]

The willingness of entrepreneurs to sponsor such races does not automatically explain the growing interest in these athletic activities. Americans had long been intrigued by feats of skill and strength, and the more formal contests of the 1830s built on this existing interest by giving the sport greater publicity and providing greater opportunity for betting on the outcome. The popularity of pedestrianism in England and two modernizing elements — records and nationalism — further encouraged the sport's growth. While these variables acted independently they were interrelated in the sense that John Bull often served as the standard by which Americans measured their own sports achievements.[6] Precisely when men began timing running races is unknown, yet this procedure was an integral part of English running and walking contests by the start of the nineteenth century and probably earlier. A letter to a New York newspaper in 1821 indicates the stimulant of time in the growth of pedestrianism and its relationship to nationalistic feelings. The author noted that he had witnessed an Englishman run 10¼ miles in 58:23 minutes. He believed that American runners were equal, if not superior, to any on earth and hoped to see an American lop 23 seconds off this time. The requirement that Stevens's runners in the 1835 race go a shorter distance in more time indicates the absence of permanent records at this stage of the sport's development in America. After 1835, however, the public was made aware of the fastest times via the growing number of sports journals.[7]

Nationalism undoubtedly played a part in the growth of pedestrianism. Evident in the 1835 contest, it was instrumental in a series of important long-distance races held at the Beacon Course in 1844. The $1,000 in prize money attracted a large field of American runners to the first contest, again won by Stannard. Before the race the *Herald* noted that "nothing is talked of now, in the sport circle, but this race," and the *Spirit* predicted that "all the world and his wife will be assembled." The huge crowd, estimated at 30,000 spectators, was enough to convince the promoter to sponsor another contest. He again offered $1,000 in prize money and this time placed notices of the upcoming race in newspapers here and abroad to lure an international field. The race attracted thirty-seven entrants (only seventeen started), including three Englishmen, three Irishmen, and an American Indian, John Steeprock, of the Seneca tribe. Stannard was the runner to beat, which is exactly what John Gildersleeve, a New York chair builder, did. He overtook John Barlow and John Greenlaugh, both

Englishmen, on the tenth and final mile in a race one newspaper asserted was one of the greatest that ever took place in America or England.[8]

Newspaperman Nathaniel P. Willis, exploring the implications of the race and why it was the talk of the town even among New York's elite, noted that unlike horse racing, which at least had some *"submerged utility,"* there was "no utility in speed of foot, no dignity in it, and no improvement of the race." Although the novelty of the contest partially contributed to the enthusiasm, the tremendous interest *"arose from the accidental contact of several of the circumstances of the race with strong under-current of natural interest."* Elaborating on this theme he claimed, "It was a trial of the Indian against the white man, on the point in which the red man most boasts his superiority. It was the trial of the peculiar American *physique* against the long held supremacy of the English muscular endurance." The excitement derived from the fact that the white man beat the red man and the American defeated the Englishman.[9]

Two more races were held in 1844, with Englishmen prevailing on each occasion. Of the first of these contests the *Spirit* doubted "if so many spectators have ever been assembled on an American race course as was present on this occasion." In an extraordinary performance Barlow covered the ten miles in what was considered a world record time of 54:21 minutes. The other contest took place in mid-December, with inclement weather holding down both the number of competitors and the size of the crowd. The hardy spectators witnessed a classic confrontation as Greenlaugh and Gildersleeve battled neck and neck until the last few yards, when the Englishman pulled ahead to win the twelve-mile race.[10]

The tremendous excitement created by the Beacon Course contests spurred the rise of pedestrianism throughout the nation. During the next decade all kinds of pedestrian events were held, most of them between competitors but a few solely against time. On several occasions both elements were employed with extra money to be won if a runner completed a certain distance in a specific time. Endurance races remained the most popular, although sprints and hurdle races did take place. At times these contests took on a carnival atmosphere. For example, on one occasion a man was matched against a horse in a hurdle race. Besides running races, walking contests also occurred in New York City, although they were not as popular. The latter were solely endurance races, and distances of twenty miles or more were common.[11]

With the national growth of the sport, professional pedestrians began touring the country in search of financial rewards. Major races usually were run for $1,000, but the prize money was frequently divided, although unequally, among a certain number of finishers. Most contests were for less than $200, and sprints and dashes could earn the winner as little as $30. Besides races for prize money put up by promoters, professional runners also issued challenges in the leading sports journals. Match races generally went for $100–$500. As was the case in rowing, backers usually put up the money for these races and reaped most of the profits. It is difficult to say how much money professional runners earned. While the incomes of leading pedestrians probably exceeded the national norm, there is no evidence to support the conclusion of one scholar that these "were affluent men by contemporary standards, with annual incomes many times above the average."[12]

The limited biographical information on New York's professional runners suggests that they came from the manual classes, but how many were artisans or semiskilled and unskilled laborers cannot be determined. Very few of them, such as John Gildersleeve, toured the country; most confined their racing to the metropolitan area. For the latter group running served as a means of supplementing their regular incomes. Most of the professional runners in New York were from the lower-middle class, although members of respectable society also engaged in walking and running contests, even if they did not enter purse races.[13]

While the Beacon Course races of 1844 may have spurred the growth of pedestrianism they represented at the same time, paradoxically, the climax of professional pedestrianism in antebellum New York. The number of running and walking contests increased, but none attracted the interest or crowds of the 1844 races. These contradictory trends persisted until the mid-1850s when the popularity of the sport declined severely in New York.[14] Among other contributing factors, in early 1845 the Beacon Course proprietor, who was the major promoter of the sport, was forced to close the track. Other groups continued to sponsor races, but the prize money they offered was far less than what the Hoboken proprietor had put up. With the loss of this entrepreneur there was a sharp rise in match races and a corresponding decrease in purse races between 1845 and 1855. The shift reflected the economic weakness of pedestrianism since the promotion of the sport and the profits that derived from it now depended on those directly involved (runners and backers) rather than commercial interests (spectators).[15] Simultaneously, and quite possibly because of it, there was a decrease in the number of good runners, and the absence of native-born American runners with national reputations further reduced interest in long-distance running. The sport also suffered from charges of fixed races, its association with gambling, and certain carnival-like and dangerous contests.[16] Finally, the continued growth of harness racing, the revival of thoroughbred racing, and the surge of baseball also added to the decline of professional pedestrianism in New York just prior to the Civil War.

The rise of the Scottish Caledonian games in the mid-1850s corresponded with the decline of professional pedestrianism. The sponsors compensated the winners; hence, the games were considered professional affairs. The nature of the sport at that time and the organizational structure of the games radically differed from earlier pedestrianism. The Caledonian games, as Gerald Redmond accurately notes, had "an important influence in the early development of track and field in the United States." They marked the beginning of organized track and field in this country, nurtured interest in the sport, and influenced its development on both the collegiate and club level.[17]

The first reference to the traditional Scottish games being held in America dates back to 1836 when the Highland Society of New York met to "renew the Sport of their Native Land." Although other Scottish societies held games from time to time during the next decade and a half, the Highland games in America became identified mainly with the Caledonian clubs. In 1853 the first such club was organized in Boston, and three years later another was established in New York. During the next twenty-five years the number of Caledonian clubs increased until they and their games became a national institution. As early as 1867 Caledonian clubs in the United States and Canada held the first international games in New York, and three years later they established the North American Caledonian Association in an attempt to standardize the rules governing the games. The birth of what was the first international sporting organization indicated "the tremendous popularity of the Caledonian games in both countries and the financial benefits of consistent public patronage."[18]

The New York Caledonian Club was the wealthiest and probably the most influential Scottish society in America. Although the annual games were not its only concern, they became an ever-increasing source of publicity and a major source of revenue. Initially the admission fee was a quarter, but by the post–Civil War years the price had risen to fifty cents. Spectators came mainly from the city's Scottish community, although contingents from Scottish societies outside the metropolitan area were also represented. The large crowds that were attracted to these events would not have materialized except for the presence of a significant number of Americans and other non-Scottish foreigners.[19]

The Caledonian clubs represented a new form of sponsorship for commercialized spectator sports. Heretofore, such sports were universally promoted by entrepreneurs seeking personal profit, with the occasional exception of horse racing. The sponsorship of commercialized track and field meetings by these quasi-athletic clubs marked an important break with this policy, however. During the Civil War decade other athletic organizations, most notably baseball clubs, began to charge admission to their contests, and by the 1870s almost all athletic clubs with commercial potential had ventured into the business side of sport.[20]

The program of the New York Caledonian Club varied significantly from the pedestrianism with which Americans had become familiar. The major contribution of the Scots to American track and field was the emphasis they placed on the field events, such as putting the heavy stone and the long jump. Following the traditions of their native land Caledonian clubs offered prize money as an incentive to compete. While the amount was small at first, it increased markedly in the post–Civil War years as commercialism took hold of the games. Even in the later years, however, the winnings per event rarely exceeded $100 and certainly never approached the amounts earlier runners had won in major long-distance races. An athlete still could earn a tidy sum in a single day by winning several events, which often occurred because of their similarity. With the rising number of games, several participants were able to join the circuit, although from their inception the games in New York always attracted competitors from outside the metropolitan area. In 1869 the chieftain of the New York club recommended that it bring over Donald Dinnie, the champion athlete of Scotland, in the hopes that he would lure an even larger crowd. Dinnie first competed in New York in 1871, and during the remainder of the decade other Scottish athletes crossed the Atlantic as well.[21]

Naturally, the majority of the competitors at the New York games were Scottish, although participants of other nationalities and races were permitted, to varying degrees, to compete in the annual affair. Biographical information on the competitors is nonexistent, but it can be assumed that their social backgrounds differed from earlier runners in that the Scots were more likely to be drawn from the middle class. Although the Caledonian games in the post–Civil War years took on an increasingly professional dimension as they grew nationally and added to the prize money, the majority of the competitors used their winnings merely to supplement their regular incomes. Only a small number of star athletes made a considerable sum from a tour of the Caledonian games, and this probably did not occur until the 1870s.[22]

From its inception the New York Caledonian Club was praised by the sports and daily presses. Journalists felt that Americans should emulate these Scots since their activities promoted health and fostered patriotism. In 1858 *Porter's Spirit* clearly articulated this sentiment, maintaining that these manly pastimes "give not only health and vigor to the frame, but place a large share on contentment in the mind, and make men fond of the soil on which they are enjoyed." Such athletic activities "are wiser than statesmanship, and more wholesome to the heart than preachers' prayers." The press also took note of the club's meticulous organization, the perfect decorum that existed despite the huge crowds, and its concern for, and encouragement of, the physical training of youth.[23]

After the Civil War long-distance races among professionals reemerged as a spectator sport in New York City and other parts of the country, although these contests were mainly walking races. Edward P. Weston's walk in 1867 from Portland, Maine, to Chicago in twenty-six days, for which he won $10,000, was the major impetus to "pedestrian mania." A year later the *Clipper* noted an increase in the number of walking contests. However, the *Times* wondered why the public sustained Weston or "what particular gratification they derived from the spectacle of a usually unattractive-looking person in tights, doing in excess what each of them is in the habit of doing in moderation everyday of his life." It also rejected the argument that professional walking contests were "an incentive to physical culture," claiming that they were "an incentive to idle young men to get a shiftless living in a desultory way, and to be generally as useless as possible." Others disapproved of these contests because of the suspicion of a fix.[24]

The seeds for the destruction of professional pedestrianism had been sown prior to 1870 with the beginnings of amateur track and field on both the club and collegiate levels. Informal footraces had long taken place at American colleges, and the first formal intercollegiate track and field program was established at Columbia College in New York City. In 1868 George Rives, a Columbia graduate who was visiting England, was so impressed with the track meets held there that he penned an enthusiastic letter to friends back home advocating the formation of an athletic association. The result was the creation in 1869 of the Columbia College Athletic Association and the holding of the first intercollegiate track meet there in June of that year.[25]

The creation of the New York Athletic Club in 1868 was far more significant to the future of track and field. The brainchild of John C. Babcock, Henry Buermeyer, and William C. Curtis, the new club was influenced by English sports developments as well as the local Caledonian games. Modeled after the London Athletic Club, the New York Club actively sponsored several sports, rather than focusing on only one sport as earlier athletic clubs had done. From the outset, however, its major emphasis was track and field, although its influence on amateur athletics ranged far and wide.[26] *Wilkes' Spirit* asserted in the club's first year that although still in its infancy it showed "remarkable promise of becoming the leading institution of its kind in this country, and will, doubtlessly, in the course of time, fill the same position in this country occupied by the London Athletic Club in England." Another sports journal maintained that the recently organized club was already "making its influence felt in the community." While such praiseworthy statements proved accurate in the long run, the club was less successful than predicted in its first three years. The track and field meets it sponsored drew little public attention and small crowds. For example, the games of the New York Caledonian Club attracted crowds of 10,000 or more, compared to less than 2,000 spectators at New York Athletic Club meets. The increase in the athletic club's membership was the only bright spot, with over a hundred names on the roster by 1870.[27]

The social composition of the New York Athletic Club varied significantly from the clubs of Caledonian competitors and professional pedestrians. Athletic club members were mainly from respectable society, and some of them were descendants of leading New York families, such as the Roosevelts and DePeysters. It is highly unlikely, however, that the New York Athletic Club included the men of wealth who joined other elite sports organizations, such as the New York Yacht Club, the American Jockey Club, or the New York Racquet Club; rather, the majority of them, like their rowing counterparts, were from New York's upper-middle class.[28]

As opposed to professional rowing, which declined because of its inherent inability to emerge as a commercial endeavor, track and field had the potential to become commercialized; yet amateurism triumphed in that sport during the last decades of the nineteenth century. A major reason for this development was the absence of sufficient popular appeal to encourage entrepreneurs to promote professional pedestrians on a regular basis. The economic weakness of the sport was already evident during the antebellum period, at a time when runners and walkers faced fewer challenges from other spectator sports, and the ongoing reliance on match races indicates that the earlier problems persisted even in the post–Civil War period. While a spectacular performance, such as achieved by Stannard and Weston, produced a burst of interest, the absence of adequate commercialization made it difficult to nurture professional pedestrianism on a continuing basis and contributed to the cyclical character of the sport in the years prior to 1870.[29]

Amateur track and field made rapid advances against the backdrop of the economic weakness of commercialized-professional pedestrianism, prompted in part by the rising number of amateur clubs. By the end of the 1870s nearly a hundred athletic clubs existed in the New York metropolitan area, many of which sponsored their own track and field meets. These amateur contests never drew the vast crowds that were attracted to the Caledonian games, but they were under no economic pressure to do so since their expenses were far less. While amateur clubs were concerned with the business side of sport, their real motivation for sponsoring meets was prestige and power rather than profit—their goal was to break even, or at least not lose too much money. More numerous, better organized, and better financed than professional groups, these amateur clubs had another distinct advantage: by eliminating professionals from their meets, collectively they appealed solely to the athlete's reason for existence—his desire to compete and demonstrate his skills. With limited opportunity to compete elsewhere, trackmen easily came under the control of amateur clubs.[30]

BILLIARDS

Until the post–World War II years billiards in America consisted of two generally mutually exclusive styles: the first, associated with the upper class, was played mainly in their homes and in private clubs; the other, associated with the hoi polloi, was played in neighborhood poolhalls. The former predominated until the 1820s and quite possibly until 1840; but by the mid-nineteenth century the latter tradition set the tone and direction of the sport. Between 1850 and 1870 this shift coincided with the emergence of pool as a commercialized spectator sport dominated by a small group of professional players.[31]

Since the 1730s wealthy New Yorkers had engaged in billiards in the comfort of their homes. Public poolrooms, as adjuncts to taverns and roadside inns, also date back to the colonial period; however, poolhalls per se did not come into existence until the beginning of the nineteenth century. Charles Haswell recalled in 1896 that two such establishments existed in the city in 1816, but both appear to have been connected with other types of businesses. A small number of public billiard tables were set up in New York coffeehouses and hotels: in 1808 there were eight such tables, which one observer insisted was more than in any other American city; by 1824 between twelve and twenty-four tables were available to the public in New York.[32]

Between 1820 and 1850 billiards remained an informal recreation, although the emergence of leading, possibly professional, players during the 1820s indicated the beginning of more formal contests. During this period the press totally ignored the activities of these skilled performers, and the advertisements of billiard table manufacturers were the only references to the sport in either daily newspapers or sports journals.[33] The limited evidence available suggests that playing pool became more common in New York in the 1830s, but the information on the development of the sport in the subsequent decade appears conflicting. The *Clipper* later claimed that the popularity of billiards waned during the mid-1840s because "blacklegs and professional sharpers, those vampyres of the sporting world, had begun to frequent the public billiard rooms, and men of respectability and integrity were driven from it." Clearly, the sport came under increasing criticism as a result of its association with gambling. Nevertheless, there are reasons to assume that the number of public billiard halls did not decrease—in fact, it quite possibly increased—during these years.[34]

The presence of a gambling element and the moral indignation against the sport in the 1840s drove respectable New Yorkers out of the public poolhalls, although they did not curtail their gentlemanly participation in the sport. It was no coincidence that this trend away from public play corresponded with the rise of a new institution, the elite social club, where billiard tables were usually available to members. Further insulated from the masses, upper-class involvement subsequently had no influence on the development of the sport, with one notable exception: gentlemanly participation, even in private, provided an important ideological sanction, a point to be discussed later in greater detail.[35]

The atmosphere of public poolrooms also changed during the 1840s. Ned Polsky points out that from the beginning these places "were always associated with gambling and various forms of low life." While there is some merit to his thesis, it is nonetheless true that prior to the 1840s poolrooms did not carry their later social stigma. In general, the places gentlemen frequented to play pool were attached to respectable business establishments, such as hotels. What emerged during the 1840s was a different type of billiard parlor, where pool tables were the owner's major source of revenue. These places became overwhelmingly lower-middle-class institutions and served as the focal point for the development of the sport.[36]

Billiards made significant advances as both a competitive and recreational sport during the 1850s. Michael Phelan was the major figure behind the rising interest in billiards and from 1850 until his death in 1871 was the sport's dominant personality and promoter.[37] In 1850 Phelan was responsible for two significant developments. Through the *Spirit* he issued a challenge to the English billiard champion, John Roberts, to a home-and-home series for $500 per match. The challenge, which remained open for a year, went unanswered. Phelan was probably not disturbed by the course of events, for in proposing the contests he asserted that his desire was merely to prove that he was not only the best pool player in America but worldwide. He had agreed to forego financial gain, promising to give his winnings, above his expenses, to the treasury of the New York Fire Department,[38] a curiously noble action in view of the fact that he later engaged in money contests and kept the proceeds. Ever the promoter, his challenge to Roberts was a shrewd one, for he quite possibly recognized from the outset that the matches would not take place and he would be proclaimed America's foremost player without ever picking up a cue. As the owner of a billiard parlor he succeeded in arousing public interest in the sport—his challenge was the first reference to billiards (outside of advertisements) in the New York press. He also managed to call attention to himself and the fact that he was in the midst of writing a book on billiards.

The publication of Phelan's *Billiards Without Masters* marked the second major development in the sport in 1850. The first work of its kind in America, the book examined the history of the sport, explained the rules of the various billiard games, provided instruction and diagrams on how to play them, and supplied the usual homilies on the moral and social benefits of the sport. In reviewing the book the *Spirit* claimed that "it was unquestionably the best and most complete work of its kind ever published." Relatively expensive at three dollars, the book nonetheless went through ten editions during the next quarter-century, illustrating its enduring popularity and the interest of the "better class" in the sport.[39] Phelan left New York for the gold fields of California around 1851 or 1852, returning to the city in 1854 or 1855. He soon began manufacturing billiard tables, entering into a partnership with Hugh Collender. In 1856 he published the *Billiard Cue,* the first billiard periodical. A four-page monthly, the publication went out of print in 1874. There do not appear to be any copies still in existence.[40]

In 1855 Phelan and his partner proposed a grand billiard tournament if eight or ten leading players could be assembled, another case of an unanswered challenge that did more to promote business than determine skill. In 1858 Phelan defeated Ralph Benjamin of Philadelphia for $1,000 in the first recorded billiard match in America. And his contest with John Seeriter of Detroit the following year evoked considerable interest in, and discussion about, the sport, probably for the first time. Even the *Times,* which heretofore had virtually ignored billiards, noted the tremendous public excitement and devoted several columns to the match, which Phelan won. Originally scheduled for $5,000, the purse was later raised to $15,000 per man, and admission was charged for the first time. All 500 seats in Detroit's Fireman Hall were filled, and it was reported that more tickets could have been sold if there had been additional space.[41]

With Phelan's title as America's billiard champion firmly established, reports of an upcoming confrontation with Roberts began to circulate in the sports journals. These proved to be nothing but rumors.[42] The arrival of Monsieur Berger, reputed to be the French champion, the following year caused a sensation in New York sports circles. *Wilkes' Spirit* noted that the "desire to witness his extraordinary performances, had brought a large number of billiards celebrities to this neighborhood." Phelan took advantage of the unique situation by promoting a week-long round-robin tournament among the leading players. In early 1861 the *Clipper* wrote that billiards "had been the subject of much attention during the past few months" and the arrival of Berger, coupled with Phelan's tournament, gave "an impetus to the game, and popularized it to an extent hitherto unknown."[43]

The increasing number of professional contests revealed one side of the sport's growth; the rise in the number of billiard manufacturers and public poolrooms revealed another. By 1858 at least four firms were producing billiard tables in New York and the rivalry was often bitter. In a letter to the *Clipper* one manufacturer took exception to Phelan's recent involvement in the business, conceding that he himself was not a "crack player" but instead had devoted his entire life to his trade and no other. While hard data are not available, most observers believed that, for better or worse, the number of poolrooms increased annually in New York City. In 1861 the *Clipper* stated that "where billiard tables, billiard rooms and billiard players were a few years since numbered by the tens, they may now be counted by hundreds."[44]

Several factors contributed to the rise of billiards in the mid-nineteenth century. In addition to the forces that stimulated the growth of sport in general, pool emerged as a popular pastime at the same time that bowling was declining in popularity. In 1869 Dudley Kavanaugh, a professional pool player and billiard manufacturer, claimed that during the previous decade the appeal of tenpins had "yielded to the superior attraction of billiards." His economic interest may have clouded his perspective, although two other observers also suggested that the greater skill required in billiards contributed to the respective fates of the two sports. These statements are credible but they run counter to our general knowledge of the relationship between skill level and participation in a recreational activity.[45] While there is no confirming evidence, billiards quite possibly was a less expensive sport than bowling. In addition, the upper-class tradition in billiards, which was absent in bowling, may have made the former more appealing to the masses.

Ned Polsky has already demonstrated that the popularity of pool and poolhalls was intimately tied to a "bachelor subculture," which was linked to various institutions ranging from fraternal organizations and middle- and upper-middle-class men's clubs to boardinghouses and hobo life. These urban residents regularly visited prostitutes and sustained all-male gathering places such as gambling parlors and saloons. They cultivated a variety of sports while playing an important, although less critical, role in the development of others. Of the numerous refuges from women, Polsky insists, the poolroom "was not just one of these places: it was *the* one, the keystone."[46] His thesis is convincing, but it requires certain minor modifications as an explanation for the initial surge of billiards, since this development occurred prior to the rise of the bachelor subculture. What Polsky does not recognize is that the creation of a bachelor subculture in the last quarter of the nineteenth century was itself part of a broader change in male-female relations.[47]

The profound impact of the changing nineteenth-century economy on masculine values and masculine institutions played a paramount role in the growth of billiards. Several scholars have shown recently that industrialization altered masculine values and "heightened the importance of defining the criteria of manhood and of fulfilling those criteria." While the masculine response to this change depended on social class, there emerged among working-class youth in particular a vigorous subculture designed to prove masculinity through fighting, wenching, and sometimes drinking. In addition, the shifting modes of production created a division of leisure that was based increasingly on sex.[48] The all-male recreational pattern, although present among all classes, emerged initially and was most firmly entrenched within the life-style of the working class.

Cultural influences alone do not explain why pool and the poolhall became such an important part of the lower-middle-class masculine subculture. The inexpensive and individualistic nature of billiards provided an advantage over some sports, but it was not the only one to possess these characteristics. The historical association of billiards with the tavern and with lowlifes played a part, but even more important was the atmosphere of the poolhall: secluded, open day and night, in use all year long, and in virtually all neighborhoods. The poolhall was unmatched by any other sports facility, with the exception of the gymnasium and the bowling alley. However, the gym could be eliminated as a serious competitor because of the unpopularity of the activities that took place there, because it catered to the middle class and to ethnic groups, and because its members were required to pay an annual subscription fee. The bowling alley, even when the sport was popular, never seemed to better the poolhall as a place to hang out.

Since colonial days moralists had attacked billiards because they associated the sport with gambling and idleness. However, as long as the game remained essentially the prerogative of the wealthy it was an acceptable diversion. Criticism of billiards did not intensify until its public form became popular among the masses. The president of the New York Society for the Suppression of Gambling claimed that fewer games are of "a more deceptive character than billiards." Its perception "as an elegant and innocent amusement, in which even persons of the most respectable character can indulge in without damage to their reputations made the sport particularly dangerous." This pretense of fashion made "verdant youth" susceptible to the "nefarious swindles of the professed gamblers."[49]

While gambling remained the essential reason for objections to billiards a more subtle factor entered into the debate. At a time when new social forces were creating all-male institutions, the view of women as refining and civilizing agents of society was also taking hold. Thus, it is not surprising that throughout the nineteenth century sports promoters actively encouraged the presence of women at their athletic events as a means of tempering the crowd and providing middle-class respectability.[50] Furthermore, moral and social reformers believed that since they and people like them, obviously meaning the middle class, had provided their children and society with the proper principles of morality and discipline, their all-masculine institutions would not create deviant behavior or threaten home and family. The lower class was a different story, however. They did not possess the proper characteristics of control, so moralists viewed their masculine hangouts, whether taverns or billiard parlors, as evil, not just because of the activity that occurred there but because such places were perceived as breeding grounds for other and more serious social ills.

Supporters of billiards responded to such criticism by drawing on the sport's upper-class tradition and ignoring the issue of the public poolhall as a den of iniquity. Billiard promoters frequently pointed to the famous men who played the game in a never-ending search for respectability. The *Herald* noted that even clergymen, such as Henry Ward Beecher, participated in the sport and attended billiard matches. Proponents also sought to downplay the association of the sport with gambling. When two professional players donated the gate receipts from their match to charity, *Wilkes' Spirit* happily noted that "billiards does not in America, as in other countries, lead to the practice of gambling among its votaries, but on the contrary, when any great match among its professors take place, the cause of charity is served." Others conceded that gambling on billiard games took place, but they justified the practice on the grounds that wagering was not an inherent part of billiards and therefore did not detract from its value. Dudley Kavanaugh pointed out the divergent view of baseball's versus billiards' association with gambling and wondered why betting tarnished one and not the other.[51]

Besides refuting the negative, devotees of billiards emphasized the positive contributions of the sport. The *Clipper* maintained that no other game was "so well adapted to the needs of dwellers in the cities as that of billiards." *Wilkes' Spirit* voiced a similar theme, noting that "billiards is a mathematical game, and affords scope and exercise for those faculties which discipline and strengthen the mind. A steady hand, a clear head, quick perception and a pleasurable exercise of the calculation powers are the requisite of an accomplished billiard-player." While promoters and sports journals were the major proponents of the positive value of billiards, some daily newspapers also encouraged the sport. The *Herald* insisted that billiards was "well worth introducing into the household" and that it was particularly well suited for women since it forced them to walk, use their arms, and expand their chest. It was "much better for ladies and gentlemen to sit together in a game of 'pool' after dinner, than for gentlemen to sit discussing politics in the dining room, while the ladies are left to amuse themselves in the drawingroom." Finally, all billiard supporters insisted that a major benefit of the sport was that it could be played during all seasons, as well as at night. The *Clipper* called billiards the best winter amusement.[52]

Billiards made significant advances as both a recreational and competitive sport during the 1860s. Unlike many other sports it did not suffer during the Civil War years, thanks to the individualistic nature of participation, the inexpensiveness, and the fact that it could be played at any time or in any season. Hard data on the rise of billiards are not available, but reports from contemporary observers are clear with regard to this development. In 1861 the *Clipper* claimed that billiards "has attained a degree of popularity in this country that is truly marvelous." Four years later the *Times* wrote that the game "was never in a more prosperous condition than at the present time, and it is really becoming a most popular amusement." By the end of the decade the *Herald* insisted that the "popularity which the game of billiards has already attained in this city is largely on the increase. Unquestionably it stands number one as a scientific and recreative amusement."[53]

The low cost of playing pool was a major factor in its widespread popularity and contributed to the easy access almost all social classes had to the game. Prior to the Civil War New Yorkers were charged an average of twenty-five cents per game; after the war proprietors began charging sixty cents per hour to prevent customers from playing "short" (i.e., intentionally delaying the end of the game). The hourly rate was hardly universal, however, and as late as the end of the 1860s some poolhall owners still charged as little as ten cents per game.[54]

The comfortable living that proprietors of billiard parlors reportedly earned also suggests the popularity of this recreational activity. First-class establishments were especially rewarding, and *Wilkes' Spirit* claimed that half a dozen poolrooms in New York City cleared $10,000–$15,000 annually. In 1862 Michael Phelan asserted that the capital investment in billiards was $2 million; four years later it was reported that 12,000 people nationwide supposedly earned their livelihood from pool. Recognizing that these figures were probably inflated, they nonetheless point to the prosperity of billiards.[55]

The growth of billiards as a professional-commercial spectator sport corresponded with an increase in recreational participation. In 1862 *Wilkes' Spirit* maintained that the tremendous excitement generated by the activities of professional players settled "any lingering doubts about the great popularity of the game of billiards among our people." Michael Phelan's retirement from active competition in 1863 sparked further interest in the sport and even more contests. The *Clipper* claimed that the tournament held to establish a new champion, won by Dudley Kavanaugh, "was the most important that has ever taken place in connection with this scientific game."[56]

Problems associated with professional billiards soon surfaced, with Phelan at the center of the controversy. Although his playing days had ended he remained the sport's leading figure both in New York and nationally. By 1865 several sports journals and players accused him of heading a clique which sought to dominate professional pool. In March of that year Kavanaugh, still the American champion, sharply criticized Phelan for monopolizing the sport. Three months later he was forced to forfeit his champion cue, although it is not perfectly clear what the grounds for forfeiture were. In September Phelan was the prime mover behind the formation of the American Billiard Players Association, open to professional players, poolroom proprietors, and skilled amateurs. The association's stated objectives were the "supervision of the interest of billiards, the encouragement and advancement of players, and the general welfare of the billiard profession at large," which was Phelan's way of solidifying his position in the face of mounting criticism. One sports journal charged that the group had been formed with the interests of certain manufacturers, not the players, in mind. Anti-Phelan forces established their own group, the National American Billiards Association, a year later, electing Kavanaugh their president and promising to revise the rules of the game and regulate competition in an open and free manner.[57]

Although championship contests on a state and national level took place with increased frequency in the years immediately following the Civil War, the controversy between the Phelan- and Kavanaugh-led groups quieted down until 1870. Then *Wilkes' Spirit* led a savage attack against Phelan, charging that he sought to dominate the sport, control all the professional players, dictate the winners of all matches, and claim the right to manufacture and sell all the billiard tables used in America. The journal further asserted that Phelan had collected a ring of leading players "between whom he fostered matches, and by whose assistance he constructed tournaments in his name, putting up, for the most part, paltry ornaments as prizes." Phelan also supposedly cheated players out of their winnings: on one occasion a tournament winner was to earn roughly $1,250 but eventually received only $364 after expenses were deducted. Finally, *Wilkes' Spirit* maintained that Phelan encouraged a luxurious life-style among professionals in order to keep his minions in bondage.[58] The exposé naturally won the support of the anti-Phelan faction, but since the issue was otherwise ignored the accuracy of the charges is open to speculation. While *Wilkes' Spirit* probably overstated certain points there appears to be little doubt that at times Phelan used his influence and well-established reputation to serve his own financial interests.

Despite the Phelan controversy billiards was comparatively free of the criticism that accompanied the professionalization of other sports. For example, the press usually reported that crowds at the leading matches were respectable and orderly. Although participation was widely based, spectators were mostly white-collar workers since an admission fee of at least $1.00, sometimes more, was charged. When ruffians attended one contest *Wilkes' Spirit* recommended that the price be raised to $2.50 and possibly $5.00 to ensure that such groups would be excluded. Charges of fixed contests also were rarely heard. Almost on principle the *Times* disapproved of professional billiards, but it admitted that, like baseball, billiards was in its proper sphere an enjoyable recreation; however, "converted into a trade it fosters idleness and ultimately depravity." The more democratic newspapers offered no criticism of the players or, like the *Clipper*, noted that they were generally honorable men.[59]

While billiards grew nationally during the 1860s New York remained the sport's capital. Many of the major matches and tournaments were held there despite the charge that the city lacked good playing facilities, and thirteen of the twenty-seven leading professional players resided at one time or another in New York (although Maurice Daly is the only known player to have been born there). Of the migrants to the city half came prior to 1860, arriving with their families while still quite young; others moved there in the 1860s to open, or more likely be employed in, billiard parlors. The late arrivals generally stayed only briefly in New York before moving on to other cities where they engaged in the same line of work.[60]

Wilkes' Spirit insisted that the large majority of the leading billiard players were of "Hibernian extraction." Phelan and Kavanaugh, the two dominant figures, were Irish by birth, but only two other players (of the twenty-three whose birthplaces could be ascertained) were from Ireland; of the remaining nineteen, eight were American-born, six were either French or French-Canadian, four were born in Germany, and one in England. Kavanaugh's nephew, Maurice Daly, was born in America but of Irish descent. The ethnic backgrounds of other players are unknown, although their names are as much English or German as Irish.[61] In spite of differences in players' nationalities, their class backgrounds were probably very similar. Of five players for whom biographical data are available, four had fathers or close relatives in the billiard business. It would not be surprising if this pattern held true for most skilled players. Both Kavanaugh, in 1869, and Polsky, in 1969, noted that the overwhelming majority of professional players of their respective eras were playing pool regularly by at least their early teens. Polsky further points out that many of the more recent great players, including Willie Hoppe and Willie Mosconi, were the sons of poolroom owners. If this was true for the earlier period, then it may be suggested that the majority of billiard players during the 1860s came from lower-middle- to middle-class backgrounds.[62]

The income of a professional player during the 1860s was comparable to that from most middle-class occupations. Many older players whose active careers ended in the 1860s already were involved in a billiard-related business, either as poolhall owners or billiard manufacturers, prior to the first decade of professional billiards. For this group, their business, not the money won in competition, was their major source of income, providing them, by all accounts, a comfortable, although not opulent, life-style. Younger players derived their income from two sources: as a supervisor or "house pro" for a certain billiard parlor—although how widespread this practice was is unknown—and via contest money. In 1866 Melvin Foster received $2,000 for supervising Kavanaugh Hall, an amount that was, according to one sports journal, about twice the going rate for this type of job. The amount earned in a contest depended on who won, and professional players in most cases had backers who put up the money in match contests and reaped most of the profits. Discrepancies between the amounts reportedly won in tournaments and the amounts actually received make it difficult to calculate the annual earnings of these professionals, but $1,500–$2,500 per year would probably be a reasonable figure.[63]

Despite this commercial-professional growth and the creation of two national billiard organizations, as late as 1870 the rules of the sport remained "an unknown quantity, varying at the caprice of irresponsible and interested parties." The various games that could be played on a billiard table further complicated the codification of rules. (Interestingly and uncharacteristically, *Wilkes' Spirit* believed that the French version was superior to the American since it required more skill.[64]) Clearly, the sport was still in a transitional stage between premodern and modern by 1870, as evidenced by the lack of standardized rules but the presence of national organizations, national champions, and coverage in national sports journals. These latter modern elements did not yet exist at a sophisticated enough level, however. The national organizations were weak in the sense that the development of the sport was more a result of Michael Phelan's personal power and influence than an effective central administration. When one considers that by 1870 professional-commercial billiards was only a decade old, that it had been marred by personal and financial squabbles, and that the sport faced middle-class disapproval, it is somewhat amazing that it had progressed so far as both a competitive and recreational sport. The foundation for the tremendous growth of billiards during the last three decades of the nineteenth century was clearly in place.[65]

BOXING

Boxing matches which occurred during the colonial period were generally of the rough-and-tumble sort and were not governed by anything approaching stringent rules. During the Jacob Hyer–Tom Beasley fight in 1816, recognized as the first American boxing match, "some attempt at uniform observance of rules were kept in view"; hence the significance of the contest in the history of American boxing.[66] Over the next fifty-five years the sport grew significantly in New York City and throughout America, mainly in two waves: slow but steady gains until the early 1840s, and rapid advances after 1850 as the number of contests and combatants markedly increased. Various social, economic, and communications changes that stimulated the development of other sports were also at work here, as was the fact that boxing was an urban product and New York was the sport's capital. In addition, massive immigration and the beginning of the modern political system influenced the rise of pugilism. By 1870 prizefighters emerged as leading sports figures despite public criticism and various legal attempts to prohibit the sport altogether.

During the 1820s boxing was linked to the emergence of the gymnasium movement. One of several skills taught in the gym, boxing was proclaimed the "manly art of self defense," a frequently echoed justification for teaching young men to fight. At least one proprietor claimed that "sparring with gloves is an athletic amusement, and not withstanding the hue and cry that has often been raised against it," there is "no reason why the Gymnasium should be discouraged because some of its members may choose to include this among their exercise."[67] Gentlemanly sparring declined during the 1830s, however, as the popularity of the gym waned and boxing came under increasing criticism. A small number of respectable New Yorkers continued to spar, but as with billiards this had almost nothing to do with the essential development of the sport except that it provided supporters with an important justification for boxing and a key to the never-ending search for respectability.

Several prizefights, each marked by an increasing regard for rules, characterized boxing in the 1820s. The press ignored local bouts, however, and when they discussed the sport at all it was always in negative terms. In 1824 one writer noted in the *Spectator* that he had accidently witnessed a boxing match and judged it a brutal affair, rife with foul play. He advocated that measures be taken to stop prizefighting. A letter to the *Post* two years later expressed a similar opposition to boxing: "Such practices are brutal and detestable in themselves and disgraceful to the country in which they are suffered to take place. What is called by its advocates the science of defense, is only the commission, always of horrible violence, and sometimes murder."[68]

During the 1830s prizefighting in New York increased despite constant criticism. Although the number of contests never exceeded more than three annually, by 1835 the *Mirror* was warning that "the detestable practice of prize fighting" threatened to take root in America. The *Herald* expressed the opinion that prizefighting was "not without merit" and "in some degree tends to benefit the community at large." While possessing certain demoralizing tendencies the sport also elicited "a feeling of courage—of proud manly self-dependence" and was "far preferable to the insidious knife . . . , or the cowardly and brutal practice of biting, kicking or gouging, now so prevalent."[69] The number of boxing contests and exhibitions rose further still in the early 1840s. Tom Hyer, Jacob's son, defeated Country McCleester in 1841 to become the first recognized heavyweight champion of America, and by the summer of 1842 the "rage for prize fighting" had reached new heights—"scarcely a week passed that there was not a grand set-to at some public house about town, at which hundreds were in attendance, giving their countenance and support." Then tragedy struck in September when Thomas McCoy became America's first boxing fatality in a fight in nearby Westchester County.[70]

The light heavyweight battle between McCoy and Christopher Lilly evolved from a personal quarrel, as so many fights of this period did. Each man represented a different New York boxing faction, and the fight took on nationalistic overtones as well (McCoy was Irish and Lilly was British). The contest lasted 120 rounds, slightly more than two hours and forty minutes. McCoy, who was obviously no match for Lilly, was urged to leave the ring as early as the 60th round, but he reportedly had committed himself to win or die. By the 86th round both of McCoy's eyes were swollen shut. In the 120th round he died after receiving eighty-one heavy blows.[71]

To the opponents of boxing McCoy's death was not an unfortunate accident but the logical extension of the sport's brutality and a reflection of the kind of people involved and the overall environment in which fighting occurred. The *Tribune,* a leading critic, noted that McCoy and Lilly met in a grogshop "where pugilism is the stable of excitement and . . . the promoters of the sport are gamblers, brothelkeepers and saloonkeepers." It found comfort only in the fact that boxing's promoters and participants were almost entirely foreigners and that the American environment itself was not congenial to the growth of the sport.[72] Now, in the aftermath of the Lilly-McCoy fight, the rest of the press and many New Yorkers joined the *Tribune* in condemning boxing. Over the next several years a few second-rate matches took place, but pugilism virtually disappeared from the New York sports scene until Tom Hyer and James "Yankee" Sullivan met for the heavyweight championship in 1849. The first of four heavyweight championship fights between 1849 and 1860, these battles indicated the revived interest in boxing as well as the changing character and setting of the sport.[73]

The Hyer-Sullivan battle had been brewing since Sullivan's arrival in New York City a decade earlier. In fact, several newspapers insisted that the increasing pugilistic activity of the early 1840s was directly linked to his presence in New York. Arrested as a result of his part in the Lilly-McCoy fight, Sullivan promised never to fight again, but in 1847 he returned to the ring to defeat Robert Caunt at Harper's Ferry for $1,000. While Hyer had not fought since 1841 he remained in the minds of many the best fighter in America. In early 1848 the two met in a saloon, drank too much, and got into a scuffle, all of which led to a proposed match for $5,000 per man.[74] The upcoming fight became the talk of the town for nearly six months, with heavy betting on both sides. Large throngs, including many respectable gentlemen, paid fifty cents each to witness the prefight sparring exhibitions of each of the combatants. The actual contest, held in February 1849 near Baltimore, was "a hurricane fight." Hyer won in only sixteen rounds (seventeen minutes and eighteen seconds) when Sullivan failed to answer the bell. *American Fistiana* noted that "never had the American ring shown so much fighting in so little time."[75]

The personal nature of the feud, the large amount of money staked and wagered, and the reputations of the fighters all contributed to the tremendous interest in the Hyer-Sullivan bout. Foreshadowing great battles of the future, the excitement this prizefight generated was in part due to a perception of the combatants as symbols of certain social groups. The *Herald* noted that Sullivan "had been the chief and champion of a class of society comprised of persons similar in every respect to himself—not refined." By contrast, Hyer was "the pet of fashionable society in this city . . . and in appearance and symmetry of person, almost equals the statue of Apollo." While certain class differences existed between Hyer's and Sullivan's fans, partisanship was not divided mainly along economic lines. Instead, the fighters' nationalities were the symbolic key: Sullivan, the representative of Irish immigrants, and Hyer, the native New Yorker and "Great American Hope," made the contest not just a prizefight but an extension of the growing tension between these two groups.[76]

In the late 1850s *Porter's Spirit* asserted that the Hyer-Sullivan match marked "the actual rise of pugilism in America, into anything like importance." Before this battle fights were few and far between; now they were innumerable, and by the eve of the Civil War one newspaper noted that four sparring matches took place in New York each week. The gradual shift of the boxing arena from taverns to theaters, to accommodate more fans, further indicated the rising spectator appeal of the sport during the 1850s. Since the admission fee to these exhibitions ranged from fifty cents to a dollar, boxing's spectators did not come from the economically deprived class but mainly from the bachelor subculture discussed earlier. Although many of these Runyonesque characters were of lower-class origin, they had money in their pockets, even if it often burned a hole there.[77]

Of all the boxing matches that took place, heavyweight championship fights generated the most excitment and attracted the largest number of spectators, even though they were held far away from population centers to avoid police interference. The title bout between Sullivan and John Morrissey in 1853 "made as much town talk as if it were some great achievement of science or wonderful exhibition of strategic skill on the battlefield." The fight between the two Irishmen had an interesting twist to it which added to the general appeal: since Morrissey had become Hyer's rival, Sullivan was seen as the bearer of American pride in a "comical juxtaposition of . . . the usual lines of popular partisanship." The stakes were $1,000 per man and the match attracted an estimated 2,000–6,000 spectators to the New York–Massachusetts border. Morrissey won the fight in the thirty-seventh round when Sullivan was disqualified on a foul.[78] When Morrissey fought James Camel Heenan in 1858 for $2,500 per man, the contest was "looked upon with the keenness of interest" in every city throughout the nation. *Porter's Spirit* pointed out that "not only are the usual sporting circles much excited about the issue, but the interest is rapidly pervading classes of society which are in the habit of viewing ordinary contests with indifference, if not distaste." More money supposedly was wagered than on any previous boxing match, and the *Times* claimed that every major sports figure attended the battle. In eleven rounds, lasting just twenty-one mintues, Morrissey easily whipped the challenger, whereupon he retired and the "Benica Boy," as Heenan was called, assumed the championship.[79]

The surge of boxing at the end of the antebellum period reached a roaring, dramatic climax in 1860 with the first international heavyweight championship fight. Heenan's confrontation with Tom Sayers, England's titleholder, for $1,000 and the championship belt, drew more public comment than any other single sports event between 1820 and 1870. *Wilkes' Spirit* and Frank Leslie's *Illustrated News* sent reporters to England to cover the fight, while the *Times* and *Herald* received regular reports from their English correspondents. The *Times* noted that "all classes of people seem to share this anxiety to hear the results — not all in the same degree or the same extent, but with the masses of the people it is just now the great topic of speculation of interest — eclipsing the Charleston Convention and throwing completely into shade all political themes, and everything else which can afford to wait." While this development was "not very creditable to our tastes or culture," the paper felt that it was due in part "to the fact that we are a very excitable people — always craving a sensation of some sort — and partly to the equally palpable and still important fact that Muscle is King."[80]

The nationalistic overtones surrounding the contest were the major stimulant for this great concern over the outcome. "The ordinary objections to vulgar pugilism are waived in the real importance of this first-class struggle," *Wilkes' Spirit* wrote, "and there is scarcely a mind that is amenable to the influence of national pride, which does not once lay aside its prejudice against fighting, in the hope to see the American champion win." The reason for this attitude, it continued, stemmed from the longstanding British assumption that physical vigor had deteriorated on this continent. An American victory would therefore testify to the nation's physical superiority. The *Herald* poked fun at such sentiment: "In the language of the bruisers' and dog beaters' organization, this fight will settle the question of national superiority between England and the United States. If Heenan whips Sayers then the commercial importance of the United States is greater than that of England, then the British government is humbug, and our Congress are the only palledum of popular liberty." While this rebuttal illustrates the ludicrous association of sports supremacy with a certain superior national character, the theme has been a pervasive one for modern sport and lends itself readily to boxing because of its highly combative nature. Not until the Joe Louis–Max Schmeling fight in the 1930s was any boxing match, or quite possibly any international sports contest in which an American was involved, so highly charged with nationalistic sentiments.[81]

The fight pitted Heenan's youth and his height and weight advantage against Sayers's experience and savvy. The American broke Sayers's arm early in the fight while the Englishman cut one of Heenan's eyes, yet both fighters continued gamely until the thirty-seventh round when the ropes were mysteriously cut and the police rushed in to break up the fight. Who was winning at the time depended on which side of the Atlantic you lived on. English journalists believed that Sayers would have eventually won; American reporters were even more adamant that Heenan was on the verge of victory. The *Times* correspondent reported that an Englishman had told him before the fight that there was "too much money bet at odds in favor of Sayers for Heenan to be permitted to gain the contest." Other New York newspapers were unanimous in their belief that a conspiracy had deprived Heenan of the victory even as they overlooked the financial consequences of the fight. *Wilkes' Spirit* dramatically placed full responsibility for the debacle squarely on the doorstep of the British government, since it was "thoroughly alive to the great political injury it might work to English prestige, should the people of the Continent, over whose race she has always domineered in physical comparison, should behold some stranger from beyond the seas bear off the emblem of her superiority in prowess." The *Times,* while not as passionate, echoed a similar theme: "England has lost so much prestige in great matters during the last few years, that the trivial circumstances of an English boxer found physically inferior to an American had evidently assumed in English eyes an importance ludicrously disproportionate to its real significance. . . . They have been worsened by sea and land in so many diverse ways and sundry manners that they cling with desperation to the ropes of the Prize Ring."[82]

The fight was declared a draw and each fighter was awarded a championship belt. Then Sayers retired and Heenan emerged as the heavyweight champion, an inadequate solution for most Americans. With nationalism running high only a firm English acceptance of Heenan's victory would suffice. Amid increasing anti-English sentiments on other fronts, Americans seemed to feel that the fight reflected the true English character, that the English applied their oft-stated belief in fair play only to themselves. The *Eagle* picked up the theme and paralleled the conspiracy against Heenan to the "foul play" of British foreign policy. Although the controversy gradually subsided the issue was often revived on the pages of *Wilkes' Spirit,* which for the next decade repeatedly pointed to the outcome of this fight as an indication of the "true" English character.[83]

Ever since the days of Tom Hyer pugilists had been popular sports figures, and the reception New Yorkers gave Heenan on his return to the city did not prove otherwise. An estimated crowd of 50,000 turned out to honor Heenan, much to the dismay of the *Herald,* which complained that the reception was a "glorification of brutality and vice and its exaltation over the noblest sentiments of the human heart." The presence of the sports fraternity was understood, but participation by city officials and other politicians was unwarranted, according to the paper—which nonetheless devoted four columns on the front page to the occasion.[84]

Just as changing urban forces stimulated the rise of boxing in the two decades prior to the Civil War, so did immigration and politics. At first the press generally insisted that neither boxers nor their sport were indigenous to America. In 1837 the *Herald* claimed that it was erroneous to suggest that the sport was confined solely to foreigners, but twenty years later *Porter's Spirit* still asserted that the majority of professional boxers in America were of European descent. An examination of the nationalities of thirty-two New York boxers between 1840 and 1860 confirms the latter thesis: twenty-four of these men were Irish (56.3 percent) or English (18.8 percent) by birth; five of the eight Americans were sons of immigrants, and another was black. The Irish clearly dominated New York boxing, with 71.9 percent of the boxers having at least one Irish parent.[85]

The nationalities of New York boxers and the data on their occupations between 1840 and 1860, while limited, indicate that they came from the lower and lower-middle classes.[86] The general absence of American-born fighters, as *Porter's Spirit* recognized, stemmed from their ability to find "more profitable ways of using their physical advantages, than standing up to be knocked about a twenty-four foot ring for a few scores of dollars." While money lured lower-class youth to boxing, ethnic, personal, and political animosities also played a part in bringing fighters into the ring. Moreover, most boxers did not as yet perceive the sport as a career. Even the leading fighters rarely entered the ring more than five times in a lifetime, excluding sparring exhibitions, but when they did fight they could earn in one contest, if they won, as much as a skilled craftsman made in a year or more.[87] Although boxing has traditionally provided lower-class youth with a means of escaping the ghetto, it has long been noted that at best the sport serves as a temporary source of mobility, even among those who fight for large purses. Despite limited data this appears to have been the case in the two decades preceding the Civil War. The *Clipper* clearly felt that most boxers wound up poor, although exceptions did exist.[88]

Historians have paid almost no attention to the relationship between the emergence of mass politics and the growth of boxing,[89] a connection that was not lost on early observers of the sport. In 1842 the *Tribune* insisted that our citizens should "ascertain what terms of mutual consideration and service exists between the most lawless and dangerous combination of our city on the one hand, and our highest Executive authority." At times the press went so far as to claim that the prizefighters in this country would be "its governing class in due course of time, if they are not so already." The *Clipper* denied this, noting that fighters "have been used and abused by politicians as the occasion demanded." While both statements are exaggerations, they reflect what was the accepted relationship between boxing and politics, a connection that played a subtle, but definite, part in the opposition of the press to the sport during these years.[90]

The link between pugilists and politicians grew out of the New York gangs that were spawned in the second quarter of the nineteenth century amid the dismal tenements of a growing immigrant community, although they also existed in other sections of the city. Many of the same social forces that produced these urban gangs also changed the very nature of New York politics. By the early 1820s Tammany Hall was the vanguard of increased democratization in the political process and the development of the modern party system. In the next decade Tammany Hall politicians began to actively seek the immigrant vote, just as they began to see "the practical value of the [gang member], and to realize the advisability of providing them meeting and hiding places, that their favors might be curried and their peculiar talents employed on election day to assure government of, by, and for Tammany." Capt. Isaiah Rynders, the Tammany boss of the Sixth Ward and a leading sports figure, was the first to organize the gang chieftains. His powerful Empire Club, established in 1843, was the center of political activity in his ward as well as "the clearing house of all [gang] activities which had to do with politics." By 1855 an estimated 30,000 men owed their allegiance to the gang leaders. And while these political "repeaters" and performers of other political services were tied mainly to Tammany Hall, other factions of the Democratic party, the Know-Nothing (or Nativist) party, and even to some extent the Whig and Republican parties, all had their "shoulder hitters."[91]

Almost all of the leading boxers and probably quite a few other sporting figures were aligned with one or another of these quasi-political gangs. For example, John Morrissey and Country McCleester were members of Rynders's Empire Club; the Bowery Boys' Tom Hyer and Bill Harrington, a leader in New York sports, were connected with the Nativist party. Many prizefights actually originated in and took their symbolic importance from these political and ethnic differences. Even more importantly the new political system gave aid and comfort to the environment that nurtured the pugilist, making politicians and elected officials indirect patrons of the sport. These men either owned or had a strong influence on the owners of the boxers' hangouts, and they provided young fighters with jobs when they were not in the ring. Some of Rynders's men, such as Morrissey (during his early years in New York), were emigrant runners; others worked in saloons, either as taverners or bouncers; and some were given patronage jobs, such as Dan Kerrigan, who was a policeman on New York's docks.[92]

By and large these fighters were heroes in wards where violence was a way of life and a man was measured by his physical prowess. In 1863 Morrissey enhanced his position in the Irish community when he brought together Irish fighters for an exhibition, with the proceeds going for the relief of the poor in his native country.[93] The funeral procession of the Bowery Boys' "Butcher" Billy Poole, which was one of the largest ever in New York, indicated that such hero worship was not confined solely to the immigrant community. Shot by a member of Rynders's gang, Poole stated on his deathbed, "Good-bye boys, I die a true American." The political overtones of the murder of this native street fighter and close friend of Tom Hyer was largely responsible for his cannonization. While the press was disgruntled by Poole's emergence as a political martyr, there is little doubt that he, along with Hyer and Harrington, were quite influential within the butcher community and among other segments of the city's lusty street life.[94] It is no wonder that politicians courted such men.

The changing nature of the urban press and the emergence of sports journals also aided the rise of boxing. In 1867 the *Chronicle* declared that there was "no incentive to the growth of prize fighting, like that presented by the notoriety given pugilists in the long, detailed reports of their brutal meeting which appear in the metropolitan dailies." This claim exaggerated the impact of the press on boxing, since it responded to the growth of the sport as much as caused it. Nevertheless, from 1840 to 1870 boxing received more newspaper coverage than any other sport, with the exception of baseball.[95] Granted, a good deal of newspaper space was devoted to denouncing the sport because of its brutality, including calls for stricter laws to prevent fights from taking place. Boxing was proclaimed antireligion, anticivilization, and anti-American; its intended purpose, as far as the press was concerned, was to encourage gambling. Objection to the sport also derived from the press's dim view of the class and ethnic backgrounds of the participants, sponsors, and spectators, and from the belief that boxers held a "privileged position" within the community and wielded undue political influence. Yet despite their disapproval of boxing many newspapers, most notably the *Herald,* provided detailed accounts of the leading matches. When a letter to the *Times* asked why a respectable paper carried so much news on the Heenan-Sayers fight, the editors replied — perhaps speaking for the media — that boxing was news and therefore must be reported; that details of such events would convince the public of the essential brutality of boxing; and that the public interest in the results of fights would cause them to go to other newspapers for the information if the *Times* did not cover the sport.[96]

The lion's share of boxing news was found in the sports journals, however, such as the *Clipper,* which catered to the more "democratic element."[97] From the very beginning Frank Queen, the *Clipper's* editor, was the leading supporter of boxers and boxing. On several occasions he argued that the character of these men had been grossly misrepresented, and he railed against the hypocrisy of the press, which gave details of the fights but decried boxing in editorials and other articles in the "bitterest manner." The *Clipper* frequently pointed to the positive contribution of pugilism, maintaining that knowledge of the sport led to manliness, confidence, and courage, and furthermore discouraged the use of knives and guns during street fights. In addition, boxers led Spartan lives — "the privation, the hardship, and the self-denial, which a man must practice before he can arrive at his physical climax" — in preparation for a fight.[98]

Such arguments did not induce any vocal supporters among the press, but there was a slow, subtle shift in the media's attitude toward the sport. While newspapers continued to carry denunciations of pugilism, they also began to include articles that spoke of the positive values of boxing. In 1848 the *Herald* declared that a boxing contest could teach a moral lesson, that the self-denial, temperance, daily exercise, and beautiful regimentation fighters undergo for months prior to a match "present the elements of a system of life which is equal to any system of morality or human conduct that can be picked out of the historical romances of the last thirty centuries." By the post–Civil War years the same paper described boxing as a "judicious, healthful and manly exercise," and insisted that knowledge of the sport infuses a feeling of confidence and gives strength to the weak and courage to the timid. It distinguished between two kinds of prizefighters, the bruiser and the scientific fighter: while the "punch-it-out" style was more common, the latter style involved "intellectual operations" and raised "the combat from its brutal character."[99]

Even the conservative *Times* found some positive value in boxing, pointing out that the sport encouraged physical development and helped banish the knife. By 1870 the *Times* was ready to admit that there were two sides to the boxing question, a change of heart influenced by a doctor who noted that prizefighting was beneficial because of the severe training it required, that it did for man what racing did for horses. While the paper conceded that "prize fighting has its merits," it nonetheless insisted that "its demerits greatly outweigh them." It acknowledged a certain admiration for "the physical advantage of training for the ring" but felt that "the moral disadvantages which are its inseparable concomitants are immensely greater." In exploring the negative consequences of boxing it is noteworthy that the *Times* focused as much, if not more, on the lifestyle of boxers as on the brutality of the sport.[100]

The contention that boxing had positive values originated in the concept of the sport as the "manly art of self defense," but it was not until the middle of the nineteenth century that respectable newspapers cautiously acknowledged the benefits of the sport. This gradual shift in attitude derived from several factors, including the growing concern for the physical well-being of urban residents. The evolving concept of manhood during the nineteenth century—from moral to physical—was the major impetus behind the changing perception of boxing.[101] While proponents of other sports claimed that their activities also contributed to physical well-being and manliness, this was the prime argument for boxing advocates. The rigorous discipline and training required of a fighter, and the courage and confidence that emerged from the ability to defend oneself, appealed to even those who denounced pugilism. Opponents could not point to any other sport that inculcated these characteristics to the same degree as boxing.

During the 1860s, as prizefighting continued to grow in terms of the number of contests and combatants, interest in the sport leveled off. Major contests still attracted considerable attention but none created the excitement of the Hyer-Sullivan or the Heenan-Sayers bouts. Boxing in New York declined during the first year of the Civil War, but this may have been a natural letdown following the excitement of the 1860 international contest. By 1862 pugilistic activity was on the rise, and the following year the *Clipper* noted that the two previous seasons would "long be remembered for the number and character of sparring exhibitions in this city." In 1863 New Yorker Joe Coburn defeated St. Louisan Mike McCool for the heavyweight championship, a fight that sparked considerable interest because of its intersectional overtones.[102]

When James Heenan came out of retirement in late 1863 to fight English champion Tom King, the international character of the contest, the high stakes, and the heavy wagering produced considerable discussion but did not create nearly the same degree of interest that the earlier international contest had, probably because of the war and a distrust of the English sporting character. Heenan's unwillingness to join the North in its battle also resulted in sharp criticism of this American-born heavyweight fighter and made it difficult for his former supporters to accept him as the champion of the American cause.[103] The out-of-shape Heenan was no match for his English challenger, leading some people to suggest that Heenan, or more likely his trainers and backers, had dumped the fight; others blamed British injustice for the outcome, as they had done earlier. The public outcry was limited, however, in both duration and scope, with most of the postfight analysis confined to sports journals.[104]

Boxing underwent a three-year period of general inactivity, the *Clipper* claiming that "the palmy days of the prize ring have gone forever." In 1867 there was a resurgence in interest and the number of contests, causing that same journal to state that it did not "remember a time when the prize ring was in such favor as it is at present, or when there was such animation among the young lambs." The *Herald* echoed these sentiments, noting that "papers team with accounts of fights . . . and benefits are held even in our theatres." *Wilkes' Spirit* maintained that the excitement created by the scheduled rematch in 1868 between Colburn and McCool was comparable to that which had surrounded the Hyer-Sullivan fight. At the last minute, however, the fight was cancelled when threats were made that the police would intervene.[105] When a contest was proposed in 1870 between two recent English immigrants, heavyweights Jem Mace and Tom Allen, the *Herald* hoped that it would not take place in New York, an attitude that did not prevent them, along with the *New York Sun* and *Wilkes' Spirit*, from sending reporters to New Orleans to cover the fight. The tremendous nationwide interest in a contest between two foreign fighters testified to the appeal of boxing, particularly major heavyweight bouts.[106]

ANIMAL SPORTS

Various animal sports, also called blood sports, had existed in New York since the earliest colonial days, although in the generation following the Revolution efforts were made to curtail such activity. Some citizens characterized these cruel diversions as "disgraceful and beastly," believing that they "debase the mind of the spectator, deaden the feelings and extinguish every spark of benevolence." By 1820 bear and bull baiting had virtually disappeared from New York's sporting scene, their demise a result of the physical growth of the city and the dangers such large animals presented to the expanding urban population.[107] Influenced primarily by those who encouraged billiards and boxing, cockfighting and other animal sports continued and experienced significant growth between 1850 and 1870. In the immediate post–Civil War years, however, changing attitudes and various social forces, symbolized by the formation in 1866 of the American Society for the Prevention of Cruelty to Animals, began to undermine these bloody sports, although their full impact would not be felt for another two decades.

In 1823 an English visitor pointed out that in New York "it is perfectly common for two or three cockfights to regularly take place every week." Although the sport no doubt was commonplace, nearly a quarter-century passed before it was referred to in the New York press. In 1847 the *Spirit* noted a battle between New York and Philadelphia cocks, and two years later it mentioned a cockfight between Troy and New York birds, strongly suggesting that intercity cockfights were also a common practice.[108] During the 1850s the media took note of other animal sports as well, a reflection of not only the changing nature of the urban press and the increasing number of sports journals but the growth of these sports. Promoters of animal sports began advertising in various sports journals, and in 1857 the *Clipper* even devoted an entire section to rat baiting and dogfighting. Although New York State had banned all blood sports the previous year, law enforcement was lax and "hardly a night passed in the city without a tournament held in amateur or professional pits."[109]

Animal sports continued to be popular during the Civil War decade, as the *Clipper* noted in 1861: "Notwithstanding the arrests that have been made from time to time, the Fancy still continue their canine 'sport' as if regardless of all laws." Cockfighting was said to be "very exciting and is becoming more popular than formerly."[110] Kit Burns's Sportsman Hall was the best known of New York's numerous animal pits. A barroom hangout for some of the city's leading ruffians and criminals, its location behind the bar and through a narrow passage made it easy to defend against the police and other intruders. The amphitheater seated 250 comfortably, although usually 400 spectators were packed around the center pit to witness rat baiting and dogfighting. Another attraction was Jack the Rat, who would bite off the head of a mouse for a dime and decapitate a rat for a quarter."[111]

Most of the spectators at Kit Burns's hall and other such places were from the lower and lower-middle classes, although individuals from other

A Sporting Time

social strata did not hesitate to pay as much as three dollars to see a cockfight. Among the spectators at one of these events the *Herald* noted "several members of our past and present municipal board, a bevy of junior members of the bar, certain ward politicians [and] a considerable assortment of fast and fancy men." In 1861 some 250 people paid three dollars each to witness a cockfight between birds owned by John Morrissey, the boxer, and Mr. Genet, the president of the board of alderman. Reporting the event under the derogatory title "Amusements of the Ruling Class," the *Times* maintained that $50,000 had changed hands on the outcome. Frederick Van Wyck claimed in his memoirs that attendance at animal contests and other bawdy sporting events was a rite de passage for the sons of the old aristocracy. At Tommy Norris's livery stable he witnessed rat baiting, a cockfight, a prizefight between two billy goats, and a boxing match between two topless women: "Certainly, for a lad of 17, such as I, a night with Tommy Norris and his attraction was quite a night."[112]

In the five years following the Civil War animal sports remained a popular pastime in the New York City area, although the law prohibiting these bloody contests became stricter and was more readily enforced. *Wilkes' Spirit* claimed that cockfighting was "all the rage and embraces all sorts of people from the millionaires of the highest respectability down to the lowest roughs." The *Herald* agreed, noting that "never before was there such universal interest in the sport" both in New York and nationally. Other animal sports also had their devotees, which prompted one writer to declare, "Those who are not interested in such contests can form but little idea of the excitement which such produce among one class of the sporting fraternity, nor will they probably appreciate the delight with which they are enjoyed and the amount of money which is staked upon the results."[113]

Objections to these cruel, bloody sports date to colonial days. During the antebellum period an infiltration of changing English attitudes toward animal sports, a general national reform movement, and the effects of urbanization and a shifting economy reinforced these older objections. The various social and intellectual pressures coalesced in 1866 with the formation of the American Society for the Prevention of Cruelty to Animals (ASPCA) in New York. Henry Bergh, the son of a wealthy New York shipbuilder, was for more than twenty years the major force behind the ASPCA, which was modeled after England's Royal Society for the Prevention of Cruelty to Animals, founded forty-two years earlier. Few public figures "labored with a greater zest for battle, or a more flamboyant sense of the dramatic."[114]

The policies of the ASPCA with regard to animal sports of all kinds took on class overtones. Although the organization condemned many upper-class activities such as pigeon shooting and fox hunting, Bergh was forced against his best judgment to prosecute "the 5th Avenue 'Sport'" with greater caution than those of Water Street," since many gentlemen sportsmen were also friends and supporters of the ASPCA. His battles with the upper class took on the nature of a sparring match, according to his biographer, with Bergh frequently retreating and only occasionally "driving home a body blow to the slow-changing public opinion."[115] This pressure to focus on the lower classes' involvement in animal sports was indicative of the general nature of criticism of blood sports. While many people had long been disgusted by the cruelty involved, others were equally, if not more, concerned with gambling and misspent time among the working class and the unemployed. The *Times,* the most outspoken critic of blood sports, noted that these contests existed solely for gambling purposes and that the amusement was "reprobated by decent people."[116] As in many other things, participation by the upper class was often overlooked when fingers were being pointed.

Bergh and the ASPCA, bolstered by changing attitudes and a more enforceable anticruelty law, began an intensive campaign to shut down the various animal pits in New York, particularly Kit Burns's place. By 1870 only a modicum of success had been achieved, for despite numerous raids the organization was unable to count on many prosecutions. The failure of Bergh and his cohorts "reflected less upon the zeal of these stout-hearted crusaders than upon the political affiliations of the sporting tribe." The *Herald* believed that "as far as preventing this sort of sport is concerned Mr. Bergh and his numerous corp of deputies may well throw up the sponge . . . ; for beyond causing a little inconvenience and conveyance to those who frequent and participate in the enjoyment, they will never accomplish anything." Although unable to win many convictions, Bergh's efforts proved to be more than minor inconveniences. One raid set Burns back $800, while other New York sportsmen, always fearful that Bergh was waiting in the wings, began to frequent pits in Brooklyn, Williamsburgh, and Hoboken for their evening entertainment.[117]

By 1870 Bergh's harassments placed animal sports on the defensive. Although certain segments of New York's sporting society continued to frequent various pits, the power of public sentiment, the clergy, and the ASPCA became too great in the 1880s. By the last decade of the nineteenth century animal sports disappeared from the city's sporting scene for all intents and purposes. Having existed in New York for more than 250 years, these cruel, bloody sports were no longer compatible with urban society.[118]

PROFESSIONAL ATHLETES AND THE MODERNIZATION
OF SPORT

The premodern character of pedestrianism, billiards, boxing, and animal sports broke down with their emergence as spectator sports both in New York and nationally. By 1870 all four sports contained certain modern elements, but none of them were transformed into a modern sport despite the presence of a professional element. Although the professional athlete emerged as one of the dominant symbols of modern sport, the limited impact that professionalization had on the modernization of sport is not surprising since there were paid athletes even during the premodern period. For those sports in which professional athletes comparatively flourished in earlier times, elements similar to modern sports can be discovered and to a certain degree were linked to the presence of these paid athletes. For example, as far back as ancient Greece professional athletes were involved in specialization, training routines, and coaching. While professional athletes sought to rationalize their sport skills, their presence did not affect the rationalization of the sporting institution.[119]

The inability of professionalization to act as an agent of rationalization derives from the fact that professional athletes merely affect the sports contest, not the institution of sport. In essence, the professional athlete is a specialized sports product (i.e., a better or more skilled player). The changing nature of ownership or sponsorship of the "means of production" (or contest) provides the impetus for the rationalization of the sport. What distinguished the sponsorship of premodern professional sport from modern professional sport was the shift from match or private sponsorship to commercial sponsorship.[120] It was precisely because of the limited commercial growth of these sports that modern elements, most notably the organizational structure, emerged so slowly.

The reasons for the limited commercialization of these professional sports varied. Legal sanctions inhibited the commercialization of boxing. While pugilism was a spectator sport, there was no admission fee charged to boxing contests held in open fields usually far away from police intervention. Gate receipts were collected at local sparring matches, but these fights were exhibitions, not contests. Pedestrianism was a commercial-spectator sport, but interest in it was insufficient to nurture entrepreneurship to any significant degree. Where commercial pedestrianism was profitable, notably the Caledonian games, the maturation of modern structures, especially on the organizational level, made significant advances. Similarly, it is no coincidence that billiards was the only other sport among these four to have a national organization, even if it was ineffective in regulating the sport. While the creation of the American Billiard Players Association was rooted in part in the recreational growth of the sport and the economic interest of billiard manufacturers, the commercialization of billiard contests also played a role in this development.

Ice skating on the Central Park pond, in New York City. From a drawing by Currier and Ives.

10

A Host of Leisure Sports

Between 1820 and 1870 New Yorkers engaged in a wide variety of recreational activities that were basically participatory and noncompetitive in nature. The social backgrounds of the participants varied from sport to sport, as the wealthy laid claim to some while particular ethnic groups dominated others. Women joined men in several of these sports, and others included participants from more than one social class. The popularity of the different sports also varied considerably; for example, fencing and lacrosse had a limited following while more people participated in skating than in baseball. None of these sports attracted much press coverage, and they were generally less modern than competitive sports: by 1870 thirteen of twenty-one sports had some form of local organization but other modern characteristics were present only to a very minor extent. Yet collectively these sports revealed the diversity of New York's athletic experience and the growth of sport during these fifty years.

FIELD SPORTS

While New Yorkers had always enjoyed field sports such as hunting, fishing, and shooting, changing urban conditions in the nineteenth century produced a new relationship between city residents and rural recreation. Prior to 1850 New York sportsmen had access to sufficient hunting and fishing areas in nearby New Jersey, in Harlem, and in Westchester County, although Long Island was by far their favorite spot. The latter was often referred to as "one of the finest sporting countries in the world," and the *Spirit* noted that "there are few sections of the country where the delightful recreation of Trout fishing may be enjoyed in greater perfection than upon Long Island."[1] After 1850 it is likely that a smaller proportion of the city's residents engaged in field sports. The cost of traveling from the city proper, limitations of time, and for some — especially unskilled, manual laborers — the requirements of work restricted general participation in these pastimes.

Three related changes in fishing and hunting occurred right around mid-century. First, although field sports once had constituted a large portion of the sporting news, especially in the *Spirit*, the amount of space daily newspapers and sports journals devoted to hunting and fishing began to decrease.[2] Second, Long Island began to lose its aura as a hunting and fishing mecca. New York sportsmen continued to frequent this nearby region during the next two decades, but the more well-to-do sportsmen increasingly went upstate, particularly to the Adirondacks, to hunt and fish.[3] Third, wealthy sportsmen established a number of hunting and fishing clubs which, though limited in number, marked the introduction of a modern element into the two sports that heretofore symbolized the informal and spontaneous character of athletics. As early as 1844 a group of gentlemen had established the New York Sportsmen Club, which remained the city's leading hunting and shooting club for the next quarter-century. Fishing associations evolved more slowly, but in 1866 *Wilkes' Spirit* noted the creation of two such clubs in New York, and five years later it pointed out that several fishing organizations existed in the metropolitan area.[4]

The implementation of more effective game laws was a major objective of New York's fishing and hunting clubs. Game laws dating to at least 1795, and subsequent enactments, were rarely enforced because of "a democratic prejudice versus the very name of a game law." To combat this prejudice and win support for more effective legislation, Henry W. Herbert set about to distinguish between the purpose of such laws in the United States and in England. He claimed that in America these laws were "confined solely to the protection of game and differ therein from the game laws of England, which as they formerly existed not only limited the right of killing game to a privilege class, actions prohibiting the owners of the soil from fish or fowl on his own land." In 1848 Herbert drafted a petition for the preservation of game in New York State, although he hoped it would be passed by New Jersey, Pennsylvania, and Connecticut as well. Robert B. Roosevelt was an even more active champion of game laws, one-time president of the New York Sportsmen Club, author of several works on America's fish and birds, and the uncle of Theodore Roosevelt. The elder Roosevelt devoted much of his energy "to the organization of clubs for the preservation of game and obtaining the legislative restrictions on the vandalism that threatened the complete extermination of the food tenants of woods and water." When the New

York Fishery Commission was established in 1867 Roosevelt was appointed one of the state commissioners.[5]

The press supported the efforts of Herbert, Roosevelt, and other conservationists. The *Tribune* asserted that divine law obligated all people to protect the animal species. By 1870, however, those who sought to protect fish and fowl had made only minor gains at best, much like those who opposed cruelty to animals and sought an end to organized blood sports. The absence of any significant enforcement agencies and the vagueness of existing legislation, combined with popular objection to game laws in general and the view that game reserves were plentiful, severely undermined the efforts of conservationists.[6]

Fox hunting was a far more esoteric activity than everyday hunting or fishing, but it was also far less popular. Only a small number of New Yorkers participated in fox hunting in the antebellum years, and it never enjoyed the appeal among New York's upper class that it had among their southern and Philadelphia counterparts. In 1856 several leading New York City and Brooklyn sportsmen established the Brooklyn Fox Hunt Club, the majority of the members being trotting horse enthusiasts who, "having one sport to their liking, determined on another so there would be no dull moment in their lives." The organization dissolved with the outbreak of the Civil War and was never revived despite several attempts to do so. There are no references to fox hunting having been in vogue during the 1860s. Residents of New York apparently did not resume the chase until the next decade, when F. Gray Griswold and other wealthy area gentlemen became involved in the sport.[7]

Shooting contests had always been a popular pastime, and New Yorkers seemed to appreciate good marksmanship. As urbanization increasingly cut city residents off from hunting and fishing, shooting became even more popular. Pigeon shooting was a favorite among certain New York sportsmen, and during the antebellum period contests regularly took place at the Red House Tavern in Harlem. Trials of skill also occurred at a variety of other places throughout the metropolitan area. After the Civil War pigeon shooting became fashionable, especially on the grounds of Jerome Park (the racecourse), among an increasing number of wealthy New Yorkers. The American Society for the Prevention of Cruelty to Animals (ASPCA) attempted to suppress the sport, arguing that birds were often left injured and helpless in the field, but to no avail. In 1869 the ASPCA invoked both the state's anticruelty law and a municipal ordinance to prevent a match between leading shooters, but the participants simply moved across the river to New Jersey. ASPCA president Henry Bergh, in battling the pigeon shooters, found himself confronting another reformer,

Robert Roosevelt, who defended both the sport and the sportsmen, proclaiming that they had done more to protect and preserve game than any other group. When some of the more influential pigeon shooters announced that they were prepared to challenge Bergh in court and threatened to obtain an injunction against him, he became fearful of losing their important support for the ASPCA and backed off from further interference with their sport.[8]

Target shooting proved to be less costly and more popular than pigeon shooting. The city's leading "cracks" often engaged in trials of skill, either with rifle or pistol, that were usually privately arranged and almost always included side bets. At times gun and rifle manufacturers engaged in contests as a means of demonstrating the superiority of their weapons, while on other occasions a promoter, usually a taverner, would put up the prize and collect an entry fee from each competitor. Until 1850 shooting contests in New York were confined to local marksmen, but eventually competitors from outside the metropolitan area came to New York for matches with local talent. A novel international contest occurred in 1842 between two Swiss sharpshooters and Samuel Lloyd, reputed to be the best rifle shot in America. The New Yorker won the match after each competitor shot in his native country and sent his scores to the others.[9]

In addition to privately arranged contests, three different types of rifle clubs promoted shooting in New York between 1820 and 1870. There were groups of men who shot on a regular basis, generally on their own property. There were never very many of these organizations, although they reached a high point in the 1830s when several existed in New York City. By the 1850s only two such clubs remained in the city, and both seem to have been discontinued before the outbreak of the Civil War. While efforts to reestablish rifle clubs in general began in the late 1860s, such organizations apparently were not revived in New York until the following decade.[10] In 1871 the National Rifle Association was formed, its major objective being the improvement of marksmanship in New York. This suggests that a few rifle clubs probably existed in the city during the late 1860s, although National Guard companies were the major force behind the new association.

Target companies, which probably evolved from military training days, as promoters of shooting contests, were far more numerous and far more enduring, but unlike the dedicated members of rifle clubs each company met only once a year to test their skills. Although prizes were offered to the best shot, the annual event was more a social occasion than a sporting one, with its marching bands and food and drink. Some companies were linked to militia units, but most were not. There is also little evidence to support one newspaper's claim that target companies were products of the festivities of volunteer fire companies.[11]

Observers were impressed in general with the number of target companies and were positive that they increased annually, particularly after 1850. In 1869 the *Herald* estimated that 5,000 men were under arms, which gave New York's target companies more members than any of the city's other sports organizations, including baseball. These marksmen appear to have come from a broad spectrum of the city's social strata, with the middle and artisan classes comprising an ever larger proportion of members after about 1850. This trend was partially due to the restrictions that changing urban conditions placed on their participation in the traditional field sports of hunting and fishing. Yet even as target companies served as a substitute for other field sports, their democratic base would have been less extensive had local politicians not been willing to promote and finance these organizations.[12]

During the antebellum period the press viewed the city's target companies in a positive light, an attitude that changed in the years immediately following the war. "Queer institution are these target corps," the *Times* wrote in 1868. They always put on a fine show, but unfortunately they "are never made to serve any good — not even to accustom young men to the use of arms, and to some restraint of organic discipline." The companies supposedly drew men away from the volunteer militia and their members couldn't shoot worth a lick. The *Herald* disapproved of the growing affiliation between target companies and politicians, arguing that they "are now to some extent a part of the machinery for 'striking' politicians and candidates for all minor offices. All would-be Alderman, Assemblyman and every Congressman must prove themselves 'sound on the goose' by liberal contributions to the prize list."[13] The growing disenchantment of the press with target companies was more strongly linked to the excitement these companies created in public areas. The press demanded that they be forced to obtain permits to march down the city's streets. With companies parading, as the *Times* complained, at a rate of two to six per day throughout the spring and summer months, they were seen more and more as a public nuisance, undermining and disturbing the business community's growing need for order. Many of the companies, increasingly populated by the lower-middle classes, had the audacity to march through the residential neighborhoods of New York's wealthier inhabitants to reach their grounds.[14]

Ethnic groups constituted the third type of organized shooting club. Both German and Swiss immigrants had brought with them a love of shooting and reputations as proficient marksmen. The Hebretian Rifle Club, a Swiss group, sponsored at least two shooting festivals during the 1850s, and in 1863 a recently organized Swiss club held a shooting match to raise money for the widows and families of fallen Swiss-born Civil War soldiers. At some point Germans established a *Schutzen* corp in New York and by 1863 had sponsored at least one *Schutzenfest,* a popular sports festival in their native land. This festival became an annual affair after 1865 for the 125 members, "mostly merchants, and a very respectable class of citizens," of the *Schutzen* corps and the large crowds that attended. The *Schutzenfest* became a ten-day affair by 1868, with German delegations coming from all over the country. Both the *Herald* and the *Times* praised the foreigners' festival, in sharp contrast to their criticism of the city's target companies. The *Herald* pointed out that the festival "was a demonstration which only Germans could have got up; and . . . the German population of this city, and indeed the whole United States, has just cause to be proud of." The *Times* noted the perfect decorum despite huge crowds and an abundance of alcoholic beverages.[15]

BALL GAMES

Besides baseball, cricket, and billiards, New Yorkers participated in five other ball games — racquets, bowling, football, lacrosse, and croquet — in the period 1820–70. With the exception of bowling none of these sports enjoyed a significant degree of popularity during the colonial period; in fact, lacrosse and croquet did not arrive in New York until the 1860s, and football was nothing more than an informal, unorganized kicking game until that time. While the historical development of each of these sports and the three ball games discussed in earlier chapters followed different paths, together they marked the emergence of America as a ball-playing society.

Racquets was introduced to New Yorkers after 1750 and was initially connected with several taverns. New York's first racquet court, the Allen Street Court, was built in the early nineteenth century and was the center of the sport in Manhattan for forty years. Use of the facilities was restricted to "the old Knickerbocker and most aristocratic families of the city." There is no record of a governing committee at the Allen Street Court, but apparently a chancellor was appointed to settle disputes. By the 1830s there may have been a couple hundred members, although no precise membership figures exist.[16]

During the Jacksonian period New York butchers also had their own racquet club. In a rare display of interclass mingling in sport during the antebellum years, New York's two racquet clubs reportedly interacted, although it is not known to what extent or why. However, such mingling does confirm the high regard in which this artisan class was held, even among the city's more prominent and affluent residents. The butchers' foray into racquets was clearly an aberration of the sport's historical association with a wealthier clientele. How long their club existed is unknown, but it almost certainly was defunct by the 1840s. Similar games, such as fives and handball, were more common among the middle and artisan classes at that time. Jennie Holliman and Robert Henderson both note that these games were exceedingly popular in New York early in the nineteenth century, although between 1820 and 1870 there were only two newspaper references to these games, both occurring in 1856.[17]

Shortly after 1840 several members of the Allen Street Court expressed dissatisfaction over the admittance of uncongenial visitors who frequented the courts not to play but to gamble, usually for high stakes. The criticism was not specifically directed at the butchers who played racquets, although some members clearly disapproved of intermingling with men of that ilk. In 1845 these dissenters, led by Robert Emmet, established the Racket Court Club, the stated objectives of which were to provide a place where the members could have the benefits of athletic exercise, enjoy judicious recreations and relaxation without being compelled to mix with uncongenial guests, and strictly adhere to restrictions on gambling. While the new club was a direct response to the older club's policies, an overlap in membership no doubt occurred to some degree. By 1848, however, the *Herald* described the Racket Court Club as one of New York's most exclusive groups.[18]

The press virtually ignored racquets in the last two decades of the antebellum period, probably because the sport remained an informal pastime whose contests were confined, with one known exception, to local players. An international match was held in 1847 between Robert Knox II, the son and grandson of the proprietors of the Allen Street Court, and Edward Lamontaigne, who won two of the three contests.[19] By the late 1850s three racquet courts existed in New York, each being supported by private subscription and each with a large membership, yet each being more a social gathering place than a promoter of the sport. By the next decade interest in racquets began to revive, and members of the Gymnasium Club acquired the services of English racquet player Frederick Foulkes. In 1867 Lamontaigne backed Foulkes in a contest against William Gray, England's leading player. Although the match, won by Gray, attracted considerable attention, the sport declined the following year when Foulkes died and, more importantly, the Gymnasium Club disbanded.[20]

No game is more closely identified with the Dutch settlers of New Amsterdam than bowling. Throughout the colonial period the game was very popular among New Yorkers, from clergymen to slaves, and it retained its broad appeal during the first half of the nineteenth century. In 1850 one newspaper estimated that there were 400 alleys in the city.

But the popularity of the sport dramatically declined during the next two decades, possibly due to the increasing interest in billiards. In 1864 one writer lamented the game's demise, blaming the greed of bowling proprietors for this development. Both sports "partook somewhat of the peculiarities of 'science and art,'" and the small pins initially used for bowling made it necessary for serious bowlers to acquire considerable skill; bowling also "required some time to make a full score." None of which suited the economic interest of the alley proprietors, with the result that big bottle-shaped pins were substituted for the smaller ones. Owners believed that the new game would bring in more money, but the public soon abandoned bowling when they perceived a decline in the degree of skill necessary to play the game.[21]

By the post–Civil War period football, as one of many popular kicking games, began a slow ascent toward the prominent position it currently holds in America's athletic universe. Such games existed throughout the colonial period and continued to be played by schoolboys and collegians, despite faculty condemnation, on an informal, unorganized, and irregular basis well into the nineteenth century. Nevertheless, in 1857 the *Clipper* reported that football was not popular in New York, and little came of the recommendation by *Porter's Spirit* to the city's baseball clubs that they take up the sport, pointing out that "during the winter recess, it takes the place of cricket in the old country." During the next decade two other sports journals also encouraged football, the *Clipper* advocating the creation of football clubs since the sport was such an exhilarating pastime, and *Turf, Field and Farm* noting that "football is a rough, burly game, but then, it is a game thoroughly enjoyable in spite of its roughness."[22]

In 1860 the New York Football Club was formed; when the *Clipper* published the rules of the game four years later, it claimed that two football clubs existed in the metropolitan area. However, it was Columbia College that emerged as the center of football in New York City, where an informal, unorganized version of the sport had existed for some time, as it did at other colleges. In 1866 the *Times* reported that the game "has become quite an institution" among Columbia's students, who participated in football contests according to academic class. In 1870 Columbia accepted a football challenge from Rutgers University, and on November 20 a twenty-man team journeyed to New Brunswick, New Jersey, only to lose to the home team, 6–3, in the fourth recorded intercollegiate football game.[23]

The ancient Indian game of lacrosse, unknown in antebellum New York, emerged as an organized sport with the establishment of the New York Lacrosse Club in 1865. Roughly forty members, mainly Canadian artisans, made up the club. In 1869 Thomas G. Van Cott, a New York lawyer and prominent baseball figure, brought two teams of Canadian Indians to New York in the hope that lacrosse would win public favor. Although the Knickerbocker Lacrosse Club was formed in the aftermath of this exhibition, the sport did not win much of a following among the city's residents.[24]

In sharp contrast to lacrosse, a croquet craze swept through New York and other parts of the country in the immediate post–Civil War years. In 1862 a leading New York sporting goods dealer advertised croquet equipment, noting that it was a new game recently imported from England. Five years later the *Chronicle* claimed that "never in the history of out-door sports in this country had any game achieved so sudden a popularity with both sexes, but especially with the ladies, as Croquet has." The journal offered four reasons for croquet's phenomenal rise: it was gentle and healthful exercise; it was exciting; it required judgment and skill; and it allowed for social intercourse. Of the various explanations participation by both men and women was far and away the most significant and the one promoters and manufacturers most strongly emphasized. Having broader public appeal than baseball, croquet "was more than a game; it was a social function."[25]

SEASONAL RECREATIONS

Since the earliest colonial days New Yorkers participated in three forms of seasonal recreations—swimming, sleigh riding, and ice skating—and they continued to engage in these sports between 1820 and 1870. Benjamin Franklin's mid-eighteenth-century treatise on swimming proclaimed it a healthful and practical recreation, and the New York press continued to advocate its values. The *American* asserted that swimming was a useful branch of education and should be taught to every young boy; the *Herald* noted that "the acquirement of the art of swimming gives health and pleasure to the pupil"; and *Wilkes' Spirit* maintained that "perhaps there is no branch of physical education of youth so health-invigorating, so necessary, and so conducive to the development of the physical man or woman, as . . . the acquirement of the art of swimming."[26] Despite this support, swimming was not really popular among New Yorkers. Sports journals contrasted the large number of swimming schools and clubs in Europe with their limited number in New York, noting, "The lack of such an establishment on a comprehensive scale has long been felt, and we trust that the deficiency will be supplied forthwith; it would not only be a boon to society, but an ample remunerative speculation." Earlier, and to no avail, the *Times* had called on the city government to construct a large basin on each side of Manhattan "expressly for a public swimming bath, and kept in a suitable condition at public expense."[27]

New Yorkers of both sexes enjoyed sleigh riding. The press made frequent references to this informal recreation, almost always presenting it in a positive light. The editor of *Harper's Magazine* maintained that "there is scarcely any sense of *life* that can surpass the bustle and excitement of a great city in 'sleigh time.' " In 1863, in an article entitled "The Sleighing Carnival," the *Herald* claimed that "no stranger visiting this metropolis for the first time, could have been induced to believe that all this splendid merriment and costly display was during the most momentous crisis of the most desperate Civil War." It pointed out that "among the various outdoor amusements which exist in the comparative bleak winter months there is none which is more counted upon by the inhabitants of this city than that of sleighriding."[28]

As with croquet, the main reason for sleigh riding's popularity was its social and courting function. Let "every gallant get a good sleigh," one newspaper told its readers on Christmas, "and treat his lady to a ride today." Despite the mingling of the sexes, this recreation "was carried on without much scandal when many other diversions which might seem more innocent to us were a source of gossip or criticism." Even more surprising, the *Herald* did not object to sleigh riding on Sunday, considering it "an especially pleasurable dispensation of Providence." Sunday was considered the best day for sleigh riding since there were more horses available and more people on the road.[29] Indeed, the city's livery stable did a thriving business on sleigh-riding day. On one occasion, the *Gazette* reported, all the horses were rented and the inns were doing fabulously well. The *Herald* noted that while "livery keepers charge exhorbitant prices . . . every available bit of horseflesh was engaged in sleighing." The cost of renting a horse and vehicle varied, but the price generally ranged from three to five dollars, which strongly indicates that the sport could not have had the broad popular appeal that the press sometimes suggested it did. Middle-class, white-collar workers most likely represented the lower limit of the participants in this pastime.[30]

Ice skating was another sport the first Dutch settlers introduced into New York. A popular pastime during the colonial period, the overwhelming majority of participants were boys and young men, although adults at times engaged in the sport, usually on holidays. As skaters took to the frozen ponds the danger of falling through the ice and drowning or freezing to death was always present, no doubt a source of anxiety for many parents.[31]

Just prior to the Civil War a skating mania swept New York and other northeastern cities. In slightly more than a decade it became not only the leading winter sport but, if the figures and impressions are anywhere near accurate, New York's leading participatory sport during any season. The opening of the Central Park skating pond in the winter of 1858–59 was the major stimulant for the surge in New York.[32] The *Spirit* insisted that Central Park was "destined to change the entire character of winter amusements," and the *Clipper* proclaimed that never before had there been such interest in skating. Throughout the 1860s the growth of the sport was linked to New York's man-made park. The *Herald* declared that "skating in the Central Park has become an extensive institution," while the *Times* noted that the park "had directly encouraged habits of exercise in both old and young and indirectly has stimulated inventions and assisted in the development of a new branch of home manufacturing."[33]

Each year the press claimed that the number of participants and the popularity of skating in New York had reached new heights. In 1860 the *Spirit* reported that the number of people at the Central Park pond on any given day ranged from a weekday low of 100 to an estimated crowd of 100,000 on Christmas Day, with 12,000 being the average daily attendance. Six years later the *Times* estimated that as many as 20,000 skaters could be found in Central Park on any given day, and the *Herald* claimed that there were 80,000 skaters in New York City, 8,000 of them women.[34] While the accuracy of these figures must be questioned, they do provide an indication of the perceived popularity of the sport. The boom in skating equipment was another good indicator, the *Times* reporting in 1859 that since the skating mania had begun, 60,000 skates were sold in New York, some for as little as twenty-five cents. The number of manufacturers and the types of skates also increased in the next decade, so that by the post–Civil War years a good pair of skates cost between thirteen and thirty dollars. Poorer quality, cheaper merchandise was available, however, placing the sport of skating well within the economic range of almost all of the city's inhabitants.[35]

During the 1860s two major structural changes occurred in conjunction with the growth of the sport: the trend toward private ponds and clubs, and the extraordinary participation of women on a grand scale. Private skating areas, supported by subscription and run by businessmen, resulted from the desire of the well-to-do to segregate themselves from the masses. The Fifth Avenue Pond was reported to be "the resort of the higher class, who desire to be select in their skating as well as in everything else." A season's ticket cost five dollars for gentlemen and three dollars for ladies and children. To ensure proper conduct, given the comparatively low price, tickets were not sold to anyone of doubtful character and only one-quarter of those who wanted them were actually able to obtain them. In 1867 Leonard Jerome flooded an area next to the racecourse named in his honor so that his friends and their guests could skate; and by 1870 there were three or four other private skating ponds in New York as well. The number of private and public skating areas led one newspaper to conclude that "there is now perhaps no city in the world which furnishes such facilities to the skating public, or those who admire this sort of amusement as New Yorkers."[36]

When the skating boom materialized in the late 1850s the *Spirit* claimed that skating clubs were already being formed; however, the New York Skating Club, the city's first such organization, was not established until 1863. The club reportedly had about 175 members as of 1866; and a large number of its officers were connected with the city's baseball clubs. These men were prosperous white-collar workers of varying social backgrounds, unlike the more exclusive patrons of the Fifth Avenue and Jerome Park ponds. The new club encouraged fancy skating and also sponsored speed-skating competitions. By 1868 the Empire Skating Club had come into existence, and in that year or the next the two New York clubs joined with organizations from other northeastern cities to form the American Skating Congress. This new association sought to promote fancy skating and to formulate the canons of the art. Despite skating's great popularity in this country, however, figure skating never reached the heights it did in Europe.[37]

To observers of the sport the participation by women in skating was a most significant achievement. Henry Chadwick, a leading sportswriter, noted after the Civil War that "ten years ago a lady on skates was not only a rare and novel sight in this vicinity," but that any native women "who dared brave the opinion of 'her set' and to have outraged their senses of feminine propriety by appearing in public on skates would have been driven forth from the sacred circles of the then fashionable coteries of the city in disgrace." The situation had reversed itself, he continued, since "the selfsame fair is now tabooed as 'slow' and not 'up to the times' if she cannot do the 'outside circle' or the 'grapevine twist' on skates in the best style of the art."[38] When it was reported that a woman had left the ladies pond at Central Park to skate with the men, the *Herald* hailed the move, claiming that the men would not object to it. Their statement infers that skating had to a certain extent been segregated by sex, a pattern that broke down rapidly. The ensuing co-recreational nature of the sport contributed significantly to its popularity in the 1860s.[39]

Since the press urged women to participate in outdoor exercise during the antebellum period, they naturally gave their unconditional support to female involvement in skating. When Central Park opened the *Times* made a special effort to encourage women to take advantage of the area. In 1862 the *Herald* wrote, "If our female population comprehended the value of outdoor enjoyment which skating furnishes, and the pernicious effect of confinement in heated rooms, we should have more carnation cheeks and happy faces." Later it charged as absurd the arguments of some physicians that skating was injurious to the health of women; rather, it proclaimed the sport, now and forever, "one of the most agreeable and healthful institutions for the benefit of American ladies." Henry Chadwick also pointed to the sport's salutary effects for women, noting that the female life-style frequently prevented the proper exhalation of carbon and inhalation of oxygen so vital to health, something skating would remedy.[40]

The significance of women's active involvement in skating went far beyond their contribution to the growing popularity of the sport. In the pre–Civil War years women occasionally participated in "male" sports, but such action was considered quite bold and was overwhelmingly frowned on. Women participated in sleigh rides, of course, but their role was passive. Horseback riding was another exception, considered a suitable feminine exercise mainly on utilitarian grounds as much as the healthful benefits to be derived from the sport; however, few women in urban areas rode horses.[41] Skating was thus the first nonutilitarian physical recreation in which women actively participated in large numbers. As such it established a pattern for women's gradually increasing involvement in sport in general. During the next century the constraints of feminine propriety would continue to affect the nature and type of women's sporting involvement, but by the mid-1860s at least the idea of women's participation in outdoor sports was accepted by a large segment of society.

A POTPOURRI OF SPORT

Besides field sports, ball games, and seasonal sports, New Yorkers engaged in a variety of other sporting activities that cannot be placed into any single category. The gymnasium was the setting for two of these sports, fencing and gymnastics. It is unclear when the first gym was opened in New York, but several came into existence between 1820 and 1840. The increasing interest in sport, the changing nature of the city, the growing concern for the health of urban dwellers, and the influence of German liberalism and gymnastics all contributed to the rising number of gyms. The press constantly encouraged the use of these facilities, pointing to the benefits offered to persons of sedentary habits.[42]

By the 1840s there were at least four gyms, possibly a few more, in New York City. During the next three decades the number of such facilities clearly did not keep pace with the increasing population. By 1871 the *Times* pointed out that more gymnasiums were needed since it was "difficult for busy men in large towns to procure exercise" and since they "would surely prove more beneficial to those who frequent them than the enormous billiard establishments."[43] But there were valid reasons for the limited expansion that occurred after 1840. While a variety of sports took place in the gym, many of them, such as billiards, increasingly were moved to their own establishments. More significantly, the sports unique to the gym never achieved a wide degree of popularity. Cost also played an inhibiting role. These facilities operated on a subscription basis, usually twelve dollars annually, an amount that was not prohibitive for white-collar workers. But with the growing number of sports and recreational alternatives, some less expensive, the gym had difficulty inducing many subscribers.[44]

Fencing was taught at New York's gymnasiums, and in 1820 there were several exhibitions of the sport. But in the next decades there was no mention of fencing except to note that the skill was taught at several gymnasiums and that it was popular among members of New York's German gymnastic societies.[45] By contrast, gymnastics and calisthenics were at the heart of the gymnasium. From the outset supporters pointed out that such exercise was mandatory to counterbalance the sedentary nature of urban life. By 1869 the *Herald* insisted that "there is no class, no calling, no sex, no age, which should altogether dispense with gymnastics."[46] Although the press continued to extoll the value of gymnastics, the sport had only a small following, being most widely practiced in the city's German community.

German immigrants brought with them a love of gymnastics, and starting in 1848 established turnvereins, or gymnastic clubs, in such cities as Cincinnati, Louisville, and New York. By 1853 some 70 turnvereins had been formed throughout America, and by the end of the 1850s that number increased to 157. In 1850 one New York gymnastic club urged a "closer union of all societies in order to insure their own existence, and to furnish a basis for mutual cooperation." The three turner societies in New York City and Brooklyn then decided to invite delegates to a national convention, with the creation of the American *Turnerbund* the result. It must be noted that the growth of German gymnastic clubs during the 1850s occurred despite increasing attacks by members of the Nativist party, especially in the Midwest. The *Turnerbund*'s antislavery stance in 1855 proved divisive as many German societies refused to join the national association while others split from the group. After the Civil War the *Turnerbund* flourished as a result of an increased number of German immigrants, the respect won by the German clubs because of their overwhelming support of the Union, the elimination of the Nativist party, and the removal of slavery as a source of division. By 1867 the national association counted over 150 societies and more than 10,000 members.[47]

The New York gymnastic clubs suffered from some of the same problems that affected the national organization. Despite a rising German population in New York, turner societies during the 1850s experienced only limited growth. By the Civil War the *Socialischer Turnvereins* of Brooklyn and New York City had collapsed, even though they had not been subjected to nativistic attacks. In 1863 the New York societies sought to reconcile the split among members on a national level and to rejuvenate the *Turnerbund*. They established a school in 1866 for the training of gymnastic teachers to supply other societies with competent men grounded in the theoretical and practical study of gymnastics. As was the case on the national level, interest and membership in New York's turnvereins increased following the war, and by 1870 there were once again two turner societies in New York City, the oldest having roughly 250 members.[48]

While gymnastics was at the heart of the turnverein, these societies were more than sports organizations. They also served as a means of preserving national identity and cultural form, while at the same time providing assistance to German immigrants in adjusting to their new home. By performing such communal functions these gymnastic societies went further than any other ethnic-based sports group, even the Caledonian clubs, in catering to a specific clientele. The political and philosophical origins of the turnvereins in Germany were partially responsible for their social flavor in America. Yet other factors that distinguished the German community from English-speaking immigrants played an even more decisive role in the structure of gymnastic clubs. A large segment of the clubs' earliest members came to America as political refugees rather than individuals seeking new economic opportunities. Germans also did not share the sports heritage of the native-born population, unlike the English, Scots, or even the Irish. Finally, and perhaps most importantly, the language barrier encountered by most German immigrants served to insulate and isolate them from the general population, thus fostering greater group dependency.

Given the attitude of the press toward gymnastics in general, it is not surprising that New York newspapers held the turnvereins in high regard. The *Tribune* hoped that German gymnastics would be introduced into the city's educational system and minimized "the alleged radical political and religious notions entertained by the masses of the Turners." Instead, the paper emphasized the physical and cultural benefits these German societies offered and encouraged Americans to emulate them. In addition, the press always spoke well of the turner's annual festival.[49]

Wrestling was also taught at the gymnasium, but it was more associated with the tavern and the village green. In 1832 the *Spirit* made note of a wrestling exhibition to be held in New York. While spontaneous, unorganized contests, generally of a rough-and-tumble nature, probably continued to take place in the antebellum years, the press made no other reference to the sport until the 1860s, when several matches were reported.[50]

Roller skating was initially introduced into New York in 1838, at least according to one observer. However, the sport did not become popular until the 1860s, when Englishman James L. Plimpton made improvements in the kind of skates being used. New York's social leaders quickly adopted this new equipment, and in 1869 several gentlemen emulated their ice skating cohorts by establishing the New York Skating Association.[51]

Of the immediate post–Civil War sporting crazes none took hold more quickly than the velocipede boom. Beginning in the fall of 1868, no less than 16,000 bicycles were reportedly sold nationwide during the first four months of the boom, one-fifth of the purchases occurring in New York. In March 1869 the *Times* claimed that when the velocipede furor had broken out, it was believed to be nothing more than a "nine day wonder." Far from showing any sign of decline, interest in the sport increased. Even "the few who first introduced the new sensation, and who were pecuniary interested in its success, little dreamed of their achievement so suddenly becoming popular." Two velocipede clubs were established in New York City and two others in the immediate vicinity. Match races took place, and schools were opened to teach the skill, experiencing good patronage. New York had three or four velocipede manufacturers by 1869, selling these machines for $50 to $150 or more. These prices obviously confined the sport to New York's well-to-do.[52]

Quoits and curling were popular New York pastimes generally associated with immigrants from the British Isles, and from Scotland in particular. Quoits had been played in America since the earliest colonial days and was one of New York's many tavern sports. In 1850 three quoiting clubs—the St. Andrew, the Thistle, and the New York—were established in Manhattan, although clubs may have existed in the city even earlier. The *Times* claimed in 1864 that "quoit playing of late years have become decidedly a most popular game among our admirers of athletic sports." Precisely when curling was introduced into America is unknown, although a New York merchant of Scottish descent noted that he played the game around the first decade of the nineteenth century. The first reference to this basically Scottish game in the New York press occurred in 1845. New Yorkers formed curling clubs in the 1850s, possibly earlier; by 1865 there were four established curling clubs in the city and a dozen throughout the metropolitan area by 1869. Since every Scottish community in the

North had a curling club, contests during the 1860s were not confined to local competition.[53]

During the antebellum period New Yorkers demonstrated their love for fast horses, but they showed little interest in horseback or pleasure riding; neither did they have the same appreciation for equestrian skill that could be found among the European aristocracy. Horseback riding was considered a proper, indeed a beneficial, female pastime, as the press readily noted: "We admire nothing so much as a women with a horse"; since "health in the gentler sex is so important to our race" let every able parent "*complete* his daughter by giving her the side saddle and steed." *Wilkes' Spirit* asserted that horseback riding was "a useful as well as graceful means of exercise" and a "most admirable promoter of female beauty and health." Amid the praise, however, was criticism of the equestrian skills of New York's women riders: "It may be thought an ungallant expression," the *Post* reported, "but we must say that, with scarce an exception, the ladies of New York who make the attempt, do not sit a horse either gracefully or safely." The editor of *Harper's Magazine* said women should be taught that "good horsemanship involves the utmost thoughtfulness, tenderness, and care; and that they are not to jump upon a horse as if he were a machine to be wound up by the whip to run at the highest possible speed."[54]

A small number of riding schools existed in New York throughout the antebellum years as a means of teaching and improving the equestrian skills of women, as well as men. Colonel Fritz Dickel, who opened a school in the late 1850s, was said to be the "first and the greatest of the riding academicians in New York." William H. Disbrow's school, which was begun in the early 1840s, also enjoyed some degree of success. Nevertheless, the fact that there were only three such establishments in New York by 1860 indicates the limited appeal of riding schools, even in a large and prosperous city, a probable lack of interest in improving equestrian skills.[55]

One other step taken to improve the horsemanship of women was the organization in 1858 of a festival "designed to bring into competition the most distinguished and graceful of female amateur equestrians." The *Clipper* stated that "the high character and honorable social position of the gentlemen forming the Committee of Management, are a sufficient guarantee that the entire affair will be conducted in the most honorable manner, and with the most perfect propriety." Unfortunately, the event was universally considered "a bomb," the *Spirit* noting that only two of twenty-two female competitors knew how to ride. The journal's reporter hoped that he would "never again be called to attend a scene so repugnant to the feelings of *a man* as that witnessed on the Union Course."[56]

While riding skills were noticeably poor, interest in horseback riding increased with the opening of the Central Park bridle path at the end of the 1850s. The lack of places to ride in New York City had clearly been one deterrent to participation, particularly after 1840. The *Times* predicted that the new park would be a favorite place for riders, and in 1860 the *Spirit* maintained that it was "already beginning to produce a marked effect upon the taste of the New York public and the use of the saddle horse is becoming one of the most popular pursuits in which pleasure and healthful exercise are admirably combined." The *Herald* reported that the taste for riding had grown "almost into a passion" and that few persons who could own or hire a horse did not turn out when the weather permitted.[57]

In 1859 several gentlemen, led by newspaperman Charles A. Dana, established the Saddle Horse Club in an effort to encourage the practice of horsemanship and the breeding of saddle horses. A decade later the New York Riding Club was created to promote the enjoyment of riding. While the press continued to allude to the increasing taste for riding, the *Times* pointed out that "considering that this is a City of a million inhabitants, the rarity of riders in our public places, still more the rarity of good riders, only serves to prove that the pastime is not really popular." Even among the wealthy class there was a preference for the fast roadster rather than demonstrations of equestrian skill.[58]

Steeplechase racing first occurred in New York in the 1840s when the Beacon Course held several such races. The *Herald* noted that this form of racing "will be very interesting but it is not sufficiently understood in the sporting circles of this latitude to create much excitement." The sport succumbed to a tragedy in 1845, when Cyrus Browning, the proprietor of the Beacon Course, died from a spill during a steeplechase. After the Civil War the American Jockey Club tried to revive hurdle racing, but the sport and the club came under severe criticism in 1867 when another rider died. The *Herald* called for the end of the steeplechase, arguing that no benefits accrued from it, and the *Times* declared it was "at best a dangerous sport," inspiring "quite as much anxiety as interest with the spectators." *Turf, Field and Farm* rushed to the defense of both the steeplechase and the American Jockey Club, insisting that the rider who had died used "more reckless daring than judgment and skill," and that he, not the jockey club, was responsible for the tragic accident. Despite mounting criticism the American Jockey Club, largely with the encouragement of Leonard Jerome, continued to offer hurdle races in conjunction with thoroughbred races. Although the sport continued in New York and elsewhere for another two decades, it did not win much of a following.[59]

Coaching was still another sport wealthy New Yorkers imported from

England in the immediate post–Civil War years. Leonard Jerome introduced four-in-hand driving among his cohorts after learning that the Duke of Beaumont had revived the sport in England. While coaching emerged as a leading sport among the city's elite by 1870, another five years would pass before sufficient interest led to the formation of the New York Coaching Club.[60]

MODERNIZATION OF LEISURE SPORTS

By 1870 these leisure sports had achieved only a limited degree of modernization. Several factors inhibited this process, although the variables differed from sport to sport. Among the hindrances were limited popularity, recent origins, the lack of or local nature of competition, and the individual or dual nature of participation. The participatory and recreational orientations of these sports were the major reasons for the minor evolution of modern structures. Given the nature of these sports, the emergence of their initial stage of modernization, not the continuation of many of their premodern characteristics, was the most important historical development of these sports during this era.

These diverse leisure sports only gradually assumed modern characteristics. Rules remained essentially local as a result of the general absence of national competition, the individual nature of participation, and the small number of clubs in most contest sports. Nevertheless, the publication in sports journals of rules for several athletic activities produced some degree of uniformity. Moreover, the newer sports emerged with their own established rules, although local variations probably crept in during the early years of the sport. While there were no records in any of these sports, historical information and newspaper coverage markedly increased, although the amount of space devoted to these recreational activities fell far below that found for the highly competitive sports. The number of sporting works and manuals rose. Books on various field sports existed in America even prior to the nineteenth century. The initial works were imported from England, but various American field sports books appeared between 1820 and 1870, although the English expatriate, Henry W. Herbert, was this country's leading authority until he committed suicide in the 1850s.[61] Books and guidebooks on several other sports also emerged, mainly during the 1860s. Similar to their baseball or billiard counterparts, these works usually gave a brief history of their respective sport, discussed the health and moral benefits that accrued from participation, gave the rules, and instructed the reader on how to perform the sport skill.[62]

By 1870 more than 90 percent of the leisure sports were organized at least locally. That eight of thirteen activities were organized between 1850 and 1870 indicates the increasing presence of this modern element in

American athletics. Equally revealing was the rapidity with which clubs were established in the newer sports.[63]

The creation of clubs in the non-contest-oriented sports dramatizes the modernization of sport in a way that contest-oriented sports clubs could not.[64] Fostering competition was an important reason for forming clubs in contest sports, but that was obviously not the case for leisure sport clubs. The complexities of modern urban life made it increasingly difficult to participate in recreations that were informal and casual, so clubs became necessary to promote and facilitate such activities. The recreational clubs performed one or more of three different functions: they facilitated participation in sports outside of the city (e.g., hunting and fishing); they promoted the segregation of participants (e.g., skating); and they saw to the allocation of space (e.g., velocipede).[65] Club members had at least white-collar occupations and often represented the more prosperous residents of the city.

The formation of these recreational clubs foreshadowed the increasing dependence of city residents on outsiders, whether voluntary organizations, private entrepreneurs, or various government agencies, to facilitate participation in athletics and leisure sports. What distinguished the formal structures of highly competitive sports from those of recreational sports was the relationship to modernization: for the former, institutionalization derived from the growth of the sport and an increasing emphasis on competition, both of which were by-products of modernization; for the latter, the emergence of formal structures was in response to modern society's need for order. Leisure sports increasingly lost their informality and spontaneity, a trend that continued well into the twentieth century.[66]

WILKES' SPIRIT of the Times.

A Chronicle of the Turf, Field Sports, Literature and the Stage.

OFFICE, No. 207, William Street, corner of Frankfort Street. | NEW YORK, SATURDAY, AUGUST 24, 1861. | WHOLE NO. 103. VOL. IV.—NO. 25

NEW YORK CLIPPER

THE OLDEST AMERICAN SPORTING AND THEATRICAL JOURNAL.

NEW YORK, SATURDAY, SEPTEMBER 12, 1868.

Spirit of the Times

A Chronicle of the Turf, Field Sports, Literature and the Stage.

OFFICE 1st Translation-st., two doors from Broadway directly opposite the Astor House. | NEW-YORK, SATURDAY, JULY 29, 1843. | VOL. XIII.—N° 22.

A sampling of the sporting publications of the mid-1800s.

CONCLUSION

The Press and the Ideology of Modern Sport

The changes that occurred in the structure and nature of sport between 1820 and 1870 were a reflection of, although not caused by, the simultaneous emergence of new attitudes toward athletics. Prior to 1820 the American view of sport was shaped by a Puritan legacy of ambivalence and suspicion. While Puritans objected to sport on the Sabbath and disliked certain recreations because they were rooted in popish and pagan practices or were associated with gambling, they were never totally opposed to sport. Most Puritan leaders recognized that some recreation was essential to refresh the mind and body, but their "detestation of idleness" and their fears that sport would seduce the flock away from their worldly and religious duties produced a clear distrust of sport in general. Given the view that athletic activities were at best necessary evils, they demanded that these be moral and serve some utilitarian benefit.[1]

In the eighteenth century this harsh, Puritan attitude toward sport was muted with the decline of Puritanism, the economic growth of the colonies, and the more secular and liberal spirit of the age. The essential framework nevertheless persisted. Although attitudes toward sport varied during this century according to social class and geographical location, moral and religious leaders remained suspicious of athletics and particularly frightened by the excesses of sport. They continued to insist that sports participants demonstrate tangible gain in both virtue and utilitarian skills.[2]

After 1820 there emerged a new and more positive attitude toward sport. A host of intellectual, social, and religious developments, directly and indirectly, encouraged this change, but modernization in general and the emergence of the modern city in particular were the chief stimulants. Worried by the physical deterioration of urban residents and fearful that the city's social order was also decaying, the press and popular writers increasingly advocated sport and exercise as a vital counterbalance to these social ills.

The urban press was the most vociferous and frequent champion of the sports movement. New York's daily and sports presses were unanimous in their encouragement of greater participation in sport, articulating the view that athletics had positive individual and societal benefits. In their writings the press produced a series of statements, opinions, and editorials, not a philosophical treatise of sport. As a result their arguments often lacked coherency and consistency, and their ideas were rarely original. They followed the lead of other writers in pointing to the ancient Greeks and, even more frequently, the recent writings of clergymen, physicians, reformers, and educators. The main contribution of the press to the emergence of the new sports ideology derived, then, from their role as synthesizers and popularizers of others' ideas. Between 1820 and 1870 they made every effort to articulate the three major justifications of modern sport: to promote health, to promote morality, and to instill character values.[3]

Promoting good health, particularly among urban dwellers, was the leading justification of athletics in the mid-nineteenth century. The argument was not original, but urbanization provided it with new meaning and a sense of urgency. Advocates of sport did not confine their view of health solely to its physical component, although this was the most important dimension. Increasingly, they asserted that athletics contributed to mental health as well. Proponents of the new sports ideology, like their counterparts in the closely allied public health and parks movements, argued that these physical and mental benefits in turn had important moral, economic, social, and nationalistic ramifications.

Between 1820 and 1840 the press came to fear that the nature of urban life had robbed city residents of their health, and they insisted that urbanites lacked the physical strength of their rural forebearers. "Numerous as are the benefits resulting from a dense population," the *Post* wrote in 1830, "we see that physical degeneracy and mental depravation are its too constant attendants." Five years later another newspaper insisted that "a healthy man in New York would be a curiosity."[4] Since the city's growing number of sedentary workers no longer performed the healthful activities of their rural counterparts, substitute methods had to be devised to encourage physical well-being. By the start of the 1830s specific references to the utility of sport, games, and other outdoor recreations became more frequent. One writer maintained that "various games, when properly conducted are among those species of exercises which are admirably adopted to the inhabitants of a city. They allure the sedentary forth into the field — while in their prosecution, the mind and muscles are both excited to an extent sufficient for the purpose of health."[5]

The press also advised educators that they should permit their students to engage in sport, noting that "students are apt to contact various disorders of the nerves and stomach by long continued sedentary habits and almost total neglect of exercise in the open air and too prolonged and intense application of the mind." A lengthy English article, reprinted in the *American*, concluded that "no corporeal acquirement can compensate for deficiency of intellectual excellence; but nothing is so likely to insure the possession of this . . . as the allotment of a due proportion of time to sport and exercise which invigorate the body and secure health." A letter to one New York newspaper insisted that the most striking difference between the ancient and modern educational systems was the emphasis the former placed on physical education and the current total neglect of this subject. Several writers focused specifically on the need for physical exercise among young children, insisting that at this stage of life the desire for action "is a natural instinct given for the development of the human frame in its due power and proportions, and any systematic check upon this disposition is so much deducted from bodily and mental vigor."[6]

The press also expressed concern for the health of women. The *Post* argued that calisthenics were highly useful "in counteracting the debility occasioned by prevailing [female] modes of living and dress." The sedentary life at fashionable seminaries also was blamed for young ladies' health problems, the recommendation being more recreation and less study. The *Free Enquirer* was aghast that anyone would deny exercise to girls and maintained that when their physical and moral conditions were improved the "millenium" would be realized. To win converts most supporters pointed to more immediate benefits, however: exercise and outdoor recreations would promote health, which in turn would facilitate feminine beauty and grace.[7]

The press moved cautiously in articulating this new ideology of sport and made a special effort to point out that athletics was not a waste of time, that it must be conducted properly to be beneficial, but that its importance in the scheme of life should not be overemphasized. Such qualifying statements were in part an attempt to alleviate popular prejudice against sport, but they also indicated the somewhat defensive, insecure posture of these advocates of outdoor recreation and exercise.

In the period 1840–60 the New York press became more assertive in proclaiming the health benefits to be derived from athletics. Reporters and editors frequently complained that Americans were experiencing true physical degeneracy, an issue that took on nationalistic overtones when the English press and the medical profession stated that the American climate was responsible for this condition. The *Times* insisted that the English had exaggerated the problem but conceded that the cries of physical degeneracy were partially true—although it was quick to argue that the deterioration was confined to certain social classes and only to the northeastern part of the country. *Porter's Spirit* maintained, "If we are really deteriorating from our European ancestors . . . , it is to the neglect of those manly outdoor sports, that we must attribute the physical decline, and not to any injurious quality of our climate."[8] Since the press universally accepted this thesis, they continued to recommend that sedentary workers and professional men actively engage in sport. One newspaper claimed that workers' neglect of their muscular system "has revenged itself in weak constitutions," while another insisted that such men required exercises that expand the chest, strengthen the muscles, and quicken the circulation. The press continued to register the complaint that urban dwellers emphasized mental development at the expense of the physical, and they repeatedly reminded their readers of the ancient dictum, "A sound mind in a sound body."[9]

The mercantile community in particular was warned about the health hazards that would ensue from an overzealous pursuit of money. In 1833 the *Mirror* maintained that businessmen's preoccupation with work was driving them to an early grave, a claim that increasingly became part of the rhetoric after 1840. The *Herald* charged that one of the defects of the American social system was the involvement in "the game of money making as to have no leisure or taste for those sports that serve to relax the mind, invigorate the body and give to existence the spice of variety." The *Times* asserted that the physical nature of man was almost entirely neglected in his pursuit of money, and another newspaper blamed the openness of American society for the unhealthy condition of urban residents. The greater economic opportunity afforded citizens of this country encouraged the search for wealth at an early age, at a time when the physical constitution was not sufficiently developed to resist the effects of such unhealthy and unnatural acts.[10]

Even as the press argued that the preoccupation with work and money was detrimental, they did an about-face and also asserted that healthful activities, such as sport, stimulated greater productivity both individually and nationally. In proclaiming the economic advantages of physical and mental well-being, proponents of the new ideology of sport merely repeated the arguments used by Dr. John Griscom and others to justify the public health movement. According to Griscom, a leading spokesman in New York, there was a direct relationship between the health of a man, his ability to sustain himself and his family, and the prosperity of the community. The *Times* echoed this theme in supporting the introduction of gymnastics at institutions of higher learning, claiming that health was "daily becoming more and more a condition of success."[11]

Such circular reasoning was not theoretically contradictory. In fact, a major objective of the press was to establish a closer relationship between work and play. An 1845 editorial in the *Herald*, "Too Much of a Good Thing—All Work and No Play," emphasized the need to balance work and recreation. A *Times* editorial pointed out that it "is beginning to be felt among us, that even America's power to labor has its limits." Since man "cannot live by work alone" and the "human constitution is not made of steel," the paper reminded its readers of the moral of the children's rhyme "All Work and No Play." The overemphasis on work and its accompanying health hazards necessitated that sensible people "make it a *duty* [emphasis mine] to play." A leading sports journal proclaimed that the opposite of work was play, not idleness; that people work for economic reasons, because the Creator intended that they should, but another reason for work was to "make us enjoy leisure, recreation and rest." Work dignifies man, the *Clipper* concluded, but should not be an end unto itself: the "end of work is to enjoy leisure."[12]

The press was never entirely successful in integrating work and play, for they continued to point out that play should not interfere with business.[13] Such statements were not the product of a defensive posture, but they do indicate that even proponents of the new ideology accepted a hierarchical relationship between business and pleasure. Within this stratified context the press argued that play was not synonymous with idleness, that it should be an enjoyable experience; on the surface they provided play with a sense of dignity and importance. Yet the rhetoric reveals that the significance of leisure activities was not self-contained but flowed from their relationship to productivity. When the press wrote of the values of play, particularly physical play—sport—they frequently pointed to its role in refreshing the body. The purpose of reinvigorating the body was obvious. For all the changing attitudes and more positive views, play and sport remained, in the final analysis, not the complement of work but its servant.[14]

Throughout the 1840s and 1850s the neglect of physical education in both public and private schools, as well as at institutions of higher learning, remained a popular theme in the daily and sports news.[15] No one would have been so bold as to argue forthrightly that physical education was just as important as mental education, but this train of thought worked its way into the rhetoric of sports advocates. In an article in the *American Educator*, reprinted in the *Clipper*, it was pointed out that the "advantages of a thorough physical education were so justly appreciated centuries ago, that even the training of the mind was not deemed more important than the body." The *Spirit* went one step further, noting that the "object of education is to make *men* out of boys. Real live men, not bookworms; not smart fellows, but manly fellows." Intellectual development without physical education did not prepare young people for life.[16]

The press continued to encourage women to participate in physical exercise and sport on the grounds that "exercise is as necessary to the health and physical development of the female as the male." A woman doctor protested that sports journals had restricted the outdoor movement to men and that the ladies columns only dealt with fashion and sentimental stories. She insisted that women "ought to have such recreations as are acknowledged to be so beneficial to the other sex" and declared that "if men would give half the attention to the improvement of the physical condition of women that they are giving to the improvement of the horse and dog, they would find growing up in her . . . the qualities they so much prize in these noble animals — strength, endurance, beauty and intelligence, and with them true refinement and womanliness; and would hear less about nervousness, headaches, weak lungs and etc."[17]

While the sedentary nature of urban life was one deterrent to health, the conditions of urban life were another. Since the early nineteenth century, but increasingly after 1840, public health spokesmen, as well as other writers, warned New Yorkers of the dangers of poor sanitation, congested living conditions, and a host of other problems related to the changing environment of the city. The absence of clean air was the most frequently articulated health problem, New York being referred to as a city of arteries but no lungs. The *Times* maintained that a lack of pure air "causes a depression of the powers of the system," leading directly to the use of ardent spirits and therefore indirectly to prostitution and other vices. John Griscom asserted that foul air burdened the blood and prevented it from imparting to the system "the qualities demanded by nature for the due maintenance of health and strength." All that was necessary to prove this point, the public health advocate maintained, was a stroll in the country,[18] a perspective that clearly had positive implications for the new sports ideology since many athletic activities required the participant to leave the city. Even though the press felt that all sports had some health value, they favored outdoor recreations to indoor ones, and some advocates argued that spectator sports also carried health benefits simply by removing the observer to the countryside.[19]

The park movement also had positive implications for sport. William C. Bryant, the editor of the *Post,* was among the initial proponents of New York's Central Park, and the remainder of the city's press overwhelmingly supported the project as well. A variety of reasons were offered for the need to build the park, but its role in promoting health was the one most frequently cited. By providing city residents with a place in which to breathe clean, fresh air, Central Park would serve as a counterbalance to the problems of the changing urban environment. This ruralization of the city was for several of its advocates an expression of antiurban feelings, although the press perceived the park as an attempt to incorporate the best of both worlds. The *Tribune* captured this sentiment when it wrote that an urban park was "the finest luxury which a city is capable; for it is the transference into the town of that which is peculiar to the countryside, so that the citizens enjoy at once the excitement of the streets and the charm of woods and fields."[20]

All New Yorkers would benefit from the park, but the press expected that those who could not afford to escape to the countryside for rest, relaxation, and recreation would be the major beneficiaries. In supporting the construction of Central Park the *Times* stated, "a large majority of our best population—the numerous class on which we depend for our everyday necessities—is doomed to a city life perpetually." For them "we should provide an accessible country whereto they may wander in their spare half hour of their toilsome lives." The *Herald* argued that the park would do its most important work "among the degraded and unbrutified young men and boys who form the underground of the city," while others pointed out that it would provide recreational areas for the laboring class. At the opening of Central Park the *Spirit* predicted that it would bring sport "within the reach of every man in New York."[21]

When advocating sport and outdoor recreations for the working class the press placed their arguments within a broader perspective of health. Unlike their sedentary well-to-do neighbors, members of the working class did not require exercise to combat physical degeneracy, but they did need sports to get them into the fresh air and, even more importantly, to help them overcome mental and physical exhaustion. The *Tribune* pointed out that "our artisans, even those whose work is sufficiently laborious, have usually had their mental and muscular energies taxed by the fixed attention required by their daily tasks, and need relaxations which shall refresh the mind as well as the body." The *Spirit* insisted that labor or even physical exercise was insufficient for the preservation of health—what was needed was not merely the development of muscles but the development of the spirit as well. "Heaving coal may be as good *exercise* as pitching quoits, or sawing wood as rowing in a regatta, but they are infinitely less inspiriting, and therefore infinitely less healthful."[22]

Using much of the rhetoric of antebellum reformers the press justified working-class participation in sport in economic terms. The *Clipper* noted that the annual cost of ill health for America's 12 million workers was $240 million, and it recommended physical exercise to combat this problem. It is significant to note that here the economic argument was stated in negative terms, while the discussion of the economic value of sport to white-collar workers, professionals, and businessmen was presented in a positive light—the contribution of sport to greater individual productivity. The difference stemmed from the fact that the press was pitching their argument to a middle-class audience, and in essence sought to convince them to allow, or at least not hinder, working-class involvement in sport. To win converts they presented their case not in terms of the benefits to the workers, but to the financial drawbacks that ill health would cause the respectable community.[23]

By the time the Civil War had descended on the nation, proponents of the new sports ideology had established a positive relationship between athletics and physical and mental health. Repeating familiar arguments in urging the masses to participate in sport, the *Clipper* declared that the war itself confirmed that the "physical education of the masses is a desideratum; neglected, the individual and the community both suffer; properly cared for general benefit is the result."[24] After the war the basic argument remained the same,[25] but the fear that Americans were physically degenerating markedly declined. "One of the blessings in disguise which accompanied the late Civil War," the *Times* maintained, was that it cultivated among the urban populace "habits of outdoor exercise, which remained a permanent gain of great value." The *Herald* reported that Americans' interest in sport had increased every year as they discovered that they could play as well as and as hard as they could work. *Wilkes' Spirit* was gratified to see that "healthy and strengthening pastimes are daily growing into favor with the community," and that the public "have learnt the inestimate worth of such relaxations, and throw themselves into them with a vigor and delight that is the real secret of their success."[26]

The press also championed sport as an adjunct of morality which was a natural extension of the link between health and morality. On the one hand this new connection was a response to the growing concern for social order. According to the press, sport assisted agencies of social control, helped to alleviate class and sectional tensions, and, most importantly, prevented the nation's urban youth from becoming enmeshed with the evils of the city. On the other hand the intrusion of sport into what had been the domain of religion could have occurred only in the face of profound changes in religious tenets.

During the antebellum period a host of reformers, particularly those associated with the evangelical Protestant sects, came to believe that "a person could not behave in a morally responsible fashion unless his or her body was unfettered and uncorrupted." The accepted notion, one scholar notes, "was that the proper care of the body was a way of strengthening the higher claims of the spirit." Such rhetoric pervaded the public health movement, as when John Griscom stated that a "depressed physical condition, and bad morals and social habits and properties have an intimate relationship to each other. — They stand clearly in the attention of cause and effect."[27] By promoting health, sport indirectly contributed to moral character; and since morality was "closely linked and depended upon health," the *Post* noted as early as 1830, "it ought to be a popular sentiment in all our large cities to establish and support institutions intended to develop our physical powers and give health and vigor to the human frame."[28]

The press also articulated a direct link between athletics, moral character, and social order on a personal, family, and national level. The *Herald* wrote that the character and workings of public amusements were "one of the most important and influential elements of order and social government." *Porter's Spirit* argued that since happiness cultivated patriotism, athletics, by contributing to the "contentment of the mind," made "men fond of the soil on which they are enjoyed." The search for a national pastime during the late 1850s indicated that the press not only viewed sport as an adjunct to morality but also as a reflection of national character. By 1866 the *Herald* claimed that a nation's sport was an important item in its national history and "their character goes a long way to prove a country's advancement in the matter of civilization."[29]

Harper's Magazine informed its readers of Swiss educator Johann Pestalozzi's belief that "if the physical advantages of gymnastics is great and uncontrovertible, the moral advantages resulting from them is as valuable." Many writers pointed to the camaraderie of the ballfield, skating pond, and other sports sites. The mercantile community was told that friends made via sports participation might afford them a business advantage. Parents were advised to play with their children as a way of building family unity. Ever since the famous horse race between Eclipse and Henry in 1823, athletic competition had been touted as a means of alleviating sectional tensions. With the emergence of international contests, the press repeated this theme, stating that sport served to bring together people of different countries. Charles Astor Bristed, the grandson of John Jacob Astor, asserted that gentlemen should join in the popular recreations as a means of reducing class tension.[30]

The most frequently cited moral argument for athletics was the role it played in removing youths from the "haunts of dissipation," most notably taverns, gambling parlors, and houses of prostitution. In the 1830s rowing was praised as the ideal sport for young men who needed and would seek recreational opportunities in whatever form they could. The *Herald* warned that "if they can't get it healthily and morally, they will seek it unhealthily and immorally at night, in drink saloons or at the gambling tables, and from these dissipations to those of a lower depth, the gradation is easy." Henry Chadwick argued that as "a remedy for the many evils resulting from the immoral associations the boys and young men of our cities are apt to become connected with baseball merits the endorsement of every clergyman in the country." *Porter's Spirit* echoed that theme in pointing out that the national pastime should be considered an "important and valuable adjunct to the church."[31]

The press initially focused on all young men in their treatment of the relationship between sport and morality, and while they continued to speak to this age group, they increasingly made reference to the moral value of amusements for the working class. The *Times* noted that workers were attracted to avenues of escape, such as dance halls and saloons, because of the numerous problems they encountered daily, and that the *"creation of innocent and virtuous amusements* for the masses" was the "true remedy" for these breeding grounds of vice. Recreation also was advocated as one way to prevent the poor from committing crimes—by removing them from the sources of evil. The contention that "no social reform among the poor will ever be successful until the healthful desire for amusements is rationally satisfied"[32] was an outgrowth of the belief that rapid change, especially urban change, was eroding the social order. The tremendous increase in New York's population, significant shifts in its social composition, vast changes in the economy, the obliteration of the system of class deference, and a host of other factors made a goodly number of New York's civic leaders apprehensive as to the potential for social disorder.[33]

Intimately linked to the rising concern for urban order and pivotal to the new relationship between sport and morality were the profound shifts taking place in religious thought and practices. During the antebellum period urban dwellers increasingly felt that the older religious principles and institutions were incapable of meeting their needs. Such feelings did not erode the importance of religion but did serve to notify religious leaders that they would have to minister to the practical as well as spiritual needs of the people. The result was significant, if not always successful, alterations in the institutional practices of organized religion. The growing need for religious groups to cope with both secular and religious problems made them more dependent on secular institutions to implement religious objectives.[34]

Shifts in Protestant thought, largely though not exclusively as a result of the Second Great Awakening, created a framework favorable to the establishment of a new association between sport and morality. The most significant change was the steady drift away from the old Calvinist view of a vengeful God to a loving and, for some Protestant denominations, rational Father; the rejection of determinism and the simultaneous emergence of an activist, individualistic, and perfectionist perspective. Accompanying this evolving theological outlook were important changes in

Protestant perceptions of the body. As one historian notes, religious reformers, despite a streak of prudishness, "seldom rejected the body in favor of the spirit" and also blurred the former distinction between body and soul, making them instead dependent on each other. Reformers, particularly those allied with the public health movement, now believed that control of the body was critical to control of society.[35]

The new religious climate allowed proponents of sport to challenge old attitudes toward athletics. In their examination of the lack of physical recreations in America the press singled out religious prejudice in general and Puritanism in particular. Puritan theology was said to create an artificial split between our spiritual, physical, and mental dimensions, and the media called for their reintegration.[36] Historians have viewed the movement known as Muscular Christianity as the primary response to the problem created by Puritan theology. The movement, which began in England, was brought to America in the late 1850s by a group of influential and respected men who wanted to articulate the need to harmonize the various sides of man.[37] While this was certainly important in the development of a more positive attitude toward sport, scholars have erroneously used the arrival of Muscular Christianity to mark the beginning of change rather than correctly seeing it as a more coherent synthesis of preexisting ideas. Indeed, the ease with which the new movement won popular acceptance indicated that supporters were repeating familiar notions. The shifting Protestant perception of the body and the writings of public health advocates had already preconditioned the public for such change. And as one historian recently pointed out, the basic precepts of Muscular Christianity were in place as early as the start of the Victorian period. It is not surprising that these newer attitudes filtered into newspaper columns in New York even prior to the middle of the nineteenth century.[38]

The press never hesitated to point out religious prejudices against sport, just as they were always quick to quote supporting statements of clergymen. The *Clipper* summarized the arguments of one Baptist minister: "it is not a right, but a *duty* for man to indulge in recreative amusements, *providing he does not make himself a slave to them, or pervert his moral and religious nature in their indulgence.*" The *Herald* reported that Henry Ward Beecher felt men should unite "mirth with morality" and that "real amusements economize time and promote industry." In an article in the *American Messenger,* entitled "Health—A Religious Duty," one writer chastised religion for its lack of concern with the physical condition of men and women, insisting that this violation of physical law was as much a sin as the violation of moral law. In 1869 the *Times* proclaimed that the newly established YMCA marked an important break with the notion that religion must be "somber and forboding." Taking note of the organization's new gymnasium and its encouragement of Muscular Christianity, the newspaper was sure that young men would quickly discover that "they can pursue their favorite amusements [there] with pleasanter surroundings than in the public places they now frequent, so often to the great injury to their morals."[39]

The changing attitude of the press toward Sunday recreations, more than anything else, indicated their acceptance of sport as an adjunct to morality and dramatized their acceptance of the positive social benefits to be derived from sport. Prior to 1840 newspapers carried many comments from people concerned about Sabbath violators, but by the 1850s all the major New York dailies had advocated a more enlightened view of Sunday recreations. The *Tribune* claimed that the absence of physical exercise on Sunday made Monday less agreeable than Saturday. The "advantages of a day of relaxation and rest once a week are numerous and undeniable," and it was the "duty of society" to promote such relaxations to inspire physical health and a cheerful mind, and to elevate tastes and gentle habits of thought and action. The press warned that if the public could not engage in innocent amusements on Sunday, they would become involved in more serious evils, notably visiting the drinking saloons.[40]

Some newspapers argued that partaking of Sunday recreations would be sinful only if citizens had the choice of participating on another day and did not do so. "When such recreation is needed in order to sustain a man in suitable health, to support those whom the ties of nature have dependent upon him," one writer insisted, "I do not think a man sins if he takes a portion of the only day of liberty allotted to him." Because of the importance of working-class participation in sports, some newspapers called for employers to provide their workers with other times for recreation; but recognizing that few bosses would follow their advice, they were willing to break with one of the cardinal tenets of American Protestantism in the interests of a healthier, morally sound, socially well-ordered citizenry. On the eve of the Civil War the *Herald* maintained that "sensible people see that more crime is induced by confining the working class to the pestilential atmosphere, moral as well as physical of this dirty, unhealthy city, than by allowing them facilities of egress into the country and the free enjoyment of those innocent and healthful blessings without which man is reduced to the condition of a mere machine."[41] Of course, most members of the press recognized that the "controversy between those who consider all Sabbath amusements absolutely sinful and those who sought open places of recreation on that day is not likely to be settled in our generation." Indeed, the struggle lasted well into the twentieth century, and while Sabbatarians won minor skirmishes from time to time they also constantly fought a rearguard battle.[42]

A somewhat unusual strain of thought emerged in England in the 1860s which asserted that sport was not subject to the ethical considerations applied to other human activities and on occasion was even superior to life. As Thomas Hughes suggested in *Tom Brown's Schooldays,* to play rugby was to enter a higher moral plane altogether. Such assertions did not appear in the writings of Muscular Christians in America for at least another three decades, yet one senses that sports journalists subscribed to the basic outlines of this argument by the 1870s. Their conviction that baseball was an expression of national character provided a moral sanction no different than that which Hughes gave rugby. Even the conservative *Times* did its part to glorify athletes and athletics: "a people which looks upon an athlete as a useless incumberance upon the face of the earth, or a paradox in nature is not likely to hold its own for centuries." History has taught us "that it has been the superiority of the physical strength quite as much as any moral qualities which gives the Anglo-Saxon race a noble supremacy in the world." From such a perspective it is but a short climb to moral superiority of sports.[43]

Another assertion was that athletics helped to instill character values. This relationship was evident in the works of Renaissance writers and Enlightenment thinkers, but it emerged only gradually in America as a justification for sport. Despite its limited, albeit growing, usage, its significance cannot be minimized, for it was pivotal to sanctioning both competitive and professional sport. However, the desire to link sport to the inculcation of "manly" characteristics also had dramatic and negative effects.

Particularly after 1850 the press became concerned with the need for guaranteeing urban social order and with the impact of modernization on masculine behavior roles. Even as they proclaimed the manly virtues of sport they never coherently defined the term, instead applying it to a collage of behavioral traits, most notably self-discipline, courage, and self-denial. Almost all sports were described as manly in an effort to encourage participation, although the press focused initially on those sports with questionable reputations or a following among foreign-born residents. In the 1830s the *Herald* maintained that boxing's single benefit was that it instilled "a feeling of courage — of proud manly self dependence — . . . that otherwise would not be elicited." Throughout the 1850s supporters of the sport repeatedly claimed that a knowledge of boxing developed manliness, confidence, and courage, and opponents even conceded in the next decade that there was something positive to be found in the Spartan life and rigorous training of the fighter. Similarly, spokesmen for baseball, on the defensive because of the sport's heritage as a child's game, consciously sought to make the national pastime a more skillful, and thereby more manly, sport. One sports journal proudly proclaimed in

1867 that baseball "affords a field for the development of the manly attributes of courage, nerve, pluck [and] endurance."[44]

Advocates of cricket and gymnastics, two sports identified closely with foreigners, also maintained that these activities encouraged manly behavior. In presenting their arguments they repeated claims made on behalf of these sports in their native countries, one writer noting that Pestalozzi himself had encouraged students to become involved with gymnastics at an early age because he felt that the sport facilitated "the habits of industry, openness and frankness of character, personal courage and a manly condition in suffering pain." Cricket supporters incorporated the rhetoric of Muscular Christianity in their defense of the sport, and one writer pointed out that the game was not "mere exercise of the mind nor mere play" but possessed a spice of danger—"courage meets and scorns its hardship—coolness avoids its danger." Success at cricket required discipline and proper obedience to the captain, and even served to educate the eye, nerves, and temper; in fact, "it educates the character." Henry Chadwick also justified cricket on these grounds, declaring that the sport called into play "most of the cardinal virtues," as players must be sober and even-tempered, and success required fortitude, self-denial, and self-control. He concluded that cricket "teaches a love of order, discipline and fair play."[45]

Just prior to the Civil War the press increasingly incorporated the character value argument into their discussion of the benefits of all sports, outdoor recreations, and physical education. *Porter's Spirit* maintained that sport rendered the individual fit for the battle of life; another sports journal insisted that it helped to produce real men. The *Clipper* reported favorably on the educational ideas of Sir Edwin Chadwick, the English reformer who urged that the school day be cut by thirty minutes and the time given over to gymnastics or, even more preferable in his view, military drill. Such activities were not only healthful but provided "an early initiation to all that is implied in the term discipline; namely, duty, self-restraint, order, punctuality, obedience to command and patience." In 1862 the *Times* came out in support of military training because it instilled discipline and because it would make every young boy "feel manly and behave like a man." Military training never won the support of American educators, but the public increasingly saw a relationship between sport and militarism during the last quarter of the nineteenth century.[46]

In using the character value argument to justify sport the press merely borrowed claims already being articulated abroad and incorporated them into their own rhetoric because they served to express values Americans had long shared. In addition, the argument used by the press was an extension of the call for a more integrated view of man. Since health and morality were allied with, and dependent on, proper character development, the promotion of one naturally reinforced the encouragement of the others. Also, the health and morality arguments by themselves could not justify the full gamut of sporting experiences. While they served to legitimate sport as a recreational activity they could not provide the ideological sanction for sport as competition.[47] Clearly, it was no coincidence that the connection between sport and discipline emerged as many sports became more competitive.

The frequency with which writers began to assert that sport could serve as a means of promoting manliness was in direct response to both the impact of modernization on urban society and the role of modernization in redefining the masculine role and creating a new middle-class view of proper sexual behavior. In recent years several scholars have shown how modernization during the nineteenth century heightened "the importance of defining the criteria of manhood and of fulfilling those criteria."[48] Within this context sport obviously had a special attraction; however, the character value argument was more than an attempt to sanction sport as an arena for displaying manhood. Given the belief that rapid change was eroding institutions of socialization, the press came to view sport as an effective means of instilling those values consistent with middle-class manhood. Intertwined with this objective was also a desire to have sport perform what initially would appear to be two opposite functions: act as a substitute for sexual activity and guard against effeminacy. Direct statements on the usage of sport to control the sexuality of adolescent males are nonexistent, which is not surprising in view of the Victorian moral climate and the probable belief on the part of sports journalists that a discussion of sexual behavior did not belong in their columns. However, such a link can be implied from the changing sexual mores of the times and a shift in the accepted ideals of middle-class manhood.

Starting in the 1830s Americans increasingly saw sex in negative terms and several outspoken reformers perceived chaste behavior as necessary to combat and eventually overcome the problems brought on by the rapidly changing urban environment. For these reformers bodily control was linked to self- and social control; to allow the passions "to act themselves out, was to destroy any hope of creating a truly Christian personality." They actively sought to repress childhood and adolescent sexuality and especially to abolish the secret vice, masturbation. Enmeshed with the changing sexual attitude was a new view of manliness. The new Christian man, as Charles Rosenberg points out, "was the athlete of continence, not coitus, continuously testing his manliness in the fires of self-denial."[49]

Sport was obviously not the only means of inculcating those character values needed to overcome passion and other sexual appetites. Historians have long recognized that the emergence of public schools was tied to the failure of other social institutions to instill greater self-control in residents of the increasingly impersonal and fragmented urban areas.[50] Fostering self-discipline solely in the classroom would have occurred at the expense of good health, however, since it was believed that excessive mental stimulation created the type of physical tension that sports participation sought to reduce. Sexual continence was seen not as a rejection of the body but rather as mastery over it. Since man was assumed to have an instinctive need for sexual activity, and since such activity was traditionally linked to manhood, reformers saw the need to control sexuality by offering other activities that would be testaments to manhood. In other words the ballfield, not the bedroom, was where manhood should be earned.

The growing fear of effeminacy dramatized the desire to have men retain those physical characteristics such as ruggedness and hardiness. Unlike the idea of sport as a sex substitute, the press clearly articulated the view that athletics served to counteract this negative trend. As the *Herald* noted, the "absence of those athletic and muscle developing sports so common among the youth of England undoubtedly tended to reduce our young men to effeminacy." The *Times* encouraged sport because it checked feminine ways by leading men into God's open air where manhood could be earned. *Wilkes' Spirit* justified athletics on the grounds that it substituted the feats of man for "the freak of the fop," hardiness for effeminacy, and dexterity for luxurious indolence.[51] America's destiny was linked to its physical prowess in terms consistent with the rhetoric of the imperial jingoists of the 1890s. In 1869 the *Times* noted that, "A weakly, sickly, flabby race may be a pleasing spectacle to theorists who live chiefly in the clouds, but for the destiny yet lying before us we cannot have too much of the attributes which are popularly included in the word 'manliness.' " Sometimes directly, sometimes not, the view was advanced that sport produced real men and real men were athletes.[52]

The rise of competitive athletics, as earlier noted, coincided with the emergence of the character value argument. Unfortunately, historians have paid scant attention to the ideological reasons for the surge of competitive sports after the middle of the nineteenth century, in part because they probably believed that competition was always an integral part of American society and in part because they could point to the existence of sporting contests in America prior to 1820. They concluded, therefore, that competitive athletics was a natural by-product of the growth of sport in general, facilitated by technological and economic changes. While it is easy to concede that the tremendous expansion of competitive sport was part and parcel of the profound alterations occurring in America's material base, it is vital to recognize as well that the growth of this athletic form was tied to the emerging ideology of modern sport, especially the theme of character development.

The importance of competition as a component of the American personality prior to 1820 should not be overemphasized, for only with the onset of modernization did Americans firmly come to accept competition as a valued mechanism for achieving social progress. As I use the term here, competition does not mean struggle; it is more rule-defined and implies a greater degree of equality between willing opponents. Competition was often viewed as socially dysfunctional in premodern America, and what little competitive sport there was existed in a weakened state. Contests were mostly spontaneous, the participants underwent limited, if any, training, the events derived largely from daily work activities, and they rarely received social sanction. Only those sporting events that demonstrated some practical, utilitarian benefits, notably horse racing, achieved some degree of legitimation. Given the early American attitude that sport was a necessary evil, the general distrust of competitive athletics is not surprising. Moralists who sanctioned sport merely as a way to refresh the mind and body could hardly justify the seriousness implicit in competitive sport.

The more positive view of athletics that emerged between 1820 and 1870 helped to erode the former suspicions of sport, altered the nature in which it could be used, and, most significantly, attached new importance to it. It accomplished this via a two-pronged approach. By proclaiming that sport served health and morality, proponents continued to insist that sport promoted utilitarian benefits without requiring it to be linked any longer to day-to-day work-oriented activities. As already pointed out, the health and morality arguments were insufficient to legitimate competitive sport. The character development argument added the missing part. By insisting that the playing field was a laboratory where proper behavioral traits were taught and tested, the press could assert that sport was no longer a simple diversion unworthy of serious attention or effort but an arena in which to train for the competitive struggle of life.

The sanctioning of competitive athletics helped to legitimate professional sport. Opposition to professionalism in the antebellum period was partially linked to the belief that money corrupted "true" sport and to a class bias against the working-class origins of most professional players. The dominant reason, however, was the belief that sport should be a recreation, not a business; that professionalism was the result of taking sport too seriously. By declaring that sport was more than just play, the character value argument eliminated a major objection to professional sport.

These new ideas did not create an immediate acceptance of professional sport, perhaps with the notable exception of baseball. Opponents of professionalism in sport created new rationales for their objections and embodied them in amateur codes, although it became an uphill battle. The hypocrisy and inconsistency that have plagued the amateur movement were inevitable, given the fact that the movement itself was—and still may be—inconsistent with the dominant values of modern America. Neither do the underlying principles of amateurism receive any sanction from the ideological justification of modern sport.

Justifying competitive sport in terms of its role as an inculcator of manly traits obviously eliminated women from this athletic form well into the twentieth century. While the press encouraged women to participate in recreational sports for health reasons, they provided no similar rationale for them to enter into competition with one another. Since competitive sport was a place where manhood was earned, women had nothing to gain and everything to lose by trying to join in.[53]

The association between competitive sport and manliness carried a high psychic price tag. Young men who did not play well, or even worse did not enjoy sport, had their masculinity called into question. Even the better players had to "pay the piper." This cost originated in the logical outcome of competition—the desire to achieve victory. While the press was quick to object to the undue importance attached to victory on the playing field, their perception of sport as an arena in which to teach and test manhood encouraged this all-or-nothing competition. The ramification of the linkage would have been far less in a society where social distinctions were more clearly defined. In a modern, open, and competitive society manhood is acknowledged not as part of any ceremonial rite de passage but through a visible demonstration of achievement. Since nineteenth-century Americans established sport as a place where manhood was earned, victory became the outward sign that it had been achieved. The problem with this approach is that competitive sport is an endeavor that creates few winners and many losers. The drawback becomes more severe when it is recognized that the proponents of character development hoped that young boys would learn socialization lessons from sport. However, this age group is precisely the one that is often emotionally and psychologically unprepared to deal with the strains and consequences of competitive sport.[54]

APPENDIX

Collecting and Collating
Occupational Data

To create an occupational profile of ball players on New York City and Brooklyn baseball teams between 1850 and 1870 I attempted to identify these players from a variety of sources; check their occupations in city directories; and devise an occupational classification system. The players' names came from club records, guidebooks, newspaper accounts, and published box scores. Unfortunately, the box scores, which were the major source for obtaining names, and some of the other sources generally listed the player by last name only, or sometimes last name and first initial, both of which proved insufficient in the absence of corroborating data. As a result I could not discover the occupations of a large proportion of those individuals engaged in organized baseball.

It is impossible to say whether the absence of information on these ball players biases the occupational profile I have constructed, but several observations can be made. Certain types of men involved in organized baseball — officers and delegates of clubs, those engaged in baseball for an extended period of time, and the more active and skilled players — were overrepresented since the various sources would sooner or later identify these more visible individuals by their first and last names. Officers and delegates were more likely to have white-collar middle-class positions than nonofficers; active and skilled players were more frequently from the artisan class. As for all the other players, the ability or inability to identify them does not seem to be related to socioeconomic considerations. I suspect that if the "missing" players could have been identified, only minor changes in the occupational structure of New York City and Brooklyn ball players would have resulted.

Once the full name of the player could be determined I assumed that players on Brooklyn and New York City teams lived in the city in which they played (although I was aware that there were New York players who lived in Brooklyn or in New Jersey but worked in Manhattan). The players' occupations were then determined by checking city directories, supplemented by a handful of contemporary discussions of the topic. Certain players were eliminated when there was more than one individual in the directory with that name and a process of elimination could not be used to discover the occupations of those who played for several years. For example, if an individual played on one or more teams between 1861 and 1868 I assumed he lived in the city during that period. If only one individual with that name was listed in the directory during the entire period I assumed it was the ball player I was interested in.

Scholars have recognized that certain drawbacks exist when city directories are used to construct occupational profiles,[1] three of which concern us here. The occupational designation given an individual in the directory often varied from year to year, without any apparent change in the nature of the work. Since I chose to divide players into broader occupational categories than those given, these shifts generally did not change my data. For the small number of players who did change occupations, the more lucrative category was recorded and probably had little effect on the profile.

The systematic discrimination by the compilers of these directories against the lower class was a more serious problem. Did the apparent lack of involvement of the lower class in the national pastime stem from the fact that they were not listed in the directories and thus could not be counted? I strongly suspect that the impact of such bias was at best minimal, if not nonexistent. First, the lower class was virtually absent from most other organized sports; and second, the professional and more active ball players—the group that one would have expected to most likely come from the lower class—were from no further down the social ladder than the artisan class. Since information on the occupations of these players frequently came from sportswriters' observations—reputable men like Henry Chadwick—it is possible to eliminate bias as a reason for the absence of the lower class among ball players.

An even more serious drawback of the directories is that they focused mainly, although not exclusively, on heads of households, making it difficult to identify many of the ball players who were young and single. Here, too, the problem seemed to be universal and not based on the economic or occupational class of the ball player. Finally, the occupations of young players on highly competitive and professional teams were sometimes listed in newspapers, making it easy to include them in the survey. I do not believe that the presence of this visible group affected the occupational profile to a significant degree because a sizable minority of these players were from white-collar groups and because this particular group of players comprised only a small proportion of the players whose occupations were known.

Initially, I used two different classification systems: that of Carl Kaestle in his study of education in New York City, adapted from Robert Ernst's work on that city's immigrants[2]; and Theodore Hershberg's system from his five-cities study.[3] The first system facilitated a broadly conceived view of the occupations of ball players; however, it had the disadvantage of being cumbersome when examining the changing occupational structure of players during the varying time periods. The advantage of the second system was its manageability in examining the changing occupations of ball players. More importantly, it provided the best indicator of the relationship that existed between occupation and class in mid-nineteenth-century America.

Notes

INTRODUCTION

1. For the recent literature on the history of sport in America, see Melvin L. Adelman, "Academicians and American Athletics: A Decade of Progress," *Journal of Sport History* 10 (Spring 1983): 80–106.

2. Dale Somers, *The Rise of Sport in New Orleans, 1850–1900* (Baton Rouge: Louisiana State University Press, 1972); John R. Betts, *America's Sporting Heritage, 1850–1950* (Reading, Mass.: Addison-Wesley, 1974), 88–111; Frederic L. Paxson, "The Rise of Sport," *Mississippi Valley Historical Review* 4 (1917): 143–68; Foster R. Dulles, *A History of Recreation: America Learns to Play* (New York: Appleton-Century-Crofts, 1965), 182–89; John A. Lucas and Ronald A. Smith, *Saga of American Sport* (Philadelphia: Lea and Febiger, 1978), 125–249; William J. Baker and John Carroll, eds., *Sports in Modern America* (St. Louis: River City Publishers, 1981).

3. Dulles, *Recreation*, 84–99; Betts, *America's Sporting Heritage*, 5–48; Lucas and Smith, *Saga*, 55–121; Benjamin G. Rader, *American Sports: From the Age of Folk Games to the Age of Spectators* (Englewood Cliffs, N.J.: Prentice-Hall, 1983), 24–43. For changing attitudes toward sport in antebellum America, see John R. Betts, "Mind and Body in Early American Thought," *Journal of American History* 54 (1968): 787–805; Peter Levine, "The Promise of Sport in Antebellum America," *Journal of American Culture* 2 (1980): 623–34; John A. Lucas, "A Prelude to the Rise of Sport: Ante-Bellum America, 1850–1860," *Quest* 11 (1968): 50–57; Roberta J. Park, " 'Embodied Selves': The Rise and Development of Concern for Physical Education, Active Games and Recreation among American Women, 1776–1865," *Journal of Sport History* 5 (Summer 1978): 5–41.

4. Richard D. Brown, *Modernization: The Transformation of American Life, 1600–1865* (New York: Hill and Wang, 1976), 122–58. For changing economic conditions, see Stuart Bruchey, *The Roots of American Economic Growth, 1607–1861, An Essay in Social Causation* (New York: Harper and Row, 1968); Douglass C. North, *Growth and Welfare in the American Past: A New Economic*

History (Englewood Cliffs, N.J.: Prentice-Hall, 1966), 75–89; George R. Taylor, *The Transportation Revolution, 1815–1860* (New York: Harper and Row, 1968).

5. The sole discussion of the impact of industrialization on behavioral patterns in sport revolves around the relationship between the rise of sport and the emergence of the machine. Two scholars assert that sport was a corrective, although inadequate, response to the dictates of the machine. See Arnold J. Toynbee, *A Study of History*, 11 vols. (London: Oxford University Press, 1934–59), 4:242; Lewis Mumford, *Techniques and Civilization* (New York: Harcourt, Brace and World, 1963), 303–4. Jacques Ellul went one step further, maintaining that "sport is linked with the technical world because sport itself is a technique." See *The Technological Society* (New York: Random House, 1964), 382. By contrast, several sport historians argue that sport was a positive product of industrialization. See John R. Betts, "The Technological Revolution and the Rise of Sport, 1850–1900," *Mississippi Valley Historical Review* 40 (1953): 256; Somers, *Rise*, 275–76. While the link between the machine and sports developments might become important in the post-1870 period, the emergence of the machine and the routinization that accompanied it did not cause the initial sports surge. Modern sport did not find its first home in the factory town of Lynn but in commercial cities like New York.

6. Brown, *Modernization*, 20–22. Also see E. A. Wrigley, "The Process of Modernization and the Industrial Revolution," *Journal of Interdisciplinary History* 3 (1972): 225–60; David Ward, *Cities and Immigrants: A Geography of Change in Nineteenth-Century America* (New York: Oxford University Press, 1971), 3; Bert F. Hoselitz, "The City, the Factory, and Economic Growth," *American Economic Review* 43 (1955): 167.

7. The tendency on the part of historians to ignore the institutional character and structure of sport in their studies also derives from two trends at work within this scholarly area of inquiry. As one historian accurately notes, "One of the paradoxes of the growing academic interest in sport is the unwillingness of scholars to actually inquire into sport *per se*. Rather, sport is used as a vehicle through which insights into other, apparently more relevant, phenomena can be gained." See Braham Dabscheck, " 'Defensive Manchester': A History of the Professional Footballers Association," in Richard Cashman and Michael Mc-Kernan, eds., *Sport in History: The Making of Modern Sporting History* (Queensland: University of Queensland Press, 1979), 227. Since historical studies on sport have tended to extrapolate from developments within sport to gain an understanding of other facets of American life, scholars have found little reason to examine the institutional character of sport beyond simply taking note of leagues and associations and chronicling their changes. Historians also have examined sport mainly from the perspective of cultural and intellectual history (and to a lesser extent within the context of American studies) rather than the social sciences. This orientation has led scholars to explore the meaning of sport by investigating its interconnection with broader cultural, social, and intellectual trends and results in their ignoring vital internal structural developments, thus creating a distorted mirror approach to understanding the causes of sports change.

8. For criticism of modernization, see James A. Henretta, "Modernization: Towards a False Synthesis," *Reviews in American History* 5 (1977): 445–52;

Raymond Grew, "Modernization and Its Discontents," *American Behavioral Scientist* 21 (1977): 289–311; Daniel Scott Smith, "Modernization and American Social History," *Social Science History* 2 (1978): 361–78. For supporting statements, see Peter Stearns, "Modernization and Social History: Some Suggestions, and a Muted Cheer," *Journal of Social History* 14 (1980): 189–209; Richard D. Brown, "Modernization: A Victorian Climax," *American Quarterly* 22 (1975): 533–48; Tamara Hareven, "Modernization and Family History: Perspective on Social Change," *Signs* 2 (1976): 190–206; Richard Jensen, "On Modernizing Frederick Jackson Turner," *Western Historical Quarterly* 11 (1980): 307–22; Jayme A. Sokolow, *Eros and Modernization: Sylvester Graham, Health Reform, and the Origins of Victorian Sexuality in America* (Rutherford, N.J.: Associated University Press, 1983), 21–22.

9. Brown, *Modernization*, 7–22; Allen Guttmann, *From Ritual to Record: The Nature of Modern Sports* (New York: Columbia University Press, 1978), 15–55; Eric Dunning, "The Structural-Functional Properties of Folk Games and Modern Sport," *Sportwissesnschaft* 3 (1973): 215–32. Also see Alan G. Ingham, "Methodology in the Sociology of Sport: From Symptoms of Malaise to Weber for a Cure," *Quest* 31 (1979): 198–212.

10. While premodern and folk games share similar characteristics, I use the former because the social setting that gave rise to and nurtured folk games in Europe was largely absent in America. Clearly, the link between folk games and ritual was virtually eliminated from most of the physical contests taking place in America even before the onset of modernity. For the connection between sport and secularism, see Gutmann, *Ritual*, 16–26.

11. David Q. Voigt, *America's Leisure Revolution: Essays in the Sociology of Leisure and Sport* (Reading, Pa., 1971), 24.

12. Ellul, *Technological Society*, 382.

13. For an outstanding review of the literature on sport and the city, see Stephen Hardy, "The City and the Rise of American Sport, 1820–1920," *Exercise and Sports Sciences Reviews* 9 (1981): 183–219. For his study of Boston, see *How Boston Played: Sport, Recreation and Community, 1865–1915* (Boston: Northeastern University Press, 1982). The latter ranks as the most thoughtful application of social theory to the study of American sport history to date. His examination of the relationship between sport and the city focuses on the link between sport and the search for community, but it pays far less attention to the impact of the changing city on the evolution of the institutional structures of athletics. For a discussion of the difference between urban as "site" and "process," within the context of the new urban history, see Theodore Hershberg, ed., *Philadelphia: Work, Space, Family and Group Experience in the Nineteenth Century, Essays Towards an Interdisciplinary History* (New York: Oxford University Press, 1981), 3–35; Eric Lampard, "American Historians and the Study of Urbanization," *American Historical Review* 67 (1961): 49–61; Roy Lubove, "The Urbanization Process: An Approach to Historical Research," *Journal of the American Institute of Planners* 33 (1967): 33–36; Charles Tilly, "The State of Urbanization, Review Article," *Comparative Studies in Society and History* 10 (1967): 100–103.

14. Oscar Handlin, "The Modern City as a Field of Historical Study," in Oscar

Handlin and John Burchard, eds., *The Historian and the City* (Cambridge, Mass.: Harvard University Press, 1963), 1–9; Louis Wirth, "Urbanism as a Way of Life," *American Journal of Sociology* 44 (1938): 1–24.

15. I want to emphasize here that nowhere in this study am I suggesting that a modern system, either in society or sport, could or did automatically impose its requirements or needs. To make this claim would reduce modernization to the mechanistic and deterministic model that I reject. Actions and attitudes were the product of human agencies, whether individually or collectively, whose decisions and beliefs did at times run counter to the requirements of the modern system. While recognizing the human dimension as the agent of the historical process, it is also true that human behavior and decisions increasingly took place within the context and boundaries established by modern institutions.

16. Don Harrison Doyle, *The Social Order of a Frontier Community: Jacksonville, Illinois, 1825–70* (Urbana: University of Illinois Press, 1978), 178–93; Stephan Thernstrom, *Poverty and Progress: Social Mobility in a Nineteenth Century City* (New York: Atheneum, 1972), 169; Walter S. Glazer, "Participation and Power: Voluntary Associations and the Functional Organization of Cincinnati in 1840," *Historical Methods Newsletter* 5 (1972): 151–68. For changes in social relationships, see Peter Goheen, "Industrialization and the Growth of Cities in Nineteenth-Century America," *American Studies* 14 (1973): 49–65; Zane Miller, "Scarcity, Abundance, and American Urban History," *Journal of Urban History* 4 (1978): 141.

17. My discussion of class in this study uses the familiar divisions upper, upper-middle, middle, lower-middle, and lower. While I employ these groupings I am aware of the limitations of discussing class in these terms. For discussion of these limitations, see Michael Katz, "Social Class in North American Urban History," *Journal of Interdisciplinary History* 11 (1981): 579–605.

18. As part of my dissertation research I did a prosopography of the members of the American Jockey Club in 1866 and 1867. See "The Develoment of Modern Athletics: Sport in New York City, 1820–1870," (Ph.D. diss., University of Illinois, 1980), 180–250.

19. John W. Loy, "The Nature of Sport: A Definitional Effort," *Quest* 10 (1968): 1–15; Guttmann, *Ritual*, 3–18. It is significant to note that organizational developments are of primary importance in the institutionalization of sport. In his classic study Johan Huizinga viewed the formation of permanent clubs as the starting point for modern sport. See *Homo Ludens: A Study of the Play Element in Culture* (Boston: Beacon, 1955), 196.

20. Richard S. Gruneau, "Sport as an Area of Sociological Study: An Introduction to Major Themes and Perspectives," in Richard S. Gruneau and John G. Albinson, eds., *Canadian Sport: Sociological Perspectives* (Don Mills, Ont.: Addison-Wesley, 1976), 20.

CHAPTER 1: THE CHANGING CHARACTER OF NEW YORK CITY

1. Bayrd Still, "The Essence of New York City," *New-York Historical Society Quarterly* 43 (1959): 423. The purpose here is not merely to examine New York in 1820 and 1870 but to summarize the factors that shaped the city at these two

dates. For the sake of convenience the terms New York and New York City refer to the city as it existed in 1870, or what is currently the borough of Manhattan.

2. Ira Rosenwaike, *Population History of New York City* (Syracuse, N.Y.: Syracuse University Press, 1972), 14-19, 22, 33-35 (quote from p. 19). For New Englanders' influence on New York, see Robert G. Albion, *The Rise of New York Port, 1815-1860* (New York: Scribner's, 1939), 241-51; David M. Ellis, "The Yankee Invasion of New York," *New York History* 32 (1951): 9-11.

3. Rosenwaike, *Population*, 20-23, 39. The 1825 census did not ascertain birthplace, merely citizenship. Consequently, the exact number of foreign-born residents can only be estimated. Also see Robert Ernst, *Immigrant Life in New York City, 1825-1863* (New York: King's Crown, 1949), 23; Sidney I. Pomerantz, *New York: An American City, 1783-1803. A Study of Urban Life* (New York: Columbia University Press, 1938), 203-9.

4. Bayrd Still, *Mirror for Gotham: New York as Seen by Contemporaries from Dutch Days to the Present* (New York: New York University Press, 1956), 88; Dorothy C. Barck, ed., *Letters from John Pintard to His Daughter Eliza Noel Pintard Davidson, 1816-1833*, 4 vols. (New York: New-York Historical Society, 1937-40), 1:216-17; Ernst, *Immigrant*, 1-24; Raymond A. Mohl, *Poverty in New York, 1783-1825* (New York: Oxford University Press, 1971), 60-62; Pomerantz, *New York*, 207-9. For the impact of ethnicity during the colonial period, see Patricia U. Bonomi, *A Factious People: Politics and Society in Colonial New York* (New York: Columbia University Press, 1971), 25-26; Virginia D. Harrington, *The New York Merchant on the Eve of the Revolution* (New York: Columbia University Press, 1935), 17-18.

5. Albion, *Rise*, 1-8; Robert G. Albion, "The Port of New York in the New Republic, 1783-1793," *New York History* 21 (1940): 388-403; Pomerantz, *New York*, 147-99; David T. Gilchrist, ed., *The Growth of Seaport Cities, 1790-1825* (Charlottesville: University Press of Virginia, 1967); Myron H. Luke, *The Port of New York. 1800-1810, The Foreign Trade and Business Community* (Hempstead, N.Y.: Salisbury, 1953).

6. Albion, *Rise*, 1, 8, 236-37; John Lambert, *Travels Through Canada and the United States of North America in the Years 1806, 1807 & 1808*, 2 vols. (London, 1804), quoted in Still, "Essence," 403. Also see Frederic C. Jaher, *The Urban Establishment: Upper Strata in Boston, New York, Charleston, Chicago, and Los Angeles* (Urbana: University of Illinois Press, 1982), 178; David Montgomery, "The Working Class of the Pre-Industrial American City, 1780-1830," *Labor History* 9 (1968): 6.

7. Albion, *Rise*, 12-13, 38-42, 276-80; Robert A. Davison, "Comments: New York's Foreign Trade," in Gilchrist, *Seaport*, 69-70.

8. Albion, *Rise*, 13-15; Herman E. Krooss, "Financial Institutions," in Gilchrist, *Seaport*, 105-15; Davidson, "Comments," 70.

9. Pomerantz, *New York*, 35-75; I. N. Phelps Stokes, *The Iconography of Manhattan Island, 1498-1909*, 6 vols. (New York: Dodd, 1915-28), 2:519-22; James G. Wilson, ed., *The Memorial History of the City of New York*, 4 vols. (New York: New York Historical Company, 1892-93), 3:381-85.

10. Edmund P. Willis, "Social Origins of Political Leadership in New York from the Revolution to 1815" (Ph.D. diss., University of California at Berkeley,

1967); Bruce M. Wilkenfield, "The New York City Common Council, 1689–1800," *New York History* 52 (1971): 264–73.

11. Edward D. Durand, *The Finances of New York City* (New York: Macmillan, 1898), 7–65; Pomerantz, *New York*, 355–71; Richard B. Morris, "The Metropolis of the State," in Alexander C. Flick, ed., *History of the State of New York*, 10 vols. (New York: Columbia University Press, 1933–37), 10:197–98.

12. Edward Pessen, *Riches, Class and Power Before the Civil War* (Lexington, Mass.: Heath, 1973), 292–94.

13. Stokes, *Iconography*, 1:331, 517; Pomerantz, *New York*, 19–20, 226–36; Daniel Curry, *New York: Historical Sketch of the Rise and Progress of the Metropolitan City of America* (New York: Carleton and Phillips, 1853), 145–46; *Blunt's Stranger's Guide to the City of New York* (New York: Edmund M. Blunt, 1817), 38–39; Myron H. Luke, "Some Characteristics of the New York Business Community," *New York History* 34 (1953): 393–94.

14. John W. Reps, *The Making of Urban America: A History of City Planning in the United States* (Princeton, N.J.: Princeton University Press, 1965), 298–99; Raymond A. Mohl, "Poverty, Pauperism, and Social Order in the Preindustrial American City, 1780–1840," *Social Science Quarterly* 52 (1972): 936; Pomerantz, *New York*, 246–58; Curry, *New York*, 167–68.

15. *Blunt's Guide*, 36–37; Luke, "Some Characteristics," 395–96.

16. George R. Taylor, "The Beginnings of Mass Transportation in Urban America," *Smithsonian Journal of History* 1 (1966): 37–40; Luke, "Some Characteristics," 398.

17. Jaher, *Urban*, 201–8; Willis, "Social Origins," 119; Douglas T. Miller, *Jacksonian Aristocracy: Class and Democracy in New York, 1830–1860* (New York: Oxford University Press, 1967), 80. For the view that wealthy New Yorkers were men of inherited wealth, see Pessen, *Riches*, 138–47.

18. Pessen, *Riches*, 172.

19. Edward Pessen, *Jacksonian America: Society, Personality and Politics* (Homewood, Ill.: Dorsey, 1969), 48. For the emergence of a middle-class consciousness, see Carl Bridenbaugh, *Cities in Revolt: Urban Life in America, 1743–1776* (New York: Oxford University Press, 1971), 350–52.

20. Sean Wilentz, *Chants Democratic: New York City & the Rise of the American Working Class, 1788–1850* (New York: Oxford University Press, 1984); Howard B. Rock, *Artisans of the New Republic: The Tradesmen of New York City in the Age of Jefferson* (New York: New York University Press, 1979); Walter Hugins, *Jacksonian Democracy and the Working Class: A Study of the New York Workingmen's Movement, 1829–1837* (Stanford, Calif.: Stanford University Press, 1960). For discussion of changing economic conditions, see George R. Taylor, *The Transportation Revolution, 1815–1860* (New York: Harper and Row, 1968); Douglass C. North, *The Economic Growth of the United States, 1790–1860* (Englewood Cliffs, N.J.: Prentice Hall, 1961), 61–121, 156–203.

21. Carrol S. Rosenberg, "Protestants and Five Pointers: The Five Point House of Industry, 1850–1870," *New-York Historical Society Quarterly* 48 (1964): 328. Also see Mohl, *Poverty*, 14–34; Ernst, *Immigrant*, 48–60; Carroll S. Rosenberg, *Religion and the Rise of the American City: The New York City Mission Movement, 1828–1870* (Ithaca, N.Y.: Cornell University Press, 1971), 33–36. For

poverty in colonial New York, see Raymond Mohl, "Poverty in Early America, A Reappraisal: The Case of Eighteenth-Century New York City," *New York History* 50 (1969): 5–27.

22. Mohl, "Poverty, Pauperism and Social Order," 934–48; Mohl, *Poverty,* 159–70, 241–63; Still, *Mirror,* 79, 96; James F. Richardson, *The New York Police, Colonial Times to 1901* (New York: Oxford University Press, 1970), 15, 25–26; Carl F. Kaestle, *The Evolution of an Urban School System: New York City, 1750–1850* (Cambridge, Mass.: Harvard University Press, 1973), 110–12, 158–59.

23. Still, *Mirror,* 98; Charles N. Glaab and A. Theodore Brown, *A History of Urban America* (New York: Macmillan, 1967), 86; Joseph Dorfman, "Economic Thought," in Gilchrist, *Seaport,* 157; John A. Dix, *A Sketch of the Resources of the City of New York* (New York: Carvill, 1827).

24. For New York's cultural life, see James T. Callow, *Kindred Spirit: Knickerbocker Writers and American Artists, 1807–1855* (Chapel Hill: University of North Carolina Press, 1967), 3–7; Robert July, *The Essential New Yorker: Gulick Crommelin Verplanck* (Durham, N.C.: Duke University Press, 1951), 90. For New York's journalistic developments, see Allan R. Pred, *Urban Growth and the Circulation of Information: The United States System of Cities, 1790–1840* (Cambridge, Mass.: Harvard University Press, 1973), 43, 49; Frank Mott, *American Journalism: A History, 1690–1960* (New York: Macmillan, 1962), 133.

25. Pomerantz, *New York,* 372–95; Jaher, *Urban,* 226–29, 238–40, 243; William W. Cutler III, "Status Values and Education of the Poor: Trustees of the New York Public School Society, 1805–1853," *American Quarterly* 24 (1972): 69–85; M. J. Heale, "From City Fathers to Social Critics: Humanitarianism and Government in New York," *Journal of American History* 63 (1976): 21–41.

26. Constance M. Green, *The Rise of Urban America* (New York: Harper and Row, 1965), 18–19; James Hardie, *The Description of the City of New York* (New York: Marks, 1827), 339.

27. Pomerantz, *New York,* 460–64, 468–85; Martha J. Lamb, *History of the City of New York,* 2 vols. (New York: Barnes, 1877), 2:433; Timothy Dwight, *Travels in New England and New York,* ed. Barbara M. Solomon, 4 vols. (Cambridge, Mass.: Belknap, 1969), 3:332.

28. Pomerantz, *New York,* 485–88; Carl Bridenbaugh, *Cities in the Wilderness: The First Century of Urban Life in America* (New York: Oxford University Press, 1971), 434–35; Bridenbaugh, *The Colonial Craftsman* (Chicago: University of Chicago Press, 1961), 165; Rock, *Artisans,* 295–300.

29. Bridenbaugh, *Cities in the Wilderness,* 119–21; Alice M. Earle, *Colonial Days in Old New York* (New York: Scribner, 1906), 208–9; Ester Singleton, *Social New York under the Georges, 1714–1776* (New York: Appleton, 1902), 259–71; Foster R. Dulles, *A History of Recreation: America Learns to Play* (New York: Appleton-Century-Crofts, 1965), 33–34, 51–52; Herbert Manchester, *Four Centuries of Sport in America, 1490–1890* (New York: Derrydale, 1931), 30–33, 38–41.

30. Earle, *Colonial,* 222–24; Oscar T. Barck, Jr., *New York City During the War for Independence: With Special Reference to the Period of British Occupation* (New York: Columbia University Press, 1931), 183–85; Dulles, *Recreation,* 65–66; Pomerantz, *New York,* 393–94, 497–500; John A. Krout, *Annals of American*

Sport (New Haven, Conn.: Yale University Press, 1929), 26; John Hervey, *Racing in America, 1665-1865*, 2 vols. (New York: The Jockey Club, 1944), 1:131.

31. Rosenwaike, *Population*, 33-48, 63-66, 71.

32. Pessen, *Jacksonian*, 297-99; Robert Ernst, "Economic Nativism in New York City During the 1840s," *New York History* 29 (1948): 170-86; Leo Hershkowitz, "The Native American Democratic Association in New York City, 1835-1836," *New-York Historical Society Quarterly* 46 (1962): 41-59; Ira P. Leonard, "The Rise and Fall of the American Republic Party in New York City, 1843-1846," ibid. 50 (1966): 151-92.

33. Rosenwaike, *Population*, 55; Blake McKelvey, *Amerian Urbanization: A Comparative History* (Glenview, Ill.: Scott, Foresman, 1973), 59, 73. For the emergence of New York as America's leading metropolis, see Edward K. Spann, *The New Metropolis, New York City, 1840-1860* (New York: Columbia University Press, 1981).

34. Spann, *New Metropolis*, 2-22, 94-116, 205-41; Still, *Mirror*, 171; Glaab and Brown, *Urban*, 38-39; Stokes, *Iconography*, 3:645-49; Jaher, *Urban*, 187-96; Albion, *Rise*, 384-86; Allan R. Pred, *The Spatial Dynamics of United States Urban Industrial Growth, 1800-1914: Interpretive and Theoretical Essays* (Cambridge: M.I.T. Press, 1966), 20, 151; Thomas C. Cochran and William Miller, *A Social History of Industrial America* (New York: Harper, 1961), 85-86.

35. Pessen, *Riches*, 33-34; Rufus S. Tucker, "The Distribution of Income among Taxpayers in the United States, 1863-1935," *Quarterly Journal of Economics* 52 (1938): 547-62; *The Income Record, a List Giving the Taxable Income for the Year 1863, of the Residents of New York* (New York: American News, 1865). For the contention that there were 115 millionaires in New York, see Reuben Vose, *The Rich Men of New York*, 2d ser. (New York, 1861), quoted in Spann, *New Metropolis*, 205. For the increasing concentration of wealth, see Peter H. Lindbert and Jeffrey G. Williamson, "Three Centuries of American Inequality," in Paul Uselding, ed., *Research in Economic History: An Annual Compilation of Research* (Greenwich, Conn.: Jai, 1976), 102-6.

36. Jaher, *Urban*, 201-8; Albion, *Rise*, 235-59. For a dissenting view, see Pessen, *Riches*, 84-85.

37. Pessen, *Riches*, 225-30; Jaher, *Urban*, 234-35, 245-46, 263-81.

38. Alexander B. Callow, Jr., *The Tweed Ring* (New York: Oxford University Press, 1965), 4-7, 76-81 passim; Spann, *New Metropolis*, 45-66, 341-61; Seymour J. Mandelbaum, *Boss Tweed's New York* (New York: Wiley, 1965), 40-41, 67-75; Jerome Mushkat, *Tammany: The Evolution of a Political Machine, 1789-1865* (Syracuse, N.Y.: Syracuse University Press, 1971), 208-9, 364-70; Leo Hershkowitz, *Tweed's New York: Another Look* (Garden City, N.Y.: Doubleday, 1977); Pessen, *Riches*, 286-88.

39. Tucker, "Distribution," 548; Spann, *New Metropolis*, 243-44; Selma Berrol, "Who Went to School in Mid-Nineteenth Century New York? An Essay in the New Urban History," in Irwin Yellowitz, ed., *Essays in the History of New York. A Memorial to Sidney Pomerantz* (Port Washington, N.Y.: Kennikat, 1978), 48.

40. Lee Soltow, *Men and Wealth in the United States, 1850-1870* (New Haven, Conn.: Yale University Press, 1975), 36; Glaab and Brown, *Urban*, 93-95; Ernst,

Immigrant, 59; Miller, *Jacksonian,* 135–38; Taylor, "Beginnings," 37–40; Mandelbaum, *Boss,* 8.

41. Spann, *New Metropolis,* 18. For studies dealing with various New York problems and responses to them, see Rosenberg, *Religion;* Kaestle, *Urban School System;* John Duffy, *A History of Public Health in New York City, 1625–1865* (New York: Russell Sage Foundation, 1968); Richardson, *New York Police;* Stephen F. Ginsberg, "The Police and Fire Protection in New York City: 1800–1850," *New York History* 52 (1971): 133–50; Roy Lubove, "The New York Association for Improving the Condition of the Poor: The Formative Years," *New-York Historical Society Quarterly* 43 (1959): 307–27. Also see Paul Boyer, *Urban Masses and Moral Order* (Cambridge, Mass.: Harvard University Press, 1978), 3–122. The phrase "search for order" is derived from Robert H. Wiebe's classic study on societal changes in the post–Civil War years. See *Search for Order, 1877–1920* (New York: Hill and Wang, 1967).

42. Mohl, "Poverty, Pauperism, and Social Order," 943–44; Mohl, *Poverty,* 137–58; Glaab and Brown, *Urban,* 90–91; Rosenberg, *Religion,* 37–38. Also see Allan Stanley Horlick, *Country Boys and Merchant Princes: The Social Control of Young Men in New York* (Lewisberg, Pa.: Bucknell University Press, 1975).

43. Spann, *New Metropolis,* 35–36, 60–66, 255–77; Rosenberg, *Religion,* 184–85; Stokes, *Iconography,* 3:756. The new governmental institutions did not solve many of the problems New Yorkers confronted. The increasing complexities of urban life combined with financial, political, and ideological considerations to frequently check urban reform. Nevertheless, these permanent organizations created an essential framework to which all later reform, in one way or another, had to conform.

44. *New York Herald,* 24 Sept., 28 Aug. 1854, 21 Oct. 1861; *New York Times,* 31 Jan. 1867; Russell B. Nye, *Society and Culture in America, 1830–1860* (New York: Harper and Row, 1974), 148; Still, *Mirror,* 93–95, 138–40, 156, 176–77; Francis G. Fairfield, *The Clubs of New York* (New York: Hinton, 1873), 7; Pessen, *Riches,* 225–30; *New York Tribune,* 31 Mar. 1852; Glaab and Brown, *Urban,* 254–55; Thomas Bender, *Toward an Urban Vision: Ideas and Institutions in Nineteenth-Century America* (Lexington: University Press of Kentucky, 1975), 173–80.

SECTION I: SPORTS OF THE TURF: THOROUGHBREDS AND TROTTERS

1. *New York Post,* 26 May 1823; *New York American,* 22 Nov. 1822; *New York Spectator,* 26 May 1823; *New York Statesman,* 24 May 1823.

2. The reported size of crowds attending sports contests between 1820 and 1870 was grossly exaggerated. Nonetheless, I note throughout this study the estimated crowd sizes the press reported since they provide insight into the media's perception of the appeal of a sport or a particular event, and because they permit, within certain limits, a comparison of the popularity of various sports and sporting events.

3. *American,* 23–27 May 1823; *Post,* 26–27 May 1823; *Spectator,* 26 May 1823; *Statesman,* 24, 28 May 1823; *New York Gazette,* 28 May 1823.

4. John Hervey, *Racing in America, 1665–1865,* 2 vols. (New York: The

Jockey Club, 1944), 1:6, 8, 12–25, 42–108; John R. Betts, *America's Sporting Heritage, 1850–1950* (Reading, Mass.: Addison-Wesley, 1974), 5–8; Francis B. Culver, *Blood Horses of Colonial Days* (Baltimore, 1922), 25–48, 99–139; John A. Lucas and Ronald A. Smith, *Saga of American Sport* (Philadelphia: Lea and Febiger, 1978), 18, 29–30, 43–46.

5. Hervey, *Racing*, 1:29–42, 120–22; Carl Bridenbaugh, *Cities in Revolt: Urban Life in America, 1743–1776* (New York: Oxford University Press, 1971), 364–65; Alice M. Earle, *Colonial Days in Old New York* (New York: Scribner, 1906), 218–26; Herbert Manchester, *Four Centuries of Sport in America, 1490–1890* (New York: Derrydale, 1931), 33–34, 45; John Austin Stevens, "Early New York Racing History," *Wallace's Monthly Magazine* 3 (Oct. 1877): 782–88; Jessie T. Merritt, *Ascot Heath, U.S.A. An Epoch in Second Century of Long Island's Turf History During British Occupation* (Farmingdale, N.Y., 1945); Henry R. Stiles, *A History of the City of Brooklyn*, 3 vols. (Brooklyn, N.Y.: Subscription, 1867–70), 1:319–28.

6. *Laws of New York, 25th Session* (Albany, N.Y., 1802), 69–70; Hervey, *Racing*, 1:111–12, 131–39; Betts, *Sporting Heritage*, 9–10.

7. *Spirit of the Times* 27 (27 Sept. 1857): 364; Hervey, *Racing*, 1:136–40, 253–60. Hervey noted that in an 1811 editorial the *Post* "bewailed the law against racing in the Empire State, taking the position that the sport should be maintained to improve the breed of horse, which was of the utmost importance." See ibid., 1:255. Also see *United States Sporting Magazine* 1 (Nov. 1835): 32–33.

CHAPTER 2: THE EARLY MODERNIZATION OF HORSE RACING, 1820–45

1. Dwight Akers, *Drivers Up: The Story of American Harness Racing* (New York: Putnam's, 1938), 34; *New York Assembly Journal, 44th Session, 1820–1821*, 1053–56; *Laws of the State of New York, 44th Session*, 175.

2. *New York American*, 23, 30 Mar. 1821; *New York Post*, 15, 20 Mar. 1821; *New York Gazette*, 17, 31 Mar. 1821; *New York Spectator*, 14 Mar., 3 Apr. 1821. I could not locate the argument that the antiracing legislation had been ineffective in newspaper accounts of the debate on the bill. Contemporary discussions of this subject illustrate that this was a popular justification for the return of legitimate racing. See *Post*, 28 Nov. 1826; *United States Sporting Magazine* 1 (Nov. 1835): 33.

3. *New York Assembly Journal, 44th Session, 1820–1821*, 1056.

4. John Hervey, *Racing in America, 1665–1865*, 2 vols. (New York: The Jockey Club, 1944), 2:100.

5. *Post*, 17–18, 20, 23 May 1823, 7 Sept. 1821; *American*, 16 Oct. 1821, 12 Oct. 1822; *Gazette*, 17 Oct. 1821, 22 May 1822, 22–23 Oct. 1823; *New York Statesman*, 22–23 Oct. 1823.

6. For discussion of Eclipse's early racing career, see Hervey, *Racing*, 1:258–60; *New York Sporting Magazine* 2 (Sept. 1834): 77–79; *American Turf Register and Sporting Magazine* 1 (Feb. 1830): 269–70. It is not known who sponsored racing on Long Island during the years the sport was prohibited. Quite possibly, racing was linked to the activities of a local agricultural society. Whether this was the case or not, the fact that races took place illustrates that enforcement of the

antiracing legislation was lax. While the legislation did not totally curtail racing, it clearly hindered the sport. It is significant that southern horses were absent from Long Island tracks during the years the sport was illegal but appeared there immediately after the passage of the 1821 racing legislation.

7. *Amerian,* 21 Mar., 15 Apr. 1820; *Post,* 7 Jan., 14 Apr. 1820.

8. *Post,* 22 May 1822; *Gazette,* 27 Oct. 1821; *Spectator,* 28 May 1822. While no figures exist, contemporary reports make it quite clear that attendance rose on the days that Eclipse raced. For discussion of Eclipse's return to racing and his races, see *American,* 18 Oct. 1821; *Gazette,* 22 May 1822; *Post,* 15, 18 Oct. 1821, 17 May, 16 Oct. 1822; *Spectator,* 20 Oct. 1821.

9. *American,* 16 Oct. 1822; *Post,* 12, 16 Oct. 1822. Van Ranst did not put up the entire stake, but the other backers of Eclipse are unknown.

10. For the initial quote, see Max Farrand, "The Great Race—Eclipse Against the World," *Scribners Magazine* 70 (Oct. 1921): 458. Also see *American,* 22–23 Nov. 1822; *Post,* 22–23, 26 Nov. 1822; *Gazette,* 25 Nov. 1822; *Spectator,* 23 Nov. 1822.

11. *American,* 23 Nov. 1822; *Gazette,* 23 Nov. 1822; *Post,* 23, 26–27 Nov. 1822. John C. Stevens put up $6,000 of the $20,000 wagered by the North. For the other backers of Eclipse, see Hervey, *Racing,* 1:261–62. For the racing career of William R. Johnson, see ibid., 1:262, 2:77–88.

12. *American,* 26 May 1823; Dorothy C. Barck, ed., *Letters from John Pintard to His Daughter Eliza Noel Pintard Davidson, 1816-1833,* 4 vols. (New York: New-York Historical Society, 1937-40), 2:136–37. Also see *Gazette,* 27 May 1823; *Spectator,* 26 May 1823.

13. For the selection of Henry as the southern choice, see Hervey, *Racing,* 1:263–65; Charles E. Trevathan, *The American Thoroughbred* (New York: Macmillan, 1905), 143–44.

14. *American,* 29 May 1823; *Post,* 28 May 1823. Crafts never got over the charge that he mismanaged Eclipse and felt that the criticism was unjust. See *Spirit of the Times* 11 (23 Oct. 1841): 402. For discussion of Purdy's background and the events surrounding his involvement in the Eclipse-Henry race, see Melvin L. Adelman, "The Development of Modern Athletics: Sport in New York City, 1820–1870" (Ph.D. diss., University of Illinois, 1980), 81.

15. For contemporary discussion of the race, see *Post,* 28 May 1823; *Statesman,* 28 May 1829; *American,* 29 May 1823; *American Turf Register* 2 (Sept. 1830): 8–11.

16. *American,* 27–28 May 1823; *Post,* 27–28 May 1823; *Statesman,* 28–29 May 1823; *Gazette,* 10 June 1823; *Spectator,* 3 June 1823.

17. *Statesman,* 27–28 May 1823; *Baltimore Niles Weekly Register,* 31 May 1823, quoted in John R. Betts, *America's Sporting Heritage, 1850-1950* (Reading, Mass.: Addison-Wesley, 1974), 11; *Post,* 29 May 1823. Cadwallader R. Colden estimated that the South lost $200,000 on the outcome of the race. See, *American Turf Register* 2 (Sept. 1830): 11. Since his account of the race has been the most popular one, his figure, which was probably high, has been repeated by virtually all other racing historians. The *Richmond Inquirer* maintained that including the $20,000 stake the South lost $60,000–$75,000, which was probably closer to the truth. The *Inquirer* article was reprinted in the *Post,* 7 June 1823.

18. Southern excuses for Henry's defeat included: (1) Colonel Johnson's absence from the course because he was ill; (2) the distance traveled by the southern horse to New York; (3) the incorrect age of Henry under New York rules; and (4) the poor racing conditions caused by the crowd spilling out onto the track. See *American*, 5 June 1823; *Gazette*, 10 June 1823; *Post*, 2, 5, 7 June 1823, 31 July 1824; *Spectator*, 6 June 1823; *Statesman*, 5, 7 June 1823.

19. *Post*, 2 June 1823. For southern challenges, see *American*, 1 July 1823, 10 Feb. 1824; *Gazette*, 2 July 1823, 10 Feb. 1824; *Post*, 21 Feb., 31 July 1824. For the news media's acceptance of Eclipse's retirement, see *American*, 29 May 1823; *Gazette*, 5 Feb. 1824; *Post*, 28 May, 2 June 1823; *Statesman*, 28 May 1823.

20. *American*, 9 June 1823; Josiah Quincy, *Figures from the Past, from the Leaves of Old Journals*, rev. ed. (Boston: Little, Brown, 1926), 85. Also see *Spectator*, 30 May 1823, 29 Nov. 1822.

21. *American*, 22 Dec. 1823, 15 Oct. 1832; *Gazette*, 3 June 1825; *Post*, 30 May 1823; *Wallace's Monthly Magazine* 3 (Mar. 1877): 160–64.

22. *Post*, 8 Oct. 1825; *American*, 11 Oct. 1825; *Gazette*, 10 Oct. 1825; *Spirit* 17 (7 Aug. 1847): 278.

23. *American*, 18 Oct. 1823, 24 May 1824, 27 May 1825; *Gazette*, 21–23 Oct. 1823, 25 May 1824; *Post*, 17 Oct. 1823, 26 May 1824, 27 May 1825; *Statesman*, 18, 22–23 Oct. 1823.

24. *American*, 1 Nov. 1825; *Post*, 1 Nov. 1825; *Spectator*, 4 Nov. 1825. For further discussion of the Ariel-Flirtilla race, see Hervey, *Racing*, 1:274–76; Trevethan, *American Thoroughbred*, 165–67.

25. *Post*, 4 Oct. 1825, 8 Feb., 28 Nov. 1826; *American*, 11 Oct. 1825. Two newspapers claimed that New York was the biggest winner in the Henry-Eclipse race since 20,000 strangers came to the city to see the intersectional contest, and each visitor spent approximately twenty dollars. See *Spectator*, 26 May 1823; *Post*, 29 May 1823.

26. [Cadwallader R. Colden], *An Exposé of the Measures which Caused a Suspension of the Races on the Union Course, in October 1830; and the Proceedings since October 1828; of the Association and Managers in Their Respective Relations by the Late Manager* (New York, 1831), 6–9; *Spirit* 8 (Dec. 8, 1838): 344.

27. [Colden], *Exposé*, 8–10, 30, 38.

28. *Post*, 21 Oct. 1830.

29. [Colden], *Exposé*, 11–22, 31–33, 37–44; *Post*, 10 Sept. 1831.

30. *Standard*, 15 Oct. 1830; *American*, 20 Oct. 1830; *Post*, 21 Oct. 1830; *Spectator*, 23 Oct. 1830. For Colden's view of the riot, see *Exposé*, 33.

31. Hervey, *Racing*, 2:102–3; John Dizikes, *Sportsmen and Gamesmen* (Boston: Houghton Mifflin, 1981), 133.

32. Hervey, *Racing*, 2:103; *Spirit* 9 (25 May 1839): 133.

33. Hervey, *Racing*, 2:91–135; Betts, *Sporting Heritage*, 11–12.

34. *Spirit* 2 (9 Feb. 1833), (30 Mar. 1833), 21 (28 June 1851): 222; *Post*, 15 Feb. 1833, 4 Nov. 1835. Produce stakes were races in which the nominations were made at least a year in advance, sometimes longer.

35. *American*, 30 Sept., 30–31 Oct., 1 Nov. 1833; *Post*, 1 Nov. 1836. For discussion of the intersectional contest between Post Boy and John Bascombe,

representing the North and South, respectively, see *American Turf Register* 7 (July 1836): 511; *Spirit* 6 (28 May 1836): 117, 6 (5 June, 1836): 124; *The New Yorker,* 1 June 1836; Hervey, *Racing,* 2:117–19.

36. *Spirit* 8 (8 Dec. 1838): 344.

37. Ibid. 7 (9 Sept. 1837): 236, (11 Nov. 1837): 308, 8 (21 Apr. 1838): 76; *New York Herald,* 5 June 1837; Hervey, *Racing,* 2:99–100, 103.

38. *Spirit* 8 (8 Dec. 1838): 344, (26 Jan. 1839): 396, 10 (10 Oct. 1840): 378. For the impact of the economic depression on New York's economy, see Edward Spann, *New Metropolis: New York City, 1840-1857* (New York: Columbia University Press, 1981), 10–13; Margaret G. Myers, *The New York Money Market* (New York: Columbia University Press, 1931), 94–99.

39. *Spirit* 8 (26 Jan. 1839): 396, 9 (13 Apr. 1839): 66.

40. For revamping the New York Jockey Club, see ibid. 9 (13 Apr. 1839): 66, (27 Apr. 1839): 90.

41. Ibid. 11 (6 Nov. 1841): 426, (13 Nov. 1841): 438; *Herald,* 10 May 1842; Hervey, *Racing,* 2:156–57.

42. See the *Spirit of the Times,* Dec. 1841–May 1842.

43. *Spirit* 12 (12 May 1842): 126, (21 May 1842): 133, 138–39; *American Turf Register* 13 (July 1842): 367–74; *Herald,* 6, 10–11 May 1842.

44. *Spirit* 12 (21 May 1842): 139.

45. Ibid. 13 (3 June 1843): 162, 14 (5 Oct. 1844): 378; *Herald,* 9 May, 5 June 1844, 18 May 1845; *American Turf Register* 14 (Dec. 1843): 734.

46. *Spirit* 15 (10 May 1845): 122, (17 May 1845): 134–35; *Herald,* 6, 12–14 May 1845; *New York Tribune,* 14 May 1845; Hervey, *Racing,* 2:167–73.

47. *Spirit* 15 (31 May 1845): 158.

48. John Hervey noted that as late as the 1830s "if an average meeting started off with from thirty to forty horses on the grounds, its success was assured, while many were glad to have as many as twenty." See *Racing,* 2:104.

49. Ibid, 2:106–8, 153–54.

50. Ibid., 2:153–54; Betts, *Sporting Heritage,* 13. Also see *American Turf Register* 10 (Jan.-Feb. 1839): 61–63, 8 (Sept. 1837): 484; *Herald,* 28 Apr. 1847. Precise figures for the impact of the depression of 1837 on the interrelationship between racing and the breeding industry are unavailable. However, the close connection between these variables may be drawn from the figures in the years surrounding the Great Depression of 1929. See, Rienzi W. Jennings, "Taxation of Thoroughbred Racing," *Bulletin of the Bureau of Business Research, College of Commerce* 20 (Lexington: University of Kentucky, 1949): 11–12.

51. For the decline of racing in the Old South, see Hervey, *Racing,* 2:154–55. For the rise of horse racing in New Orleans, see Dale A. Somers, *The Rise of Sport in New Orleans, 1850-1900* (Baton Rouge: Louisiana State University Press, 1972), 24–34.

52. Nancy L. Struna, "The North-South Races: American Thoroughbred Racing in Transition, 1823-1850," *Journal of Sport History* 8 (Summer 1981): 42.

53. For the development of the American stud book, see Fairfax Harrison, *The Background of the American Stud Book* (Richmond, Va.: Old Dominion Press, 1933); Hervey, *Racing,* 1:95–98.

54. Hervey, *Racing,* 1:250; *Spirit* 12 (4 June 1842): 157.

55. There is no list of New York horsemen. Names of individuals who entered horses in races were drawn from the newspapers. The majority of entrants were non–New York residents. Of the horsemen living in the metropolitan area, the majority resided outside the city, generally in the rural regions of Long Island and New Jersey where there was space to breed and raise horses. For the list of the wealthiest New Yorkers in 1828 and 1845, see Edward Pessen, *Riches, Class and Power Before the Civil War* (Lexington, Mass.: Heath, 1973), 320–26.

56. For the classic study of the connection between status and consumption, see Thorstein Veblen, *The Theory of the Leisure Class: An Economic Study of Institutions* (New York: Mentor, 1953), 41–80. For discussion of the relationship between sport, wealthy men, and status, see Somers, *Rise,* 23–24; Dennis Brailsford, *Sport and Society: Elizabeth to Anne* (London: Routledge and Kegan Paul, 1969), 173–95; Benjamin G. Rader, *American Sports: From the Age of Folk Games to the Age of Spectators* (Englewood Cliffs, N.J.: Prentice-Hall, 1983), 50–60.

57. *Spirit* 10 (10 Oct. 1840): 378; Struna, "North-South Races," 50–53; Adelman, "Modern Athletics," 82. Wray Vamplew claims that while English horsemen were primarily motivated by social considerations, they never lost sight of the economic dimensions of the sport. See *The Turf: A Social and Economic History of Horse Racing* (London: Lane, 1976), 183.

58. For the view that religion inhibited the growth of racing, see *Spirit* 27 (27 June 1857): 235; *American Turf Register* 12 (Dec. 1841): 649–50; *Wilkes' Spirit of the Times* 11 (Dec. 24, 1864): 268. The absence of a thoroughbred racing heritage in New England was largely responsible for the failure of wealthy New Yorkers of New England descent to become involved in racing. To a lesser extent this pattern held throughout the post–Civil War years. See Adelman, "Modern Athletics," 183–84.

59. *Spirit* 6 (3 Dec. 1836): 332.

60. Ibid. 7 (9 Sept. 1837): 236, 6 (7 May 1836): 92. Also see *Post,* 18 Oct. 1821; *American,* 28 May 1833; *Herald,* 5 June 1837, 6 May 1836. For a discussion of the current relationship between attendance at the racecourse and the availability of quick, low-cost transportation, see David Novick, *An Economic Study of Harness Horse Racing* (Santa Monica, Calif., 1962), 17.

61. For changes in English racing, see Vamplew, *Turf,* 23–33.

62. [Colden], *Exposé,* 8–11, 39–41; *Post,* 10 Sept. 1831. The following are estimates of Colden's expenses. Purses were $5,390 yearly (during the Botts administration they averaged $6,800 yearly). In two years Colden spent $6,750 to improve the Union Course, or $3,375 annually. To obtain the deed to the land he paid $2,708, or $1,354 yearly. He claimed that his rent was approximately $300, but this seems exceptionally low (the annual rent of the Beacon Course was $6,000 yearly); thus I estimated annual rent for the Union Course at $6,000. Finally, Colden estimated that his additional expenses on racing days were $100 per day, or $1,000 for the ten-day racing calendar. The total annual expenses thus come to $17,119.

63. *New York Sporting Magazine* 1 (June 1833): 182–83.

64. Hervey, *Racing,* 1:249.

65. *American Turf Register* 3 (July 1832): 571; *New York Sporting Magazine*

2 (Aug. 1834): 54; *Spirit* 8 (16 Feb. 1839): 421, 9 (1 June 1839): 150. For publication of the jockey club rules, see ibid. 6 (30 Apr. 1836): 85, 12 (24 Sept. 1842): 357.

66. Hervey, *Racing*, 2:92–95. For the early development of America's sports journalism, see Jack W. Berryman, "The Tenuous Attempts of Americans to 'Catch-up with *John Bull*': Specialty Magazines and Sporting Journalism, 1800–1835," *Canadian Journal of History of Sport and Physical Education* 10 (May 1979): 40–61.

CHAPTER 3: HARNESS RACING AS THE FIRST MODERN SPORT

1. *New York Herald*, 28 Apr. 1847; *American Turf Register and Sporting Magazine* 14 (Apr. 1843): 227; *Spirit of the Times* 13 (18 Mar. 1843): 25.

2. For the sake of convenience the terms "trotting" and "harness racing" will be used interchangeably, although technically there are differences between the two. Trotting is a style of racing and may occur in saddle (the dominant form until the 1840s) or in harness. Harness racing is a method of racing which consists of trotting and pacing gaits. For the development of harness racing in the first quarter of the nineteenth century, see Dwight Akers, *Drivers Up: The Story of American Harness Racing* (New York: Putnam's, 1938), 27–36.

3. *Spirit* 1 (12 May 1832), 26 (8 Mar. 1856): 38.

4. Akers, *Drivers*, 27–30 (quote from p. 29); Jennie Holliman, *American Sport, 1785–1835* (Durham, N.C.: Seeman, 1931), 121; John Hervey, *The American Trotter* (New York: Coward-McCann, 1947), 27.

5. Hervey, *American Trotter*, 19.

6. For a discussion of racing and taverns on Third Avenue, see Akers, *Drivers,* 39–31; Abram C. Dayton, *Last Days of Knickerbocker Life in New York* (New York: Putnam's, 1897), 237–58; Charles Astor Bristed, *The Upper Ten Thousands: Sketches of American Society* (New York: Stringer and Townsend, 1852), 23–24; *American Turf Register and Sporting Magazine* 8 (Sept. 1836): 41.

7. Until the emergence of the standard-bred light harness horse in 1879 the trotter was a "mongrel horse," although certain well-recognized families, such as the Morgans, Bellfounders, and Messengers, existed in 1825–50. The trotting horse of this period was thus at best from "a group of horse families that had a common characteristic, their ability to trot." See Akers, *Drivers*, 106–9; Hervey, *American Trotter*, 12.

8. Frank A. Wrench, *Harness Horse Racing in the United States and Canada* (New York: Van Nostrand, 1948), 21; Hervey, *American Trotter,* 21–22; Akers, *Drivers*, 28; Dayton, *Last Days,* 245–60. As late as 1847 the Harlem Course was still viewed as the beginner's track for New York's roadsters. See *Herald*, 28 Apr. 1847.

9. Thomas Floyd-Jones, *Backward Glances: Reminiscence of an Old New Yorker* (Somerville, N.J.: Unionist Gazette Association, 1941), 71; Akers, *Drivers,* 13; Hervey, *American Trotter,* 22–23.

10. For the formation of the New York Trotting Club, see Akers, *Drivers,* 37–38; Holliman, *American Sport,* 122. For the relationship between the NYTC

and the NYAIB, see the speech of the NYTC president in the *New York Post,* 20 May 1825.

11. *Spirit* 5 (12 Dec. 1835); Henry W. Herbert, *Frank Forester's Horse and Horsemanship of the United States and the British Provinces of North America,* 2 vols. (New York: Stringer and Townsend, 1857), 2:158. Also see *American Turf Register* 7 (Sept. 1836): 41; Dayton, *Last Days,* 245–47; Akers, *Drivers,* 59–60. For the rising cost of good trotters, see Peter C. Welsh, *Track and Road: The American Trotting Horse. A Visual Record 1820 to 1900 from the Harry T. Peters "America on Stone" Lithography Collection* (Washington, D.C.: Smithsonian Institution, 1967), 18.

12. *Herald,* 11 Oct. 1838. For the popularity of trotting as a spectator sport, see *Post,* 19 Sept. 1832; *Spirit* 1 (15 Sept. 1832), 11 (31 July 1841): 258; *New York Spectator,* 9 Oct. 1829; *New York American,* 2 Oct. 1832.

13. Akers, *Drivers,* 152.

14. *New York Clipper* 1 (19 Nov. 1853); *New York Times,* 14 Nov. 1853.

15. Herbert, *Frank Forester's,* 2:123, 126–27. Also see *American Turf Register* 14 (Apr. 1843): 216–17; *Turf, Field and Farm* 4 (22 June 1867): 387.

16. In contrast to the view that the trotter was the horse of the masses, in 1826 only one New Yorker in thirty owned any kind of horse; by 1853 this ratio had increased to one in twenty-three. See *Herald,* 25 Apr. 1853.

17. For the involvement of men in New York's various food markets with trotting, see Floyd-Jones, *Backward,* 9. Frank Forester maintained that prior to 1840 (or before commercialization) trotting was "as completely in the hands of gentlemen sportsmen as the turf proper." See Herbert, *Frank Forester's,* 2:158. The evidence does not confirm this thesis. While the owners of thoroughbreds in the New York metropolitan area were from wealthy and/or prominent families, only three New Yorkers actively involved in trotting were members of the city's elite. To make this assessment the names of individuals involved in trotting were extracted from newspapers and checked against Edward Pessen's list of the wealthiest New Yorkers in 1828 and 1845. See "The Wealthiest New Yorkers of the Jacksonian Era: A New List," *New-York Historical Society Quarterly* 53 (1970): 155–72.

18. *Herald,* 16 May, 25 Apr. 1849, 30 May 1848, 21 June 1853, 4, 10 June 1859, 15 Mar. 1869.

19. Welsh, *Track,* 75.

20. *Herald,* 25 Apr. 1853.

21. For the differences in the development of harness racing in England and the United States, see Hervey, *American Trotter,* 19.

22. For Holmes's statement, see John A. Lucas and Ronald A. Smith, *Saga of American Sport* (Philadelphia: Lea and Febiger, 1978), 93. For the view of the trotter as an American horse, see Robert Bonner, "Papers," Box 12, 19 Feb. 1895, New York Public Library; Hervey, *American Trotter,* 20; Akers, *Drivers,* 29. Harness racing also never suffered from the religious opposition which checked the growth of horse racing in various regions of the country. See ibid., 29; Peter C. Welsh, "The American Trotter," *American Heritage* 23 (Dec. 1966): 31.

23. Arthur H. Cole, "Perspectives on Leisure-Time Business," *Explorations in Entrepreneurial History,* 2d ser., 1 (Summer 1964): 23, 27–28. It would be

erroneous to perceive these commercialized "popular" amusements as "mass" institutions because working-class men rarely patronized them. Their support was overwhelmingly drawn from the middle classes.

24. *Spirit* 13 (18 Mar. 1843): 25; *Turf, Field and Farm* 4 (22 June 1867): 387.

25. *Porter's Spirit of the Times* 1 (25 Oct. 1856): 132.

26. For the career of Lady Suffolk, see John Hervey, *The Old Grey Mare of Long Island* (New York: Derrydale, 1936); Hiram Woodruff, *The Trotting Horse of America: How to Train and Drive Him. With Reminiscences of the Trotting Turf*, ed. Charles J. Foster, 19th ed. (Philadelphia: Porter and Coates, 1874), 211–47; Akers, *Drivers*, 49–56.

27. For the impact of Messanger on American thoroughbreds and trotters, see John Hervey, *Racing in America, 1665-1865*, 2 vols. (New York: The Jockey Club, 1944), 1:259–60; Hervey, *American Trotters*, 28–43.

28. Akers, *Drivers*, 49. Bryan's long-term ownership of Lady Suffolk was a rarity. During this period most trotters, including some of the best horses, had several owners during their careers.

29. Akers, *Drivers*, 50. For a comparison between the earnings, number of races, and miles raced of Lady Suffolk and the three competitors in the intersectional horse races of the 1840s (Fashion, Boston, and Peytonia), see Melvin L. Adelman, "The First Modern Sport in America: Harness Racing in New York City, 1825-1870," *Journal of Sport History* 8 (Spring 1981): 41.

30. *Porter's Spirit* 3 (23 Jan. 1858): 39. For the emergence of harness racing at county fairs, see John R. Betts, *America's Sporting Heritage, 1850-1950* (Reading, Mass.: Addison-Wesley, 1974), 34–36; Akers, *Drivers*, 105–8; Welsh, "Trotter," 31.

31. For the career of Flora Temple, see Woodruff, *Trotting*, 247–335; Akers, *Drivers*, 78–89.

32. *Spirit* 7 (21 Oct. 1837): 284.

33. *Times*, 16 Apr. 1857. Also see *Clipper* 1 (25 June 1853), (25 Mar. 1854), 5 (26 Sept. 1857): 117, 7 (25 June, 1859): 74, 6 (9 Apr. 1859): 402; *Herald*, 18 Oct. 1845, 17 Sept. 1853, 4 June 1859; *Wilkes' Spirit of the Times* 2 (13 Aug. 1860): 360, 4 (10 Aug. 1861): 36, 5 (23 Nov. 1861): 184, (7 Dec. 1861): 213, 6 (21 June 1862): 249, (2 Aug. 1862): 344, 7 (8 Nov. 1862): 153, 14 (7 July 1866): 297.

34. In his history of harness racing Dwight Akers devoted an entire chapter, "Sharps and Flats," to the crisis created by the fixing of races. He conceded that "not all races, probably not most of them, were dishonestly driven. . . . Much of the ugly gossip could be set down as the malicious imagination of fanatics who looked upon racing and betting as vices." Despite this brief statement Akers left the impression, through his choice of a chapter title and the disproportionate amount of space devoted to the fixing of races, that he believed the manipulation of contests was a widespread practice on trotting tracks. See, *Drivers*, chap. 11. Contrast Akers's view with Adelman, "First Modern Sport," 30. Also see *Spirit* 30 (28 July 1860): 298; *Turf, Field and Farm* 5 (30 Nov. 1867): 338; *Herald*, 6 Apr. 1860.

35. For examples of the obvious drawbacks of such a method in determining the integrity of a contest, see Woodruff, *Trotting*, 262–63, 296–98.

36. By contrast, there were almost no charges of fixing contests in thoroughbred racing in New York between 1820 and 1870, even though jockeys were professional athletes and large amounts of money depended on the outcome of a race. Upper-class control of the sport was largely responsible for the different attitudes.

37. *Clipper* 6 (9 Apr. 1859): 402, 1 (25 Mar. 1854), 7 (25 June 1859): 74; *Wilkes' Spirit* 2 (11 Aug. 1860): 356; *Herald*, 4 June 1859, 6 Apr., 3 Aug. 1860.

38. *Spirit* 30 (28 July 1860): 298.

39. Woodruff, *Trotting*, 288; *Clipper* 7 (16 July 1859): 103.

40. Harold Seymour, *Baseball*, 2 vols. (New York: Oxford University Press, 1960–71), 1:60. For the changing style of professional drivers, see Akers, *Drivers*, 152.

41. *Wilkes' Spirit* 12 (25 Mar. 1865): 57, (18 Mar. 1865): 41, (11 Mar. 1865): 24. For road racing in New York between 1850 and 1870, see *Clipper* 18 (16 Apr. 1870): 13; Akers, *Drivers*, 90–92; John A. Krout, *Annals of American Sport* (New Haven, Conn.: Yale University Press, 1929), 55; Wheaton J. Lane, *Commodore Vanderbilt, An Epic of the Steam Age* (New York: Knopf, 1942), 162–63.

42. While there is no comprehensive list of Elm Park Association members there is a register for 1859–60. It is perfectly clear that not all those who signed the register were members of the club, one being Sen. Stephen Douglas of Illinois; nevertheless, the repetition of names indicates that the majority were members. The New York City directories revealed occupational data for fifty-three members: twenty-five (47.1 percent) were merchants or brokers; twenty-three (43.3 percent) engaged in service occupations, twelve of them in the food and drink industry; three were lawyers; and two were clerks. Biographical data on these turfmen were limited but indicated that they came mainly from the prosperous segment of the middle class. See Elm Park Pleasure Garden Association, "Visitor Book," New-York Historical Society.

43. Akers, *Drivers*, 90–104 (quote from p. 95). For background material on Bonner, see his "Scrapbook of Newspaper Clippings, 1850–1899," 2 vols., New York Public Library; Stanwood Cobb, *The Magnificent Partnership* (New York: Vintage, 1945); Charles Morris, ed., *Makers of New York* (Philadelphia: Hamersly, 1895), 236. Notices of Bonner's death on July 6, 1899, were probably in every major American newspaper.

44. *Wilkes' Spirit* 6 (16 May 1862): 188–89; Lane, *Commodore*, 163.

45. Bonner, "Papers," 1:66; Hervey, *American Trotter*, 77; Akers, *Drivers*, 95.

46. *New York Tribune*, 7 July 1899; Akers, *Drivers*, 93, 95. Also see Bonner, "Scrapbook," 2:163–231; Lane, *Commodore*, 164. While New York's elite were never supporters of trotting, it is doubtful that their opposition to either the sport or trotting men was as monolithic as some writers have suggested. See Dayton, *Last Days*, 237–58; Bristed, *Upper*, 23–24.

47. I know of only one individual involved in trotting prior to 1870 (excluding the three noted in the 1830s, see n. 17) who was a descendant of New York's antebellum elite. George B. Alley was not, however, a product of the new respectability the ownership of trotting horses won. Involved with trotting prior to Bonner, Alley was "one of the most prominent patrons of the trotter in the Metropolis, if not the foremost among them all" between 1850 and 1870. Hervey, *American Trotter*, 131. For biographical material on Alley, see *Times*, 17 Oct.

1883. For a discussion of the New York elite, see Frederic C. Jaher, *The Urban Establishment: Upper Strata in Boston, New York, Charleston, Chicago and Los Angeles* (Urbana: University of Illinois Press, 1982), 201-8, 245-50, 252-59, 275-81.

48. John Elderken, "Turf and Trotting Horse of America," in *Every Owners' Cyclopedia*, ed. Robert McClure (Philadelphia, 1872), 553, quoted in Welsh, *Track*, 18; Akers, *Drivers*, 168-69.

49. Akers, *Drivers*, 105. For the story of William M. Rysdyk and Hambletonian, see ibid., 115-19; Hervey, *American Trotter*, 44-88.

50. Akers, *Drivers*, 168-69.

51. For a very good discussion of these developments, see Hervey, *American Trotter*, 272-92.

52. The quote is from Betts, *Sporting Heritage*, 145. For the persistence of the utilitarian argument, see Melvin L. Adelman, "The Development of Modern Athletics: Sport in New York City, 1820-1870" (Ph.D. diss., University of Illinois, 1980), 118-20.

53. For the tremendous popularity of harness racing at county fairs in the immediate post–Civil War years, see Betts, *Sporting Heritage*, 144.

54. *Clipper* 12 (17 Dec. 1864): 282, 11 (6 June 1863): 63; *Herald*, 11 Sept. 1862; *Times*, 11 Sept. 1862, 16 Oct. 1864, 8 Sept. 1865; *Wilkes' Spirit* 8 (2 May 1863): 140, 10 (16 July 1864): 313, 11 (8 Oct. 1864): 78-79, 12 (29 Apr. 1865): 132-33.

55. For the figures, see *Times*, 18 Mar. 1862; *Wilkes' Spirit* 22 (16 Apr. 1870): 138; *Herald*, 1 May, 5 July 1870.

56. *Wilkes' Spirit* 10 (26 Mar. 1864): 56.

57. *Clipper* 17 (20 Nov. 1869): 258, 9 (10 Aug. 1861): 130, (31 Aug. 1861): 154; *Herald*, 6 Apr. 1860, 25 Sept., 9, 17 Nov. 1869; *Times*, 5 June 1863; *Wilkes' Spirit* 2 (11 Aug. 1860): 360, 4 (10 Aug. 1861): 36, 7 (8 Nov. 1862): 153, 14 (7 July 1866): 297.

58. National Association for the Promotion of the Interest of the Trotting Turf, *Rules and Regulations, Adopted February 4, 1870* (Providence, R.I.: Providence, 1870), 19; John Hervey, "American Harness Horse and Horsemen," in *American Harness Racing* (New York: Hartenstein, 1948), 32.

59. Hervey, "American Harness Horse," 32; Wrench, *Harness*, 16-18; Akers, *Drivers*, 161-66.

60. *Wilkes' Spirit* 21 (29 Jan. 1870): 370-71.

61. *Porter's Spirit* 3 (23 Jan. 1858): 329.

62. *Wilkes' Spirit* 21 (29 Jan. 1870): 370; *Times*, 12 June 1862; Akers, *Drivers*, 138-39.

63. *Wilkes' Spirit* 22 (26 Feb. 1870): 20-21. John L. Cassady wrote under the name of Larkin. For publication of the New York rules, see *Spirit* 8 (21 Apr. 1838): 80, 11 (29 Jan. 1842): 569, 18 (6 May 1848): 128. Dale Somers notes that the New Orleans Trotting and Pacing Club adopted the rules used at the Beacon Course. See *Rise of Sport in New Orleans, 1850-1900* (Baton Rouge: Louisiana State University Press, 1972), 35.

64. *Times*, 14 Jan. 1885. For information on Rynders and his political involvement, see Alexander B. Callow, Jr., *The Tweed Ring* (New York: Oxford University

Press, 1966), 58; Herbert Asbury, *The Gangs of New York: An Informal History of the Underworld* (New York: Capricorn, 1970), 43–44.

65. *Wilkes' Spirit* 19 (30 Jan. 1869): 377; *Times*, 31 Jan. 1870. The newer racing schedule affected only purse races; match races, sweepstakes, and some specially arranged contests continued to be held throughout the year. I found no evidence that the National Trotting Association, in 1870 or after, emerged with a *formal* racing calendar. Nevertheless, the creation of systematic schedules, through the federation of local trotting clubs, began in the 1870s. The first and by far most important of these associations was the Grand Circuit established in 1873, the success of which "led local associations elsewhere to form similar combinations." In time an organizational pattern emerged that remains in existence today: "In a truer sense than before, harness racing became a 'national sport.' " Akers, *Drivers*, 141.

66. Marshall B. Davison, *Life in America*, 2 vols. (Boston: Houghton Mifflin, 1951), 2:35.

CHAPTER 4: HORSE RACING COMES OF AGE, 1845–70

1. *New York Herald*, 4 June 1846, 1 Oct. 1847; *Spirit of the Times* 19 (2 Feb. 1850: 50.

2. John Hervey, *Racing in America, 1665–1865*, 2 vols. (New York: The Jockey Club, 1944), 2:229–30.

3. *Spirit* 23 (12 Nov. 1853): 462, 468, 24 (29 Apr. 1854): 126, (20 May 1854): 162, (24 June 1854): 222; *Herald*, 16 May 1854; *New York Times*, 1, 24 May 1854.

4. *Spirit* 24 (29 Apr. 1854): 132, (24 June 1854): 222; *New York Clipper* 1 (3 June 1854). For Boyden's challenge, see *Spirit* 24 (24 June 1854): 222.

5. *Clipper* 1 (1 July 1854), (8 July 1854): *Spirit* 24 (8 July 1854): 246; *Herald*, 27, 30 June, 2 July 1854; *New York Tribune*, 27 June 1854; *Times*, 27 June 1854.

6. *Clipper* 1 (16 Sept. 1854), (7 Oct. 1854); *Times*, 30 Sept. 1854; *Spirit* 24 (12 Aug. 1854): 306, (10 Feb. 1855): 618; *Tribune*, 19 Jan. 1855.

7. *Spirit* 25 (12 May 1855): 150, (28 Apr. 1855): 126, (26 May 1855): 174; Hervey, *Racing*, 2:229.

8. *Herald*, 11 June 1856, 21 Feb. 1857; *Spirit* 26 (12 Apr. 1856): 102, 27 (21 Feb. 1857): 18, (11 Apr. 1857): 102, (18 Apr. 1857): 126, (10 Oct. 1857): 405; *Porter's Spirit of the Times* 1 (25 Oct. 1856): 132; *Clipper* 5 (2 May 1857): 12, (13 June 1857): 59, (26 Sept. 1857): 178, (24 Oct. 1857): 210.

9. *Spirit* 27 (15 Aug. 1857): 318, 28 (1 May 1858): 138, (6 Mar. 1858): 42, 29 (9 July 1859): 313; *Clipper* 6 (8 May 1858): 18. The editor of *Porter's Spirit* poked fun at Purdy's effort to link himself to the city's turfmen of the previous period. See *Porter's Spirit* 2 (22 Aug. 1857): 392, (29 Aug. 1857): 408.

10. *Herald*, 23 June 1860, 10 July 1862; *Clipper* 8 (6 Oct. 1860): 199, 9 (15 Mar. 1862): 78, 10 (12 July 1862): 98; *Times*, 23 June 1860, 6, 8 July 1862, 25 June 1863; *Wilkes' Spirit of the Times* 2 (30 June 1860): 265, 6 (15 Mar. 1862): 20, 25, (19 Apr. 1862): 101, 104, (19 July 1862): 313, 316, 9 (6 Feb. 1864): 365, 10 (25 June 1864): 265, (9 July 1864): 291.

11. *Times,* 12 Apr. 1866; *Herald,* 27 June 1863, 27 Sept. 1866; *Clipper* 9 (5 Apr. 1862): 402; *Porter's Spirit* 2 (4 Apr. 1857): 72; Henry W. Herbert, *Frank Forester's Horse and Horsemanship of the United States and British Provinces of North America,* 2 vols. (New York: Stringer and Townsend, 1857), 1:168–69.

12. *Porter's Spirit* 6 (16 Apr. 1859): 105; *Spirit* 29 (3 Sept. 1859): 355. For developments within the northern breeding industry, see Hervey, *Racing,* 2:227–28.

13. While the data on the social backgrounds of the club officials are far from complete, at least a little more than a third of the officers (thirteen of thirty-eight) residing in the New York metropolitan area were not related to New York's antebellum elite.

14. A year prior to the beginning of racing at Saratoga a racecourse was opened in Paterson, New Jersey. Historians have overlooked this fact, although observers at the time viewed it as significant to the revival of northern racing. See *Wilkes' Spirit* 15 (8 Sept. 1866): 25; *Times,* 26 Apr. 1868; *Clipper* 12 (20 Aug. 1864): 146. By comparison to Saratoga, however, the Paterson course had neither an immediate nor long-term impact on the growth of horse racing.

15. For the development of horse racing at Saratoga, see *Herald,* 6 Aug. 1863, 20 May, 14 Oct. 1865; *Times,* 8 Aug. 1864, 30 June, 3 Aug. 1865; *Wilkes' Spirit* 8 (22 Aug. 1863): 393, 10 (13 Aug. 1864): 372–73, 377, 12 (19 Aug. 1865): 388–89, 392; Hugh Bradley, *Such Was Saratoga* (New York: Doubleday, Doran, 1950), 142–45; William H. P. Robertson, *The History of Thoroughbred Racing in America* (Englewood Cliffs, N.J.: Prentice-Hall, 1964), 102–3. For background material on John Morrissey, see Edward James, *The Life and Battles of John Morrissey* (New York, 1879); Bradley, *Such Was Saratoga,* 136–40; Herbert Asbury, *The Gangs of New York: An Informal History of the Underworld* (New York: Capricorn, 1970), 90–100; Nat Fleischer, *The Heavyweight Champion: An Informal History of Heavyweight Boxing from 1719 to the Present Day* (New York: Putnam's, 1961), 55–62; *Times,* 2 May 1878.

16. Anita Leslie, *The Remarkable Mr. Jerome* (New York: Holt, 1964); Allen Churchill, *The Upper Crust: An Informal History of New York's Highest Society* (Englewood Cliffs, N.J.: Prentice-Hall, 1970), 56–57; Ralph G. Martin, *Jennie: The Life of Lady Randolph Churchill, The Romantic Years, 1854–1895* (Englewood Cliffs, N.J.: Prentice-Hall, 1969), 14–28 passim; *Wilkes' Spirit* 8 (22 Aug. 1863): 393; *Times,* 5 Mar. 1891.

17. During the 1850s there had been talk of building a course in Westchester County, but nothing came of the project. See *Porter's Spirit* 2 (4 Apr. 1857): 72; *Clipper* 5 (26 Sept. 1857): 178. For the construction of Jerome Park, see Leslie, *Mr. Jerome,* 78–80; John A. Krout, *Annals of American Sport* (New Haven, Conn.: Yale University Press, 1929), 34; Robertson, *History,* 103; Francis G. Fairfield, *The Clubs of New York* (New York: Hinton, 1873), 167–69.

18. Leslie, *Mr. Jerome,* 79; *Herald,* 26 Sept. 1866; *Times,* 26 Sept. 1866; *Tribune,* 26 Sept. 1866; Martin, *Jennie,* 26–27.

19. *Herald,* 6 Oct. 1870, 3 Oct., 26 Sept., 22 Apr. 1866, 22 May, 7 June 1868; *Times,* 12 Oct. 1867, 11 Oct. 1868; *Spirit* 27 (27 June 1857): 235; *Wilkes' Spirit* 17 (7 Sept. 1867): 51, (12 Oct. 1867): 151, 21 (22 Jan. 1870): 364. For the new fashion and respectability of racing in New York, see ibid. 15 (12 Jan. 1867): 298; *Times,* 24 June 1867; *Herald,* 6 Oct. 1870.

20. *Herald*, 27 Sept., 3 Oct. 1866, 21 May 1867, 6 Oct., 13 Nov. 1870; *Times*, 22 Apr. 1866, 24 May 1869; *Clipper* 12 (10 Aug. 1864): 146; Fairfield, *Clubs*, 168; John B. Irving, *The American Jockey Club* (New York: Thitchner and Glastaner, 1866), 1–5. Also see, W. S. Vosburgh, *Racing in America, 1866–1921* (New York: The Jockey Club, 1922), preface, 10–11; Krout, *Annals*, 34, 36; John R. Betts, *America's Sporting Heritage, 1850–1950* (Reading, Mass.: Addison-Wesley, 1974), 143.

21. Six editors and/or publishers of newspapers and journals were among the members of the American Jockey Club in 1866 and 1867. While they comprised a small fraction of the overall membership of the club, Henry Raymond of the *Times,* Manton Marble of the *World,* and James G. Bennett, Jr., of the *Herald* were among the club's fifty life members, the powerful ruling group of the organization. The presence of these newspapermen did not always guarantee that their papers supported club policies. For the composition of the jockey clubs, see Melvin L. Adelman, "The Development of Modern Athletics: Sport in New York City, 1820–1870" (Ph.D. diss., University of Illinois, 1980), chap. 4.

22. *Herald*, 25 May 1863. For the impact of the Civil War on southern racing and breeding, see Hervey, *Racing*, 2:343–56; Robertson, *History*, 87–88. For racing in New Orleans in the immediate postwar period, see Dale A. Somers, *The Rise of Sport in New Orleans, 1850–1900* (Baton Rouge: Louisiana State University Press, 1972), 75–79, 92–98.

23. Six of the club's fifty life members were southern horsemen and breeders. See Adelman, "Modern Athletics," 181–82.

24. The four New Yorkers were John G. Hecksher, John Hunter, Lewis Gouverneur Morris, and Charles Lloyd. Hunter and Hecksher were listed as descendants of the wealthiest residents of the city in 1828 and again in 1845. While Morris and Lloyd were not on either list, it was probably because their families lived outside of New York, not because they weren't wealthy. The Morris estate was in Morrisiana, in Westchester County, and the Lloyds' was at Lloyd-Neck, on Long Island. The non–New Yorkers of upper-class birth were Paul S. Forbes of Massachusetts, Roderick Cameron of Canada, and August Belmont. Of the four individuals whose class background could not definitely be determined, only one could have come from an established New York family. Therefore, at best only a third of the city's horsemen were descended from New York's antebellum elite.

25. Although breeding in the north had come to a virtual standstill by the 1850s, a few New Yorkers—Francis Morris, Lewis Morris, John Hunter, and James Bathgate—had small stud operations which they maintained in spite of the discouraging outlook. See Hervey, *Racing*, 2:227–28. With the exception of Bathgate, who died in 1859, all the horsemen named continued to race their thoroughbreds on the Jerome Park racecourse. Charles Lloyd also raced horses on the New York tracks in both the 1850s and 1860s, while John F. Purdy was an officer in New York's jockey clubs during the antebellum period. It was the increasing quantity, the better quality, and the willingness to pay huge sums for good thoroughbreds that distinguished the stables of New York horsemen in the 1860s from those of a decade earlier.

26. Given the diverse social backgrounds of the owners of thoroughbreds in

New York, the status accrued from the turf naturally had different meanings for different members of this group. For nouveaux horsemen the turf served as a means of proclaiming their position; for horsemen from old New York families the sport served as a vehicle for buttressing their elite status; and for horsemen born to upper-class families from outside New York the ownership of good stock served to integrate them into New York society. For all the city's horsemen the national dimension of horse racing served to integrate New York's upper class with similar gentlemen in other regions of the country.

27. The strong symbiotic relationship between the breeding industry and developments within racing makes it virtually impossible to come up with any *simple* cause-and-effect explanation. There were always New Yorkers who owned good horses, but as with other business endeavors the *more favorable climate* produced by the elimination of the southern stranglehold over the sport resulted in an increasing number of northern investors who were willing to test the market.

28. Irving, *American Jockey Club*, 1–5; *Herald*, 3 Oct. 1866; *Times*, 20 May 1867, 26 Apr. 1868.

29. New York turfmen were innovators only in the sense that they introduced the style of racing already prevalent on the English track onto the American track.

30. "Heat racing" was more than just contests run in heats. Rather, it was a system of racing which "glorified gameness and stamina above speed, *per se*, . . . was averse to handicaps (to the old-school turfmen a 'vehicle for chicanery') and races at fractional distances, and also the racing of two-year-olds until late in the season and then to but limited extent." See, Hervey, *Racing*, 2:340.

31. Ibid., 2:341–42. For developments in England, see Wray Vamplew, *The Turf: A Social and Economic History of Horse Racing* (London: Lane, 1976), 23–24, 33.

32. *Herald*, 5 July 1868, 2 Apr., 8 Aug., 7 Sept. 1869. In 1869 there was an attempt to revive the old system of racing at the Fashion Course, but the sparse attendance demonstrated that "the verdict of popular approval would be decidedly in favor of the dash races." See *Times*, 7 Sept. 1869. How long it took before heat races were totally eliminated from the New York racing card is unknown; however, by the early 1870s the American Jockey Club still had rules to govern these kinds of races. See Fairfield, *Clubs*, 188–89.

33. *Times*, 24 May 1869.

34. Hervey, *Racing*, 2:342.

35. Figures are drawn from *Wilkes' Spirit*, 1866–70.

36. Somers, *Rise*, 34. For the reasons New Yorkers adopted the dash system, see Hervey, *Racing*, 2:340; Robertson, *History*, 87. Compare Adelman, "Modern Athletics," 159–60, 176–77.

37. As early as 1858 one newspaper predicted that breeders would adopt the system of handicapping races since it was beneficial to them. See *Herald*, 30 Sept. 1858. For the trend toward the increasing importance of efficiency and financial consideration in the breeding industry, see Hervey, *Racing*, 2:342–33. Also see Somers, *Rise*, 109–10; Bradley, *Such Was Saratoga*, 164.

38. Robertson, *History*, 91; Somers, *Rise*, 94–114; Betts, *Sporting Heritage*, 142–49.

39. *Times,* 12 Oct. 1867; *Herald,* 10 Apr. 1860, 14 Apr. 1869, 3 Oct. 1870; *Wilkes' Spirit* 20 (17 Apr. 1869): 192, 2 (14 Apr. 1860): 89. Interestingly, when George Wilkes was part-owner of *Porter's Spirit* his own journal favored free admission. See *Porter's Spirit* 1 (15 Nov. 1856): 177, 2 (4 Apr. 1857): 72. For Cameron's proposal, see *Clipper* 17 (17 Apr. 1869): 10–11; *Wilkes' Spirit* 20 (10 Apr. 1869): 121. By 1900 spectators at the races "included people of all ranks." See Somers, *Rise,* 91. However, Steven A. Riess informs us that by the turn of the century a variety of factors, including the cost of admission, mitigated against lower-class attendance at professional baseball games. See *Touching Base: Professional Baseball and American Culture in the Progressive Era* (Westport, Conn.: Greenwood, 1980), 26–39. Since the masses did not attend the national pastime, a cheaper amusement and one with broader appeal, it is doubtful that they were present in any significant numbers at the races. While the commercialization of racing encouraged a broader class attendance at the track, by 1900 spectators were probably drawn from no further down the social ladder than the middle class.

40. For the persistence of the rural English aristocracy in nineteenth-century England, see Walter L. Arnstein, "The Survival of the Victorian Aristocracy," in Frederic C. Jaher, ed., *The Rich, the Well Born, and the Powerful: Elites and Upper Classes in History* (Urbana: University of Illinois Press, 1973), 203–57. There was one other major difference between racing in England and the United States: in England horse racing had long been tied to communal, and frequently agricultural, functions, a connection that remained in effect during the first half of the nineteenth century and would have made it difficult for the English aristocracy to exclude the masses from racing even if they had wanted to; in America prior to 1800, racing had been linked to agricultural activities but never to the extent it was in England, and what remained dissipated by the Jacksonian period, although it was replaced to a certain extent by the emergence of trotting contests at county fairs. Also see Vamplew, *Turf,* 17–28; Hugh Cunningham, *Leisure in the Industrial Revolution, c. 1780–c. 1880* (London: Croom Helm, 1980), 19–20.

41. Although the press favored a more liberal admission policy they had no real desire to have the masses attend the races. Despite their many charges against the jockey club's exclusive policy, they never questioned the club's right to restrict "undesirables." The issue was not one of discrimination but rather who should be included and excluded from a select group. See *Clipper* 17 (17 Apr. 1869): 10–11; *Herald,* 9 Apr. 1869; *Times,* 24 June, 13 July, 12 Oct. 1867, 11 Oct. 1868. There were also complaints against the exclusion of the public from certain special racing days sponsored by the jockey club. See ibid., 10 Nov. 1867; *Wilkes' Spirit* 17 (16 Nov. 1867): 239.

42. *Wilkes' Spirit* 16 (22 June 1867): 304, 311; *Clipper* 17 (17 Apr. 1869): 10–11, (1 May 1869): 29; *Times,* 12 Oct., 10 Nov. 1867, 11 Oct. 1868.

43. *Wilkes' Spirit* 16 (22 June 1867): 304, 311, 19 (17 Oct. 1868): 136–37, (31 Oct. 1868): 169.

44. *Turf, Field and Farm* 7 (30 Oct. 1868): 704, (6 Nov. 1868): 720.

45. *Times,* 10 Nov. 1867, 11 Oct. 1868; *Wilkes' Spirit* 17 (16 Nov. 1867): 239,

19 (14 Nov. 1868): 201, 197, 20 (8 May 1869): 185; *Clipper* 17 (17 Apr. 1869): 10–11.

46. Charles B. Parmer, *For Gold and Glory: The Story of Thoroughbred Racing in America* (New York: Carrick and Evans, 1939), 140.

47. For discussion of the pool system, see Robertson, *History*, 93–94.

48. *Wilkes' Spirit* 12 (26 Aug. 1865): 413; *Herald*, 11 June 1868; *Times*, 12 Sept. 1857; *Turf, Field and Farm* 4 (25 May 1867): 328.

49. Parmer, *Gold and Glory*, 136; *Wilkes' Spirit* 16 (10 Aug. 1867): 451; *Turf, Field and Farm* 5 (21 Sept. 1866): 184, 6 (28 Mar. 1868): 200.

50. *Turf, Field and Farm* 5 (20 July 1867): 40; *Wilkes' Spirit* 12 (19 Aug. 1865): 393. Compare *Herald*, 16 Nov. 1870.

51. *Wilkes' Spirit* 10 (16 July 1864): 313, 15 (13 Oct. 1866): 104; *Clipper* 16 (20 June 1868): 282; *Times*, 12 Sept. 1867. All acts incorporating the city's racing associations were justified on the belief that racing contributed to the improvement of the breed.

52. *Turf, Field and Farm* 7 (9 Oct. 1868): 652; *Herald*, 11 June 1868, 6 Oct. 1870; *Times*, 24 June 1867, 11 Oct. 1870; *Wilkes' Spirit* 5 (1 Mar. 1862): 409; *Spirit* 29 (10 Sept. 1859): 367, 31 (30 Mar. 1861): 120; *Porter's Spirit* 1 (8 Nov. 1856): 161.

53. For discussion of the new justifications of sport see the Conclusion.

SECTION II: BALL GAMES IN THE CITY: CRICKET AND BASEBALL

1. Harold Seymour, *Baseball*, 2 vols. (New York: Oxford University Press, 1960–71), 1:3–8. For further discussion of baseball prior to 1840, see Robert Henderson, *Ball, Bat and Bishop: The Origin of Ball Games* (New York: Rockport, 1947), 132–60; Jennie Holliman, *American Sport, 1785–1835* (Durham, N.C.: Seeman, 1931), 64–67; John A. Krout, *Annals of American Sport* (New Haven, Conn.: Yale University Press, 1929), 114–16.

2. For the development of baseball's ideology at the start of the twentieth century, see Steven A. Riess, *Touching Base: Professional Baseball and American Culture in the Progressive Era* (Westport, Conn.: Greenwood, 1980), 4–9, 221–35.

3. Albert G. Spalding, *America's National Game* (New York: American Sports, 1911), 17–26. Also see Seymour, *Baseball*, 1:8–12; Henderson, *Ball*, 170–94; Peter Levine, *A. G. Spaulding and the Rise of Baseball: The Promise of American Sport* (New York: Oxford University Press, 1985), 112–15.

4. Seymour, *Baseball*, 1:31. For the thesis that baseball evolved from rounders, see Henderson, *Ball*, 144–46, 154–57, 169.

5. Ian Tyrrell, "The Emergence of Modern American Baseball c. 1850–80," in Richard Cashman and Michael McKernan, eds., *Sport in History: The Making of Modern Sporting History* (Queensland: University of Queensland Press, 1979), 205–26.

6. Prior to reading Tyrrell's article I had reached the conclusion that national characteristics and nationalistic sentiments themselves do not create an adequate framework for understanding the fates of cricket and baseball. See Adelman, "The Development of Modern Athletics: Sport in New York City, 1820–1870" (Ph.D. diss., University of Illinois, 1980), 252–53. While there are minor differences

between my own and Tyrrell's attack on the conventional wisdom, my major criticism of his work is that the evidence does not support his conclusion that the destinies of cricket and baseball were the result of class differences. Also see Stephen Freedman, "The Baseball Fad in Chicago, 1865–1870: An Exploration of the Role of Sport in the Nineteenth-Century City," *Journal of Sport History* 5 (Summer 1978): 50–60; George B. Kirsch, "American Cricket: Players and Clubs Before the Civil War," ibid. 11 (Spring 1984): 32–34, 37–39, 41–44.

7. Tyrrell, "The Emergence of Modern American Baseball," 207–8.

8. John Higham points out that if national character is to be a useful analytic tool, historians must conceive it as fluid and changing rather than static and enduring. See *Writing American History: Essays on Modern Scholarship* (Bloomington: University of Indiana Press, 1970), 74. Also see Laurence Veysey, "The Autonomy of American History Reconsidered," *American Quarterly* 31 (1979): 455; Gene Wise, "Paradigm Dramas in American Studies: A Cultural and Institutional History of the Movement," ibid. 31 (1979): 229–338; David E. Stannard, "American Historians and the Idea of National Character: Some Problems and Prospects," ibid. 23 (1971): 202–20.

9. Allen Guttmann, *From Ritual to Record: The Nature of Modern Sport* (New York: Columbia University Press, 1978), 100.

10. There is as yet no comprehensive history of American cricket. The most complete work is John A. Lester, ed., *A Century of Philadelphia Cricket* (Philadelphia: University of Pennsylvania Press, 1951). His study focuses on the history of the sport in that city since the end of the Civil War, but it also touches on the general development of cricket in America from 1850 to 1950. Similar to other popular histories of sport, the study is unfortunately more narrative, descriptive, and anecdotal than analytic. Given the current state of the literature on cricket, George Kirsch's recent examination of the sport during the antebellum years is a welcome addition. See "American Cricket," 28–50. For the image of cricket in general histories of American sport, see Krout, *Annals*, 123–30; Foster R. Dulles, *A History of Recreation: America Learns to Play* (New York: Appleton-Century-Crofts, 1965), 186–88; John R. Betts, *America's Sporting Heritage, 1850–1950* (Reading, Mass.: Addison-Wesley, 1974), 5, 18, 29–31 passim; John A. Lucas and Ronald A. Smith, *Saga of American Sport* (Philadelphia: Lea and Febiger, 1978), 48–49, 106, 200, 204.

11. For examples of popular histories of baseball, see Arthur Daley, *Times at Bat: A Half Century of Baseball* (New York: Random House, 1950); Frederick G. Lieb, *The Baseball Story* (New York: Putnam's, 1950).

12. Spalding, *America's National Game*, 47–88; Alfred H. Spink, *The National Game* (St. Louis: National Game, 1910); Irving A. Leitner, *Baseball: Diamond in the Rough* (New York: Criterion, 1972), 15–48; Preston D. Orem, *Baseball, from Newspaper Accounts* (Altadena, Calif., 1961).

13. In his two-volume history of baseball David Q. Voight devotes only one short chapter, drawn from secondary sources, to the pre-1860 period. See *American Baseball*, 2 vols. (Norman: University of Oklahoma Press, 1966–70), 1:1–13. Harold Seymour gives more coverage to baseball's early years, but he examines this period mainly as a prelude to, or in comparison with, the professional years. See *Baseball*, 1:3–72.

14. For all the sports discussed in this book there was some association between New York teams and organizations and similar groups in the metropolitan area. By and large the New York sports scene can be understood without focusing on developments in the surrounding communities, but not in the case of cricket or baseball.

CHAPTER 5: THE FAILURE OF CRICKET AS AN AMERICAN SPORT

1. For the development of cricket in pre-1840 America, see John A. Lester, ed., *A Century of Philadelphia Cricket* (Philadelphia: University of Pennsylvania Press, 1951), 3–11; Jennie Holliman, *American Sport, 1785–1835* (Durham, N.C.: Seeman, 1931), 67–68; John Betts, *America's Sporting Heritage, 1850–1950* (Reading, Mass.: Addison-Wesley, 1974), 29–31; Jane Carson, *Colonial Virginians at Play* (Charlottesville: University of Virginia Press, 1965), 183–87; *Spirit of the Times* 26 (31 May 1856): 187; *New York Clipper* 16 (17 Oct. 1868): 220; *Porter's Spirit of the Times* 6 (26 Mar. 1859): 52.

2. *New York Post*, 16 June 1820; *New York Gazette*, 15 June 1820. For a discussion of single wicket, which is a modified form of cricket, see Eric Parker, *The History of Cricket* (London: Seeley Service, 1949), 94–100.

3. For the English influence on the development of American sporting patterns, see Holliman, *American Sport*, 1–10; Betts, *Sporting Heritage*, 19–20.

4. Robert Henderson, *Ball, Bat and Bishop: The Origin of Ball Games* (New York: Rockport, 1947), 3–38 (quote from pp. 35–36). Also see Uriel Simri, "The Religious and Magical Functions of Ball Games" (Ed.D. diss., West Virginia University, 1966); Walter Umminger, *Superman, Heroes and Gods: The Story of Sport Through the Ages*, trans. James Clark (London: Thames and Hudson, 1963), 69–83; William J. Baker, *Sports in the Western World* (Totowa, N.J.: Rowman and Littlefield, 1982), 6–7, 43–46.

5. Robert Malcolmson, *Popular Recreations in English Society, 1700–1850* (Cambridge: Cambridge University Press, 1973), 6, 13–14. Also see Dennis Brailsford, *Sport and Society: Elizabeth to Anne* (London: Routledge and Kegan Paul, 1969); Joseph Strutt, *The Sports and Pastimes of England* (London: Tegg, 1833); Winston U. Solberg, *Redeem the Time: The Puritan Sabbath in Early America* (Cambridge, Mass.: Harvard University Press, 1977), 46–52. For Puritan opposition to cricket, see S. M. Toyne, "The Early History of Cricket," *History Today* 5 (June 1955): 360; Rowland Bowen, *Cricket: A History of Its Growth and Development Throughout the World* (London: Eyre and Spottiswoode, 1970), 40.

6. Sport historians have universally recognized that ball playing was not a major component of pre-1840 American athletics. When discussing ball playing prior to this date, the thrust of their work has been to take note of its existence rather than explain why so little of it occurred. Nevertheless, they leave the distinct impression that the factors that shaped American sports patterns in general were the major reason for the paucity of ball playing.

7. Richard D. Brown, *Modernization: The Transformation of American Life, 1600–1865* (New York: Hill and Wang, 1976), 23–158 (quote from p. 48). Also see Brown, "Modernization and the Modern Personality in Early America,

1600–1865: A Sketch of a Synthesis," *Journal of Interdisciplinary History* 2 (1979): 201–28; Michael Zuckerman, "The Fabrication of Identity in Early America," *William and Mary Quarterly* 34 (1977): 183–214. For the decline of football, see Eric Dunning and Kenneth Sheard, *Barbarians, Gentlemen and Players: A Sociological Study of the Development of Rugby Football* (New York: New York University Press, 1979), 39–45.

8. Louis Hartz, *The Liberal Tradition in America: An Interpretation of American Political Thought since the Revolution* (New York: Harcourt, Brace and World, 1955), remains the classic work on the impact of the absence of a feudal heritage on American politics and political thought. Historians have paid no attention to the influence of a nonfeudal heritage on American sports developments, and it is against the background of this absence of feudalism that future research may uncover the origins of the uniqueness of the American sports experience and why it differs from English and European ones. One point, however, is clear: the absence of a traditional-feudal society made it exceedingly difficult to transplant the folk games of Europe to this country or for Americans to develop their own. While premodern sport in America was structurally similar to folk games—both were unorganized, lacked standardized rules, etc.—it was never woven into the fabric of society as traditional folk games were.

9. For the history of cricket in England prior to 1840, see Harry S. Altham, *A History of Cricket* (London: Allen and Unwin, 1926), 15–128; James Pycroft, *The Cricket Field; or, The History and Science of the Game of Cricket* (London: Longman, Green, Brown and Longman, 1854), 1–15; Bowen, *Cricket,* 27–86; Parker, *Cricket,* 17–93, 101–12; Toyne, "Early History of Cricket," 357–65; W. F. Mandle, "The Professional Cricketer in England in the Nineteenth Century," *Labour History* 23 (1972): 1–6.

10. Lester, *Philadelphia Cricket,* 15. For further discussion of the connection between gambling and cricket, see Pycroft, *Cricket,* chap. 6; Altham, *Cricket,* 38–39, 62–63; Parker, *Cricket,* 84–93; Malcolmson, *Popular Recreations,* 41; Toyne, "Early History of Cricket," 357–59.

11. "Society has its ranks and classes. These distinctions we believe to be not artificial, but natural, . . . but these lines are nowhere less wanted, than on the cricket field. . . . Cricket is a game available to poor as well as rich; it has no privileged class." Pycroft, *Cricket,* 32–34. For further discussion of the egalitarianism of the cricket field, see Malcolmson, *Popular Recreations,* 40–42; Brailsford, *Sport,* 210. Perfect equality never really existed on the cricket field. Gentlemen were more frequently the batsmen, while the lower class, the players, generally performed the more menial tasks of the bowlers.

12. Lester, *Philadelphia Cricket,* 14. For the social composition of these English-born cricketers, see ibid., 10–11; Betts, *Sporting Heritage,* 31; *Gazette,* 15 June 1820.

13. The exact origins of the St. George Club are very hazy, as contemporary accounts and later reminiscences lack clarity and are often contradictory when it comes to dates. See *New York Herald,* 16 Oct. 1859; *Spirit* 15 (29 Sept. 1855): 391; *Porter's Spirit* 6 (26 Mar. 1859): 52.

14. *Spirit* 8 (15 Sept. 1838): 244, (13 Oct. 1838): 272. I doubt that the New York Cricket Club existed prior to the New York–Long Island match. Robert

Waller, who joined the St. George Club in 1840 and was one of its most influential members, wrote that prior to 1840 cricket had been played only sporadically. For Waller's comments, see William R. Wister, *Some Reminiscences of Cricket in Philadelphia Before 1861* (Philadelphia: Allen, Lane and Scott, 1904), 140. Henry Chadwick, who knew many of the participants in the New York–Long Island contest, also made no reference to the existence of such a club. See *Chadwick's American Cricket Manual* (New York: Dewitt, 1873), 85–86.

15. For a discussion of the New York–Long Island contest, see *Spirit* 8 (27 Oct. 1838): 292; Chadwick, *Cricket Manual*, 85–86. In 1839 the press described the new cricket club as the New York Cricket Club. See *Spirit* 9 (26 Oct. 1839): 397; *Herald*, 21 Oct. 1839. This title is not surprising since the cricket club was the only one in New York, but it was not the name designated by the members themselves. For the naming of the St. George Cricket Club, see Wister, *Reminiscence*, 140–41.

16. *Spirit* 10 (25 July 1840): 241. For a discussion of the differences betwen recreational and competitive sport, see p. 11.

17. John I. Marder, *The International Series: The Story of the United States versus Canada at Cricket* (London: Kaye and Ward, 1968), 11–13; *Spirit* 10 (12 Sept. 1840): 330, (25 Aug. 1840): 289, 13 (26 Aug. 1843): 306.

18. *Spirit* 9 (24 Oct. 1839): 397. For the impact of the Canadian matches, see Henry Chadwick, "Scrapbooks," 26 vols. (New York Public Library), vol. 20.

19. *Spirit* 14 (3 Aug. 1844): 276, (10 Aug. 1844): 282, (28 Sept. 1844): 372, 15 (9 Aug. 1845): 279; *Herald*, 2, 8 Aug., 13, 25, 27 Sept. 1844; Marder, *International Series*, 11–17.

20. John Marder claims that the September 1844 (re)match was the first United States–Canada cricket contest. See *International Series*, 11. I view the 1845 contest as the first international match, although in both 1844 and 1845 the American squad was composed of cricketers who were technically St. George Club members. What distinguished the two matches was that the press claimed that the opposition in 1845 was the all-Canada team, while they viewed the 1844 opponents as members of the Toronto Club. See *Spirit* 14 (28 Sept. 1844): 372, 15 (9 Aug. 1845): 279. For events at the 1846 contest, see *Herald*, 31 Aug. 1846; *Spirit* 16 (5 Sept. 1846): 327; Marder, *International Series*, 22–23.

21. The six professionals on the St. George team included three cricketers from the Union Cricket Club of Philadelphia who were made honorary members of the St. George Club, although exactly when this occurred is unknown.

22. Of the sixty-seven club members in 1848, thirty-five (52.2 percent) could be identified through New York city directories and other sources. For the social composition of these members in 1848, 1859, and 1865, see p. 117. The 1848 roster is included in "St. George Cricket Club, New York—Register of Play, 1848–1867 [incomplete]," which is part of the Spalding collection in the New York Public Library. Also see Wister, *Reminiscence*, 11.

23. Chadwick, "Scrapbook," vol. 20.

24. For the formation of the New York Cricket Club, see ibid.; *Spirit* 14 (2 Mar. 1844): 10, (25 May 1844): 150, 22 (4 Dec. 1852): 498. To identify club members the box scores of their games were examined, but as only the last name was generally provided just a small fraction of the club members could be

identified in New York directories. Nevertheless, the association of many of the members with the *Spirit* suggests that they were drawn from the literary, artistic, and theater communities; this is also implied by the absence of newspaper statements that the club members were men of commerce—if they had been this would definitely have been mentioned.

25. George Kirsch, "American Cricket: Players and Clubs Before the Civil War," *Journal of Sport History* 11 (Spring 1984): 28. See also *Spirit* 20 (3 Aug. 1850): 288; *Herald*, 15 Sept. 1844, 7 Apr., 31 July 1845, 4 May 1846.

26. *Spirit* 23 (3 Sept. 1853): 342–43, 26 (20 Sept. 1856): 379; *Porter's Spirit* 1 (20 Sept. 1856): 37. For competition between American and Canadian cricketers in the 1850s, see Marder, *International Series*, 36–43.

27. *Spirit* 23 (30 July, 1853): 277, 27 (28 Mar. 1857): 78, (25 Apr. 1857): 126, (9 May 1857): 150, (20 June 1857): 228; *New York Times*, 10 Aug. 1853, 9 June 1857.

28. Kirsch, "American Cricket," 28–29.

29. *Brooklyn Eagle*, 20 July 1857, 1 Sept. 1858. Intercity competition began as early as 1843 when the Union Cricket Club of Philadelphia played the St. George Club. See *Spirit* 13 (16 Sept. 1843): 339; *Herald*, 13 Oct. 1843. The figures on the number of contests include any match in which a New York City or Brooklyn team participated. Since duplication was avoided (i.e., when both of the teams were from New York City or Brooklyn), the figures do not represent the sum total of all the games played by the cricket clubs of both cities.

30. *Spirit* 27 (6 June 1857): 199, (25 Apr. 1857): 126, (9 May 1857): 150; *Clipper* 5 (9 May 1857): 19; *Porter's Spirit* 2 (9 May 1857): 153, 156.

31. *Spirit* 17 (27 Nov. 1847): 471; Alexander D. Paterson, *The Manual of Cricket* (New York: Bedford, 1847); Henry Chadwick, ed., *Beadle's Dime Book of Cricket: A Desirable Cricketer's Companion, Containing Complete Instructions* (New York: Beadle, 1860).

32. *Spirit* 24 (12 Aug. 1854): 306, (7 Oct. 1854): 403, 25 (17 Mar. 1855): 55, 29 (8 Oct. 1859): 414; *Herald*, 6 Nov. 1853; *New York Tribune*, 7 Nov. 1853, 5 Aug. 1845; *Times*, 22 June 1855.

33. *Spirit* 23 (17 Mar. 1855): 53, 27 (6 June 1857): 199.

34. Ibid. 27 (20 June 1857): 219; Chadwick, *Beadle's Dime Book of Cricket*, 7; *Porter's Spirit* 6 (14 May 1859): 164.

35. *Tribune*, 7 Nov. 1853; *Herald*, 31 July 1845, 9 Sept. 1853; *Spirit* 26 (31 Jan. 1857): 603; *Clipper* 7 (18 Feb. 1860): 349; *Porter's Spirit* 4 (3 Apr. 1858): 68.

36. It is significant to note that Thomas Jefferson believed ball games had nothing to do with character values, in contrast to the horse and gun, which were instruments of discipline. Jefferson's view of ball games was probably typical at the time and goes far in explaining why the sport was not perceived as manly in pre-1840 America. For Jefferson's statement, see Dixon Wecter, *Saga of American Society* (New York: Scribner, 1937), 428. The New York press was not alone in their failure to offer a precise definition of "manly" in the context of sport. Morris Mott notes that pioneer Manitobans and other Victorians had more of an image of what it was than any coherent, uniform definition. See "The

British Protestant Pioneer and the Establishment of Manly Sport in Manitoba, 1870–1886," *Journal of Sport History* 7 (Winter 1980): 27–28.

37. Chadwick's work on the character values of cricket was itself a summary of the work of Englishman James Pycroft. Compare Chadwick, *Beadle's Dime Book of Cricket*, 7, and Pycroft, *Cricket Field*, 16–39.

38. *Times*, 15 June 1855, 7 Nov. 1853; *Clipper* 5 (16 May 1857): 26, 9 (7 Sept. 1861): 174. Also see *Herald*, 10 Aug. 1854; *Spirit* 24 (12 Aug. 1854): 306; *Porter's Spirit* 3 (17 Oct. 1857): 101.

39. *Clipper* 4 (24 May 1856): 36, (15 Nov. 1856): 236, (24 Jan. 1857): 316, 5 (16 May 1857): 26. For the popularity of cricket, also see *Tribune*, 13 Apr. 1855, 8 Sept. 1853; *Herald*, 6 Nov. 1853; *Spirit* 27 (18 Mar. 1857): 78; *Eagle*, 26 Aug. 1858. A sports manual published in 1858 devoted eighteen and a half pages to cricket and only four and a half pages to baseball. It pointed out that cricket was "the leading game played out of doors . . . the favorite game of the country village and country town, as well as of the larger commercial cities." Quoted in Harold Seymour, *Baseball*, 2 vols. (New York: Oxford University Press, 1960–71), 1:14.

40. *Spirit* 29 (3 Dec. 1859): 505. For the rise of baseball in the years after 1855 see pp. 126–34.

41. *Times*, 28 Aug. 1858; *Herald*, 22 Dec. 1856, 27 July 1859; *Porter's Spirit* 1 (6 Sept. 1856): 13, (31 Jan. 1857): 357, 3 (23 Jan. 1858): 325.

42. *Times*, 26 Aug. 1858; *Clipper* 6 (26 Mar. 1859): 388; *Eagle*, 4 May 1858.

43. *Spirit* 19 (11 Aug. 1849): 295; [John B. Irving], *The International Cricket Match Played Oct., 1859 in the Elysian Fields, at Hoboken on the Grounds of the St. George's Cricket Club* (New York: Vinten, 1859), vii–ix; Fred Lillywhite, *The English Cricketers' Trip to Canada and the United States* (London, 1860), 31–32; *Herald*, 17 Sept. 1859, 14 Nov. 1858; *Times*, 24 Aug. 1859.

44. *Times*, 3–4 Oct. 1859; *Clipper* 7 (15 Oct. 1859): 202–3; *Herald*, 5 Oct. 1859; [Irving], *International Cricket*, x.

45. *Clipper* 7 (15 Oct. 1859): 202; *Herald*, 7 Oct. 1859.

46. For the formation of the American Cricket Club, see *Clipper* 8 (15 Sept. 1860): 170, (29 Sept. 1860): 186; *Eagle*, 13, 22 Sept. 1860.

47. *Porter's Spirit* 1 (8 Nov. 1856): 165; *Spirit* 29 (23 July 1859): 282. How many ball players actually attended the contest against the English cricketers is unknown, but there can be little doubt that some of the ball players of the two cities were part of the immense crowd. See *Eagle*, 15 Mar. 1864. For a discussion of the skill level of both sports, see p. 111.

48. *Clipper* 9 (30 Nov. 1861): 259, (16 Nov. 1861): 245, 13 (23 May 1863): 48; *Times*, 25 Sept. 1863.

49. *Clipper* 10 (24 May 1862): 43.

50. *Eagle*, 7, 25 Apr. 1862.

51. *Herald*, 17 Oct. 1866. Also see *Eagle*, 4 Apr. 1867; *Wilkes' Spirit of the Times* 16 (4 May 1867): 150, 20 (24 July 1869): 360.

52. Chadwick, *Beadle's Dime Book of Cricket*, 9; *Porter's Spirit* 3 (23 Jan. 1858): 325; *Herald*, 5 Oct. 1856, 7 Oct. 1859, 17 Oct. 1866. Also see *Spirit* 28 (27 Mar. 1858): 78; *Eagle*, 4 Apr. 1867.

53. The distinction between competitive and recreational sport is discussed in

the Introduction. For an example of how differing approaches and attitudes affect sports behavior, see Hobson Bryan, "Leisure Value Systems and Recreational Specialization: The Case of Trout Fishermen," *Journal of Leisure Research* 9 (1977): 174–87.

54. *Spirit* 28 (27 Mar. 1858): 78, 29 (3 Dec. 1859): 505; *Clipper* 7 (18 Feb. 1860): 349.

55. *Clipper* 16 (17 Oct. 1868): 218. Also see *Wilkes' Spirit* 19 (12 Sept. 1868): 50; Chadwick, "Scrapbook," vol. 20; *Baseball Chronicle* 1 (26 Sept. 1867).

56. For the golden age of Philadelphia cricket, 1865–1920, see Lester, *Philadelphia Cricket*, 22–235.

57. The participation of New Yorkers in racquets prior to 1840 does not undermine the assertion that Americans lacked a manly ball-playing tradition before that date. While New Yorkers played racquets prior to the Revolution, it did not begin to emerge as a popular pastime until the first four decades of the nineteenth century. The involvement of New Yorkers in the sport suggests that the period 1800–1840 was a transitional one in the development of American ball playing. Clearly, it is not my intent to suggest that a decided break occurred in our ball-playing heritage in 1840. For the view that this period was transitional, see Henderson, *Ball*, 138.

58. Unlike other upper-class sports, cricket was not expensive.

59. In the late 1850s individuals from New York's upper class began to join cricket clubs, but their inability to affect the course of the game derived from the fact that they never assumed control of it and because the momentum for baseball's eventual supremacy was already underway. To have met the challenge of baseball, upper-class sponsorship of cricket would have been required prior to 1857.

60. One drawback of the conventional wisdom is that despite the claims that cricket was symbolic of the English character, Americans examined the sport there solely in terms of upper-class participation. For example, if the popularity of the sport in England stemmed from the greater availability of spare time, how did the English working-class manage to engage in the sport?

61. *Spirit* 19 (11 Aug. 1849): 295, 20 (12 Oct. 1850): 403; *Porter's Spirit* 3 (5 Sept. 1847): 4. In competitive sports situations there is a need to eliminate all elements of chance. Consequently, in almost all championships victory is rarely achieved by winning one game but rather the best two out of three, four out of seven, and so on.

62. The key to any successful drama is not merely its pattern but that the pattern is understood by both performer and spectator. Writers in the 1860s recognized that the comprehension of the games played a role in the fates of the two sports. One newspaper noted that cricket required "closer scrutiny for the lookers on to understand it; but, everybody, ladies and all, comprehend the game of baseball." See *Herald*, 17 Oct. 1866. David Riesman and Reuel Denney, "Football in America: A Study in Cultural Diffusion," *American Quarterly* 3 (1951): 315–16, analyze the transformation of English rugby into American football and point out the preference of American spectators for sports that are cyclical in structure. The only other sport I know of that closely approximates cricket in the length of time one side is on the offense is pocket pool. (Obviously, in

certain sports, such as handball, one player can theoretically be on the offense indefinitely. However, I am concerned here with contests in which performers are about evenly matched). An extended period of time in pool between changes in offense and defense occurs only among highly skilled players. Pocket pool was at one time a very popular spectator sport, a fact that does not disprove the contention that Americans favor sports with a cyclical character, or that pool is merely the exception that proves the rule. Rather, it illustrates that the structure of a sport is only one factor, albeit an important one, contributing to the popularity of a sport.

63. After he is put out, a baseball player is at most eight batters away from returning to the offensive action. Hence, there is no point in a baseball inning when a player cannot potentially be involved in the action of the contest, either on offense or defense (assuming he is not injured, ejected from the game, or pinch-hit for—rare occurrences in recreational sport). As a result, there is a continuing kind of involvement with the contest even during periods of seeming inactivity.

64. *Clipper* 8 (11 Aug. 1860): 130–31, (29 Sept. 1860): 186. In the late nineteenth century some Philadelphia cricketers did seek to reform the sport. See John A. Krout, *Annals of American Sport* (New Haven, Conn.: Yale University Press, 1929), 129. The absence of change stemmed neither from the fact that upper-class cricketers were Anglophiles at heart nor from the desire to keep the game as it was to distinguish them from the masses who played baseball. At best, these elements were contributory factors.

65. For this section I consulted Eric Dunning, "Industrialization and the Incipient Modernization of Football," *Stadion* 1 (1975): 103–12, 117–19, 133–39; Dunning, "The Structural-Functional Properties of Folk-Games and Modern Sports: A Sociological Analysis," *Sportwissenschaft* 3 (1973): 215–32; Riesman and Denny, "Football," 314–24.

66. For the shift from underhand to overhand bowling, see Altham, *Cricket*, 65–70; Parker, *Cricket*, 103–12; John Nygren, "The Young Cricketer's Tutor," in E. V. Lucas, ed., *The Hambledon Men* (London: Frowde, 1907), 39–41.

67. *Porter's Spirit* 1 (9 May 1857): 158.

68. Ibid. 4 (13 Mar. 1858): 21; *Clipper* 8 (11 Aug. 1860): 130–31, (15 Sept. 1860): 170, 10 (21 June 1862): 74, 6 (26 Mar. 1859): 388; *Wilkes' Spirit* 6 (17 May 1862): 173.

69. *Clipper* 6 (26 Mar. 1859): 388. For the difference between a game and a sport, see John Loy, "The Nature of Sport: A Definitional Effort," *Quest* 10 (1968): 1–15.

70. Lester, *Philadelphia Cricket*, 42–267.

71. Chadwick, "Scrapbook," vol. 10; *Times*, 29 May 1867.

72. *Turf, Field and Farm* 4 (11 May 1867): 292; *Wilkes' Spirit* 16 (27 Apr. 1867): 134; *Herald*, 3 May 1868; *Clipper* 15 (20 Apr. 1867): 10. Kirsch claims that Philadelphia had become America's cricket capital even prior to the Civil War. See "American Cricket," 29.

73. Chadwick, "Scrapbook," vol. 20.

74. Chadwick pointed out that several well-to-do English members of the club comprised the group's financial background. Ibid.

75. For the business connections between American and English Dragon Slayers, see ibid.

76. Howard Mumford Jones, *The Age of Energy: Varieties of American Experience, 1865–1915* (New York: Viking, 1970), 165.

77. David Q. Voigt, *American Baseball*, 2 vols. (Norman: University of Oklahoma Press, 1966–70), 1:7.

CHAPTER 6: THE EARLY YEARS OF BASEBALL, 1845–60

1. For a discussion of baseball's pastoral image, see Allen Guttmann, *From Ritual to Record: The Nature of Modern Sports* (New York: Columbia University Press, 1978), 100–106; Bruce Catton, "The Great American Game," *American Heritage* 10 (Apr. 1959): 16–25; Richard C. Crepeau, "Urban and Rural Images in Baseball," *Journal of Popular Culture* 9 (1975): 315, 318–24; Murray Ross, "Football and Baseball in America," in John T. Talamini and Charles H. Page, eds., *Sport and Society: An Anthology* (Boston: Little, Brown, 1973), 103–4; Steven A. Riess, *Touching Base: Professional Baseball and American Culture* (Westport, Conn.: Greenwood, 1980), 227–28.

2. For the formation of the Knickerbockers, see Harold Seymour, *Baseball*, 2 vols. (New York: Oxford University Press, 1960–71), 1:15; Robert W. Henderson, *Ball, Bat and Bishop: The Origin of Ball Games* (New York: Rockport, 1947), 161–62; Charles A. Peverelly, *The Book of American Pastimes* (New York, 1866), 339–40; Albert G. Spalding, *America's National Game* (New York: American Sports, 1911), 47–88.

3. Henry Chadwick, ed., *Beadle's Dime Base-Ball Player*, 6 vols. (New York: Beadle, 1860–65), (1861): 6. Also see Seymour, *Baseball*, 1:6, 18, 33; Henderson, *Ball*, 146–47, 161, 168; Spalding, *America's National Game*, 55; Irving A. Leitner, *Baseball: Diamond in the Rough* (New York: Criterion, 1972), 31–32; Harold Peterson, *The Man Who Invented Baseball* (New York: Scribner, 1969), 76–77. For Curry's view thirty-one years after the contest, see Alfred H. Spink, *The National Game* (St. Louis: National Game, 1910), 56.

4. *New York Herald*, 21, 25 Oct. 1845. For further discussion of this theme and an examination of the composition of the Brooklyn Club, see Melvin L. Adelman, "The First Baseball Game, The First Newspaper References to Baseball and the New York Club: A Note on the Early History of Baseball," *Journal of Sport History* 7 (Winter 1980): 132–35.

5. *Herald*, 11 Nov. 1845. In 1865 Alexander J. Cartwright wrote that the Knickerbockers were baseball's first club "for the old New York Club never had a regular organization." See his letter to Charles Debost in Peterson, *Man Who Invented Baseball*, 175. The statement suggests that the New Yorkers had some organization even if they lacked the formality of the Knickerbockers.

6. Henderson, *Ball*, 162, 167, 196; Seymour, *Baseball*, 1:17–20, 38.

7. For the conventional wisdom about the Knickerbockers, see Peverelly, *American Pastimes*, 340; Seymour, *Baseball*, 1:15–17; David Q. Voigt, *American Baseball*, 2 vols. (Norman: University of Oklahoma Press, 1966–70), 1:8; Spalding, *America's National Game*, 65–69; John A. Krout, *Annals of American Sport* (New Haven, Conn.: Yale University Press, 1929), 117–18; Foster R. Dulles, *A*

History of Recreation: America Learns to Play (New York: Appleton-Century-Crofts, 1965), 187; Leitner, *Baseball,* 33.

8. For the view that the Knickerbockers were from the upper class, see Leitner, *Baseball,* 33; Spalding, *America's National Game,* 51, 66; Robert Smith, *Baseball* (New York: Simon and Schuster, 1947), 37; Robert Boyle, *Sport—Mirror of American Life* (Boston: Little, Brown, 1963), 16. None of the Knickerbockers were among, or descendants of, the wealthiest 1,000 New Yorkers in 1845. See Edward Pessen, "The Wealthiest New Yorkers of the Jacksonian Era: A New List," *New-York Historical Society Quarterly* 54 (1970): 161–72. Harold Seymour notes that the Knickerbockers were professional men, merchants, and white-collar workers. While he never suggests that they were from the upper class, he parallels baseball's early years with the effort of the upper class to restrict other sports to its own social class. He further asserts that one fact that contributed to baseball's popularity was that "the upper class had given their imprimateur to the game." See *Baseball,* 1:16, 31. A major drawback of Seymour's discussion of the Knickerbockers is that he considers the club's development between 1845 and 1860 in a singular analysis. Although certain similarities in policies and practices persisted throughout these fifteen years, changes naturally occurred as a result of shifting membership and the overall growth of the sport. Seymour draws data for his analysis of the club members from the membership rosters for 1859 and 1860, which also give the year each member of those two teams joined the club. Since many of the Knickerbockers between 1845 and 1850 were no longer club members in 1859 and 1860, his analysis can hardly be accurate in terms of the occupational structure of baseball's pioneer team during its early years. Voigt's examination of social class among the Knickerbockers is similar to Seymour's. See *American Baseball,* 1:8.

9. Peterson, *Man Who Invented Baseball,* 53, 90–106, 164–76. When the Knickerbockers were formed in the 1840s they were not men of absolute leisure but rather from the mercantile class. See *Wilkes' Spirit of the Times* 19 (23 Jan. 1869): 359.

10. Robert W. Henderson, "Adams of the Knickerbockers," unpublished MS. in the New York Racquet and Tennis Club. The Knickerbocker club book reveals no effort to arrange a baseball game, although they did play intersquad contests during this period. See Knickerbocker Base Ball Club of New York, "Game Book, 1845–1868," 5 vols., Manuscript Room, New York Public Library.

11. Elite social clubs indicate the desire of men of eminence to "proclaim their status, to identify it to peers and inferiors as dramatically as possible." See Edward Pessen, *Riches, Class, and Power Before the Civil War* (Lexington, Mass.: Heath, 1973), 229.

12. *Porter's Spirit of the Times* 1 (3 Jan. 1857): 293, 3 (7 Nov. 1857): 148; Preston D. Orem, *Baseball, from Newspaper Accounts* (Altadena, Calif., 1961), 10.

13. *Spirit of the Times* 23 (9 July 1853): 246; Orem, *Baseball,* 10–11; Leitner, *Baseball,* 37.

14. *Porter's Spirit* 1 (10 Jan. 1857): 309; Spalding, *America's National Game,* 59–61; Leitner, *Baseball,* 38–39; Seymour, *Baseball,* 1:23–24; Dulles, *Recreation,* 187.

15. For a discussion of New York shipwrights, see Sean Wilentz, *Chants Democratic: New York City and the Rise of the American Working Class, 1788–1850* (New York: Oxford University Press, 1984), 134–37, 405–7. For the economic status of shipwrights in Philadelphia, see Stuart Blumin, "Mobility and Change in Ante-Bellum Philadelphia," in Stephan Thernstrom and Richard Sennett, eds., *Nineteenth Century Cities: Essays in the New Urban History* (New Haven, Conn.: Yale University Press, 1969), 168–69. The occupations of only eight of the eighteen Eckford players who appeared in the 1855 box scores could be identified. Of these players, four were nonmanual workers (two clerks, a doctor, and a merchant), so if every other player was a manual worker, then 22.2 percent of the club members would have been nonmanual workers.

16. *Porter's Spirit* 6 (26 Mar. 1859): 52; Chadwick, "Scrapbook," 26 vols., Spalding Collection, New York Public Library, vol. 3. Henry Eckford was among the wealthiest 300 New Yorkers in 1845. See, Pessen, *Riches*, 323. For a typology of different working-class groups and attitudes, see Paul Faler, "Cultural Aspects of the Industrial Revolution: Lynn Massachusetts Shoemakers and Industrial Morality," *Labor History* 15 (1974): 367–94; Bruce Laurie, *Working People of Philadelphia, 1800–1850* (Philadelphia: Temple University Press, 1980).

17. For the method used to collect and collate the data, and the problems that arose, see the Appendix.

18. I compared the Brooklyn work force, compiled from the *Census of the State of New York for 1855* (Albany, 1857), 178–95, with Carl Kaestle's work on New York for the same year. See *The Evolution of an Urban School System: New York City, 1750–1850* (Cambridge, Mass.: Harvard University Press, 1973), 201–2. The largest variation between the economic universe of the two cities was 6.7 percent, for common laborers; no other category had a difference larger than 2 percent.

19. For the development of Brooklyn, see Henry R. Stiles, *A History of the City of Brooklyn*, 3 vols. (Brooklyn, N.Y.: Subscription, 1867–70).

20. *Spirit* 25 (12 May 1855): 147; Seymour, *Baseball*, 1:33.

21. *Herald*, 3 Nov. 1854; *Spirit* 25 (2 June 1855): 181.

22. *Herald*, 20 July 1859. For contemporary views on the growth of baseball, see ibid., 22 Dec. 1856; *Brooklyn Eagle*, 2 Aug. 1858; *Porter's Spirit* 1 (6 Sept. 1856): 13, 3 (5 Dec. 1857): 212; *Spirit* 26 (3 Jan. 1857): 558; *New York Times*, 14 July 1858.

23. *Herald*, 7 Dec. 1855; *Porter's Spirit* 1 (11 Oct. 1856): 93. Also see ibid. 2 (7 Mar. 1857): 5; *Herald*, 22 Dec. 1856; *Spirit* 26 (3 Jan. 1857): 558, (31 Jan. 1857): 603. For the relationship between the expanded number of teams and games and the formation of a national association, see Chadwick, *Beadle's Dime*, (1860): 9.

24. *Herald*, 14 Mar. 1858; *Porter's Spirit* 4 (20 Mar. 1858): 37; *Spirit* 28 (20 Mar. 1858): 65; Henry Chadwick, "Scrapbook," vol. 7.

25. Spalding, *America's National Game*, 70; Voigt, *American Baseball*, 1:8–9; Krout, *Annals*, 118; Seymour, *Baseball*, 1:35–36.

26. *Porter's Spirit* 3 (31 Oct. 1857): 132, (5 Sept. 1857): 4, (16 Jan. 1858): 309, 2 (7 Mar. 1857): 5; *Spirit* 26 (31 Jan. 1857): 603.

27. For the view that the events at the 1858 convention were a democratic

revolt, see Krout, *Annals*, 118; Spalding, *America's National Game*, 65–70. Voigt leaves the impression that the 1858 convention was a palace revolt. See *American Baseball*, 1:8–9. For Van Cott's letter, see *Spirit* 24 (23 Dec. 1854): 534; *Tribune*, 19 Dec. 1854.

28. The term "junior club" was given to those teams whose delegates were less than twenty-one years old. With the passage of time it came to connote teams that were comprised mainly of boys and young men (usually ages fourteen to twenty-one). The NABBP had no age restrictions for members of senior clubs as long as they were not delegates. Most senior teams had some players who were less than twenty-one years old.

29. *Porter's Spirit* 4 (20 Mar. 1858): 337. For a similar view, see *New York Clipper* 5 (3 Apr. 1858): 396. Also see *Herald*, 14 Mar. 1858; *Spirit* 28 (20 Mar. 1858): 65. For the formation of the National Association of Junior Base Ball Players, see Chadwick, *Beadle's Dime*, (1861): 50.

30. *Herald*, 14 Mar. 1858; *Spirit* 28 (20 Mar. 1858): 56.

31. Seymour, *Baseball*, 1:37.

32. For the growth of baseball outside of the metropolitan area, see ibid., 1:24–29; Voigt, *American Baseball*, 1:9–10; Spalding, *America's National Game*, 62–63.

33. *Spirit* 29 (21 May 1859): 169. New Englanders had their own version of baseball and in 1858 held their own convention. For a discussion of the New England game, see *Porter's Spirit* 1 (27 Dec. 1856): 276–77, 4 (29 May 1858): 196, 3 (24 Oct. 1857): 117; Leitner, *Baseball*, 21, 46–47; Seymour, *Baseball*, 1:26–28. For the suggestion that the New York game won out because it was a better one than the New England game, see ibid., 1:37–38.

34. *Porter's Spirit* 3 (26 Dec. 1857): 261, (7 Nov. 1857): 148, 2 (7 Mar. 1857): 5.

35. Ibid. 1 (6 Dec. 1856): 229; *Clipper* 7 (31 Mar. 1860): 496, 8 (26 May 1860): 43.

36. Orem, *Baseball*, 16. See *Porter's Spirit* 1 (20 Dec. 1856): 260 for its recommendation that a game have six outs per inning and that a ball caught on the first bounce would constitute one out but if caught on the fly would count as two outs.

37. *Porter's Spirit* 2 (7 Mar. 1857): 5.

38. The concept of manliness was critical in overcoming the view that baseball was a suitable game only for children. The press described baseball as a manly amusement on numerous occasions but, as was the case with cricket, never precisely defined the term. The strong link to physical prowess and skill found in the cricket argument did not appear in the baseball argument, however, and seriously affected attempts to justify the sport as manly. It also suggests that while the press was certain that cricket was a manly sport, they were not so sure about baseball. For the contention that baseball was a manly sport, see *Porter's Spirit* 1 (31 Jan. 1857): 357, 4 (3 Apr. 1858): 68; *Clipper* 7 (18 Feb. 1860): 349; *Herald*, 3 Nov. 1854, 16 Oct. 1859; *Spirit* 26 (31 Jan. 1857): 603; *Eagle*, 28 July 1858, 3 Aug. 1859, 10 May 1860.

39. *Porter's Spirit* 1 (8 Nov. 1856): 165. The Knickerbockers, "with a view of making the game more manly and scientific . . . proposed that no player should

be out on a fair struck ball, if it was only taken by the fielder according to the old rule." Ibid. 2 (7 Mar. 1857): 5.

40. *Porter's Spirit* 2 (20 June 1857): 245.

41. Ibid. 6 (20 Aug. 1859): 388; Seymour, *Baseball*, 1:19.

42. *Spirit* 28 (27 Mar. 1858): 78, 29 (3 Dec. 1859): 505; *Porter's Spirit* 4 (3 Apr. 1858): 69, 6 (19 Mar. 1859): 35.

43. *Clipper* 7 (9 July 1859): 95; *Porter's Spirit* 6 (9 July 1859): 292, (13 Aug. 1859): 372. For Van Cott's statement, see Chadwick, *Beadle's Dime*, (1860): 45.

44. Chadwick analyzed the voting at the 1860 convention to illustrate that the players supported the fly rule. He noted that the newly admitted clubs, who voted 26–7 against the proposition, had been responsible for the defeat of the bill by 9 votes. Closer scrutiny demonstrates that among older teams the fly rule was overwhelmingly desired only by those from Brooklyn. Delegates from clubs in that city voted 18–5 in favor of the bill, but New York City clubs and teams from outside the metropolitan area voted 12–10 and 8–7 against the bill, respectively. See Chadwick, *Beadle's Dime*, (1860): 46–47. For the argument that the players favored the fly rule, also see *Porter's Spirit* 3 (16 Jan. 1858): 308; *Eagle*, 6 Aug. 1860.

45. *Porter's Spirit* 4 (12 June 1858): 228, (26 June 1858): 260, (17 July 1858): 313; *Clipper* 6 (24 July 1858): 110. Two baseball historians contend that it cost fifty cents to witness the all-star game; the only newspaper reference was to a ten-cent admission fee, with a one-horse vehicle costing an additional twenty cents and a two-horse vehicle costing an additional forty cents. The latter fee structure, rather than a flat rate, was the one commonly used at the New York tracks. See *Herald*, 11 July 1858; Spalding, *America's National Game*, 71; Seymour, *Baseball*, 1:25.

46. *Spirit* 28 (17 July 1858): 270, (24 July 1858): 288, (21 Aug. 1858): 330, (18 Sept. 1858): 373; *Porter's Spirit* 4 (24 July 1858): 332; *Times*, 14, 21 July 1858; *Eagle*, 21 July 1858; *Clipper* 6 (24 July 1858): 110.

47. *Porter's Spirit* 5 (18 Sept. 1858): 36; *Times*, 14 July 1858; *Clipper* 6 (18 Sept. 1858): 174. For the supremacy of Brooklyn teams, see *Porter's Spirit* 6 (6 Aug. 1859): 361; Seymour, *Baseball*, 1:25. For the 1861 all-star game, see *Eagle*, 3, 22 Oct. 1861; Chadwick, *Beadle's Dime*, (1862): 40–41; *Clipper* 9 (5 Oct. 1861): 194, (12 Oct 1861): 202.

48. *Eagle*, 3 Sept., 12 Mar., 10 May 1862.

49. Ibid., 30 Apr., 22, 16 July 1860. For the importance of the tour, see ibid., 9, 13 July 1860; Chadwick, "Scrapbook," vol. 1; Seymour, *Baseball*, 1:32; Spalding, *America's National Game*, 79–81.

50. For a more detailed discussion of the reconstruction of the Excelsiors, see Melvin L. Adelman, "The Development of Modern Athletics: Sport in New York City, 1820–1870" (Ph.D. diss., University of Illinois, 1980), 345–46.

51. *Eagle*, 6 Aug. 1860.

52. For the view of Creighton as the first professional baseball player, see Chadwick, "Scrapbook," vol. 7. Also see Orem, *Baseball*, 26; Seymour, *Baseball*, 1:47–48; Voigt, *American Baseball*, 1:13.

53. *Eagle*, 10, 24 Aug. 1860; *Herald*, 24 Aug. 1860; *Clipper* 8 (31 Aug. 1860): 154; *Times*, 14 Aug. 1860.

54. *Eagle*, 27 Aug. 1860; *Clipper* 8 (8 Sept. 1860): 163. For earlier problems, see *Porter's Spirit* 3 (28 Nov. 1857): 196, (5 Sept. 1857): 4, 5 (30 Oct. 1858): 135; *Clipper* 8 (21 July 1860): 107; Chadwick, *Beadle's Dime*, (1861): 53–54.

55. *Eagle*, 24 Aug. 1860; *Clipper* 8 (8 Sept. 1860): 164. The *Clipper* also noted that the problems at the Atlantic-Excelsior contest were rooted in the different social status of the two teams. The Excelsiors were reportedly American-born merchants and the Atlantics were artisans, many of them Irish-American. Also see *Wilkes' Spirit* 19 (23 Jan. 1869): 359; Spink, *National Game*, 361.

56. *Eagle*, 30 Oct. 1860; *Clipper* 8 (2 Feb. 1861): 322.

57. *Herald*, 22 Dec. 1856; *Eagle*, 18 Sept. 1858; *Times*, 28 Aug. 1858; *Clipper* 7 (18 Feb. 1860): 349; *Spirit* 27 (27 Mar. 1858): 78.

58. Guttmann, *Ritual*, chap. 4. For problems with Guttmann's view, see Adelman, "Modern Athletics," 376–77, n. 100. For other explanations of baseball's special place in American life, see Catton, "Great American Game," 16–25; Voigt, *American Baseball*, 1:80–96; Riess, *Touching Base*, 221–35; Ralph Andreano, *No Joy in Mudville: The Dilemma of Major League Baseball* (Cambridge, Mass.: Schenkman, 1965), 3–39.

59. *Eagle*, 1 Sept. 1858.

60. Guttmann, *Ritual*, 136–57. For a discussion of the connection between team sports and the character value argument, see the Conclusion.

61. *Spirit* 26 (31 Jan. 1857): 603; *Times*, 5 June 1857; *Porter's Spirit* 1 (31 Jan. 1857): 357.

62. Robin Carver, *Book of Sport* (Boston, 1834). For a discussion of Carver's work, see Henderson, *Ball*, 152–60. For the belief in the American origins of baseball, see *Porter's Spirit* 1 (31 Jan. 1857): 357, 3 (24 Oct. 1857): 117; *Spirit* 26 (31 Jan. 1857): 103; *Eagle*, 3 Aug. 1859; *Herald*, 19 Dec. 1854.

63. *Herald*, 16 Oct. 1859; Chadwick, *Beadle's Dime*, (1860): 5.

64. Chadwick, *Beadle's Dime*, (1860): 5; Chadwick, "Scrapbook," vol. 7.

65. Morris Cohen, "Baseball," *Dial* 19 (26 July 1919): 57–58; Riess, *Touching Base*, 5–8, 221–33.

66. *Eagle*, 30 May 1864; *Baseball Chronicle* 1 (6 June 1867); Seymour, *Baseball*, 1:32–34.

67. *Porter's Spirit* 3 (24 Oct. 1857): 117; Chadwick, *Beadle's Dime*, (1860); Seymour, *Baseball*, 1:44.

68. For a discussion of metropolitan industrialization and its impact on New York's various crafts, see Wilentz, *Chants Democratic*, 107–42.

69. Biographical material on New York and Brooklyn baseball players is lacking, but there is some evidence to suggest that wealthier master craftsmen within the food industry were officers of several baseball clubs. For example, Seaman Lichtenstein, the treasurer of the Gotham Club from 1857 to 1859, made his fortune in pickles and went on to become one of the city's most prominent produce merchants. A lover of fast horses, Lichtenstein was a member of the Elm Park Trotting Association and drove his horses with Cornelius Vanderbilt and other well-to-do-gentlemen. See *Times*, 25 Dec. 1902. Robert G. Cornell, an officer of the Baltic Club, was the brother of Charles G. Cornell, a wealthy butcher, carriage maker, and member of the city council. Charles Cornell was also a member of the Elm Park Trotting Association, as well as New York's

330 Notes, pages 141–49

prestigious American Jockey Club. See S. R. Harlow and H. H. Boone, *Life Sketches of the State Officers, Senators and Members of the Assembly of the State of New York in 1867* (Albany, N.Y.: Weed, Parsons, 1867), 85–86. For the relationship between master craftsmen and workers in the butcher and shipping industries, see Wilentz, *Chants Democratic*, 135–36, 139.

70. Wilentz, *Chants Democratic*, 139; Laurie, *Working People*, 54–60; Alvin F. Harlow, *The Old Bowery Days: The Chronicle of a Famous Street* (New York: Appleton, 1931), 151.

CHAPTER 7: BASEBALL MATURES AND TURNS PROFESSIONAL, 1860–70

1. *Spirit of the Times* 31 (9 Feb. 1861): 5; *Brooklyn Eagle*, 20 Mar. 1861.

2. For the influence of returning veterans, see *Eagle*, 9 Sept. 1862; Henry Chadwick, ed., *Beadle's Dime Base Ball Book*, 6 vols. (New York: Beadle, 1860–65), (1864): 33.

3. *New York Clipper* 11 (19 Sept. 1863): 180. Also see *Eagle*, 12, 22 July, 19 Sept. 1862, 4 Aug., 9 Sept. 1863; *New York Times*, 25 Sept. 1863.

4. *Times*, 4 Aug., 7 Nov. 1865; *Eagle*, 4, 15, 24 Aug. 1865; *New York Herald*, 4 Aug. 1865; *Clipper* 13 (12 Aug. 1865): 138.

5. *Herald*, 29 June 1865; Henry Chadwick, "Scrapbook," 26 vols., Spalding Collection, New York Public Library, vol. 1.

6. It was suggested in a letter to the *Clipper* that a silver ball be offered to baseball's championship team as a means of increasing interest in the sport and an incentive to improve skills among ball players. See *Clipper* 4 (6 Dec. 1856): 259.

7. *Eagle*, 4 Aug. 1863, 16 Aug. 1864.

8. *Clipper* 12 (9 July 1865): 99, 13 (12 Aug. 1865): 138. Also see *Eagle*, 12 July 1862, 17 Mar., 8 Oct. 1864, 4 Aug. 1865.

9. *Eagle*, 10 Apr., 12 May 1862; *Clipper* 10 (24 May 1862): 42; Chadwick, "Scrapbook," vol. 2.

10. *Spirit* 17 (9 Oct. 1847): 383, (6 Nov. 1847): 431, 27 (17 Oct. 1857): 426, 29 (5 Nov. 1859): 462, 30 (24 Nov. 1860): 506; *Herald*, 12 Oct. 1847, 11 Oct. 1853; *Times*, 12 Sept. 1863; *Clipper* 10 (25 Oct. 1862): 219; *Wilkes' Spirit of the Times* 9 (19 Sept. 1863): 36.

11. *Clipper* 8 (21 Apr. 1860): 7; *Wilkes' Spirit* 2 (4 Aug. 1860): 348.

12. *Clipper* 10 (24 May 1862): 42; Chadwick, "Scrapbook," vols. 2, 24; *Eagle*, 10 Apr. 1862.

13. *Herald*, 15 Aug. 1865. Also see *Times*, 1 May 1865; *Eagle*, 16 Apr., 5 Aug. 1864; Chadwick, "Scrapbook," vols. 1, 6; Alfred H. Spink, *The National Game* (St. Louis: National Game, 1910), 10.

14. For a discussion of the substitution theory, see Foster R. Dulles, *A History of Recreation: America Learns to Play* (New York: Appleton-Century-Crofts, 1965), 136–38; Fritz Redlich, "Leisure-Time Activities: A Historical, Sociological and Economic Analysis," *Explorations in Entrepreneurial History*, 2d ser., 3 (Fall 1965): 18; Dale Somers, *The Rise of Sport in New Orleans, 1850–1900* (Baton Rouge: Louisiana State University Press, 1972), vii–viii. For the rise of spectator sports, see Dulles, *Recreation*, 223–28, 344–45; John A. Lucas and Ronald A.

Smith, *Saga of American Sport* (Philadelphia: Lea and Febiger, 1978), 127–32; Somers, *Rise*, 19–20, 275–76; Benjamin G. Rader, *American Sports: From the Age of Folk Games to the Age of Spectators* (Englewood Cliffs, N.J.: Prentice-Hall, 1983), 70–86, 111–19; Frederic L. Paxson, "The Rise of Sport," *Mississippi Valley Historical Review* 4 (1917): 146.

15. Dale Somers notes that the new urban commercial leisure activities "were not entirely satisfactory substitutes for the leisure activities associated with rural living. Commercial spectacles, no matter how alluring, could not entirely supplant rural pastimes that encouraged participation and took people out-of-doors." See *Rise*, 20. For the antiurban view of American sport history, see Stephen Hardy, "The City and the Rise of American Sport, 1820–1920," *Exercise and Sports Science Reviews* 9 (1981): 185–92.

16. Although demographic and physical changes affected the sporting patterns of New York City, they did not occur until the 1840s and it was not until the next decade that these alterations made an imprint on the physical recreations of Manhattanites. By the mid-nineteenth century spectator sports had been well established in New York.

17. For the function of spectator sports, see Dolf Zillmann, Jennings Bryant, and Barry S. Sapolsky, "The Enjoyment of Watching Sport Contests," in Jeffrey H. Goldstein, ed., *Sport, Games, and Play* (Hillsdale, N.J.: Erlbaum, 1979), 297–335; R. B. Cialdini et al., "Basking in Reflected Glory: Three Field Studies," *Journal of Personality and Social Psychology* 34 (1976): 366–75; A. A. Brill, "The Why of the Fan," *North American Review* 228 (1929): 429–34; Arnold Beisser, *The Madness in Sport* (New York: Meredith, 1967), 124–41; Paul Weiss, *Sport: A Philosophic Inquiry* (Carbondale: Southern Illinois University Press, 1969), 84–85; Allen Guttmann, "On the Alleged Dehumanization of the Sports Spectator," *Journal of Popular Culture* 14 (1980): 275–82.

18. Somers, *Rise*, vi.

19. A recent reviewer of English sport history notes that several studies indicate that the commercialization of leisure there predated the Industrial Revolution. See William J. Baker, "The State of British Sport History," *Journal of Sport History* 10 (Spring 1983): 55–56. While I recognize these English antecedents, there have been critical differences between the promotion of sport in England and the United States. In England the sports promoter, frequently a tavern owner, sought to profit only indirectly from sponsorship of a contest; in America entrepreneurs sought their profits directly through gate receipts contributed by spectators. For further discussion of this theme, see Melvin L. Adelman, "The Development of Modern Athletics: Sport in New York City, 1820–1870" (Ph.D. diss., University of Illinois, 1980), 388–89.

20. Frederick C. Lieb, *The Baseball Story* (New York: Putnam, 1950), 34–35; Harold Seymour, *Baseball*, 2 vols. (New York: Oxford University Press, 1960–71), 1:47–48; David Q. Voigt, *American Baseball*, 2 vols. (Norman: University of Oklahoma Press, 1966–70), 1:15–18; Chadwick, "Scrapbook," vol. 3. For baseball's benefits, see *Eagle*, 31 Oct., 1 Nov. 1861, 14 Oct. 1864; *Times*, 28 Nov. 1865; *Clipper* 9 (9 Nov. 1861): 234, (16 Nov. 1861): 237.

21. *Eagle*, 27 Aug. 1863, 3 Sept. 1866, 17 Aug., 4 May 1864; Chadwick,

"Scrapbook," vol. 8; *Clipper* 13 (9 Dec. 1865): 274. "Muffin" refers to those ball players with very limited ability.

22. Seymour, *Baseball*, 1:47; Voigt, *American Baseball*, 1:9–10.

23. Dale Somers maintains that during the antebellum period "sportsmen defined a professional as a man who made a profit from participation in sports; an amateur, by contrast, was a gentleman sportsman who played for the pure love of sport. This definition borrowed from the English where custom and practice rigidly separated gentlemen from other players generally restricted the amateur class to America's sporting gentry whose wealth and leisure permitted them to indulge in sports with no concern for financial rewards." See *Rise*, 87. While Somers's thesis is the generally accepted one, it inaccurately portrays the division of sports participants in England—until the 1870s and 1880s social status, not financial considerations, divided participants there. In addition, the assumption that the English or American upper classes were unconcerned with profit is both romantic and inaccurate. Finally, Americans were influenced by English sports patterns but never directly imported them. The unwillingness of America's upper class to participate with other social classes, as their English counterparts did, negated any need to distinguish between professional and amateurs or gentlemen and players in the antebellum period. While vague notions of these different categories existed during the pre–Civil War years, the main point is that they had not yet solidified into an ideology.

24. Professional cricket was well established in England even prior to the nineteenth century. English-born cricketers transplanted this system when they established cricket cubs in America, and by 1857 the *Spirit* noted that all the major cricket clubs quite possibly had professional players. In the late 1850s criticism of professional cricket, particularly from those clubs with an American flavor, mounted with the increasing number of play-for-pay participants. At the 1858 cricket convention there were efforts to propose that professionals be prohibited from playing in contests as one step to Americanize the sport. Although the convention established a definition of a professional, the first sport in America to do so, the long heritage of professional cricket and the strength of the English clubs nullified reform efforts. While several clubs continued to hire professional players, organizations with large numbers of American players still refused to play paid performers in their contests. *Spirit* 27 (17 Oct. 1857): 426, (15 Aug. 1857): 320; *Times*, 25 Aug. 1860; *Porter's Spirit of the Times* 4 (8 May 1858): 148–49; *Eagle*, 18 May 1865; *Wilkes' Spirit* 6 (17 May 1862): 173.

25. *Spirit* 27 (17 Oct. 1857): 426, 29 (5 Nov. 1869): 462; *Herald*, 11 Oct. 1853; *Wilkes' Spirit* 9 (19 Sept. 1863): 36; *Clipper* 10 (25 Oct. 1862): 219; *New York Tribune*, 30 Sept. 1853; *Eagle*, 18 May 1865.

26. *Times*, 26 Aug. 1858. For a discussion of professional cricket in Philadelphia, see William R. Wister, *Some Reminiscences of Cricket Before 1861* (Philadelphia: Allen, Lane and Scott, 1904), 19; John A. Lester, ed., *A Century of Philadelphia Cricket* (Philadelphia: University of Pennsylvania Press, 1951), 378–79.

27. *Chronicle* 1 (5 Dec. 1867); *Times*, 10 Apr. 1869; *Porter's Spirit* 6 (26 Mar. 1859): 52.

28. *Clipper* 6 (26 Mar. 1859): 386; *Porter's Spirit* 6 (19 Mar. 1859): 35, (26 Mar. 1859): 52.

29. *Porter's Spirit* 6 (19 Mar. 1859): 35; *Clipper* 13 (9 Dec. 1865): 274. For the charge of hypocrisy, see Seymour, *Baseball*, 1:51.

30. *Eagle*, 28 July 1862, 19 Aug. 1863.

31. For a comprehensive breakdown of the participants in at least one baseball game, see Adelman, "The Development of Modern Athletics," 402.

32. For examples of company games, see *Eagle*, 2 Sept. 1865, 4 Aug. 1866; *Herald*, 20 Sept. 1866. Also see Horace Coon, *Columbia: Colossus on the Hudson* (New York: Dutton, 1947), 291–92; S. Willis Rudy, *The College of the City of New York: A History, 1847–1947* (New York: City College Press, 1949), 100; *Herald*, 26 July 1870; *Clipper* 9 (14 Dec. 1861): 275; *Eagle*, 5 Nov. 1861. The increasing number of baseball emporiums was another indicator of the growth of the game. See Chadwick, "Scrapbooks," vols. 1, 3, 8; *Times*, 30 Apr. 1871; *Chronicle* 1 (27 June 1867).

33. *Wilkes' Spirit* 16 (4 May 1867): 150; *Times*, 10 Apr. 1869. For the growth of baseball in the post–Civil War period, see Chadwick, "Scrapbook," vol. 7; Seymour, *Baseball*, 1:41–48.

34. *Eagle*, 25 June 1866, 4 Apr. 1867, 17 Nov. 1870; *Times*, 24 Oct. 1869, 21 Feb. 1871; *Wilkes' Spirit* 22 (11 June 1870): 263, 19 (26 Sept. 1869): 89. Also see Chadwick, "Scrapbook," vol. 7; *Herald*, 19 Feb. 1871.

35. Seymour, *Baseball*, 1:56; *Eagle*, 13 May 1868.

36. *Wilkes' Spirit* 22 (13 Aug. 1870): 407, (26 Nov. 1870): 235; *Times*, 23 Sept. 1870; *Eagle*, 8 Oct. 1867, 10 Sept. 1868.

37. *Eagle*, 27 July 1868, 16 Oct. 1866, 8 Oct., 13 Aug. 1867, 6 July 1869; *Herald*, 23 Sept. 1868; *Times*, 16 Oct. 1866, 17 Sept. 1867, 8 Sept. 1868; *Clipper* 16 (12 Sept. 1868): 178.

38. *Times*, 10 Apr. 1869, 15 Apr. 1867; *Chronicle* 1 (3 Oct. 1867); *Wilkes' Spirit* 19 (23 Jan. 1869): 359, (21 Nov. 1869): 211.

39. *Chronicle* 1 (13 June 1867), (22 Aug. 1867); *Eagle*, 1 Sept. 1865. In 1867 the Knickerbockers passed a resolution making the last Thursday of each month "Ladies Day." See Knickerbocker Base Ball Club of New York, "Club Book, 1859–1868," Manuscript Room, New York Public Library. Also see Barbara Welter, "The Cult of True Womanhood: 1820–1860," *American Quarterly* 18 (1966): 151–74.

40. *Times*, 10 Apr. 1869; *Chronicle* 1 (3 Oct. 1867); *Eagle*, 7 Oct., 4 Apr. 1866.

41. *Chronicle* 1 (29 Aug. 1867); *Eagle*, 15 Oct. 1869; *Clipper* 16 (7 Nov. 1868): 240, (14 Nov. 1868): 250, (2 Jan. 1869): 300; Voigt, *American Baseball*, 1:17.

42. *Eagle*, 15 Oct., 9 July 1869, 11 Mar. 1870; *Clipper* 16 (5 Dec. 1868): 274; *Wilkes' Spirit* 19 (21 Nov. 1868): 211.

43. *Chronicle* 1 (28 Nov. 1867), (22 Aug. 1867); *Eagle*, 15 June, 14 Sept. 1870.

44. *Clipper* 15 (27 Apr. 1867): 19; *Wilkes' Spirit* 16 (27 Apr. 1867); *Eagle*, 26 Aug. 1868; Chadwick, "Scrapbook," vol. 1; *Times*, 7 Apr. 1870; Seymour, *Baseball*, 1:52; Voigt, *American Baseball*, 1:15, 18. While the press recognized that ball players were being compensated, they disagreed on how players from different clubs were being paid.

45. For New York's role as the chief player market, see Voigt, *American Baseball*, 1:20; *Eagle*, 11 Mar. 1870. For examples of contemporary listings of

metropolitan area ball players participating outside this region, see ibid., 24 Oct. 1867, 1 May 1868, 28 Mar. 1870; *Herald,* 20 Sept. 1866; *Clipper* 18 (23 Apr. 1870): 21; *Wilkes' Spirit* 19 (30 Jan. 1869): 374. For the formation of the Cincinnati Red Stockings, see Seymour, *Baseball,* 1:56–57; Voigt, *American Baseball,* 1:23–27; Albert G. Spalding, *America's National Game* (New York: American Sports, 1911), 129–37. For the formation of the Chicago White Stockings, see *Eagle,* 27 July 1870; Chadwick, "Scrapbook," vol. 6; *Clipper* 17 (30 Oct. 1869): 237; Seymour, *Baseball,* 1:59.

46. *Times,* 10 Apr., 24 Oct. 1869. The following example illustrates the problem of dealing with contemporary figures. In the same article in which the *Times* claimed that the leading clubs divided $100,000 in gate receipts, it maintained that the leading clubs attracted 200,000 spectators. If the latter figure is accurate, then the gross receipts of the clubs would have been $50,000 since admission was only a quarter at the time. These kinds of contradictions make it necessary for historians of early professional baseball to grope for rough economic estimates. Contemporaries left the impression that it cost $10,000–$15,000 to run a professional baseball team. See *Eagle,* 21 June 1869, 13 Dec. 1870, 25 Jan. 1871. Since most clubs just covered their costs and since gate receipts constituted the major share of the net assets, it is possible to speculate on crowd attendance as follows. To make $15,000 required 60,000 fans. If a team played twenty to thirty home games per year (and assuming what they paid visiting clubs was balanced by what they made on the road), baseball contests attracted an average of 2,000–3,000 spectators per game, far less than contemporary estimates. For the contemporary view of baseball as a business, see *Times,* 16 Jan. 1871; *Wilkes' Spirit* 23 (12 Nov. 1870): 197, (26 Nov. 1870): 235.

47. *Eagle,* 4 Sept. 1865; Seymour, *Baseball,* 1:36–37.

48. *Eagle,* 4 Aug. 1866, 11 Mar. 1870; *Clipper* 16 (20 Feb. 1869): 363; *Wilkes' Spirit* 15 (1 Dec. 1866): 220.

49. *Times,* 7 Apr. 1870; Chadwick, "Scrapbook," vol. 1; *Clipper* 16 (20 Feb. 1869): 363, 17 (13 Nov. 1869): 253; Seymour, *Baseball,* 1:51–52.

50. *Clipper* 16 (20 Feb. 1869): 363; *Times,* 7 Apr. 1870; Chadwick, "Scrapbook," vol. 1; Seymour, *Baseball,* 1:52; *Chronicle* 1 (20 June 1867).

51. *Clipper* 14 (7 Nov. 1866): 234, 17 (18 Dec. 1869): 270; *Chronicle* 1 (3 Oct. 1867).

52. *Chronicle* 1 (28 Nov. 1867), (3 Oct. 1867), (27 June 1867); Chadwick, "Scrapbook," vol. 1; *Clipper* 14 (3 Nov. 1866): 234; *Times,* 16 Jan. 1871; *Wilkes' Spirit* 23 (26 Nov. 1870): 235. Hippodroming did not just mean that a team intentionally lost; at times the press also used the term to indicate that ball games billed as championship contests were actually exhibition games with many regulars absent. See ibid. 20 (10 July 1869): 329.

53. *Times,* 24 June 1869; *Herald,* 11 Oct. 1868; *Wilkes' Spirit* 18 (25 Apr. 1868): 148; *Chronicle* 1 (5 Sept. 1867). For examples of considerable betting, see *Eagle,* 12 July 1862, 17 Sept. 1867; *Times,* 17 Sept. 1867.

54. *Eagle,* 10 Apr. 1868; *Wilkes' Spirit* 18 (25 Apr. 1868): 148.

55. *Wilkes' Spirit* 13 (11 Nov. 1865): 166; *Eagle,* 30 Sept. 1868; *Clipper* 15 (27 Apr. 1867): 21 (18 May 1867): 43; *Chronicle* 1 (10 Oct. 1867).

56. *Herald,* 10 Aug., 23 Sept. 1870; *Wilkes' Spirit* 23 (1 Oct. 1870): 100; *Eagle,* 28 Sept. 1870; *Clipper* 15 (16 Nov. 1867): 250.

57. Jim Brosnan, *The Long Season* (New York: Harper, 1960); *Clipper* 17 (14 Aug. 1869): 146, 18 (20 Aug. 1870): 154; *Eagle,* 28 Oct. 1870.

58. As was the case with harness racing, the win-loss record of professional clubs is not just impressive but awesome. For example, the Atlantics had a 137–22 record from 1855–67. With the surge of professionalization after 1867 it might be expected that their record declined, but since they could still pad their schedule with second-rate clubs, they maintained a high win-loss ratio. It should be further noted that the losses of professional clubs were almost entirely against similar types of teams. Also see *Eagle,* 7 Oct. 1869; Chadwick, "Scrapbook," vol. 1.

59. Chadwick, "Scrapbook," vol. 7; *Wilkes' Spirit* 23 (3 Dec. 1870): 244; *Eagle,* 1 Dec. 1870. The resolution of the common council did not explicitly provide that the money go to the Mutuals, but in all likelihood the baseball team did receive the gift. There is no evidence, however, to support Seymour's contention that "Tweedism in baseball cost New York City $30,000 annually." See *Baseball,* 1:52.

60. *Clipper* 18 (23 Apr. 1870): 18; *Eagle,* 13 July 1869.

61. *Eagle,* 27 Aug. 1863, 16 Nov. 1865, 23 Oct. 1869, 31 Aug. 1867; *Clipper* 13 (5 Aug. 1865): 130, (9 Dec. 1865): 274, 17 (5 Feb. 1870): 347; *Herald,* 20 Sept. 1866; *Wilkes' Spirit* 4 (13 July 1861): 292; *Times,* 17 Apr. 1871; Chadwick, "Scrapbook," vol. 6.

62. *Times,* 17 Apr. 1871.

63. For a new and more complex examination of Tweed, see Leo Hershkowitz, *Tweed's New York: Another Look* (Garden City, N.Y.: Anchor, 1977); Alexander B. Callow, Jr., *The Tweed Ring* (New York: Oxford University Press, 1965).

64. *Times,* 3 July, 27 Nov., 11 Sept. 1870; Chadwick, "Scrapbook," vols. 1, 10; *Eagle,* 17 Nov. 1869; *Wilkes' Spirit* 19 (24 Oct. 1868): 148, 20 (24 July 1869): 369, 23 (26 Nov. 1870): 235; James W. Haynie, ed., *Baseball Rules and Regulations* (Chicago: Kelley, 1871), 12.

65. *Eagle,* 11, 15 Nov. 1869; *Herald,* 4 Apr. 1869; *Clipper* 14 (15 Dec. 1866): 282–83; Chadwick, "Scrapbook," vol. 1; *Wilkes' Spirit* 24 (11 Mar. 1871): 59.

66. Chadwick, "Scrapbook," vols. 1, 6; *Clipper* 14 (15 Dec. 1866): 272–73; *Chronicle* 1 (5 Dec. 1867).

67. *Times,* 10 Apr. 1869; Chadwick, "Scrapbook," vol. 5; *Clipper* 17 (18 Dec. 1869): 290; *Eagle,* 11 Mar. 1870, 10 July 1868; *Wilkes' Spirit* 19 (23 Jan. 1869): 359.

68. *Clipper* 18 (22 Oct. 1870): 228; *Wilkes' Spirit* 24 (25 Mar. 1871): 70. Several papers claimed that amateur apathy made it possible for professional teams to control the NABBP. See *Clipper* 17 (18 Dec. 1869): 290; *Times,* 14 Nov. 1870.

69. *Eagle,* 17 Nov., 1 Dec. 1870; *Times,* 14 Nov. 1870.

70. *Times,* 17 Mar. 1871; *Clipper* 18 (9 July 1870): 107, (10 Dec. 1870): 283, (24 Dec. 1870): 299, (18 Mar. 1871): 394; *Eagle,* 14 Feb., 30 Jan., 13 Mar. 1871, 1, 9, Dec. 1870; Chadwick, "Scrapbook," vols. 1, 5; *Wilkes' Spirit* 24 (25 Mar. 1871): 70.

71. *Eagle,* 20 Mar. 1871; Haynie, *Baseball,* 42; Henry Chadwick, ed., *Chad-*

wick's Convention Base Ball Manual (Boston: National Chronicle Office, 1871), 36; *Wilkes' Spirit* 24 (25 Mar. 1871): 70.

72. *Times*, 1, 13, 18 Mar. 1871; *Wilkes' Spirit* 24 (11 Mar. 1871): 59, (25 Mar. 1871): 70, 19 (21 Nov. 1868): 212; *Eagle*, 20, 26 Mar. 1871, 9 Dec. 1870; *Herald*, 12 Mar. 1871; *Clipper* 18 (11 Mar. 1871): 387–88, (18 Mar. 1871): 394, (25 Mar. 1871): 405.

73. Voigt, *American Baseball*, 1:37.

74. *Eagle*, 27 July 1868; Seymour, *Baseball*, 1:60–66; Spink, *National Game*, 58.

75. *Times*, 10 Apr. 1869, 21, 24 Oct. 1868; *Herald*, 5 July 1869, 6 Aug. 1867; Henry Chadwick, ed., *DeWitt's Baseball Guide* (New York: DeWitt, 1869), 11; *Eagle*, 21 Sept. 1868, 4 Apr. 1867. In 1859 an attempt was made to arrange a baseball game with the touring English professional cricketers. Nothing came of it, but the significant point is that the confidence baseball supporters had in the manliness of their sport in 1868 was not present when the earlier challenge was issued. See *Herald*, 21 Oct. 1859.

76. Chadwick, *DeWitt's Baseball*, 10–11.

77. *Eagle*, 14 Mar. 1864, 23 Aug. 1865, 15 Aug. 1868; Chadwick, "Scrapbook," vol. 6; Voigt, *American Baseball*, 1:19.

78. *Eagle*, 18 Aug., 19 June 1869; *Times*, 24 Oct. 1869.

79. *Wilkes' Spirit* 20 (19 June 1869): 281, 23 (24 Dec. 1870): 292; *Eagle*, 21 Mar., 7, 9 July 1864, 18 Aug., 19 June 1869, 19 June 1870, 6 Aug. 1860; Chadwick, "Scrapbook," vols. 6, 7.

80. *Eagle*, 10 Sept. 1868; Chadwick, "Scrapbook," vols. 1, 7; *Clipper* 16 (2 Jan. 1869): 306. Four of the nine leading players (Reach, Waterman, Wright, and Hatfield) were originally from the metropolitan area.

81. *Clipper* 17 (26 June 1869): 92; Chadwick, "Scrapbook," vol. 6; *Wilkes' Spirit* 20 (19 June 1869): 281.

82. *Wilkes' Spirit* 22 (18 June 1870): 277; *Eagle*, 15 June 1870; *Times*, 15 June 1870. For the rule permitting extra innings, see *Spirit* 30 (5 May 1860): 149.

83. *Eagle*, 15–16 June 1870.

84. Ibid., 24 June, 17, 19 Nov. 1870, 21 Feb., 24 Mar. 1871; Chadwick, "Scrapbook," vol. 3; Voigt, *American Baseball*, 1:33–34.

85. *Eagle*, 17 Mar., 22 Aug. 1864, 16 Mar. 1871; Henry Chadwick, ed., *Baseball Player's Book of References* (New York: Haney, 1866), vii. For the arguments that baseball promoted health, see *Eagle*, 28 July 1864; *Times*, 11 Sept. 1870; *Herald*, 17 Oct., 5 July 1869; *Wilkes' Spirit* 20 (24 July 1869): 360; Chadwick, "Scrapbook," vol. 7.

86. *Chronicle* 1 (27 June 1867). Also see *Herald*, 5 July 1869.

87. *Times*, 11 Sept. 1870.

88. *Clipper* 9 (9 Nov. 1861): 236. Frank Merriwell was America's first sports hero in juvenile literature. An American Tom Brown, Merriwell was the personification of the Christian gentleman and amateur athlete. By the twentieth century professional ball players, either directly or in fictionalized form, became the heroes in juvenile literature. As the symbol of the athlete and gentleman, Merriwell was replaced by Christy Mathewson, the great New York Giant pitcher. For the role of Mathewson as a sports hero, see Steven A. Riess, *Touching Base:*

Professional Baseball and American Culture in the Progressive Era (Westport, Conn.: Greenwood, 1980), 16, 23, 162–63. Also see Christian Messenger, *Sport and the Play Spirit in American Fiction* (New York: Columbia University Press, 1981), 114, 165–71.

89. Voigt, *American Baseball*, 1:91; Seymour, *Baseball*, 1:44–45.

90. Allen Guttmann, *From Ritual to Record: The Nature of Modern Sport* (New York: Columbia University Press, 1978), 109–14.

91. Mohican Base Ball Club of New York, *Constitution, By Laws and Minutes of Meetings from Jan. 1, 1870–Feb. 16, 1871; the List of Five Matches and the List of the Membership of 1870*, MS., New York Public Library. Among the members of the Mohicans were sons of the New York elite, such as George Alley, William A. Hadden, and Adrian Iselin. Moreover, all twenty-seven boys lived in New York's elite residential area, a third of them on Fifth Avenue. By 1860 several members of the Knickerbockers were from New York's leading families, but they constituted only a small minority of the club.

92. *Eagle*, 17 Oct. 1862; *Wilkes' Spirit* 17 (5 Oct. 1867): 133; *Clipper* 15 (26 Oct. 1867): 227; *Chronicle* 1 (3 Oct. 1867), (31 Oct. 1867).

93. Seymour, *Baseball*, 1:42; *Eagle*, 14 Nov. 1870; *Times*, 14 Nov. 1870; *Wilkes' Spirit* 21 (11 Sept. 1869): 55. There is very limited information on the attitude of New York City and Brooklyn clubs to the admission of blacks. The Star Club of Brooklyn wanted to bar them from the NABBP. See *Times*, 14 Nov. 1870. In 1867 the question was raised at a Knickerbocker meeting when James W. Davis, the club delegate, asked for instructions on this issue. One member proposed that the club oppose black membership, but after considerable discussion the Knickerbockers decided to leave the decision to their delegate. See Knickerbocker Base Ball Club of New York, "Club Book," MS., 4 Dec. 1867.

94. As a result of the increasing number of clubs joining the national association after the Civil War, the NABBP in 1867 modified its constitution. Clubs then sent representatives to a state convention and each state in turn sent delegates to the national association. The delegates included here are those who went to the national convention in 1866 and 1867 and to the state convention in 1868, 1869, and 1870.

95. For a comprehensive breakdown of participants in at least one game from 1866 through 1870, see Adelman, "Modern Athletics," 449.

96. Chadwick, "Scrapbook," vol. 6; *Eagle*, 29 Apr. 1869, 15 Aug. 1868.

97. *Times*, 24 Oct. 1869.

98. Chadwick, "Scrapbook," vols. 1, 19; *Eagle*, 15 Mar. 1869; *Clipper* 17 (1 Oct. 1869): 204; Spink, *National Game*, 59.

99. I use the term "initial professionals" when referring to the group of ball players comprised of the twenty-four active participants who joined the NAPBBP and the ten Brooklyn and New York players who participated in the 1860s and then in the NABBP but were not active participants between 1866 and 1870. There were many other New York and Brooklyn ball players in the NAPBBP, but most, if not all, of them played for some organized junior club team in the 1860s and are not included in this survey.

100. *Eagle*, 3 Dec. 1869; Seymour, *Baseball*, 1:67; Voigt, *American Baseball*, 1:56–57; David Q. Voigt, *America's Leisure Revolution: Essay in the Sociology*

of Leisure and Sport (Reading, Pa., 1971), 81; Adelman, "Modern Athletics," 473.

101. Adelman, "Modern Athletics," 473; Spink, *National Game,* 244, 246.

102. Joseph F. Kett, *Rites of Passage: Adolescence in America, 1790 to the Present* (New York: Basic Books, 1977), 151.

103. For the increasing postponement of adulthood between 1840 and 1900, see ibid., 111–215. For the uncertainty of paydays and the low prestige of professional baseball, see Voigt, *American Baseball,* 1:53; Riess, *Touching Base,* 156.

104. Riess, *Touching Base,* 151–60; Steven A. Riess, "Sport and the American Dream: A Review Essay," *Journal of Social History* 14 (1980): 295–301.

105. The classification system Riess used and which I adopted here was taken from Stephan Thernstrom, *The Other Bostonians: Poverty and Progress in the American Metropolis, 1880–1970* (Cambridge, Mass.: Harvard University Press, 1973), 290–92.

106. Ibid.

107. Voigt, *American Baseball,* 1:84; Chadwick, "Scrapbook," vol. 1.

108. It was not uncommmon for professional ball players to have several occupations after their careers ended. In discussing this theme with Riess, we both agreed that the economic condition of many former ball players could change fairly rapidly.

SECTION III: THE DIVERSITY OF SPORT IN THE CITY

1. For a discussion of the nature of leisure sport, see p. 11.

2. John R. Betts used the title "The Heyday of Yachting" to describe the growth of the sport from 1865 to the turn of the century. See *America's Sporting Heritage, 1850–1950* (Reading, Mass.: Addison-Wesley, 1974), 149. For the impact of international yachting on the growth of the sport in New York, see *New York Herald,* 18 Apr., 31 Aug., 15, 27 Sept. 1870, 27 Mar., 23 July, 4 May 1871; *New York Times,* 16 Aug. 1870, 23 June 1871; *Wilkes' Spirit of the Times* 18 (15 Aug. 1868): 472.

CHAPTER 8: WATER SPORTS: ROWING AND YACHTING

1. Robert F. Kelley, *American Rowing: Its Background and Traditions* (New York: Putnam, 1932), 14–16.

2. Ibid., 16–17; Jennie Holliman, *American Sport, 1785–1835* (Durham, N.C.: Seeman, 1931), 155; Herbert Manchester, *Four Centuries of American Sport, 1490–1890* (New York: Derrydale, 1931), 58.

3. *New York Gazette,* 10, 13 Nov. 1820; *New York Post,* 13 Nov. 1820; *New York American,* 13 Nov. 1820. Also see John R. Betts, *America's Sporting Heritage, 1850–1950* (Reading, Mass.: Addison-Wesley, 1974), 36–37; Kelley, *Rowing,* 16.

4. *Gazette,* 2 July 1824; *American,* 12 Mar., 2 July 1824; *Post,* 12 Mar. 1824. Also see *New York Clipper* 17 (29 May 1869): 61; Kelley, *Rowing,* 16; Charles A. Peverelly, *Book of American Pastimes* (New York, 1866), 243. Information

on the Whitehallers continues into the 1840s. Naturally, the members of this rowing group changed over the years.

5. *American*, 3–4, 9–10, 13, 20 Dec. 1824, 5 Jan. 1825; *Gazette*, 10, 13 Dec. 1824; *Post*, 9–10 Dec. 1824; *New York Spectator*, 14 Dec. 1824. Also see Kelley, *Rowing*, 17–18; Holliman, *American Sport*, 157–58.

6. *Post*, 20 May, 6 July 1825; *American*, 20 May 1825; *Gazette*, 11, 21 May 1825; Charles H. Haswell, *Reminiscence of New York by an Octogenarian, 1816–1860* (New York: Harper, 1896), 253, 298. For the formation of the Castle Garden Association, see Kelley, *Rowing*, 21; Peverelly, *American Pastimes*, 249; *Porter's Spirit of the Times* 3 (10 Oct. 1857): 84. For discussion of the Wave Club, see *Spirit of the Times* 7 (30 Sept. 1837): 261; Kelley, *Rowing*, 21. The statement concerning the association's opposition to competing for money was one of the few that linked amateurism to financial considerations during the antebellum period. See *Spirit* 7 (5 Aug. 1837): 197. These statements do not undermine the point made earlier, namely, that amateurism in the pre–Civil War years was linked mainly to social rather than economic factors. In 1832 the Wave and Eagle clubs of New York, both Castle Garden members, raced for $100. See Haswell, *Reminiscences*, 298. This practice probably diminished after 1832, but it never totally ceased. In 1838 there was a report of a contest between clubs "formed of the most respectable young men in the community" on which bets were placed. See *New York Herald*, 26 June 1838.

7. Kelley, *Rowing*, 21; Peverelly, *American Pastimes*, 252.

8. *Spirit* 6 (21 May 1836): 119; *New York Journal of Commerce*, quoted in *Post*, 20 Sept. 1836. Also see *Herald*, 20 June 1838; *Post*, 2 June 1838; *Spirit* 6 (24 Sept. 1836): 253.

9. *Herald*, 19 July 1837, 26 July 1836, 2 June 1838; *Post*, 16 Oct. 1835, 27 Aug., 24 Sept. 1830; *Spirit* 7 (22 July 1837): 180, 9 (13 July 1839): 222; Peverelly, *American Pastimes*, 246–48. For the beginnings of professional rowing, see ibid., 248; Kelley, *Rowing*, 27; Samuel Crowther and Arthur Ruhl, eds., *Rowing and Track Athletics* (New York: Macmillan, 1905), 8–9.

10. *Spirit* 7 (16 Sept. 1837): 241. For the rise of rowing nationally, see Betts, *Sporting Heritage*, 37; Kelley, *Rowing*, 17, 20, 22; Holliman, *American Sport*, 159; Dale A. Somers, *The Rise of Sport in New Orleans, 1850–1900* (Baton Rouge: Louisiana State University Press, 1972), 46–48.

11. *American*, 23 June 1826; *Spirit* 6 (17 Sept. 1836): 246; Holliman, *American Sport*, 159; E. Merton Coulter, "Boating as a Sport in the Old South," *Georgia Historical Society* 27 (1943): 238–39. For boating in the South, see ibid., 231–47; Somers, *Rise*, 46–48. For the sale of northern boats to southerners, see ibid., 47; Kelley, *Rowing*, 21.

12. Somers, *Rise*, 47; Melvin L. Adelman, "The Development of Modern Athletics: Sport in New York City, 1820–1870" (Ph.D. diss., University of Illinois, 1980), 519.

13. *New York Times*, 21 June 1854; *Spirit* 25 (29 Sept. 1855): 390. Stephen Roberts, the first great professional American sculler, became a member of the New York Common Council during the 1850s.

14. *Herald*, 18 Oct. 1855, 6 July 1859; *Spirit* 25 (20 Oct. 1855): 427; Peverelly, *American Pastimes*, 287–300.

15. Kelley, *Rowing*, 25–26; *Clipper* 5 (19 Sept. 1857): 171, (6 Mar. 1858): 361, 4 (27 Sept. 1856): 178; *Porter's Spirit* 1 (27 Sept. 1856): 53.

16. Irene Norsen, *Ward Brothers: Champions of the World* (New York: Vantage, 1955), 24–25; Kelley, *Rowing*, 29–30; John A. Krout, *Annals of American Sport* (New Haven, Conn.: Yale University Press, 1929), 78.

17. *Times*, 19 July, 12 Sept. 1865; *Wilkes' Spirit of the Times* 12 (22 July 1865): 328, (29 July 1865): 337, 344, 349; *Herald*, 19, 21 July 1865; *Clipper* 13 (29 July 1865): 122–23; Peverelly, *American Pastimes*, 306–12.

18. Crowther and Ruhl, *Rowing and Track*, 196; Kelley, *Rowing*, 31–47.

19. For the rise of collegiate crew, see Guy M. Lewis, "America's First Intercollegiate Sport: The Regattas from 1852 to 1875," *Research Quarterly* 38 (1967): 637–48. For rowing at Columbia, see Horace Coon, *Columbia: Colossus on the Hudson* (New York: Dutton, 1947), 302. A rowing club was also formed at City College of New York. See S. Willis Rudy, *The College of the City of New York: A History, 1847–1947* (New York: City College Press, 1949), 78.

20. *Porter's Spirit* 3 (31 Oct. 1857): 132; *Wilkes' Spirit* 2 (7 Apr. 1860): 72, 3 (6 Oct. 1860): 69; Kelley, *Rowing*, 49–52; Peverelly, *American Pastimes*, 150, 192.

21. *Wilkes' Spirit* 18 (25 Apr. 1868): 147; *Clipper* 17 (15 May 1869): 45, (11 Sept. 1869): 178; Peverelly, *American Pastimes*, 332–33. Another difference between antebellum and postbellum rowing clubs in New York was their numerical structure. During the early years each club was comprised of the exact number of rowers needed for competition, with the possible addition of one or two substitutes; consequently, rowing clubs rarely had more than ten members. In the later years many members of rowing clubs were not active competitors and club membership reached as high as forty or fifty.

22. *Herald*, 12 Sept. 1869; *Times*, 26 Aug. 1871; *Clipper* 17 (28 Aug. 1869): 168.

23. *Herald*, 29 Aug. 1869. Also see Joseph J. Mathews, "The First Harvard-Oxford Boatrace," *New England Quarterly* 33 (1960): 74–82.

24. *Wilkes' Spirit* 17 (21 Sept. 1867): 91, 23 (3 Dec. 1870): 252. For the growth of rowing nationally, see Crowther and Ruhl, *Rowing and Track*, 150–60; Kelley, *Rowing*, 52–53, 59.

25. For the formation of the National Association of Amateur Oarsmen, see Crowther and Ruhl, *Rowing and Track*, 161–65; Kelley, *Rowing*, 60–61; Krout, *Annals*, 87. For the separation of amateur and professional rowing in England, see Phillip Goodhart and Christopher Chataway, *War Without Weapons* (London: Allen, 1968), 45. Also see Crowther and Ruhl, *Rowing and Track*, 163–90.

26. William P. Stephens noted that "yacht" applies to a vessel, "not merely on account of model and equipment, but largely from her use exclusively as a pleasure craft." See *American Yachting* (New York: Macmillan, 1904), 1. While he recognizes that the sport of yachting had its origins in motivation and usage, Juan Baader points out that "it is hard to tell at what point yacht building became separated from the construction of small merchant vessels." See *The Sailing Yacht. How It Developed—How It Worked*, trans. James and Ingeborg Moore (New York: Norton, 1965), 20. For yachting in New Amsterdam, see Stephens,

American Yachting, 1; Arthur H. Clark, *The History of American Yachting, 1600-1815* (New York: Putnam, 1904), 42.

27. *Herald,* 14 June 1844, 30 July 1839, 29 Sept. 1841, 23-24 Oct. 1843; *Spirit* 13 (28 Oct. 1843): 414, 5 (30 June 1835): 156; John J. Parkinson, *The History of the New York Yacht Club from Its Founding Through 1973* (New York: New York Yacht Club, 1975), 10-11. For yachting prior to 1835, see Clark, *Yachting,* 136-37; Krout, *Annals,* 60; Parkinson, *New York Yacht Club,* 5. Although there is no evidence of yacht racing prior to 1835, sailing contests between commercial vessels occurred from time to time. See *Post,* 2 May 1827, 3 June 1828; *Herald,* 9 June 1855.

28. For the formation of the New York Yacht Club, see Parkinson, *New York Yacht Club,* 13. For the impact of the club on yachting, see Frederick S. Cozzens, *Yachts and Yachting* (New York: Cassell, 1887), 11; Stephens, *American Yachting,* 37-38; Betts, *Sporting Heritage,* 37-38. For the yacht club in Boston, see Stephen Hardy, *How Boston Played: Sport, Recreation, and Community, 1865-1915* (Boston: Northeastern University Press, 1982), 130. For claims that earlier yachting clubs existed in New York, see Stephens, *American Yachting,* 16-17; Charles Boswell, *The America: The Story of the World's Most Famous Yacht* (New York: McKay, 1967), 121. For an opposing view, see Adelman, "Modern Athletics," 522-23.

29. *Herald,* 2 Aug. 1844, 18 July 1845, 28 Mar. 1846; *Spirit* 16 (10 Oct. 1846): 390; *New York Tribune,* 18 July 1845, 17 July 1846.

30. *Herald,* 28 Apr. 1847; Parkinson, *New York Yacht Club,* 525.

31. For Stevens's involvement in sport in general and yachting in particular, see Archibald D. Turnbull, *John Stevens: An American Record* (New York: Century, 1928), 485-87, 510-12; Benjamin G. Rader, *American Sports: From the Age of Folk Games to the Age of Spectators* (Englewood Cliffs, N.J.: Prentice-Hall, 1983), 37-39; Parkinson, *New York Yacht Club,* 7-9; John Dizikes, *Sportsmen and Gamesmen* (Boston: Houghton-Mifflin, 1981), 91-120; *Herald,* 11 June 1857; *Times,* 12 June 1857; *Spirit* 8 (16 June 1838): 140, (21 July 1838): 181; *Porter's Spirit* 2 (20 June 1857): 243-44. The syndicate consisted of John C. Stevens and his brother Edwin, J. Beekman Finlay, Hamilton Wilkes, and George L. Schuyler.

32. For a discussion of Stevens's taking a yacht to England, see *Herald,* 20 July, 13 Sept. 1839, 17 Oct. 1840, 4 Mar. 1842; *Spirit* 16 (29 Aug. 1846): 313. For construction of the *America* and the preparation for taking her to England, see ibid. 20 (25 Jan. 1851): 582, 21 (28 June 1851): 221; Jerome E. Brooks, *The $30,000,000 Cup: The Stormy History of the Defense of the America's Cup* (New York: Simon and Schuster, 1958), 5-13; Boswell, *America,* 3, 17-19.

33. James A. Hamilton, *Reminiscence of James A. Hamilton: or Men and Events, at Home and Abroad, During Three Quarters of a Century* (New York: Scribner, 1869), 396. According to the conditions of the sale, the syndicate was not required to purchase the *America* unless she proved to be the fastest yacht in the country. The syndicate chose the *Maria,* owned by the three Stevens brothers and universally considered the swiftest New York vessel, to test the new yacht. Despite the *Maria's* success, the syndicate felt that work on the *America* was not complete and that the new boat "was designed for heavier work than

the waters in which the *Maria* was so comfortable." See Brooks, *$30,000,000 Cup*, 13–14. For the *Maria-America* race, also see *Spirit* 21 (21 June 1851): 221; *Tribune*, 24 June 1851.

34. *European Times*, quoted in *Spirit* 21 (16 Aug. 1851): 312. For national interest in the *America*, see ibid., (24 May 1851): 162; *Tribune*, 3, 15 May 1851. For Stevens's challenge, see *Spirit* 21 (6 Sept. 1851): 343. For gambling on yacht racing in general and the desire of the *America*'s syndicate to profit from her races in England in particular, see Brooks, *$30,000,000 Cup*, 14–15; Parkinson, *New York Yacht Club*, 20. Stevens's competitiveness contributed to the syndicate's inability to cash in on the *America*. See Hamilton, *Reminiscence*, 396; Brooks, *$30,000,000 Cup*, 20–21.

35. *London Times*, 16 Aug. 1851, quoted in *Spirit* 21 (6 Sept. 1851): 343. For the race with Stephenson, see ibid., (13 Sept. 1851): 355, (20 Sept. 1851): 367; *Tribune*, 15 Sept. 1851; Boswell, *America*, 54–57. For Stevens's discontent with developments in England, see *Wilkes' Spirit* 24 (15 Apr. 1871): 131; Brooks, *$30,000,000 Cup*, 9, 25.

36. *Spirit* 21 (13 Sept. 1851): 354–55; Herbert L. Stone and William H. Taylor, *The America's Cup Race* (Princeton, N.J.: Van Nostrand, 1958), 13–16. For the nationalistic rhetoric, see *Spirit* 21 (27 Sept. 1851): 374, (4 Oct. 1851): 388–89; *Times*, 19 Sept. 1851.

37. *Herald*, 27, 19–20 Sept. 1851; George T. Strong, *The Diary of George Templeton Strong*, ed. Allan Nevins and Milton H. Thomas, 4 vols. (New York: Macmillan, 1952), 2:65–66; *Times*, 2 Oct. 1851. Also see *New York Sun*, 9 Sept. 1851; Winfield M. Thompson and Thomas W. Lawson, *The Lawson's History of the America's Cup: A Record of Fifty Years* (Boston, 1902), 29–30.

38. *Spirit* 21 (11 Oct. 1851): 405, 27 (1 Aug. 1857): 295; *Herald*, 3 Oct. 1851; *Times*, 25 July 1857. Also see, Boswell, *America*, 96; Stephens, *American Yachting*, 105–7. For the impact of the *America* on yachting, see Douglas Phillips-Birt, *The History of Yachting* (New York: Stein and Day, 1974), 45–46; Betts, *Sporting Heritage*, 38.

39. *Clipper* 5 (1 Aug. 1857): 116; Parkinson, *New York Yacht Club*, 35. For international racing, see *Herald*, 20 Apr. 1852; *Spirit* 22 (24 Apr. 1852): 114, (12 Feb. 1853): 618. For information on the *Sylvie* and her racing in England, see *Bell's Life of London*, 28 Aug. 1852, quoted in *Spirit* 23 (24 Sept. 1853): 380; Parkinson, *New York Yacht Club*, 29; Stephens, *American Yachting*, 73, 82.

40. For general information on the backgrounds of antebellum New York Yacht Club members, see William P. Stephens, *Traditions and Memoirs of American Yachting* (New York: Motor Boating, 1945), 157; Parkinson, *New York Yacht Club*, 14, 32, 57.

41. For the social composition of the American Jockey Club, see Adelman, "Modern Athletics," chap. 4.

42. *Times*, 10 Oct. 1870; *Tribune*, 6 June 1865; Krout, *Annals*, 65. In 1871 the Seewanhaka Corinthian Yacht Club was established in response to the decline of amateur yachting, and one historian notes that probably no other yachting organization did more to encourage amateur and Corinthian yachting. Many of the members came from the New York Yacht Club. For the impact of the

Seewanhaka Club on yachting, see ibid., 68; Stephens, *American Yachting*, 126–27; Betts, *Sporting Heritage*, 150.

43. *Herald*, 3 June, 22 May 1854, 18 July 1846, 27 June 1858, 8 June 1860. The *Herald* was the major critic of the yacht club during the antebellum period, but its attitude changed after James Gordon Bennett, Jr., the son of the owner of the newspaper, joined the club.

44. For biographical information on Steers and his involvement in yachting, see *Herald*, 10 Jan. 1853, 27 Sept. 1856; *Times*, 26 Sept. 1856; Boswell, *America*, 6–11, 90–92; Stephens, *American Yachting*, 14–15, 17–22; Parkinson, *New York Yacht Club*, 11–12. For the Steers incident, see *Herald*, 22, 25 May 1854, 10 Jan. 1852; *Tribune*, 10 Jan. 1852.

45. *Herald*, 13 Sept. 1846, 22 May 1854, 12 July 1857, 27 June 1858, 7 Aug. 1859, 28 May, 8 June 1860, 9 Aug. 1868; *Tribune*, 6 June 1865; *Times*, 24 May 1855, 3 Aug. 1870.

46. *Wilkes' Spirit* 14 (21 Apr. 1866): 121, 20 (10 Apr. 1869): 120. For the connection between commercial vessels and yachting, see Stephens, *American Yachting*, 17–18. For the distinction between people involved in yachting and yacht racing, see *Times*, 3 Aug. 1870.

47. *Herald*, 12 July, 5 May, 18 Sept. 1857, 28 May, 8 June 1860, 11, 30 Mar. 1861; *Times*, 5 June 1857, 25 June 1858, 1 June 1859; *Spirit* 30 (26 May 1860): 162. Between 1855 and 1857 several smaller yacht clubs were established in the metropolitan area. See ibid. 25 (7 Apr. 1855): 90, 28 (26 June 1858): 217; Stephens, *American Yachting*, 81. For yachting in Civil War New York, see *Times*, 20 May 1861, 7 June 1862; Parkinson, *New York Yacht Club*, 525; Stephens, *American Yachting*, 87.

48. For the growth of yachting in the five years following the Civil War, see Betts, *Sporting Heritage*, 149–50; Phillips-Birt, *Yachting*, 55.

49. For the changing numbers and leadership of the yacht club, see Parkinson, *New York Yacht Club*, 47, 526; New York Yacht Club, "Scrapbook," 2 vols., 1:22; *Wilkes' Spirit* 12 (29 Apr. 1865): 140. For Bennett's involvement in sport in general and yachting in particular, see Richard O'Connor, *The Scandalous Mr. Bennett* (Garden City, N.Y.: Doubleday, 1962), 45–61; John A. Lucas and Ronald A. Smith, *Saga of American Sport* (Philadelphia: Lea and Febiger, 1978), 149, 151, 162–67.

50. *Herald*, 19 Oct. 1866; *Harper's Magazine* 34 (Mar. 1867): 525; Alfred F. Loomis, *Ocean Racing: The Great-Blue Water Yacht Races, 1866–1935* (New York: Morrow, 1936), 3–17; Stephens, *American Yachting*, 82–93.

51. *Herald*, 10–11, 17, 21 Nov. 1866; *Times*, 29 Nov., 31 Dec. 1866; *Wilkes' Spirit* 15 (17 Nov. 1866): 185, (24 Nov. 1866): 201, (1 Dec. 1866): 217; *Clipper* 14 (24 Nov. 1866): 258.

52. *Herald*, 30 Dec. 1866; *Clipper* 14 (5 Jan. 1867): 306. For a dissenting view, see *Wilkes' Spirit* 15 (5 Jan. 1867): 297. For the development of ocean racing, see Loomis, *Ocean Racing*, 33ff.

53. Stephens, *American Yachting*, 87. Stephens used the phrase "the Day of the Great Schooner" to describe yachting in the immediate post–Civil War years. See ibid., chap. 7. For the list of New York Yacht Club yachtsmen, see Peverelly, *American Pastimes*, 30.

54. *Herald,* 23 June 1867; *Wilkes' Spirit* 18 (15 Aug. 1868): 472.

55. *Herald,* 6 Jan. 1867, 12 Apr., 3 June 1866, 28 Aug. 1868; *Bell's Life of London,* quoted in New York Yacht Club, "Scrapbook," 1:86; *Wilkes' Spirit* 14 (21 Apr. 1866): 121; Stephens, *American Yachting,* 93–95; R. D. Burnell, *Races for the America's Cup* (London: Macdonald, 1965), 30–31.

56. *Herald,* 19, 29 Nov. 1868, 1 June, 22 Aug. 1869, 15, 24 Jan., 23 Mar. 1870; *Times,* 23 Nov., 10 Dec. 1868; *Wilkes' Spirit* 19 (13 Feb. 1869): 406, (21 Nov. 1868): 213, 215, (12 Dec. 1868): 264, 20 (20 Mar. 1869): 71, 21 (28 Aug. 1869): 32; *Report of the Committee Appointed by H. G. Stebbins, Esq., Commodore of the New York Yacht Club, to Take Action in the Matter of the Challenge of James Ashbury, Owner of the Yacht "Cambria" to Contest for the Possession of the Challenge Cup, Won by the "America" in 1851* (New York: Amerman, 1870). Also see Parkinson, *New York Yacht Club,* 63–64; Phillips-Birt, *Yachting,* 47–48; Roland F. Coffin, *The America's Cup. How It Was Won by the Yacht "America" in 1851 and Has Been since Defended* (New York: Scribner, 1885), 25–32.

57. For discussion of the deed, see Brooks, *$30,000,000 Cup,* 43; Stephens, *American Yachting,* 107–8, 119–22.

58. *Herald,* 24, 15 Jan., 25 Mar., 31 July 1870. To support this position, proponents noted that the preamble to the deed specifically pointed to the conditions under which the Cup had been won. Stephens accurately pointed out the difference between the two: the *America* "sailed on perfectly even terms with her competitors, each racing for the possession of a prize. In the case of the *Cambria* and the fleet, while she was racing for the possession of a prize, the other seventeen were racing not to possess the prize, but to keep her from winning it." See, *American Yachting,* 114.

59. *Herald,* 4 July, 6 Feb. 1870; *Wilkes' Spirit* 22 (26 Mar. 1870): 83.

60. Loomis, *Ocean,* 21–29; *Herald,* 17 Nov. 1869, 5, 22–30 July 1870; *Times,* 10 Dec. 1868, 7 Dec. 1869, 20, 28–29, 31 July 1870; *Wilkes' Spirit* 21 (13 Nov. 1869): 200–201, (20 Nov. 1869): 217, (4 Dec. 1869): 249, (1 Jan. 1870): 313, 22 (30 July 1870): 373, 377, (6 Aug. 1870): 385–86, 393; *Clipper* 18 (6 Aug. 1870): 138.

61. *Herald,* 9 Aug. 1870; *Times,* 9 Aug. 1870; *Wilkes' Spirit* 22 (13 Aug. 1870): 404, 408–9.

62. *Report of Committee of Arrangements, and Correspondence with Commodore Ashbury, in Relation to Races with the "Livonia" for the America's Cup* (New York: Biglow, 1872): *Herald,* 27 Apr., 6, 28 May, 18 June, 30 July, 6–7, 10–11 Oct. 1871; *Times,* 19 Mar., 22 May, 13 June 1871; *Wilkes' Spirit* 24 (15 Apr. 1871): 131, (18 Feb. 1871): 8, (18 Mar. 1871): 67, (24 June 1871): 296, 25 (19 Aug. 1871): 9; Coffin, *America's Cup,* 48–59.

63. *Herald,* 10, 19–20, 22–24, 26 Oct. 1871; *Wilkes' Spirit* 25 (21 Oct. 1871): 152–53, (28 Oct. 1871): 168, 170–71; *Times,* 26 Oct. 1871; Coffin, *America's Cup,* 66–80.

64. *Report of the Committee of Arrangements; and Commodore Ashbury's Reply to the Report of the New York Yacht Club in Relation to the Race with "The Livonia" for the America's Cup, in October, 1871* (London: Waterlow, 1872). Also see Coffin, *America's Cup,* 86–88; Brooks, *$30,000,000 Cup,* 65.

Although English yachtsmen did not try for the America's Cup until 1885, challenges came from Canadian yachtsmen in 1876 and 1881.

65. The nationalistic rhetoric that was part of the growth of international yachting in general and the Ashbury challenges in particular was considerable. For examples, see *Herald*, 26 Oct., 12 Dec. 1866, 21 May, 15 Aug. 1870; *Wilkes' Spirit* 22 (28 May 1870): 225, 232. For the formation of the modern Olympic Games, see John J. MacAloon, *This Great Symbol, Pierre de Coubertin and the Origins of the Modern Olympic Games* (Chicago: University of Chicago Press, 1981).

CHAPTER 9: PEDESTRIANISM, BILLIARDS, BOXING, AND ANIMAL SPORTS

1. *New York Post*, 8 July, 3 Sept. 1824, 3 June 1834; *New York American*, 2, 23 July 1824. Also see John Cumming, *Runners and Walkers: A Nineteenth Century Sports Chronicle* (Chicago: Regnery Gateway, 1981), 5–8; John R. Betts, *America's Sporting Heritage, 1850–1950* (Reading, Mass.: Addison-Wesley, 1974), 36; George Moss, "The Long Distance Runners of Ante-Bellum America," *Journal of Popular Culture* 8 (1974): 370; Jennie Holliman, *American Sport, 1785–1835* (Durham, N.C.: Seeman, 1931), 152–54. For running races prior to 1820, see ibid., 152; Foster R. Dulles, *A History of Recreation: America Learns to Play* (New York: Appleton-Century-Crofts, 1965), 26, 34.

2. *Post*, 14 Jan., 17 Apr. 1835; *Spirit of the Times* 5 (18 Apr. 1835). Also see Allan Nevins, ed., *The Diary of Philip Hone, 1828–1851* (New York: Arno, 1970), 156; Archibald D. Turnbull, *John Stevens: An American Record* (New York: Century, 1928), 510–11. Samuel L. Gouveneur was from one of New York's wealthiest families and an active member of the city's horse-racing community during the 1820s and 1830s. The exact amount of the Gouveneur-Stevens wager is unknown.

3. Nevins, *Diary*, 156–57. The *Post* reported that the crowd at this contest was not as large as the one at the Eclipse-Henry race; this race attracted 16,000–20,000 spectators. See *Post*, 25 Apr. 1835.

4. *Post*, 17, 25 Apr. 1835; *American Turf Register and Sporting Magazine* 6 (May 1835): 478; *Spirit* 14 (1 June 1844): 162; *New York Spectator*, 27 Apr. 1835. For the background of the runners, see *Post*, 25 Apr. 1835. Francis Smith, a black runner, wanted to compete but was declared ineligible because he had not filled out the entry form before the deadline. See Moss, "Long Distance," 371, 378; *American Turf Register* 6 (June 1835): 518–20.

5. For pedestrianism in New York between 1835 and 1844, see *Spirit* 8 (16 June 1838): 140, (8 Sept. 1838): 236, 10 (6 Aug. 1840): 265, 11 (11 Dec. 1841): 468.

6. For the lure of gambling, see Henry Chafetz, *Play the Devil: A History of Gambling in the United States, 1492–1955* (New York: Potter, 1960), 223–24; Moss, "Long Distance," 370. For pedestrianism in England, see Melvyn Waterman, *History of British Athletics* (London: Hale, 1968), 15–18; Harold Harris, *Sport in Britain: Its Origins and Development* (London: Paul, 1975), 136–38.

7. *American*, 15 June 1821. Richard Mandell claims that the first use of the term "record" in connection with a sporting event appeared in an 1868 track

and field manual. See "The Invention of the Sports Record," *Stadion* 2 (1976): 259. Prior to this date, however, Americans were familiar with both the term and the concept of a sports record. See *Spirit* 24 (23 Nov. 1844): 462. Nevertheless, there was at this time no agency for keeping records, authenticating performances, or making sure of standardized conditions. While all records were unofficial and a published list of sports records did not as yet exist, the swiftest times could be found by consulting back issues of sports journals.

8. *Spirit* 14 (1 June 1844): 162, (8 June 1844): 169; *New York Herald*, 1, 4 June, 13, 17–18 Oct. 1844; *American Turf Register* 15 (July 1844): 436–38, (Nov. 1844): 684–90.

9. *Spirit* 14 (2 Nov. 1844): 426.

10. Ibid., (23 Nov. 1844): 462–63, (21 Dec. 1844): 510; *American Turf Register* 15 (Dec. 1844): 730–35, 738–43; *Herald*, 18, 20 Nov. 1844.

11. *Spirit* 14 (22 June 1844): 202, 19 (1 Dec. 1849): 486, 15 (9 Aug. 1845): 278; *Herald*, 14 July 1841. For walking contests, see *Spirit* 7 (16 Sept. 1837): 244, 10 (4 Apr. 1840): 49, 11 (6 Mar. 1841): 6; *American Turf Register* 12 (Mar. 1841): 162. For the growth of pedestrianism nationally, see Moss, "Long Distance," 375–82; Cumming, *Runners*, 30–34, 40–41, 48–62; Betts, *Sporting Heritage*, 36; Dulles, *Recreation*, 143–44; Dale A. Somers, *The Rise of Sport in New Orleans, 1850–1900* (Baton Rouge: Louisiana State University Press, 1972), 61–62.

12. Moss, "Long Distance," 373. For examples of the size of New York purses, see *Spirit* 8 (8 June 1838): 128, 11 (11 Dec. 1841): 468, 14 (12 Oct. 1844): 387, 15 (5 July 1845): 213, 18 (18 Nov. 1848): 462, 24 (18 Mar. 1854): 54; *Herald*, 12 Apr. 1856.

13. For the involvement of respectable New Yorkers in the sport, see *Spirit* 14 (8 June 1844): 169, 11 (6 Mar. 1841): 6; *American Turf Register* 12 (Mar. 1841): 162.

14. For racing in New York between 1845 and 1855, see *Spirit* 15 (5 July 1845): 213, 18 (18 Nov. 1845): 462, 20 (10 Aug. 1850): 294, 24 (18 Mar. 1854): 54; *Herald*, 3 Jan., 25 Mar., 9, 26 June, 8 July 1845, 5 Sept. 1854; *New York Times*, 4 Aug., 5 Sept. 1854; *New York Clipper* 2 (12 Aug. 1854).

15. The economic implications of commercial versus participant money is discussed in chapter 3. The Beacon Course was closed "because most of the inhabitants of its surrounding area did not like races or the characters that patronize them." See Harry B. Weiss and Grace M. Weiss, *Early Pastimes in New Jersey* (Trenton, N.J.: Pastime, 1960), 124. While these elements quite possibly contributed to the demise of the Beacon Course, the death of Cyrus Browning, the proprietor, was probably more significant. Whatever the exact reason, the closing of the Beacon Course raises questions of the profitability of the race-course—if it had been a financial success, other investors would have stepped in to challenge the closing; and if it was not a profitable venture, then the crowd sizes must have been grossly exaggerated. In any event it is easier to understand why there was a shift from promoter to match money.

16. *Times*, 1 June 1857; *Herald*, 25 Mar., 1, 10 July, 4 Oct. 1845; *Clipper* 1 (18 Mar. 1854), (25 Mar. 1854).

17. Gerald Redmond, *The Caledonian Games in Nineteenth-Century America* (Cranbury, N.J.: Associated University Press, 1971), 20. Also see Rowland Berthoff,

British Immigrants in Industrial America, 1790-1950 (New York: Russell and Russell, 1953), 151; Robert Korsgaard, "A History of the Amateur Athletic Union of the United States" (Ed.D. diss., Teacher's College, Columbia University, 1952), 28-29.

18. Redmond, *Caledonian*, 37-45, 59-60; Berthoff, *British*, 151, 168; *Times*, 2 July 1867; Korsgaard, "Amateur," 22-23.

19. Redmond, *Caledonian*, 40-41; Berthoff, *British*, 151. Crowds at the Caledonian games in New York during the 1860s were almost always estimated at 10,000 or more. For examples, see *Wilkes' Spirit of the Times* 23 (10 Sept. 1870): 54; *Times*, 10 Sept. 1864.

20. Sport historians have easily linked the commercialization of sport with professionalization. Unfortunately, they have paid scant attention to the role that amateur athletic clubs played in this development.

21. *Clipper* 7 (24 Sept. 1859): 183; *Wilkes' Spirit* 23 (10 Sept. 1870): 54; Redmond, *Caledonian*, 20-21, 42, 62-66, 116-17. Field events were known in America before the Caledonian games but rarely engaged in at track and field meets. Similarly, running races in the Scottish games were more on the order of dashes, in contrast to the passion of Americans for endurance races.

22. Redmond, *Caledonian*, 53-54, 59-60, 62-67; Melvin L. Adelman, "The Development of Modern Athletics: Sport in New York City, 1820—1870" (Ph.D. diss., University of Illinois, 1980), 593.

23. *Porter's Spirit of the Times* 5 (4 Sept. 1858): 9; *Clipper* 4 (29 Nov. 1856): 252, 13 (16 Sept. 1865): 176; *Wilkes' Spirit* 11 (17 Sept. 1864): 36, 1 (24 Sept. 1859): 45, 23 (10 Sept. 1870): 54; *Times*, 12 Oct. 1867, 24 Sept. 1858, 10 Sept. 1864; *Herald*, 8 Oct. 1858, 16 Sept. 1859.

24. *Clipper* 16 (30 May 1868): 58, 15 (14 Dec. 1867): 282, 17 (10 Apr. 1869): 5; *Times*, 24 Sept. 1870, 28 July 1868, 1 Dec. 1867; *Herald*, 24 Nov. 1869; *Wilkes' Spirit* 15 (1 Sept. 1866): 8, 18 (9 May 1868): 195, (30 May 1868): 252. Also see, Cummings, *Runners*, 77-100.

25. Redmond, *Caledonian*, 76. Korsgaard notes that informal track meets took place at Columbia College as early as 1864. See "Amateur," 32-33.

26. John A. Krout, *Annals of American Sport* (New Haven, Conn.: Yale University Press, 1929), 186; Redmond, *Caledonian*, 51-52; Frederick W. Janssen, *A History of American Athletics and Aquatics, 1829-1886* (New York: Outing, 1888), 31.

27. *Wilkes' Spirit* 19 (10 Oct. 1868): 121; *Turf, Field and Farm* 7 (13 Nov. 1868): 736; *Clipper* 17 (19 Mar. 1870): 397.

28. The New York Athletic Club emerged as a sports club of the New York elite in the 1880s. See Benjamin G. Rader, *American Sports: From the Age of Folk Games to the Age of Spectators* (Englewood Cliffs, N.J.: Prentice-Hall, 1983), 55-57.

29. Redmond also pointed out that financial considerations were an important reason for the decline of the Caledonian games during the 1880s. See *Caledonian*, 99-110.

30. For the rise of athletic clubs in New York during the 1870s, see Korsgaard, "Amateur," 32-33, 50. As was the case with rowing, amateur control over track and field did not occur overnight. See ibid., 43-69; Redmond, *Caledonian*, 67.

31. For a discussion of the two billiard styles, see Ned Polsky, *Hustlers, Beats and Others* (Garden City, N.Y.: Anchor, 1969), 7–18. While professional pool players dominated the sport after 1850, billiards is the only sport discussed in this chapter to also have a significant recreational dimension. In this chapter the terms "billiards" and "pool" are used interchangeably to describe various types of billiard and pool games.

32. Ibid., 6–16, 24; Louise C. Belden, "Billiards in America Before 1830," *Antiques* 87 (Jan. 1965): 99–101; Charles Haswell, *Reminiscence of New York by an Octogenarian, 1816–1860* (New York: Harper, 1896), 59; *Clipper* 9 (23 Nov. 1861): 250, 16 (9 May 1868): 37, (16 May 1868): 44.

33. For a discussion of skilled pool players in the 1820s, see *Clipper* 9 (23 Nov. 1861): 250, 16 (16 May 1868): 44. For billiard advertisements, see *Herald*, 21 Dec. 1837, 5 June 1846; *Spirit* 7 (2 Sept. 1836): 231.

34. *Clipper* 16 (16 May 1868): 44, (23 May 1868): 5; J. H. Green, *An Exposure of the Arts and Miseries of Gambling; Designed Especially as a Warning to the Youthful and Inexperienced Against the Evils of that Odious and Destructive Vice*, 5th ed. (Philadelphia: Zieber, 1847), 206–7.

35. For the growth of club life in New York, see Edward Pessen, *Riches, Class and Power Before the Civil War* (Lexington, Mass.: Heath, 1973), 225–29.

36. Polsky, *Hustlers*, 6, 17–21. New York merchant N. T. Hubbard fondly recalled that he played billiards at the New York Hotel. See *Autobiography of N. T. Hubbard with Personal Reminiscences of New York City from 1795–1875* (New York: Trow, 1875), 69–70.

37. Phelan was born in Ireland around 1814, and his family emigrated to America when he was seven or eight years old. At one time an apprentice jeweller, Phelan became the proprietor of the Arcade Billiard Saloon in New York in 1846, if not earlier. See *Herald*, 5 June 1846, 8 Oct. 1871; *Times*, 7 Oct. 1871; Betts, *Sporting Heritage*, 41–42.

38. *Spirit* 20 (23 Feb. 1850): 6, (1 Mar. 1851): 18.

39. Michael Phelan, *Billiards Without Masters* (New York: Winant, 1850); *Spirit* 20 (17 Aug. 1850): 312.

40. Polsky, *Hustlers*, 24; Betts, *Sporting Heritage*, 75.

41. *Spirit* 25 (8 Dec. 1855): 516, 27 (30 May 1857): 187, 29 (16 Apr. 1859): 109; *Times*, 19 Mar., 11 Apr. 1859; *Porter's Spirit* 3 (9 Jan. 1858): 293, 6 (26 Mar. 1859): 53, (23 Apr. 1859): 115–17; Michael Phelan, *The American Billiard Record. A Compendium of Important Matches since 1854* (New York: Phelan and Collender, 1870), 11.

42. *Spirit* 29 (27 Aug. 1859): 342; *Wilkes' Spirit* 1 (15 Oct. 1859): 89.

43. *Wilkes' Spirit* 3 (10 Nov. 1860): 153, (6 Oct. 1860): 73, (13 Oct. 1860): 88, (27 Oct. 1860): 121, 5 (21 Sept. 1861): 37; *Clipper* 8 (12 Jan. 1860): 314. Also see *Times*, 1 Oct. 1860; Phelan, *American Billiard*, 12. Americans were led to believe that Berger was the champion billiard player of France, and the ease with which he defeated professional pool players in America gave credence to the claim. However, a letter written to the editor of *Wilkes' Spirit* from Paris claimed that Berger was not the best French player. See *Wilkes' Spirit* 5 (28 Sept. 1861): 57.

44. *Clipper* 6 (29 Jan. 1859): 327, (12 Feb. 1859): 343, 9 (23 Nov. 1861): 252,

7 (21 Jan. 1860): 314; *Herald*, 4 Feb. 1858; *Spirit* 29 (12 Mar. 1859): 60; Phelan, *American Billiard*, 12.

45. Dudley Kavanaugh, *The Billiard World: Containing the Rules of the Games of Billiard as Played in the United States and Europe* (New York: Kavanaugh and Decker, 1869), 27; *Wilkes' Spirit* 7 (10 Jan. 1863): 292, 11 (26 Nov. 1864): 202. For similar developments in New Orleans, see Somers, *Rise*, 65. It is interesting to note that one of the explanations offered for bowling being more popular today than billiards is that it is easier to learn. For the relationship between mastery of a physical skill and involvement in a recreational activity, see p. 111.

46. Polsky coined the term "bachelor subculture" to describe a group "that has become increasingly rare and unimportant to America—the hetero-sexual but all male subculture." The bachelor subculture originated from the increasing proportion of single males in the population during the latter part of the nineteenth century. See Polsky, *Hustlers*, 20-25. For the bachelor subculture and its relation to sport, see Somers, *Rise*, 52-53; Rader, *American Sports*, 97-98.

47. Polsky points out that American historians "seem never to have assayed, indeed to be oblivious of, the swiftly growing role of a confirmed bachelor subculture in the social history of nineteenth-century America." Unfortunately, he does not explore this theme in any depth. He simply shows that a casual relationship existed between marriage statistics and the emergence of the bachelor subculture and states that changing economic conditions and immigration affected America's sexual patterns. See *Hustlers*, 21-24. For a discussion of the changing sexual patterns, see Jayme A. Sokolow, *Eros and Modernization: Sylvester Graham, Health Reform, and the Origins of Victorian Sexuality in America* (Cranbury, N.J.: Associated University Press, 1983), 11-39, 77-99; Stephen W. Nissenbaum, *Sex, Diet, and Debility in Jacksonian America: Sylvester Graham and Health Reform* (Westport, Conn.: Greenwood, 1980), 3-38; Charles N. Rosenberg, "Sexuality, Class and Role in 19th Century America," *American Quarterly* 25 (1973): 131-53; Barbara Welter, "The Culture of True Womanhood, 1820-1860," ibid. 18 (1966): 151-74; Nancy Cott, "Passionlessness: An Interpretation of Victorian Sexual Ideology, 1790-1850," *Signs* 4 (1978-79): 219-36; Ronald G. Walters, *Primers for Prudency: Sexual Advice to Victorian America* (Englewood Cliffs, N.J.: Prentice-Hall, 1974). Dale Somers applies the concept of the bachelor subculture to explain sporting developments in antebellum New Orleans. He avoids the problem found in Polsky's argument by merely pointing to the discrepancy in the number of men and women in that city's population. See *Rise*, 52-53. In New York, however, the male-female ratio was roughly even. See United States Bureau of the Census, *Eighth Census of the United States (1860): Population of the United States in 1860* (Washington, D.C., 1864), 322, 328, 337.

48. Peter Stearns, *Be a Man! Males in Modern Society* (New York: Meier and Holmes, 1979), 39-112 (quote from p. 38); Joe L. Dubbert, *A Man's Place: Masculinity in Transition* (Englewood Cliffs, N.J.: Prentice-Hall, 1979), 29-30, 111-12; E. Anthony Rotundo, "Body and Soul: Changing Ideals of American Middle-Class Manhood, 1770-1920," *Journal of Social History* 16 (1983): 23-38.

49. Green, *Art and Miseries*, 206-7; J. H. Green, *Green's Report No. 1 on*

Gambling and Gambling Houses in New York (New York, 1851), 79–81; *New York Tribune*, 25 Dec. 1850; Polsky, *Hustlers*, 6; Marshall B. Davidson, *Life in America*, 2 vols. (Boston: Houghton-Mifflin, 1951), 2:31.

50. Welter, "Cult," 151–74; Barbara Welter, "The Feminization of American Religion, 1800–1860," in Lois Banner and Mary Hartman, eds., *Clio's Consciousness Raised* (New York: Harper and Row, 1974), 137–57; Nancy Cott, *Bonds of Womanhood: "Woman's Sphere" in New England, 1780–1835* (New Haven, Conn.: Yale University Press, 1977), 149–54. In 1866 *Wilkes' Spirit* claimed, "We have always advocated the presence of ladies at these matches, . . . as the most reliable means of conferring tone upon the necessarily heterogeneous masculine assemblage." See *Wilkes' Spirit* 14 (19 May 1866).

51. Michael Phelan, *The Game of Billiards*, 3d ed. (New York: Appleton, 1858), 13–28; *Herald*, 5 Apr. 1862; *Wilkes' Spirit* 10 (16 Apr. 1864): 99; Kavanaugh, *Billiard World*, 68.

52. *Clipper* 11 (19 Dec. 1863): 29, 5 (19 Dec. 1857): 276; *Wilkes' Spirit* 15 (24 Nov. 1866): 204; *Herald*, 11 June 1864; *Times*, 13 Feb. 1870.

53. *Clipper* 9 (23 Nov. 1861): 252; *Times*, 17 Jan. 1865; *Herald*, 21 Feb. 1869, 11 June 1864. Also see *Wilkes' Spirit* 5 (21 Sept. 1861): 37, 6 (28 June 1862): 260, 11 (21 Jan. 1865): 324.

54. *Clipper* 7 (21 Jan. 1860): 314, 12 (1 Oct. 1864): 194; *Turf, Field and Farm* 5 (31 Aug. 1867): 138; Kavanaugh, *Billiard World*, 67.

55. *Wilkes' Spirit* 6 (22 Mar. 1862): 37, 15 (5 Jan. 1867): 292; *Clipper* 14 (3 Nov. 1866): 235.

56. *Wilkes' Spirit* 6 (12 Apr. 1862): 89, (15 Mar. 1862): 20–21, 8 (2 May 1863): 141; *Clipper* 11 (27 June 1863): 84; *Times*, 19 Mar., 10 June 1863, 21 June 1861; *Herald*, 5 Apr. 1862; Phelan, *American Billiard*, 18.

57. *Wilkes' Spirit* 12 (4 Mar. 1865): 4, (17 June 1865): 249, 15 (15 Sept. 1866): 41, 48, (29 Sept. 1866): 77, (3 Nov. 1866): 156; *Clipper* 12 (11 Feb. 1865): 347, (25 Feb. 1865): 362, 14 (3 Nov. 1866): 235; *Times*, 2 Sept. 1865; Phelan, *American Billiard*, 34.

58. *Wilkes' Spirit* 23 (1 Oct. 1870): 101, 105, (8 Oct. 1870): 117, 120, (22 Oct. 1870): 155–56, (7 Jan. 1871): 325, 22 (23 July 1870): 356–57.

59. Ibid. 10 (25 June 1864): 260; *Herald*, 5 Apr. 1862, 11 June 1864; *Times*, 20 Jan. 1871; *Clipper* 11 (24 Oct. 1863): 218.

60. For a discussion of professional billiard players coming to New York, see *Wilkes' Spirit* 6 (12 Apr. 1862): 84. The names of leading players were taken mainly from newspaper accounts of major billiard contests. Also see ibid. 13 (23 Dec. 1865); Phelan, *American Billiard*, 11; Kavanaugh, *Billiard World*, 23–64.

61. *Wilkes' Spirit* 8 (2 May 1863): 141. Polsky also shares the view that "most of the early non-WASP billiard professionals are of Irish origin," although he realizes that German-Americans were involved in the sport to a far greater extent than earlier billiard historians recognized. See *Hustlers*, 25. Polsky makes no mention, however, of the contribution of the French or French-Canadians to the development of the sport in America, possibly because their influence was not far-reaching and was confined to the initial decade of professional billiards, and because these skilled performers, unlike other immigrant players, rarely stayed in the United States for any extended period of time.

62. Polsky, *Hustlers*, 19; Kavanaugh, *Billiard World*, 69.

63. *Wilkes' Spirit* 15 (29 Sept. 1866): 77, 6 (12 Apr. 1862): 84–85; Kavanaugh, *Billiard World*, 54. For further discussion of the financing and earnings of professional poolplayers, see Melvin L. Adelman, "Neglected Sports in American History: The Rise of Billiards in New York City, 1850–1870," *Canadian Journal of History of Sport* 12 (Dec. 1981): 23, n. 67.

64. *Wilkes' Spirit* 20 (22 May 1869): 201, 23 (20 Aug. 1870): 4, 13 (14 Oct. 1865): 104. Also see *Times*, 13 Feb. 1870. For the rules and various types of billiard games, see Phelan, *Billiard*, 172–97.

65. Betts, *Sporting Heritage*, 205; Polsky, *Hustlers*, 19, 25–26.

66. For boxing in America prior to 1820, see Elliot Jacob Gorn, "The Manly Art: Bare-Knuckle Prize Fighting and the Rise of American Sport" (Ph.D. diss., Yale University, 1983), 1–61, 118–26; Holliman, *American Sport*, 138–43; *American Fistiana, Containing All the Fights in the United States from 1816 to 1860* (New York: DeWitt, 1860), 5–6; Nat Fleischer, *The Heavyweight Championship: An Informal History of Heavy-Weight Boxing from 1719 to the Present Day* (New York: Putnam, 1961), 41. Newspapers during the antebellum period agreed that the Hyer-Beasley fight was the first American prizefight. See *Herald*, 24 Sept. 1842, 9 Feb. 1849; *Times*, 13 Dec. 1855; *Porter's Spirit* 5 (23 Oct. 1858): 118.

67. *American*, 19, 1 Mar. 1822. Also see Gorn, "Manly Art," 141–54.

68. *Spectator*, 19 Oct. 1824; *Post*, 14 Dec. 1826, 28 June 1823. For boxing contests during the 1820s, see *American Fistiana*, 6–7; *Herald*, 9 Feb. 1849; Gorn, "Manly Art," 126–32; Holliman, *American Sport*, 143.

69. For the *New York Mirror's* criticism of boxing, see Davidson, *Life*, 2:33; *Herald*, 22 Aug. 1837. Also see *Spirit* 6 (15 Oct. 1836): 275. For boxing contests in New York in the 1830s, see *Herald*, 21 Aug. 1837, 24 Sept. 1842, 9 Feb. 1849; *Porter's Spirit* 5 (23 Oct. 1858): 118; *Post*, 30 Aug. 1830; Holliman, *American Sport*, 147; Gorn, "Manly Art," 135–41.

70. *Herald*, 24 Sept. 1842; *Spirit* 12 (3 Sept. 1842): 322; *Times*, 13 Dec. 1855; *Clipper* 9 (4 Jan. 1862): 304; Fleischer, *Heavyweight*, 41.

71. *Herald*, 13–16 Sept. 1842; *Tribune*, 19 Sept. 1842; *Spirit* 12 (17 Sept. 1842): 342; *Clipper* 1 (25 Feb. 1854); Thomas M. McDade, "Death in the Afternoon," *Westchester Historian* 46 (Winter 1970): 2–4. Some writers claimed that McCoy's mother told him not to return home a loser, but others insisted that his mother opposed his fighting. See *Herald*, 15 Sept. 1842; *Spirit* 12 (17 Sept. 1842): 342; *Tribune*, 17 Sept. 1842. Under the boxing rules of the day a round lasted until one of the fighters was knocked down; the next round started thirty seconds later.

72. *Tribune*, 19–20 Sept. 1842; *Herald*, 16–17 Sept. 1842.

73. For the negative view of pugilism, see Nevins, *Diary*, 619–20, 636–37, 640; George T. Strong, *The Diary of George Templeton Strong*, ed. Alan Nevins and Milton H. Thomas, 4 vols. (New York: Macmillan, 1952), 1:185–86. For the damper the Lilly-McCoy fight put on pugilism and second-rate fights in New York, see *Porter's Spirit* 5 (23 Oct. 1858): 118; *Herald*, 26 June 1843; *Tribune*, 27 June 1843, 1 Sept., 19 Oct. 1847.

74. Sullivan was neither a Yankee nor a Sullivan—he was born James Ambrose in Ireland in 1813. For biographical material on Sullivan, his impact on the rise

of pugilism, and his boxing career, see Gorn, "Manly Art," 172–80; Fleischer, *Heavyweight,* 51–59; *Times,* 30 June 1856, 13 Dec. 1855; *American Fistiana,* 16–17; *Herald,* 9 July, 14 May 1847, 9 Feb. 1849, 22 Oct. 1858; *Spirit* 16 (19 Sept. 1846): 354; *Clipper* 4 (5 July 1856): 82–83; *Porter's Spirit* 5 (23 Oct. 1858): 118; *Times,* 13 Dec. 1855.

75. *American Fistiana,* 19; *Herald,* 11 Jan., 9 Feb. 1849; *Spirit* 18 (23 Sept. 1848): 366, (25 Nov. 1848): 474, (17 Feb. 1849): 615, 618–19; *Times,* 13 Dec. 1855; *Clipper* 9 (8 Feb. 1862): 341.

76. *Herald,* 7, 9, 11 Feb. 1849; *Porter's Spirit* 5 (23 Oct. 1858): 118; *American Fistiana,* 19.

77. For the impact of the Hyer-Sullivan fight, see *Porter's Spirit* 5 (23 Oct. 1858): 118; *Clipper* 9 (8 Feb. 1862): 341. For the growth of boxing during the 1850s, see ibid. 1 (25 Feb. 1854), (15 Apr. 1854), 4 (9 Aug. 1856): 122, 7 (11 June 1859): 58; *Herald,* 23 Feb. 1858; *Tribune,* 7 Feb. 1855. Also see *Clipper* 1 (4 Feb. 1854), 5 (12 Dec. 1857): 267, 6 (13 Nov. 1858): 234; *Wilkes' Spirit* 1 (10 Dec. 1859): 221.

78. *Herald,* 13–14 Oct. 1853; *Times,* 11, 14 Oct. 1853; *American Fistiana,* 20–21; *Tribune,* 20 Oct. 1853; *Spirit* 23 (22 Oct. 1853): 421; *Clipper* 1 (15 Oct. 1854), (22 Oct. 1854). The heavyweight championship fights between Floyd Patterson and Muhammad Ali, and Ali and Sonny Liston, had some of the same symbolic characteristics as the Sullivan-Morrissey contest a century earlier. See Adelman, "Modern Athletics," 600.

79. *Porter's Spirit* 4 (31 July 1858): 345, 349, (7 Aug. 1858): 357; *Times,* 18 Sept., 18, 22–23 Oct. 1858; *Herald,* 22 July, 26 Sept., 15, 21 Oct. 1858; *American Fistiana,* 59; *Clipper* 6 (30 Oct. 1858): 222–23, (13 Nov. 1858): 234. The backgrounds of Heenan and Morrissey were remarkably similar: both grew up in Troy, New York; both had Irish parents; and both went to California during the 1850s, eventually returning to New York. For biographical material on Heenan, see *John C. Heenan of Troy, N.Y., Champion Pugilist of America* (New York: Fox, 1882), 6–9; *Herald,* 22 Oct. 1858. Heenan was the American representative in this fight because he was born in America and because nativists disliked Morrissey.

80. *Times,* 25, 28, 30 Apr., 9 Mar. 1860; *Herald,* 11 Mar., 24 Apr., 13, 28 May, 9 Nov. 1859, 13, 18 Feb., 30 Apr. 1860; *Wilkes' Spirit* 2 (14 Apr. 1860): 84–85; *Clipper* 7 (12 Nov. 1859): 234, (7 Jan. 1860): 398; *Harper's Magazine* 20 (May 1860): 844. For a popular history of the Heenan-Sayers fight, see Alan Lloyd, *The Great Prize Fight* (New York: Coward, McCann and Geoghegan, 1977).

81. *Herald,* 8 Dec. 1859, 25 Apr. 1860; *Clipper* 7 (24 Mar. 1860): 386; *Wilkes' Spirit* 1 (21 Jan. 1860): 313. Also see Anthony O. Edmonds, "The Second Louis-Schmeling Fight," *Journal of Popular Culture* 7 (1973): 42–50.

82. For an American view of the fight, see *Times,* 30 Apr., 3, 17 May, 16 July 1860; *Herald,* 29 Apr. 1860; *Wilkes' Spirit* 2 (5 May 1860): 129–35, 137–41, (12 May 1860): 143–49, 153, (2 June 1860): 201, (21 July 1860): 330, 5 (28 Dec. 1861): 264. For a discussion of the fight, see ibid. 2 (29 Apr. 1860): 114–20; *Clipper* 8 (5 May 1860): 18–20, (12 May 1860): 26–27; Lloyd, *Great,* 137–59; Fleischer, *Heavyweight,* 64–66.

83. *Brooklyn Eagle,* 12 May 1860; *Herald,* 30 Apr., 2, 8 May 1860; *Clipper*

8 (2 June 1860): 50, 52, (9 June 1860): 71, (23 June 1860): 106. For an anti-English view and a discussion of the English sporting character, see *Wilkes' Spirit* 22 (21 May 1870): 216–17.

84. *Herald*, 30 June, 15 May, 16 June 1860; *Clipper* 8 (19 May 1860): 34, (25 Aug. 1860): 145–47; *Times*, 8 May 1860.

85. *Tribune*, 20 Sept. 1842; *Herald*, 24 Aug. 1837; *Porter's Spirit* 5 (23 Oct. 1858): 118. Of the six English-born fighters in New York, it is noteworthy that four were from minority groups—two were Irish or part Irish, and two were Jewish. While there were several black fighters in New York between 1840 and 1860, Samuel Freedman was the only one on whom any information exists. Black fighters competed at times against whites in exhibitions. For black boxing in New York, see *Clipper* 9 (3 Aug. 1861): 122, 16 (27 Feb. 1869): 371; *Times*, 18 Oct. 1859.

86. The evidence on occupation indicates that boxers were employed in unskilled and semiskilled jobs, which is not surprising given the high proportion of Irish fighters. Native-born fighters were more likely to come from the artisan class, particularly the butcher community. Although many of the fighters were of lower-class origins, a few owned their own taverns and others were probably managers or bouncers. Some fighters were given patronage jobs. Even among the fighters who held white-collar jobs, the evidence strongly suggests that they had lower- or lower-middle-class origins.

87. *Porter's Spirit* 5 (23 Oct. 1858): 118. The average fighter in New York earned money by participating in numerous sparring exhibitions. How much of the gate receipts he was given is unknown, but in all probability it was not more than $25 and quite possibly as little as $10 for an evening's work.

88. *Clipper* 8 (6 Oct. 1860): 195. For this view of boxers, see S. Kirson Weinberg and Henry Arond, "The Occupational Culture of the Boxer," *American Journal of Sociology* 58 (1951): 460–69; Nathan Hare, "A Study of the Black Fighter," *Black Scholar* 3 (Nov. 1971): 2–8; John Ford, *Prizefighting: The Age of Regency Boximania* (New York: Great Albion, 1972), 57–59.

89. The connection between pugilism and politics was briefly touched on by Fleischer, *Heavyweight*, 50–51; Alvin F. Harlow, *Old Bowery Days: The Chronicle of a Famous Street* (New York: Appleton, 1931), 296, 299–301; Herbert Asbury, *The Gangs of New York: An Informal History of the Underworld* (New York: Capricorn, 1970), 95; Edward K. Spann, *The New Metropolis, New York City, 1840–1867* (New York: Columbia University Press, 1981), 345–48.

90. *Tribune*, 20 Sept. 1842, 1 Mar. 1855; *Times*, 28 July 1858, 28 Apr. 1860, 18 May 1871; *Herald*, 22, 30 Oct. 1858, 6 July, 12 Aug. 1860; *Eagle*, 27 Sept. 1858; *Clipper* 4 (14 Feb. 1857): 338, (15 Nov. 1856): 234. The amount of space given to the political ramifications of pugilism appeared to be equal to the amount given for other reasons for disapproval of the sport.

91. For the formation of New York gangs, see Asbury, *Gangs*, 1–86. For the development of Tammany Hall and the shifting nature of politics, see Jerome Mushkat, *Tammany: The Evolution of a Political Machine, 1789–1865* (Syracuse, N.Y.: Syracuse University Press, 1971), 76, 101, 202; Alexander B. Callow, Jr., *The Tweed Ring* (New York: Oxford University Press, 1965), 6–7; Spann, *The New Metropolis*, 45–66, 341–63. For the connection between gangs and politics,

see Asbury, *Gangs*, 37–44, 105–6; Callow, *Tweed*, 57–59. For the declining political importance of fighters in the post–Civil War period, see Adelman, "Modern Athletics," 573–75.

92. Harlow, *Bowery*, 296–301; Fleischer, *Heavyweight*, 50–51; Callow, *Tweed*, 56–57; Asbury, *Gangs*, 95.

93. *Clipper* 11 (25 Apr. 1863): 10; *Wilkes' Spirit* 8 (25 Apr. 1863): 122.

94. *Herald*, 23 Jan., 26–27 Feb., 9, 11, 19–20 Mar., 1855, 28 July 1854; *Tribune*, 26 July 1854, 27 Feb., 9–10 Mar. 1855; *Times*, 28 July 1854, 26–27 Feb., 12 Mar., 13, 15, 17 Dec. 1855; Asbury, *Gangs*, 99–100; Spann, *New Metropolis*, 254–55. One journal noted that Bill Harrington won the respect of the better class. See *Porter's Spirit* 6 (2 Apr. 1859): 68. A member of old-line Knickerbocker society declared that Harrington was "a protector of the weak and timid, a terror to sneak-thieves and ruffians." See Abram C. Dayton, *The Last Days of Knickerbocker Life in New York* (New York: Putnam, 1897), 338–39. Also see Harlow, *Bowery*, 151; *American Fistiana*, 80.

95. *Chronicle* 1 (22 Aug. 1867): *Turf, Field and Farm* 5 (31 Aug. 1867): 137.

96. *Times*, 20 Apr. 1860.

97. The increasing coverage boxing received in the daily press reflected the changing nature of the urban press. See James L. Crouthamel, "The Newspaper Revolution in New York, 1830–1860," *New York History* 45 (1964): 91–113; Crouthamel, "James Gordon Bennett, the *New York Herald* and the Development of Newspaper Sensationalism," ibid. 54 (1973): 294–316; Dan Schiller, *Objectivity and the News: The Public and the Rise of Commercial Journalism* (Philadelphia: University of Pennsylvania Press, 1981).

98. *American Fistiana*, 24; *Clipper* 6 (27 Nov. 1858): 250, (2 Oct. 1856): 186, (22 Jan. 1859): 314, 1 (28 Jan. 1854), 4 (23 Aug. 1856): 138, (27 Dec. 1856): 284, 5 (26 Dec. 1857): 252, 7 (25 Feb. 1860): 356, 8 (2 Feb. 1861): 330, (9 Mar. 1861): 372, 16 (6 June 1868): 68.

99. *Herald*, 26 Sept. 1848, 9 Feb., 2 June 1866, 11 May 1870, 22 Aug. 1837.

100. *Times*, 18 Sept. 1858, 9 Sept. 1870, 13 Dec. 1855, 26 Mar. 1862.

101. Rotundo, "Body and Soul," 123–38.

102. *Clipper* 11 (20 June 1863): 79; *Herald*, 20 July 1860; *Wilkes' Spirit* 8 (25 Apr. 1863): 122. For the Coburn-McCool fight, see *Herald*, 29 Apr., 6 May 1863; *Clipper* 11 (16 May 1863): 335; *Times*, 26 Mar. 1863; Fleischer, *Heavyweight*, 71.

103. *Herald*, 24 Nov. 1863; *Times*, 22 Dec. 1863; *Eagle*, 23 Aug. 1861.

104. *Clipper* 11 (21 Jan. 1864): 314, (13 Feb. 1864): 346, (27 Feb. 1864): 362, (19 Mar. 1864): 386, 12 (23 Apr. 1864): 10; *Wilkes' Spirit* 9 (2 Jan. 1864): 273–74, 280, 284–85, (9 Jan. 1864): 296–97; *Times*, 26 Dec. 1863.

105. *Clipper* 13 (16 Dec. 1865): 282, 15 (18 May 1867): 421; *Herald*, 23 Aug. 1867, 25 Aug. 1868. For the Coburn-McCool fight, see *Clipper* 16 (18 Apr. 1868): 11, (6 June 1868): 667; *Wilkes' Spirit* 18 (25 Apr. 1868): 153.

106. *Herald*, 8 Jan., 11 May 1870; *Times*, 11 May 1870; *Wilkes' Spirit* 22 (14 May 1870): 201; Fleischer, *Heavyweight*, 72–73; Somers, *Rise*, 162–63.

107. For animal sports prior to 1820, see Jack Berryman, "The Ending of American Blood Sports," paper presented at the 86th meeting of the American Historical Association, 1971, 4–7; Krout, *Annals*, 15, 23; Holliman, *American*

Sport, 128, 130, 134; Ester Singleton, *Social New York under the Georges, 1714–1776* (New York: Appleton, 1902), 266–67.

108. Isaac Holmes, *An Account of the United States* (London, 1823), quoted in Berryman, "Ending," 6; *Spirit* 17 (20 Mar. 1847): 4, 19 (10 Nov. 1849): 450; Gerald Carson, *Men, Beasts and Gods: A History of Cruelty and Kindness to Animals* (New York: Scribner, 1972), 65.

109. *Spirit* 22 (25 Dec. 1852): 540, 19 (12 Jan. 1850): 558, 20 (25 Jan. 1851): 582, 29 (8 Oct. 1859): 414; Zula Steele, *Angel in Top Hat* (New York: Harper, 1942), 141; *Tribune,* 24 Jan. 1855; *Herald,* 8 Feb., 28 May 1858; *Porter's Spirit* 6 (5 Mar. 1859): 12; *Wilkes' Spirit* 1 (17 Dec. 1859): 229, (24 Dec. 1859): 253; *Times,* 24 May 1855; *Clipper* 4 (31 Jan. 1857): 327, 6 (26 Feb. 1859): 355.

110. *Clipper* 8 (16 Mar. 1861): 378, 10 (8 Nov. 1862): 234, 12 (25 Feb. 1865): 362; *Herald,* 21 Feb. 1862; *Times,* 22 Jan., 23 Aug. 1861; *Wilkes' Spirit* 4 (22 June 1861): 245.

111. Asbury, *Gangs,* 49–51; Steele, *Angel,* 142–43; Martin and Herbert J. Kaufman, "Henry Bergh, Kit Burns, and the Sportsmen of New York," *New York Folklore Quarterly* 28 (1972): 15–20. For biographical material on Burns, see *Herald,* 24 Dec. 1870; *Clipper* 18 (31 Dec. 1870): 306; *Wilkes' Spirit* 23 (24 Dec. 1870): 293.

112. *Herald,* 8 Feb. 1858; *Times,* 22 Jan. 1861; Frederick Van Wyck, *Recollections of an Old New Yorker* (New York: Liveright, 1932), 113–14; *Tribune,* 24 Jan. 1855; *Wilkes' Spirit* 3 (2 Feb. 1861): 340.

113. *Herald,* 19, 27 Jan., 13 Mar., 1 Nov. 1870, 14 Dec. 1869, 12 Mar., 18 May 1868; *Wilkes' Spirit* 22 (19 Mar. 1870): 68, 21 (12 Feb. 1870): 406–7; Berryman, "Ending," 5, 8–9.

114. Carson, *Men,* 96–97. For biographical material on Bergh, see ibid., 97–100; Steele, *Angel,* 3; Charles B. Morris, ed., *Makers of New York* (Philadelphia: Hammersly, 1895), 66. For changing attitudes toward animal sports in England, see Robert W. Malcolmson, *Popular Recreations in English Society, 1700–1850* (Cambridge: Cambridge University Press, 1973), 123–38; Brian Harrison, "Religion and Recreation in Nineteenth Century England," *Past and Present* 38 (1968): 118–23; Carson, *Men,* 43–54.

115. Steele, *Angel,* 7, 218.

116. *Times,* 22 Mar. 1866, 7 Mar. 1867.

117. Kaufman and Kaufman, "Henry Bergh," 26–29; *Herald,* 1 Nov. 1870; Steele, *Angel,* 144–48. Also see Berryman, "Ending," 8–9, 11.

118. Berryman, "Ending," 8, 11, 13; Somers, *Rise,* 205–6.

119. For the relationship between professional athletes and the emergence of certain modern sporting characteristics prior to the nineteenth century, see Allen Guttmann, *From Ritual to Record: The Nature of Modern Sport* (New York: Columbia University Press, 1978), 36–38; Dennis Brailsford, *Sport and Society: Elizabeth to Anne* (London: Routledge and Kegan Paul, 1969), 210–17. Sport scholars have asserted that the rationalization of sport "had been greatly facilitated by commercialization and professionalization." See Alan G. Ingham, "Occupational Subculture in the Work World of Sport," in Donald W. Ball and John W. Loy, eds., *Sport and Social Order: Contributions to the Sociology of Sport* (Reading, Mass.: Addison-Wesley, 1975), 353. In examining the influence of commercial-

ization and professionalization on sporting developments, scholars have too easily tended to perceive them as two sides of the same coin. While there has been a growing interrelationship between these two elements during this century, historically they have been divergent traditions.

120. In both the private (or match) and commercial system the promoter's objective is to make a profit; however, the means to this end vary. In the former system the backer achieves his profit only through victory; in the latter system the winner is unimportant. For the entrepreneur the size of the crowd and gate receipts are the key to his profits. The differences betwen the two systems produces different relationships to the contest. While the backer is concerned with "outcome," the entrepreneur is concerned with "spectacle." It is this shifting relationship to the promotion of sporting contests that marks the initial step in the emerging rationalization of the sporting institution.

CHAPTER 10: A HOST OF LEISURE SPORTS

1. *American Turf Register and Sporting Magazine* 2 (Mar. 1831): 342; *Spirit of the Times* 7 (5 Aug. 1837): 196. For hunting and fishing in the New York metropolitan area between 1800 and 1850, see ibid. 1 (21 Apr. 1832), 2 (8 Sept. 1832), 6 (4 Aug. 1836): 206, 8 (31 Mar. 1838): 52, (21 July 1838): 180; 12 (12 Mar. 1842): 13, 13 (15 Apr. 1843): 73, (2 Dec. 1843): 474, 15 (20 Sept. 1845): 350, 17 (17 Aug. 1847): 279; *New York Post,* 4 Mar. 1826; *New York Tribune,* 27 July 1849; *American Turf Register* 11 (June 1840): 255; Thomas Floyd-Jones, *Backward Glances; Reminiscences of an Old New-Yorker* (Somerville, N.J.: Unionist Gazette Association, 1914), 139; Ralph H. Gabriel, *The Evolution of Long Island* (New Haven, Conn.: Yale University Press, 1921), 171–72.

2. The decline of fishing and hunting news corresponded with the rise of competitive sport, the emergence of "democratic" sports journals, and the demise of the *Spirit* in 1861. For the emergence in the post–Civil War years of sports journals devoted exclusively to hunting, fishing, and the outdoors, see John R. Betts, *America's Sporting Heritage, 1850-1950* (Reading, Mass.: Addison-Wesley, 1974), 58–60.

3. For hunting and fishing developments on Long Island, see *Spirit* 17 (17 Aug. 1847): 279, 21 (19 July 1851): 258, 30 (1 Dec. 1860): 513; *Post,* 11 May 1835; Robert B. Roosevelt, *The Game Birds of the Coasts and Lakes of the Northern States of America* (New York: Carleton, 1867), 25. For the rise of upstate New York as a hunting and fishing area, see *New York Times,* 2 Sept. 1858; *Journal of a Hunting Excursion to Louis Lake, 1851* (Blue Mountain Lake, N.Y.: Adirondack Museum, 1981).

4. *Spirit* 14 (15 June 1844): 186; *Wilkes' Spirit of the Times* 13 (20 Jan. 1866): 321, 23 (21 Jan. 1871): 358.

5. For game laws in New York in the pre–Civil War years, see Jennie Holliman, *American Sport, 1785-1835* (Durham, N.C.: Seeman, 1931), 52–54. For Herbert's views, see *Spirit* 15 (14 Feb. 1846): 603, 17 (22 Jan. 1848): 566. Also see, ibid. 14 (15 June 1844): 186, 16 (4 Apr. 1846): 66, 20 (29 June 1850): 223; *Wilkes' Spirit* 1 (26 Nov. 1859): 185. For Roosevelt, see Charles Morris, ed., *Makers of New York* (Philadelphia: Hammersly, 1895), 314; Roosevelt, *Game,* 1–26.

6. *Tribune,* 12 Feb. 1859. Also see, *Spirit* 29 (5 Feb. 1859): 5; *New York Herald,* 16 Apr. 1869; *Wilkes' Spirit* 22 (26 Mar. 1870): 81–82, 85.

7. For fox hunting in pre-1820 New York, see J. Blan Van Urk, *The Story of American Foxhunting: From Challenge to Full Cry,* 2 vols. (New York: Derrydale, 1940–41), 1:81–85, 116–19. For fox hunting in New York after 1820, see ibid., 1:104–7; *Spirit* 10 (7 Mar. 1840): 6, (28 Mar. 1840): 44, 15 (22 Nov. 1845): 458, 26 (18 Oct. 1856): 426; *Post,* 17 Mar. 1823, 24 Apr. 1828. For the reemergence of fox hunting in New York in the 1870s, see Dixon Wecter, *Saga of American Society* (New York: Scribner, 1937), 446–47.

8. *New York Gazette,* 30 May, 16 Nov. 1825; *Post,* 14 June 1825; *Herald,* 7 Sept. 1844; *Spirit* 2 (20 July 1833), (10 Aug. 1833), 26 (12 July 1856): 260, 27 (6 June 1857): 198, (8 Aug. 1857): 306, 28 (14 Aug. 1858): 313. For the ASPCA's objection to pigeon shooting, see Zula Steele, *Angel in Top Hat* (New York: Harper, 1942), 219, 222; *Times,* 13 Jan. 1870.

9. For shooting contests, see *Spirit* 2 (3 July 1833), 11 (20 Mar. 1841): 30, 17 (25 Sept. 1847): 362, 18 (27 May 1848): 159, 19 (17 Mar. 1849): 42; *Porter's Spirit of the Times* 1 (8 Nov. 1856): 165, (13 Dec. 1856): 237; *Herald,* 29 Aug. 1844, 8 Jan., 30 Oct. 1870; *Times,* 15 June 1864. For intercity competition, see *Spirit* 19 (22 Dec. 1849): 522, 22 (28 Aug. 1852): 330, (14 Aug. 1852): 306; *Times,* 19 July 1854. For the Lloyd match and biographical material on Lloyd, see *American Turf Register* 13 (Nov. 1842): 655–56; *Spirit* 13 (9 Dec. 1843): 486–87, 23 (24 Dec. 1853): 534.

10. For shooting clubs, see *Spirit* 6 (12 Mar. 1836): 32, 7 (16 Sept. 1837): 244, 8 (12 Jan. 1839): 381, 9 (9 Mar. 1839): 6. For the National Rifle Association see, John A. Krout, *Annals of American Sport* (New Haven, Conn.: Yale University Press, 1929), 169.

11. *New York American,* 4 Aug. 1820, 9 Aug. 1821, 30 July 1823; *Post,* 16 Aug. 1833, 14 July 1829; *Herald,* 28 Oct., 19 Nov. 1869, 5 Sept. 1835, 9 Sept. 1843, 2, 30 Oct., 2 Nov. 1853; *Tribune,* 13 Dec. 1850, 13 Nov. 1851; *New York Clipper,* 1 (31 Dec. 1853), (7 Jan. 1854).

12. *Herald,* 11 Nov. 1869. It should be kept in mind that I am speaking here only of involvement on an organized level. Clearly, there were many individuals who participated in baseball on an informal basis. For the connection between politicians and target companies, see ibid., 28 Oct. 1869; *Tribune,* 3 Oct. 1850.

13. For a view of target companies during the antebellum period, see *American,* 9 Aug. 1821; *Clipper* 1 (7 Jan. 1854); *Herald,* 5 Sept. 1835, 9 Sept. 1843, 30 Oct., 2 Nov. 1853. For the post–Civil War view, see ibid., 28 Oct. 1869; *Times,* 22 Nov. 1868, 7 July 1870.

14. *Times,* 22 Nov. 1868; *Herald,* 28 Oct. 1868.

15. For Swiss rifle clubs, see *Spirit* 24 (22 Oct. 1854): 409; *Herald,* 17 Sept. 1863; *Wilkes' Spirit* 9 (26 Sept. 1863): 60. For German rifle clubs, see ibid. 18 (27 June 1868): 339; *Clipper* 11 (8 Aug. 1863): 132; *Times,* 19, 27 June, 7 July 1868; *Herald,* 9 June 1865, 30 June, 7 July 1868, 14 June 1870; Charles D. Shanley, "Germany in New York," *Atlantic Monthly* 19 (1867): 563. Also see *Spirit* 13 (2 Dec. 1843): 474.

16. Robert W. Henderson, *Ball, Bat and Bishop: The Origin of Ball Games* (New York: Rockport, 1947), 102–9; Holliman, *American Sport,* 74–75.

17. Henderson, *Ball*, 110–11; Holliman, *American Sport*, 73–75; John A. Krout and Clifford Lord, "Sport and Recreation," in Alexander C. Flick, ed., *History of the State of New York*, 10 vols. (New York: Columbia University Press, 1937), 10:239; *Clipper* 4 (16 Aug. 1856): 134, (6 Sept. 1856): 155.

18. Racket Court Club, *Constitution and By-Laws* (New York, 1845), 5; Henderson, *Ball*, 111; *Herald*, 17 Sept. 1845, 3 Mar. 1848.

19. *Herald*, 7 June 1847; *Spirit* 17 (15 May 1847): 134, (5 June 1847): 171, (19 June 1847): 194. At the time of this contest wine merchant Edward LaMontaigne lived in Canada but subsequently moved to New York.

20. *Porter's Spirit* 4 (5 June 1858): 210–11; *Herald*, 15 Jan. 1860; *Wilkes' Spirit* 16 (23 Mar. 1867): 56, (13 Apr. 1867): 105, 18 (14 Mar. 1868): 56; Krout and Lord, "Sport," 10:239. For the Gymnasium Club's role in New York racquets, see Henderson, *Ball*, 113.

21. For bowling in colonial New York, see Foster R. Dulles, *A History of Recreation: America Learns to Play* (New York: Appleton-Century-Crofts, 1965), 33; Alice M. Earle, *Colonial Days in Old New York* (New York: Scribner, 1906), 209; Holliman, *American Sport*, 81–82. Also see *Tribune*, 14 Dec. 1850; *Wilkes' Spirit* 11 (26 Nov. 1864): 202.

22. John A. Lucas and Ronald A. Smith, *Saga of American Sport* (Philadelphia: Lea and Febiger, 1978), 192–96; *Clipper* 5 (26 Dec. 1857): 282, 13 (4 Nov. 1865): 234; *Porter's Spirit* 1 (13 Dec. 1856): 245; *Turf, Field and Farm* 5 (19 Oct. 1867): 249.

23. *Clipper* 7 (21 Jan. 1860): 314, 12 (3 Dec. 1884): 266. For football at Columbia College, see Charles H. Haswell, *Reminiscence of New York by an Octogenarian, 1816–1860* (New York: Harper, 1896), 81–82; Horace Coon, *Columbia: Colussus on the Hudson* (New York: Dutton, 1947), 293–94; *Herald*, 7 May 1866; *Times*, 20 Apr. 1866. The football played at Columbia in pre-1870 was essentially a crude form of rugby football rather than American football as we know the game today.

24. *Clipper* 13 (26 Aug. 1865): 154, 17 (2 Oct. 1869): 202; *Herald*, 11, 14 Sept. 1869; *Times*, 25 Nov. 1870; *Wilkes' Spirit* 21 (9 Oct. 1869): 122.

25. *Clipper* 10 (11 Oct. 1862): 202; *Chronicle* 1 (6 June 1867): 5; Dulles, *Recreation*, 191–92.

26. Holliman, *American Sport*, 86–94; *American*, 12 Aug. 1826; *Herald*, 20 June 1855, 12 Sept. 1838; *Wilkes' Spirit* 8 (23 May 1863): 188.

27. *Wilkes' Spirit* 8 (23 May 1863): 188, 17 (16 Nov. 1867): 241; *Times*, 30 July 1855.

28. *Harper's Magazine* 10 (Feb. 1855): 417; *Herald*, 25 Feb. 1863, 3 Jan. 1869, 25 Jan. 1837, 2 Jan. 1843, 9 Jan. 1856, 7 Jan. 1856, 7 Jan. 1860, 11 Jan. 1865; *Tribune*, 8 Feb. 1845, 26 Jan. 1855.

29. *Herald*, 25 Dec. 1839, 22 Feb. 1858; Holliman, *American Sport*, 165.

30. *Gazette*, 26 Feb. 1823; *Herald*, 7 Feb. 1862, 25 Feb. 1863, 3 Jan. 1859; Marshall B. Davidson, *Life in America*, 2 vols. (Boston: Houghton-Mifflin, 1951), 2:13; Melvin L. Adelman, "The Development of Modern Athletics: Sport in New York City, 1820–1870" (Ph.D. diss., University of Illinois, 1980), 646.

31. Dulles, *Recreation*, 34; Holliman, *American Sport*, 94–98; *Post*, 14 Jan.

1835; Henry Chadwick, ed., *Beadle's Dime Guide to Skating and Curling* (New York: Beadle, 1867), 5; Dorothy Barck, ed., *Letters from John Pintard to His Daughter Eliza Noel Pintard Davidson, 1816–1833*, 4 vols. (New York: New-York Historical Society, 1937–40), 2:215, 319–22 passim.

32. Several historians maintain that the writings of Thomas Wentworth Higginson prompted the beginning of the skating craze in America. See Davidson, *Life*, 2:43; Howard N. Meyer, *Colonel of the Black-Regiment—The Life of Thomas Wentworth Higginson* (New York: Norton, 1967), 112; John A. Lucas, "Early Apostle of Health and Fitness—Thomas Wentworth Higginson," *Journal of Health, Physical Education and Recreation* 42 (Feb. 1971): 32. While Higginson might have been responsible for the skating surge in Boston and the surrounding area, his impact on the development of the sport in New York was minimal if not nonexistent. A year before his writings came out, one journal claimed, "Skating seems to be greater than we have ever before known it." See *Clipper* 4 (10 Jan. 1857): 298. Since New York was the communication and sports capital, the skating development there was a major catalyst for the mania that swept through the North, with the exception of New England, during the Civil War decade.

33. *Spirit* 29 (24 Dec. 1859): 541; *Clipper* 6 (19 Feb. 1859): 348; *Herald*, 23 Jan. 1861, 12 Feb. 1862; *Times*, 24 Aug. 1867, 12 Jan. 1866, 2 Jan. 1860; T. Addison Richards, "The Central Park," *Harper's Magazine* 23 (Aug. 1861): 298; Chadwick, *Skating and Curling*, 5; *Wilkes' Spirit* 15 (22 Dec. 1866): 266.

34. *Spirit* 30 (10 Mar. 1860): 54; *Times*, 29 Jan. 1866, 2 Jan. 1860, 13 Dec. 1865, 3 Feb. 1862; *Herald*, 5 Dec. 1869, 23 Jan. 1861, 5 Jan. 1862. Also see *Wilkes' Spirit* 9 (23 Jan. 1864): 329, 19 (28 Nov. 1868): 227; *Clipper* 6 (19 Feb. 1859): 348, 12 (11 Feb. 1865): 365.

35. *Times*, 29 Dec. 1859, 3 Jan. 1861, 12 Jan. 1866, 24 Aug. 1867; *Clipper* 6 (19 Feb. 1859): 348; *Wilkes' Spirit* 19 (28 Nov. 1868): 227. Also see Haswell, *Reminiscence*, 77; Holliman, *American Sport*, 97.

36. *Herald*, 8 Dec. 1867, 10 Jan. 1865; *Times*, 20 Dec. 1862, 6 Feb. 1863, 12 Jan. 1866, 24 Aug. 1867; *Clipper* 12 (24 Dec. 1864): 290; *Wilkes' Spirit* 9 (19 Dec. 1863): 243, (26 Dec. 1863): 259, 15 (22 Dec. 1866): 266; Anita Leslie, *The Remarkable Mr. Jerome* (New York: Holt, 1954), 85.

37. *Spirit* 29 (24 Dec 1859): 541; *Times*, 12 Jan. 1866, 11 Feb. 1871; *Herald*, 5 Dec. 1869; *Clipper* 16 (19 Dec. 1868): 291; *Wilkes' Spirit* 9 (19 Dec. 1863): 243; Krout, *Annals*, 181.

38. Chadwick, *Skating and Curling*, 5–6. Also see *Herald*, 5 Jan. 1862; Dulles, *Recreation*, 95–96. For the absence of women in skating prior to the Civil War, see Holliman, *American Sport*, 165–66.

39. *Herald*, 13 Feb. 1860.

40. *Times*, 12 Jan. 1858, 12 Jan. 1866; *Herald*, 6 Jan. 1862, 9 Jan. 1866; Chadwick, *Skating and Curling*, 5–6; *Wilkes' Spirit* 11 (25 Feb. 1865): 410.

41. Holliman, *American Sport*, 169–72.

42. *Post*, 17 Mar. 1834, 1 Apr. 1833; *American*, 19 Mar. 1822, 3 Apr. 1830, 1 June 1831.

43. *Times*, 19 Oct. 1871.

44. For costs, see *Clipper* 7 (18 Feb. 1860): 348.

45. *American*, 19 Mar. 1822, 9 Apr. 1821, 12 Mar. 1827; *Post*, 24 June 1820.

46. *Herald*, 12 June 1869; *American*, 27 May 1831; *Spirit* 6 (15 Oct. 1836): 275, 16 (18 July 1846): 315; William Fuller, *The Elements of Gymnastics* (New York, 1830), 6, 8–11; *Post*, 20 Mar. 1827, 6 Sept. 1830; *Times*, 28 Nov. 1856; *Clipper* 9 (9 Nov. 1861): 237.

47. Henry Metzner, *A Brief History of the American Turnerbund*. trans. Theodore Stempfel, Jr. (Pittsburgh: National Executive Committee of the American Turnerbund, 1924), 7–24; Robert K. Barney, "Knights of Cause and Exercise: German Forty-Eighters and Turnvereine in the United States During the Ante-Bellum Period," *Canadian Journal of History of Sport* 13 (Dec. 1982), 62–79; Barney, "Americans First Turnverein: Commentary in Favor of Louisville, Kentucky," *Journal of Sport History* 11 (Spring 1984): 134–37.

48. Metzner, *Brief History*, 8–9; *Times*, 6 Feb. 1870.

49. *Tribune*, 31 Aug. 1854, 9, 18 Aug. 1851, 8 Sept. 1853; *Herald*, 8 June 1852, 6 Sept. 1853, 6 June 1865; *Times*, 6 Feb. 1870, 1 Sept. 1857.

50. *Spirit* 1 (3 Mar. 1832); *Herald*, 2, 14, Apr. 1863, 13 May 1868, 28 Mar. 1869; *Times*, 12 Apr. 1863; *Wilkes' Spirit* 20 (6 Mar. 1869): 36.

51. Haswell, *Reminiscence*, 35; Dulles, *Recreation*, 193–94; Krout, *Annals*, 179; *Herald*, 28 July 1869.

52. *Times*, 8, 20 Mar., 15 Feb., 11 Apr. 1869; H. J. Winser, "The Velocipede," *Galaxy* 7 (Apr. 1869): 587; *Herald*, 21, 28 Mar., 17 June 1869; *Wilkes' Spirit* 20 (17 Apr. 1869): 138, (13 Mar. 1869): 55; *Clipper* 17 (10 Apr. 1869): 3, (29 May 1869): 138.

53. *Times*, 5 Oct. 1864, 12 May 1865, 19 Apr. 1866, 31 Aug. 1855, 12 Jan. 1859, 9 Jan. 1860; Emily J. DeForest, *John Johnston of New York, Merchant* (New York, 1906), 48; *Herald*, 18 Jan. 1845; *Porter's Spirit* 2 (25 July 1857): 324, 6 (26 Mar. 1859): 57; *Spirit* 13 (18 Nov. 1843): 450, 29 (3 Dec. 1859): 489; *Wilkes' Spirit* 8 (30 May 1863): 205, 11 (14 Jan. 1865): 317, 19 (2 Jan. 1869): 311, 3 (9 Feb. 1861): 357; *Clipper* 12 (7 Jan. 1865): 306, 4 (10 Jan. 1857): 298, (14 Feb. 1857): 339, 16 (12 Dec. 1868): 283; Rowland T. Berthoff, *British Immigrants in Industrial America, 1790–1950* (New York: Russell and Russell, 1953), 152–53. For quoiting in eighteenth- and nineteenth-century America, see Holliman, *American Sport*, 78–79; Betts, *Sporting Heritage*, 30–31; Dulles, *Recreation*, 64, 73.

54. *Times*, 21 Sept. 1856; *Spirit* 25 (7 Apr. 1855): 121; *Wilkes' Spirit* 12 (6 May 1865): 147; *Post*, 17 Dec. 1824; *Harper's Magazine* 21 (Aug. 1860): 412, 3 (Oct. 1851): 709; *Herald*, 9 Aug. 1844, 11 Apr. 1869.

55. Frederick Van Wyck, *Recollections of an Old New Yorker* (New York: Liveright, 1932), 366–67. For advertisements for riding schools, see *Herald*, 23 Jan. 1843, 23 Apr. 1860; *Post*, 17 Dec. 1824; *Spirit* 14 (15 June 1844): 190.

56. *Clipper* 6 (28 Aug. 1858): 146, (18 Sept. 1858): 170; *Spirit* 28 (18 Sept. 1858): 438, (14 Aug. 1858): 338; *Herald*, 11 Sept. 1858; *Times*, 9 Sept. 1858.

57. *Times*, 17 Nov. 1859; *Spirit* 30 (28 Aug. 1860): 138; *Herald*, 23 Apr., 15 July 1860, 21 Nov. 1861; *Wilkes' Spirit* 9 (14 Nov. 1863): 164.

58. *Herald*, 24 Dec. 1859, 11 Apr. 1869; *Times*, 13 Oct. 1870, 8 June 1871; *Turf, Field and Farm* 5 (31 Aug. 1867): 134.

59. For the steeplechase in antebellum New York, see *Herald*, 29 June, 29 July, 3, 6 Nov. 1845; Elizabeth Eliot, *Portrait of a Sport: The Story of Steeplechasing in Great Britain and the United States* (Woodstock, Vt.: Countrymen, 1957), 95–101. For steeplechasing in the immediate post–Civil War period in New York, see ibid., 107–9; *Herald*, 27, 16 Oct. 1867, *Times*, 16 Oct. 1867; *Turf, Field and Farm* 5 (26 Oct. 1867): 264; *Wilkes' Spirit* 15 (13 Oct. 1866): 98; W. S. Vosburgh, *Steeplechasing in America* (New York: Burke and Lee, 1895), 8–9. Steeplechasing was not a leisure sport, but I felt that including this one paragraph on the history of the sport in either of the chapters on thoroughbred racing would have been an intrusion. It seemed to fit in better with similar sports like horseback riding and coaching.

60. Leslie, *Remarkable*, 75; Richard O'Connor, *The Scandalous Mr. Bennett* (Garden City, N.Y.: Doubleday, 1962), 47–48; Reginald Rives, *The Coaching Club, Its History, Records, and Activities* (New York, 1935), 1–2; *Herald*, 22 Apr. 1866.

61. For American dependency on English sporting works, see Holliman, *American Sport*, 7–9. For Herbert's contribution to America's field sports literature, see Luke White, *Henry William Herbert and the American Publishing Scene, 1831–1858* (Newark, N.J.: Carteret Book Club, 1943); David W. Judd, ed., *Life and Writing of Frank Forester (Henry William Herbert)*, 2 vols. (New York: Orange Judd, 1882); John Dizikes, *Sportsmen and Gamesmen* (Boston: Houghton-Mifflin, 1981), 67–87.

62. Fuller, *Elements*; Chadwick, *Skating and Curling*; Henry Chadwick, ed., *Beadle's Dime Book of Cricket and Football, being a Complete Guide to Players, and Containing All the Rules and Laws of the Ground and Games* (New York: Beadle, 1866).

63. Of the five new sports (those that first emerged during the 1860s), three (lacrosse, roller skating, and velocipeding) were organized during the 1860s, while a coaching club was established in the 1870s.

64. By noncontest sports I mean athletic activities in which no competition existed (e.g., sleighriding and coaching) or sports in which competition began to take place but played no part in the establishment of clubs or the essential thrust of the sport (e.g., skating and equestrianism). Field sports were included among the noncontest sports. In comparing the establishment of clubs in contest and noncontest sport, it might be expected that more clubs would have been organized in the contest sports; however, clubs were created in six of the nine noncontest sports, and in the contest sports clubs were formed in seven of the twelve cases.

65. Other sporting clubs to varying degrees performed these functions. The essential difference was that they were generally a means to an end, the fostering of competition. In the cases discussed in the text, they were an integral part in the formation of these clubs.

66. For the breakdown of spontaneity in our recreational sports, see Allen Guttmann, *From Ritual to Record: The Nature of Modern Sport* (New York: Columbia University Press, 1978), 159–61; Fritz Redlich, "Leisure-Time Activities: A Historical, Sociological and Economic Analysis," *Explorations in Entrepreneurial History*, 2d ser., 3 (1965): 19–20.

CONCLUSION: THE PRESS AND THE IDEOLOGY OF MODERN SPORT

1. For the Puritan view of sports in America and England, see Foster R. Dulles, *A History of Recreation: America Learns to Play* (New York: Appleton-Century-Crofts, 1965), 3-5, 8-14; Winton U. Solberg, *Redeem the Time: The Puritan Sabbath in Early America* (Cambridge, Mass.: Harvard University Press, 1977), 48, 71-74, 76-77; Peter C. McIntosh, *Sport in Society* (London: Watts, 1968), 43-44; Dennis Brailsford, *Sport and Society: Elizabeth to Anne* (London: Routledge and Kegan Paul, 1969), 128-41; Robert W. Malcolmson, *Popular Recreations in English Society, 1700-1850* (New York: Cambridge University Press, 1973), 6-10, 12; J. Thomas Jable, "The English Puritans: Suppressors of Sport and Amusements?" *Canadian Journal of History of Sport and Physical Education* 7 (May 1976): 33-40; Peter Wagner, "Puritan Attitudes Towards Physical Recreation in Seventeenth Century New England," *Journal of Sport History* 3 (Summer 1976): 139-51; Nancy L. Struna, "Puritans and Sport: The Irretrievable Tide of Change," ibid. 4 (Spring 1977): 1-21; Heintz Meyer, "Puritanism and Physical Training: Ideological and Political Accents in the Christian Interpretation of Sport," *International Review of Sport Sociology* 8 (1973): 37-51.

2. For American attitudes toward sport in the eighteenth and early nineteenth centuries, see Jennie Holliman, *American Sport, 1785-1835* (Durham, N.C.: Seeman, 1973), 178-83; John A. Lucas and Ronald A. Smith, *Saga of American Sport* (Philadelphia: Lea and Febiger, 1978), 35, 38, 59; J. Thomas Jable, "Aspects of Moral Reform in Early Nineteenth Century Pennsylvania," *Pennsylvania Magazine of History and Biography* 102 (1978): 344-68; Benjamin G. Rader, *American Sports: From the Age of Folk Games to the Age of Spectators* (Englewood Cliffs, N.J.: Prentice-Hall, 1983), 12-14.

3. Several scholars have examined the changing attitude toward sport in antebellum America. See, John R. Betts, "Mind and Body In Early American Thought," *Journal of American History* 54 (1968): 787-805; Peter Levine, "The Promise of Sport in Antebellum America," *Journal of American Culture* 2 (1980): 623-34; Stephen Hardy, *How Boston Played: Sport, Recreation, and Community, 1865-1915* (Boston: Northeastern University Press, 1982), 41-62; John A. Lucas, "A Prelude to the Rise of Sport: Ante-Bellum America, 1850-1860," *Quest* 11 (1968): 50-57; Roberta J. Park, "The Attitude of Leading Transcendentalists Towards Healthful Exercise, Active Recreation and Proper Care of the Body, 1830-1860," *Journal of Sport History* 4 (Spring 1977): 34-50. These studies have virtually ignored the press' opinions and attitudes toward sport despite John R. Betts's correct insistence that any account of the shifting view of sport would be incomplete if it did not emphasize "the indispensable role played by magazine and newspaper editors who championed the cause of sport." See "Sporting Journalism in Nineteenth-Century America," *American Quarterly* 5 (1953): 40. It should be noted that Betts's own study ("Mind and Body") is guilty of this neglect. The three arguments used to justify athletics were separated here for the purpose of clarity. This division is artificial since the press felt that the three sporting benefits were interrelated.

4. *New York Post,* 24 June, 19 Jan. 1830, 14 Sept. 1838; *New York Mirror* 10 (6 Apr. 1833): 317–18, quoted in Betts, "Mind and Body," 797.

5. *Post,* 19 Jan., 17 Mar., 6 Sept. 1830, 17 Mar., 2 Oct. 1834, 12 May 1838; *New York American,* 1 Mar. 1822, 3 Apr. 1830; *New York Statesmen,* 13 July 1823; *New York Herald,* 12 Sept. 1838.

6. *Post,* 22 Oct., 30 Nov. 1829; *American,* 8 May 1828, 27 Jan. 1830, 27 May, 1 June 1831.

7. *Post,* 1 Apr. 1833, 29 July 1830, 10 Apr., 22, 24 Oct. 1827, 17 Dec. 1835; *New York Free Enquirer* 3 (23 Apr. 1831): 205–7, quoted in Roberta J. Park, " 'Embodied Selves': The Rise and Development of Concern for Physical Education, Active Games and Recreation among American Women, 1776–1865," *Journal of Sport History* 5 (Summer 1978): 27; *Herald,* 18 Nov. 1835.

8. *Brooklyn Eagle,* 12 July, 1 Sept. 1858; *New York Times,* 17 Feb. 1858, 5 June 1857; *Porter's Spirit of the Times* 3 (20 Feb. 1858): 392. Also see *New York Tribune,* 16 Nov. 1848; *Spirit of the Times* 29 (4 June 1859): 356. For the English view of the American physical condition, see *Times,* 17 Feb. 1858, 5 June 1857; *Herald,* 27 July 1859; *New York Clipper* 2 (2 Sept. 1854), 5 (27 Feb. 1858): 356.

9. *Tribune,* 16 May 1853, 1 Jan. 1846; *Eagle,* 13 Apr., 13 June 1859, 12 July, 1 Sept. 1858; *Times,* 11 Oct. 1859, 5 June 1857, 22 June 1855; *Herald,* 4 May 1845, 23 Dec. 1846; *Clipper* 7 (4 June 1859): 49; *Spirit* 30 (24 Mar. 1868): 73.

10. *Mirror* 10 (6 Apr. 1833), quoted in Betts, "Mind and Body," 797; *Herald,* 20 July 1859; *Times,* 24 Sept. 1856, 21 May 1853, 11 Oct. 1859; *Eagle,* 12 July 1858; *Spirit* 26 (31 May 1856): 187; *Clipper* 4 (23 Aug. 1856): 140.

11. John H. Griscom, *The Sanitary Condition of the Labor Class of New York, with Suggestions for Its Improvement* (New York: Harper, 1845), 1; *Times,* 2 Feb. 1860; *Herald,* 28 Jan. 1869; *Wilkes' Spirit of the Times* 11 (17 Dec. 1864): 244.

12. *Herald,* 22 July 1845; *Times,* 28 Jan. 1854; *Clipper* 7 (25 Feb. 1860): 356.

13. *Herald,* 20 July 1859; *Clipper* 5 (24 Oct. 1857): 212, 7 (4 June 1859): 49.

14. For the link between play (leisure or sport) and work, and its ramifications in modern society, see Sebastian deGrazia, *Of Time, Work and Leisure* (New York: Twentieth Century, 1962); Bero Rigauer, *Sport and Work,* trans. Allen Guttmann (New York: Columbia University Press, 1981); David Q. Voigt, *America's Leisure Revolution: Essays in the Sociology of Leisure and Sport* (Reading, Pa., 1971), 53–54; Bennett M. Berger, "The Sociology of Leisure: Some Suggestions," in Edwin O. Smiegel, ed., *Work and Leisure: A Contemporary Social Problem* (New Haven, Conn.: College and University Press, 1963), 28, 35–36; Daniel T. Rogers, *The Work Ethic in Industrial America, 1850–1920* (Chicago: University of Chicago Press, 1974), 108–9, 123–24. For similar arguments in England, see Peter Bailey, *Leisure and Class in Victorian England: Rational Recreation and the Contest for Control, 1830–1885* (London: Routledge and Kegan Paul, 1978), 94.

15. *Clipper* 4 (3 May 1856); 10, 7 (4 June 1859): 49, 8 (4 Aug. 1860): 124; *Tribune,* 18 June 1852; *Eagle,* 13 Apr. 1859; *Times,* 30 Aug. 1860. For the reasons why New Yorkers failed to institute physical education programs despite the active support of the press and other reformers, see Melvin L. Adelman, "The

Development of Modern Athletics: Sport in New York City, 1820–1870" (Ph.D. diss., University of Illinois, 1980), 661–62.

16. *Clipper* 5 (26 Dec. 1857): 284; *Spirit* 27 (20 June 1857): 219; *Times*, 30 Aug. 1860.

17. *Clipper* 4 (21 Mar. 1857): 378, (28 June 1856): 76; *Wilkes' Spirit* 1 (4 Feb. 1860): 343; *Harper's Magazine* 13 (June 1856): 76–78; *Eagle*, 12 July 1858.

18. *Times*, 3 Apr. 1854. For Griscom's view, see Charles N. Glaab and A. Theodore Brown, *A History of Urban America* (New York: Macmillan, 1967), 70.

19. For the benefits of rural and outdoor sports, see *Post*, 9 Aug. 1833; *Herald*, 24 Aug. 1842; *Clipper* 4 (15 Nov. 1856): 238; *Spirit* 29 (4 June 1859): 193.

20. *Tribune*, 31 Mar. 1852. Also see *Herald*, 1 Apr. 1853, 26 Mar. 1854, 22 Aug., 13 Nov. 1859; *Times*, 7 Aug. 1871. For the construction of Central Park, see Ian R. Stewart, "Politics and the Park: The Fight for Central Park," *New-York Historical Society Quarterly* 61 (1977): 124–55; Glaab and Brown, *History*, 256–57; Thomas Bender, *Towards an Urban Vision: Ideas and Institutions in Nineteenth Century America* (Lexington: University Press of Kentucky, 1975), 173–75.

21. *Times*, 13 June 1853, 11 Oct. 1859; *Herald*, 13 Nov., 20 July 1859; *Spirit* 30 (10 Mar. 1860): 54–55; *Tribune*, 23 Apr., 28 June 1853, 11 Feb. 1854, 23 Apr. 1857; *Harper's Magazine* 11 (June 1855): 124–25.

22. *Tribune*, 16 May 1853; *Spirit* 30 (10 Mar. 1860): 54.

23. *Clipper* 8 (10 Nov. 1860): 234; Griscom, *Sanitary*, 1. For the middle-class audience, see Levine, "Promises," 631.

24. *Clipper* 9 (1 June 1861): 50; *Wilkes' Spirit* 7 (22 Nov. 1862): 184. John Betts maintains that the Civil War helped break down the prejudices against play and sport. See "Home Front, Battle Field and Sport During the Civil War," *Research Quarterly* 42 (1971): 130. The impact of the war on the ideology of sport was minimal. At best it provided an impetus and lent meaning to already existing sanctions.

25. *Herald*, 18 Mar. 1867, 12 June 1869; *Turf, Field and Farm* 5 (20 July 1867): 40, 7 (4 Sept. 1868): 576; *Wilkes' Spirit* 15 (24 Nov. 1866): 204, 19 (10 Oct. 1868): 121; *Clipper* 16 (24 Oct. 1868): 226.

26. *Times*, 28 Aug. 1869, 10 Apr. 1870; *Herald*, 22 Apr. 1866, 30 May 1867, 3 May 1868; *Wilkes' Spirit* 19 (10 Oct. 1868): 121, 17 (26 Oct. 1867): 190; *Clipper* 17 (17 Apr. 1869): 10.

27. Griscom, *Sanitary*, 1; Ronald G. Walters, *American Reformers, 1815–1860* (New York: Hill and Wang, 1978), 23–24. Also see Bernard Wishy, *The Child and the Republic: The Dawn of Modern American Child Nurture* (Philadelphia: University of Pennsylvania Press, 1968), 35; *Times*, 3 Apr. 1854; Russell Nye, *Society and Culture in America, 1830–1860* (New York: Harper and Row, 1974), 185–87; James C. Whorton, *Crusaders for Fitness: The History of American Health Reformers* (Princeton, N.J.: Princeton University Press, 1982), 30–32.

28. *Post*, 24 June 1830.

29. *Herald*, 29 May 1849, 12 Dec. 1866, 12 Oct. 1857; *Porter's Spirit* 5 (4 Sept. 1859): 9; *Tribune*, 16 May 1853; *Clipper* 12 (21 Jan. 1865): 332.

30. *Harper's Magazine* 1 (June 1850): 106; *Clipper* 4 (29 Nov. 1856): 25, 5 (6 June 1857): 52; *Herald*, 29 Aug. 1869; *Wilkes' Spirit* 2 (7 July 1860): 275.

31. *Post,* 2 June 1838; *Eagle,* 22 Aug., 17 Mar. 1864, 16 Mar. 1871; Henry Chadwick, *Baseball Player's Book of References* (New York: Haney, 1866), vii; *Porter's Spirit* 2 (20 June 1857): 245; *Herald,* 20 July 1859.

32. *Times,* 31 Mar. 1866, 23 July 1869.

33. Peter Levine maintains that the perception of reformers "of a constantly changing world tempered optimistic appraisals of the future," and their apprehension of the potential for social disorder "encouraged new meaning for sport as a way of controlling certain tendencies that threatened to undermine the virtues and values of the American republic." See "Promises," 624. Levine's effort to link supporters of the new sports creed to individuals who were ambivalent about their society and who sought reform as a means of restoring past values is not valid for New York newspapermen. New York editors and writers were deeply concerned about the impact of rapid change on urban order, but they remained cautiously optimistic. As a group they were overwhelmingly pro-urban, were active boosters of the city, and felt that the nation's leading metropolis had significantly contributed to individual and national progress culturally and, especially, economically. While the press recognized that there was a price to pay for rapid progress, it generally felt the benefits of urban growth far outweighed the drawbacks.

34. Carroll Rosenberg, *Religion and the Rise of the American City: The New York City Mission Movement, 1812-1870* (Ithaca, N.Y.: Cornell University Press, 1971), 184–85; Edward K. Spann, *New Metropolis: New York City, 1840-1857* (New York: Columbia University Press, 1981), 256–77; Walters, *American Reformers,* 23–24; Charles E. Rosenberg, *The Cholera Years: The United States in 1832, 1849 and 1866* (Chicago: University of Chicago Press, 1966), 220–21.

35. Whorton, *Crusaders,* 30–32; Walters, *American Reformers,* 145; Wishy, *Child,* 35; Jayme A. Sokolow, *Eros and Modernization: Sylvester Graham, Health Reform and the Origins of Victorian Sexuality in America* (Cranbury, N.J.: Associated University Press, 1983), 72–73, 81.

36. *Wilkes' Spirit* 1 (31 Dec. 1859): 258, (7 Jan. 1860): 273; *Herald,* 28 Sept. 1859; *Times,* 18 Jan. 1869.

37. For the rise of English Muscular Christianity, see Peter C. McIntosh, *Sport in Society,* 86; William E. Winn, "Tom Brown's School Days and the Development of 'Muscular Christianity,' " *Church History* 21 (1960): 64–71; Walter E. Houghton, *The Victorian Frame of Mind, 1830-1860* (New Haven, Conn.: Yale University Press, 1957), 202–4. For the rise of American Muscular Christianity, see Lucas, "Prelude," 50–57; Guy M. Lewis, "The Muscular Christianity Movement," *Journal of Health, Physical Education and Recreation* 27 (May 1966): 27–28, 42; Arthur C. Cole, "Our Sporting Grandfathers: The Cult of Athletics at Its Source," *Atlantic Monthly* 110 (July 1932): 88–96.

38. Gerald Redmond, "The First Tom Brown's Schooldays: Origins and Evolution of 'Muscular Christianity' in Children's Literature, 1762-1857," *Quest* 30 (1978): 4–18. John Betts's classic study of mind and body in the antebellum period makes it perfectly clear that the ingredients for the creation of the new sports ideology existed prior to 1850. See "Mind and Body," 787–805; Betts, "American Medical Thought on Exercise as the Road to Health," *Bulletin of the History of Medicine* 45 (1971): 138–45.

39. *Clipper* 7 (18 June 1859): 66, 6 (24 Apr. 1858): 4; *Herald,* 28 Jan. 1869; *Times,* 18 July, 9 Aug. 1869. The article in the *American Messanger* was reprinted in the *New York Sun,* 17 Aug. 1850.

40. *Tribune,* 23 Apr. 1853, 16 Nov. 1848; *Herald,* 21 Apr. 1844, 3 July, 28 Sept., 6 Nov. 1859, 22 Mar. 1860; *Times,* 10 Feb. 1858.

41. *Tribune,* 23 Apr. 1853; *Herald,* 22 Mar. 1860; *Times,* 21 May 1853, 31 May 1866.

42. *Times,* 3 Apr. 1860; *Wilkes' Spirit* 15 (24 Nov. 1866): 200.

43. *Times,* 28 Aug. 1869; Brian Dobbs, *Edwardians at Play: Sport, 1890-1914* (London: Pelham, 1973), 16.

44. *Herald,* 22 Aug. 1837; *Clipper* 5 (26 Dec. 1857): 282; *Baseball Chronicle* 1 (27 June 1867). Also see *Spirit* 6 (15 Oct. 1836): 275; *Clipper* 1 (28 Jan. 1854), 4 (23 Aug. 1856): 138, 7 (25 Feb. 1860): 356; *Herald,* 9 Feb. 1849, 22 June 1866, 11 May 1870; *Times,* 9 Sept. 1870, 18 Oct. 1858, 26 Mar. 1862.

45. *Harper's Magazine* 1 (June 1850): 106; *Spirit* 27 (20 June 1857): 219; Henry Chadwick, ed., *Beadle's Dime Book of Cricket: A Desirable Cricketer's Companion, Containing Complete Instruction* (New York: Beadle, 1860), 7; *Porter's Spirit* 6 (14 May 1859): 164.

46. *Porter's Spirit* 3 (12 Sept. 1857): 24; *Spirit* 27 (20 June 1857): 219; *Clipper* 8 (4 Aug. 1860): 124; *Times,* 9 Mar. 1862. For contemporary statements on sport and militarism, see *Wilkes' Spirit* 4 (17 Aug. 1861): 377; *Herald,* 27 July 1859; *Times,* 9 Mar. 1862. For further discussion of this theme, see Dale A. Somers, *The Rise of Sport in New Orleans, 1850-1900* (Baton Rouge: Louisiana State University Press, 1972), 276-77.

47. For a discussion of this theme, see pp. 173-74.

48. Peter Stearns, *Be a Man! Males in Modern Society* (New York: Holmes and Meier, 1979), 40-112; Joe L. Dubbert, *A Man's Place: Masculinity in Transition* (Englewood Cliffs, N.J.: Prentice-Hall, 1979), 27-33; E. Anthony Rotundo, "Body and Soul: Changing Ideals of American Middle-Class Manhood, 1770-1920," *Journal of Social History* 16 (1983): 23-38.

49. Charles N. Rosenberg, "Sexuality, Class and Role in Nineteenth Century America," *American Quarterly* 25 (1973): 133-34, 139. For further discussion of the changing attitudes toward sex during the antebellum period, see citations in chapter 9, note 47.

50. Michael Katz, *The Irony of Early School Reform: Education and Innovation in Mid-Nineteenth Century Massachusetts* (Boston: Beacon, 1968); Carl F. Kaestle, *The Evolution of an Urban School System: New York City, 1750-1850* (Cambridge, Mass.: Harvard University Press, 1973).

51. *Herald,* 27 July 1859; *Times,* 21 June 1854; *Wilkes' Spirit* 11 (11 Feb. 1865): 372, 1 (31 Dec. 1859): 258, (7 Jan. 1860): 273-74.

52. *Times,* 28 Aug. 1869.

53. For further discussion of this theme, see Stephanie L. Twin, "Introduction," in Stephanie L. Twin, ed., *Out of the Bleachers: Writings on Women and Sport* (Old Westbury, N.Y.: Feminist, 1979), xv-xxii.

54. Sport was obviously not the only area where manhood could be demonstrated or earned—success in business, as measured by wealth, had the same implications. It should be kept in mind, however, that while writers spoke of

manhood and manliness, they hoped boys of nonworking age would develop character values. For a discussion of manliness and youth, see Joseph F. Kett, *Rites of Passage: Adolescence in America, 1790 to the Present* (New York: Basic, 1977), 167–68, 173. The members of this group were often emotionally unprepared to deal with the tension of competitive athletics; for them the link between manliness, victory, and sport had its most dire and unfortunate consequences.

APPENDIX: COLLECTING AND COLLATING OCCUPATIONAL DATA

1. Stephan Thernstrom, *Poverty and Progress: Social Mobility in a Nineteenth-Century City* (New York: Athenum, 1972), 31; Edward Pessen, *Riches, Class and Power Before the Civil War* (Lexington, Mass.: Heath, 1973), 49–51.

2. Carl F. Kaestle, *The Evolution of an Urban School System: New York City, 1750–1850* (Cambridge, Mass.: Harvard University Press, 1973), 102–3; Robert Ernst, *Immigrant Life in New York City, 1825–1863* (New York: King's Crown, 1949), appendix 7, 206–12. For the application of this classification system to the creation of an occupational profile of New York City and Brooklyn baseball players, see Melvin L. Adelman, "The Development of Modern Athletics: Sport in New York City, 1820–1870" (Ph.D. diss., University of Illinois, 1980), 331, 356, 398, 445.

3. Theodore Hershberg et al., "Occupation and Ethnicity in Five Nineteenth Century Cities: A Collaborative Inquiry," *Historical Methods Newsletter* 7 (1974): 185–87.

A Guide to Relevant
Bibliographical Material

Primary Sources

Daily newspapers and sports journals from the period 1820–70 comprised the major sources of information on sports developments in New York City. It is important to note, however, that the journalists of that time were not neutral observers. Their reports were colored by their reliance on the good will of sports promoters, their occasional vested interest in sports, either directly or indirectly, and because they shared the class and ethnic prejudices of their period. At times they were also given to sensational journalism, and their judgments suffered no doubt from the all-too-common problem of drawing hasty conclusions in the rush to make a deadline. While historians of nineteenth-century sport must rely heavily on the print media for information, we must be sensitive to these limitations and examine and interpret such sources judiciously.

Sports journals of this period generally were published on a weekly basis, although some monthlies existed, and focused on a variety of athletic activities. While they made an effort to report on events throughout the country, because these journals were based in New York City they paid a disproportionate amount of attention to sports developments within the metropolitan area. Any examination of antebellum sport in America must begin with the *Spirit of the Times* (1831–33, 1835–61), as well as *Porter's Spirit of the Times* (1856–60), *Wilkes' Spirit of the Times* (1859–71), and the *New York Clipper* (1853–70). The *New York Sporting Magazine* (1833–34) and its successor, the *United States Sporting Magazine* (1835–36), and the Baltimore-based *American Turf Register and Sporting Magazine* (1829–44) were useful in terms of horse racing developments. *Turf, Field and Farm* (1867–71) and the *Baseball Chronicle* (1867–68), among other later journals, were studied also.

New York's daily newspapers provided much information on sports developments that did not appear in the sports journals and added a local flavor. The most beneficial of the many dailies examined were the *New York Herald* (1835–71), the *Brooklyn Eagle* (1850–71), and the *New York Times* (1851–71). Sport received only minimal coverage prior to the creation of the penny press in the late 1830s, and here the *New York American* (1820–35) and the *New York Post* (1820–40) were the most useful.

Guidebooks and scrapbooks were valuable supplements to newspapers and sports journals. Guidebooks for several sports were published after 1860, the most important being the annual publications on baseball, almost always edited by Henry Chadwick. Several scrapbooks were consulted which contained clippings usually from New York City newspapers but occasionally from papers outside the metropolitan area as well. The most important of these were Henry Chadwick's twenty-six volumes, located in the New York Public Library. In all likelihood most, if not all, of the articles in these scrapbooks were written by Chadwick, although this has not been proven. His scrapbooks were particularly helpful because they contained post-1870 reminiscences about the early years of baseball and what had happened to the ball players of that era.

A variety of club records proved valuable in supplying the names of club members, but they included virtually no information on the inner workings of these organizations. The notable exception was a two-volume correspondence book (1846–76) of the Knickerbocker Base Ball Club of New York, located in the New York Public Library.

General Historical Works

My understanding of the link between changing societal conditions and the modernization of sport was influenced to a great extent by Richard Brown, *Modernization: The Transformation of American Life, 1600–1865* (New York: Hill and Wang, 1976), and by two of his articles, "Modernization and the Modern Personality in Early America: A Sketch of a Synthesis," *Journal of Interdisciplinary History* 2 (1972): 201–28 and "Modernization: A Victorian Climax," *American Quarterly* 22 (1975): 533–48; indeed, Brown's work inspired this study by illustrating the usefulness of modernization as a conceptual framework for examining social change. E. A. Wrigley, "The Process of Modernization and the Industrial Revolution," *Journal of Interdisciplinary History* 3 (1972): 225–60 helped to distinguish between these two processes. Other informative works included Peter Stearns, "Modernization and Social History: Some Suggestions, and a Muted Cheer," *Journal of Social History* 14 (1980): 189–209; Tamara Haraven, "Modernization and Family History: Perspective on Social Change," *Signs* 2 (1976): 190–206.

Several articles sensitized me to the need to examine the city as process in order to comprehend the urban impact on social change: Eric Lampard, "American Historians and the Study of Urbanization," *American Historical Review* 67 (1961): 49–61; Roy Lubove, "The Urbanization Process: An Approach to Historical Research," *Journal of American Institute of Planners* 23 (1967): 33–36; Theodore Hershberg, "Introduction," in *Philadelphia: Work, Space, Family and Group Experiences in the Nineteenth Century. Essays Toward an Interdisciplinary History* (New York: Oxford University Press, 1981), 3–35. While these were insightful critiques of historical research on the city, they did not help in establishing a framework to comprehend the link between urban change and sports change. Far more beneficial in that regard were Oscar Handlin, "The Modern City as a Field of Historical Study," in Oscar Handlin and John Burchard, eds., *The Historian and the City* (Cambridge, Mass.: Harvard University Press, 1963), 1–26, and Louis Wirth, "Urbanism as a Way of Life," *American Journal of Sociology* 44 (1938): 1–24.

This work profited from several historical studies of the city, particularly Charles N. Glaab and A. Theodore Brown, *A History of Urban America* (New York: Macmillan, 1967), and several valuable chapters in David T. Gilchrist, ed., *The Growth of the Seaport Cities, 1790–1825* (Charlottesville: University Press of Virginia, 1967). Thomas Bender, *Towards an Urban Vision: Ideas and Institutions in Nineteenth Century America* (Lexington: University of Kentucky Press, 1975), and Peter G. Goheen, "Industrialization and the Growth of Cities in Nineteenth-Century America," *American Studies* 14 (1973): 49–63, examine the changing image of the city and how industrialization impacted on urban social class. Geographer Allan Pred's work was invaluable to my concept of the city and the various roles it played; *The Spatial Dynamics of United States Urban-Industrial Growth, 1800–1914: Interpretive and Theoretical Essays* (Cambridge: M.I.T. Press, 1966); *Urban Growth and the Circulation of Information—The United States System of Cities, 1790–1840* (Cambridge, Mass.: Harvard University Press, 1973); "Manufacturing in the American Mercantile City, 1800–1840," *Annals of the American Association of Geographers* 56 (1966): 307–25.

My understanding of the cultural, social, and intellectual developments in nineteenth-century America was heightened by the insightful overviews of American life found in the classic works of Louis Hartz, *The Liberal Tradition in America: An Interpretation of American Political Thought since the Revolution* (New York: Harcourt, Brace and World, 1955), and David M. Potter, *People of Plenty: Economic Abundance and the American Character* (Chicago: University of Chicago Press, 1963). Edward Pessen, *Jacksonian America: Society, Personality and Politics*, rev. ed. (Homewood, Ill.: Dorsey, 1978) also provided a useful overview. Ronald G. Walter, *American Reformers, 1815–1860* (New York: Hill and Wang, 1978) is outstanding, as is Paul Boyer's comprehensive historical examination of the concern for social order in the city, *Urban Masses and Moral Order in America, 1820–1920* (Cambridge, Mass.: Harvard University Press, 1978). I was also influenced by Robert H. Wiebe, *Search for Order, 1877–1920* (New York: Hill and Wang, 1967). Don Harrison Doyle, *The Social Order of a Frontier Community: Jacksonville, Illinois, 1825–70* (Urbana: University of Illinois Press, 1978), and Stephan Thernstrom, *Poverty and Progress: Social Mobility in a Nineteenth Century City* (New York: Atheneum, 1972), were valuable in my understanding of voluntarism in nineteenth-century America. Russell Nye, *Society and Culture in America, 1830–1860* (New York: Harper and Row, 1974), a bit dated, is still useful. I also consulted two popular histories of social life in America: Dixon Wecter, *Saga of American Society* (New York: Scribner, 1937), and Marshall B. Davidson, *Life in America*, 2 vols. (Boston: Houghton-Mifflin, 1951).

George Rodgers Taylor's classic work, *The Transportation Revolution, 1815–1860*, rev. ed. (New York: Harper and Row, 1968), remains the starting point for comprehending economic change during the antebellum period. Lee Soltow, *Men and Wealth in the United States, 1850-1870* (New Haven, Conn.: Yale University Press, 1975), explores the impact of economic change on different social groups, and Daniel T. Rogers, *The Work Ethic in Industrial America, 1850-1920* (Chicago: University of Chicago Press, 1974), was significant to comprehending shifting attitudes toward work. Theodore Hershberg et al., "Occupation and Ethnicity in Five Nineteenth Century Cities: A Collaborative Inquiry," *Historical Methods Newsletter* 7 (1974): 174-216, was instrumental to the creation of my profile of the social classes of baseball players.

On the issue of manliness I examined Peter Stearns, *Be a Man! Males in Modern Society* (New York: Holmes and Meier, 1979); Joe L. Dubbert, *A Man's Place: Masculinity in Transition* (Englewood Cliffs, N.J.: Prentice-Hall, 1979); E. Anthony Rotundo, "Body and Soul: Changing Ideals of American Middle Class Manhood, 1770-1920," *Journal of Social History* 16 (1983): 23-38. For changing sexual attitudes in Victorian America, Charles N. Rosenberg, "Sexuality, Class and Role in Nineteenth Century America," *American Quarterly* 25 (1973): 131-53, is a good starting point; more in-depth discussion can be found in Jayme A. Sokolow, *Eros and Modernization: Sylvester Graham, Health Reform, and the Origins of Victorian Sexuality in America* (Cranbury, N.J.: Associated University Press, 1983); Ronald G. Walters, *Primers for Prudency: Sexual Advice to Victorian America* (Englewood Cliffs, N.J.: Prentice-Hall, 1974); Stephen W. Nissenbaum, *Sex, Diet and Debility in Jacksonian America: Sylvester Graham and Health Reform* (Westport, Conn.: Greenwood, 1980).

New York City History

For an overview of the city's history see I. N. Phelps Stokes, *The Iconography of Manhattan Island, 1498-1909,* 6 vols. (New York: Dodd, 1915-28). Bayard Still, *Mirror for Gotham: New York as Seen by Contemporaries from Dutch Days to the Present* (New York: New York University Press, 1966), provides an interesting examination of how the city was perceived during different time periods, and Sidney I. Pomerantz, *New York: An American City, 1783-1803: A Study of Urban Life* (New York: Columbia University Press, 1938), remains the best work to consult on New York in the two decades following the Revolution. Edward Spann, *The New Metropolis, New York City, 1840-1857* (New York: Columbia University Press, 1981), is a balanced account of the trials and triumphs of the city and solidified many of my ideas about New York's emergence as America's premier metropolitan area. Alice M. Earle, *Colonial Days in Old New York* (New York: Scribner, 1906), and Ester Singleton, *Social New York under the Georges, 1714-1776* (New York: Appleton, 1902), explores the social life of the city during the colonial era.

Ira Rosenwaike, *Population History of New York City* (Syracuse, N.Y.: Syracuse University Press, 1972) examines the changing demographics of New York City and vicinity. Robert Albion, *The Rise of New York Port, 1815-1860* (New York: Scribner, 1939), and Robert Ernst, *Immigrant Life in New York City, 1825-1863* (New York: King's Crown, 1949), are both unsurpassed in their respective areas of discussion. My understanding of the New York elite was strongly influenced by Edward Pessen, *Riches, Class and Power Before the Civil War* (Lexington, Mass.: Heath, 1973), but I tend to subscribe to the view of a somewhat more fluid class structure as presented in Frederic C. Jaher, *The Urban Establishment: Upper Strata in Boston, New York, Charleston, Chicago and Los Angeles* (Urbana: University of Illinois Press, 1982). Howard B. Rock, *Artisans of the New Republic: The Tradesmen of New York City in the Age of Jefferson* (New York: New York University Press, 1979), and the recent outstanding work of Sean Wilentz, *Chants Democratic: New York City and the Rise of the American Working Class, 1788–1850* (New York: Oxford University Press, 1984), were vital to my comprehension of working-class culture and behavior.

Several studies aided my understanding of political development and political leadership in New York: Edmund P. Willis, "Social Origins of Political Leadership in New York from the Revolution to 1815" (Ph.D. diss., University of California, Berkeley, 1967); Jerome Mushkat, *Tammany: The Evolution of a Political Machine, 1789–1865* (Syracuse, N.Y.: Syracuse University Press, 1971); Alexander B. Callow, Jr., *The Tweed Ring* (New York: Oxford University Press, 1966); Leo Hershkowitz, *Tweed's New York: Another Look* (Garden City, N.Y.: Doubleday, 1977).

For New Yorkers' responses to the changing social order I relied on Carrol S. Rosenberg, *Religion and the Rise of the American City: The New York City Mission Movement, 1812–1870* (Ithaca, N.Y.: Cornell University Press, 1971); Raymond Mohl, *Poverty in New York, 1783–1825* (New York: Oxford University Press, 1971); William W. Cutler III, "Status, Values and the Education of the Poor: The Trustees of the New York Public School Society, 1805–1853," *American Quarterly* 24 (1972): 69–85; M. J. Heale, "From City Fathers to Social Critics: Humanitarianism and Government in New York," *Journal of American History* 63 (1976): 21–41; Allen Stanley Horlick, *Country Boys and Merchant Princes: The Social Control of Young Men in New York* (Lewisberg, Pa.: Bucknell University Press, 1975). Institutional developments in New York are treated in Carl F. Kaestle, *The Evolution of an Urban School System: New York City, 1750–1850* (Cambridge, Mass.: Harvard University Press, 1973); John Duffy, *A History of Public Health in New York City, 1625–1866* (New York: Russell Sage Foundation, 1968); and James G. Richardson, *The New York Police: Colonial Times to 1901* (New York: Oxford University Press, 1970).

A variety of nineteenth-century accounts proved beneficial, including Charles Astor Brinsted, *The Upper Ten Thousands: Sketches of American Society* (New York: Stringer and Townsend, 1852), and Abram C. Dayton, *Last Days of Knickerbocker Life in New York* (New York: Putnam, 1897), both of which provided colorful descriptions of social life in New York as well as information on the city's sporting life. Francis G. Fairfield, *The Clubs of New York* (New York: Hilton, 1873), served as a guide to these organizations. John H. Griscom, *The Sanitary Condition of the Labor Class of New York, with Suggestions for Its Improvement* (New York: Harper, 1845), proved to be an important pamphlet by New York's leading health reformer of the time.

A variety of published diaries, autobiographies, and biographies supplied valuable information on New York's social and sporting life. Anyone researching New York City life in the nineteenth century must consult Allan Nevins, ed., *The*

Diary of Philip Hone, 1828-1851, 2 vols. (New York: Arno, 1970); George Templeton Strong, *The Diary of George Templeton Strong,* ed. Allan Nevins and Milton H. Thomas, 4 vols. (New York: Macmillan, 1952); Dorothy Barack, ed., *Letters from John Pintard to His Daughter, Eliza Noel Pintard Davidson, 1816-1833,* 4 vols. (New York: New-York Historical Society, 1937-40). Among the most useful biographies and autobiographies were Charles H. Haswell, *Reminiscence of New York by an Octogenarian, 1816-1860* (New York: Harper, 1896); James A. Hamilton, *Reminiscence of James A. Hamilton: or Men and Events, at Home and Abroad, During Three Quarters of a Century* (New York: Scribner, 1869); Francis Brinkley, *Life of William T. Porter* (New York: Appleton, 1860); David W. Judd, ed., *Life and Writings of Frank Forester (Henry William Herbert),* 2 vols. (New York: Orange Judd, 1882); Wheaton Lane, *Commodore Vanderbilt, An Epic of the Steam Age* (New York: Knopf, 1942); Anita Leslie, *The Remarkable Mr. Jerome* (New York: Holt, 1954); Richard O'Connor, *The Scandalous Mr. Bennett* (Garden City, N.Y.: Doubleday, 1962); Archibald D. Turnbull, *John Stevens: An American Record* (New York: Century, 1926).

The occupations of a goodly number of area sports participants were found in the various New York City and Brooklyn directories for 1820-70. Lists of wealthy New Yorkers were also a valuable source, the best and most accurate being Edward Pessen, "The Wealthiest New Yorkers of the Jacksonian Era: A New List," *New-York Historical Society Quarterly* 54 (1970): 155-72. The appendix in Brian J. Danforth, "The Influence of Socioeconomic Factors in Political Behavior: A Quantitative Look at New York City Merchants, 1828-1844" (Ph.D. diss., New York University, 1974), also contained valuable data.

Sports Histories

The ideas expressed in Allen Guttmann, *From Ritual to Record: The Nature of Modern Sports* (New York: Columbia University Press, 1978), and Eric Dunning, "The Structural-Functional Properties of Folk Games and Modern Sports: A Sociological Analysis," *Sportwissenchaft* 3 (1973): 215-32, were instrumental to my understanding of the characteristics of modern sport and how it differed from premodern sport and folk games. Several articles helped me to differentiate between competitive and recreational sport, including James W. Keating, "The Two Faces of Sport," in *The First Canadian Symposium on the Philosophy of Sport and Physical Activity* (Ottawa: Sports Canada Directorate, Department of Health and Welfare, 1972), 103-18; Richard S. Gruneau, "Sport as an Area of Sociological Study: An Introduction to Major Themes and Perspectives," in Richard S. Gruneau and John Albinson, eds., *Canadian Sport: Sociological Perspectives* (Don Mills, Ont.: Addison-Wesley, 1976), 8-43; and John W. Loy, "The Nature of Sport: A Definitional Effort," *Quest* 10 (May 1968): 1-15.

In "Academicians and Athletics: Historians' View of American Sport," *Maryland Historian* 4 (1973): 123-37, and "Academician and American Athletics: A Decade of Progress," *Journal of Sport History* 10 (Spring 1983): 80-106, I have discussed the growth and status of scholarly (i.e., by professional-academic historians) research on the history of American sport. While sport history as a field of serious inquiry has made significant progress over the last decade, the wide gaps that still exist in the literature necessitate that academic historians continue to rely on popular (i.e., by nonacademic historians) histories of various sports. These works tend to be descriptive rather than analytic and only superficially relate sports to societal change. Often they are penned by individuals connected in some way with that particular sport, resulting in glaring biases. Despite this weakness, such works do contain useful information and for many sports are the only accounts in existence. Nevertheless, academic historians must use these sources carefully, forever on guard against factual errors and unsubstantiated claims that are frequently passed on from one writer to the next.

The early studies of Frederic L. Paxson, "The Rise of Sport," *Mississippi Valley Historical Review* 4 (1917): 143–68; John A. Krout, *Annals of American Sport* (New Haven, Conn.: Yale University Press, 1929); and Foster R. Dulles, *A History of Recreation: America Learns to Play,* rev. ed. (New York: Appleton-Century-Crofts, 1965), all remain valuable, although in them the rise of sport is perceived as a post–Civil War development. John R. Betts, *America's Sporting Heritage, 1850–1950* (Reading, Mass.: Addison-Wesley, 1974), shares a similar view, even as it gives more attention to sport in the antebellum period. Despite the encyclopedic nature of Betts's work, I am in awe of the incredible amount of research he undertook; the volume remains an important starting point for students of American sport history. John A. Lucas and Ron A. Smith, *Saga of American Sport* (Philadelphia: Lea and Febiger, 1978), contains valuable information, and Benjamin G. Rader, *American Sports: From the Age of Folk Games to the Age of Spectators* (Englewood Cliffs, N.J.: Prentice-Hall, 1983), is the most analytic of the historical surveys of sport. Arthur H. Cole, "Perspectives on Leisure-Time Business," *Explorations in Entrepreneurial History,* 2d ser., 1 (Summer 1964, supplement): 1–38; Fritz Redlich, "Leisure-Time Activities: A Historical, Sociological and Economic Analysis," *Explorations in Entrepreneurial History,* 2d ser., 3 (1965): 3–23, provide valuable overviews.

Dale A. Somers, *The Rise of Sport in New Orleans, 1850–1900* (Baton Rouge: Louisiana State University Press, 1972), and Stephen Hardy, *How Boston Played: Sport, Recreation and Community, 1865–1915* (Boston: Northeastern University Press, 1982), are thoughtful examinations of sports developments in other urban locales. Stephen Hardy, "The City and the Rise of American Sport, 1820–1920," *Exercise and Sports Sciences Reviews* 9 (1983): 183–219, is an outstanding review of the scholarly literature on the relationship between sport and the city.

Historians have generally ignored sports developments between the Revolution and the Civil War, with the notable exception of Jennie Holliman, *American Sport, 1785–1835* (Durham, N.C.: Seeman, 1931); John Dizikes, *Sportsmen and Gamesmen* (Boston: Houghton-Mifflin, 1981); and Sorern S. Brynn, "Some Sports in Pittsburgh During the National Period," *Western Pennsylvania Magazine,* pt. 1, 51 (1968): 345–68, pt. 2, 52 (1969): 57–69. A far more extensive literature on changing attitudes toward sports during the antebellum period includes John R. Betts, "Mind and Body in Early American Thought," *Journal of American History* 54 (1968): 787–805; Peter Levine, "The Promise of Sport in Antebellum America," *Journal of American Culture* 2 (1980): 623–34; Roberta J. Park, " 'Embodied Selves': The Rise and Development of Concern for Physical Education, Active Games and Recreation among American Women, 1776–1865," *Journal of Sport*

History 5 (Summer 1978): 5–41. James Whorton, *Crusaders for Fitness: The History of American Health Reformers* (Princeton, N.J.: Princeton University Press, 1982), and John R. Betts, "American Medical Thought on Exercise as the Road to Health," *Bulletin of the History of Medicine* 45 (1971): 138–45, should be consulted on the issue of sports and health.

While this study focused on American sports developments, an understanding of and comparisons with English trends were both necessary and inevitable. For a discussion of recent studies of British sport history during the last decade, see William J. Baker, "The State of British Sport History," *Journal of Sport History* 10 (Spring 1983): 53–66. Other valuable works include Robert W. Malcolmson, *Popular Recreations in English Society, 1700–1850* (Cambridge: Cambridge University Press, 1973); Dennis Brailsford, *Sport and Society: Elizabeth to Anne* (London: Routledge and Kegan Paul, 1969); Peter Bailey, *Leisure and Class in Victorian England: Rational Recreation and the Contest for Control, 1830–1885* (London: Routledge and Kegan Paul, 1978); H. E. Meller, *Leisure and the Changing City, 1870–1914* (New York: St. Martin, 1980); Eric Dunning and Kenneth Sheard, *Barbarians, Gentlemen and Players: A Sociological Study of the Development of Rugby Football* (New York: New York University Press, 1979).

To my knowledge there does not exist any comprehensive scholarly overview of either horse or harness racing in America. Authors of any future work on this subject would be wise to consult Wray Vamplew, *The Turf: A Social and Economic History of Horse Racing* (London: Lane, 1976), for an examination of horse racing in England and for useful information paralleling English and American developments. Nancy Struna, "The North-South Races: American Thoroughbred Racing in Transition, 1823–1850," *Journal of Sport History* 8 (Summer 1981): 28-57, is a thoughtful look at antebellum racing, but it focuses mainly on shifting elite attitudes toward the sport rather than institutional developments. Popular nineteenth-century histories of horse and harness racing include Henry William Herbert, *Frank Forester's Horse and Horsemanship of the United States and the British Provinces of North America*, 2 vols. (New York: Stringer and Townsend, 1857), and Hiram Woodruff, *The Trotting Horse of America: How to Train and Drive Him with Reminiscence of the Trotting Turf*, ed. Charles J. Foster, 19th ed. (Philadelphia: Porter and Coates, 1874).

John Hervey, *Racing in America, 1666-1866*, 2 vols. (New York: The Jockey Club, 1944), is among the best of the more recent works, providing a comprehensive and balanced overview of racing developments despite the weaknesses associated with this genre. It's quite evident that Hervey examined in detail the racing literature of the period. William H. P. Robertson, *History of Thoroughbred Racing in America* (Englewood Cliffs, N.J.: Prentice-Hall, 1964), also contains useful information; W. S. Vosburgh, *Racing in America, 1866-1921* (New York: The Jockey Club, 1922), is less satisfying as it offers a slanted view of the American Jockey Club's role in racing reform. Cadwallader R. Colden's pamphlet, *An Expose of the Measures which Caused a Suspension of the Races on the Union Course in October 1839* (New York: 1831) is a must for understanding the racing conditions in New York, although it contains only the author's views. Dwight Akers, *Drivers Up: The Story of American Harness Racing* (New York:

Putnam, 1938), is the best overview of the history of trotting, even though the book was published nearly a half-century ago. John Hervey, *The American Trotter* (New York: McCann, 1947), and Peter G. Welsh, *Track and Road: The American Trotting Horse. A Visual Record 1820 to 1900 from Harry T. Peters "American On Stone" Lithography Collection* (Washington, D.C.: Smithsonian Institution Press, 1967), both contain much useful data.

Historians have paid more attention to baseball than any other sport. The first volume of Harold Seymour's two-volume study on *Baseball: The Early Years* (New York: Oxford University Press, 1961) is the standard history of the sport. David Q. Voigt, *American Baseball: From Gentleman's Sport to the Commissioner System* (Norman: University of Oklahoma Press, 1966), also provides a thoughtful look at nineteenth-century baseball, generally following Seymour's lead in examining the sport in the pre-1870 period. Steven A. Riess, *Touching Base: Professional Baseball and American Culture in the Progressive Era* (Westport, Conn.: Greenwood, 1980), is an outstanding examination of the sport and a pioneer work in the application of quantification techniques to sport history. He also offers valuable comparative data on the social characteristics of baseball players, as does Stephan Freedman, "The Baseball Fad in Chicago, 1865–1870: An Exploration of the Role of Sport in the Nineteenth-Century City," *Journal of Sport History* 5 (Summer 1978): 42–64.

Ian Tyrrell, "The Emergence of Modern American Basball, c. 1850–80," in Richard Cashman and Michael McKernan, eds., *Sport in History: The Making of Modern Sporting History* (Queensland: University of Queensland Press, 1979), 205–26, raises good questions about the efforts to explain baseball's popularity in terms of national characteristics and nationalistic sentiments; but the evidence does not support his assertion that class differences were responsible for the divergent fates of baseball and cricket. Robert W. Henderson's unpublished paper, "Adams of the Knickerbockers," in the New York Racquet and Tennis Club, was pivotal to my understanding of the early development of baseball's pioneer club. In "The First Baseball Game, the First Newspaper References to Baseball and the New York Club: A Note on the Early History of Baseball," *Journal of Sport History* 7 (Winter 1980): 132–35, I also shed new light on these developments. The most useful of the many popular histories of baseball were: Albert G. Spalding, *America's National Game* (New York: American Sports, 1911); Alfred H. Spink, *The National Game* (St. Louis: National Game, 1910); Irving A. Leitner, *Baseball: Diamond in the Rough* (New York: Criterion, 1972); Preston D. Orem, *Baseball from the Newspaper Accounts* (Altadena, Calif., 1966); Harold Peterson, *The Man Who Invented Baseball* (New York: Scribner, 1969).

There are only a couple of scholarly works on the history of cricket in America. Tyrrell's "The Emergence of Modern American Baseball c. 1850–80" (above) contained useful information, but George Kirsch, "American Cricket: Players and Clubs Before the Civil War," *Journal of Sport History* 11 (Spring 1984): 28–50, is a more thoughtful examination of the sport, detailing its developments in nearby Newark, New Jersey. Popular studies on American cricket are also limited, but see John A. Lester, ed., *A Century of Philadelphia Cricket* (Philadelphia: University of Pennsylvania Press, 1951), and William R. Wister, *Some Reminiscences of Cricket in Philadelphia Before 1861* (Philadelphia: Allen, Lane and

Scott, 1904). John I. Marder, *The International Series: The Story of the United States Versus Canada at Cricket* (London: Kaye and Ward, 1968), is an interesting account of the first international sports competition. Robert W. Henderson, *Ball, Bat and Bishop: The Origin of Ball Games* (New York: Rockport, 1947), and Uriel Simri, "The Religious and Magical Functions of Ball Games" (Ed.D. diss., West Virginia University, 1966), were crucial to my understanding of the evolution of ball games.

Robert F. Kelley, *American Rowing: Its Backgrounds and Traditions* (New York: Putnam, 1932), provided a popular overview of rowing developments, while Samuel Crowther and Arthur Ruhl, eds., *Rowing and Track Athletics* (New York: Macmillan, 1905), also contained much valuable information. I also profited from several scholarly articles on various aspects of rowing history: Guy M. Lewis, "America's First Intercollegiate Sport: The Regattas from 1852 to 1875," *Research Quarterly* 38 (1967): 637–48; Joseph J. Mathews, "The First Harvard-Oxford Boatrace," *New England Quarterly* 33 (1960): 74–82; and E. Merton Coulter, "Boating as a Sport in the Old South," *Georgia Historical Society* 27 (1943): 231–47.

There are several popular histories of yachting as well as examinations of the challenges for the America's Cup. The most useful were: Douglas Phillips-Birt, *The History of Yachting* (New York: Stein and Day, 1974); William P. Stephen, *American Yachting* (New York: Macmillan, 1904); Charles Boswell, *The America: The Story of the World's Most Famous Yacht* (New York: McKay, 1967); Jerome E. Brooks, *The $30,000,000 Cup: The Stormy History of the Defense of the America's Cup* (New York: Simon and Schuster, 1958); Roland F. Coffin, *The America's Cup. How It Was Won by the Yacht America in 1851 and Has Been since Defended* (New York: Scribner, 1885). Alfred F. Loomis, *Ocean Racing: The Great Blue-Water Yacht Races, 1866–1935* (New York: Morrow, 1936), proved valuable in understanding the early beginning of this phase of yacht racing, as did John Parkinson, Jr., *The History of the New York Yacht Club from Its Founding Through 1973* (New York: New York Yacht Club, 1975).

Ned Polsky's discussion of billiards in *Hustlers, Beats and Others* (Garden City, N.Y.: Doubleday, 1969), was critical to my study of this sport, and Louise C. Belden, "Billiards in America Before 1830," *Antiques* 87 (Jan. 1965): 99–101, aided my understanding of the early developments of billiards. John Cumming, *Runners and Walkers: A Nineteenth Century Sports Chronicle* (Chicago: Regnery Gateway, 1981), is adequate as a survey of track and field developments, and George Moss, "The Long Distance Runners of Ante-Bellum America," *Journal of Popular Culture* 8 (1970): 371–82, describes the popularity of this sport. Gerald Redmond, *The Caledonian Games in Nineteenth Century America* (Cranbury, N.J.: Associated University Press, 1971), is the definitive study of Scottish games in America and their impact on American track and field, and Rowland Berthoff, *British Immigrants in Industrial America, 1790–1950* (New York: Russell and Russell, 1953), also contains useful information on the sporting practices of Scots. Robert Korsgaard, "A History of the Amateur Athletics Union of the United States" (Ed.D. diss., Teacher's College, Columbia University, 1952), offers valuable information on the early development of track and field.

Elliot Jacob Gorn, "The Manly Art: Bare-Knuckle Prize Fighting and the Rise of American Sport" (Ph.D. diss., Yale University, 1983), has emerged as the place to look to understand nineteenth-century pugilism. Nat Fleischer, *Heavyweight Championship: An Informal History of Heavyweight Boxing from 1719 to the Present Day* (New York: Putnam, 1961), is a good popular history of the sport, and *American Fistiana, Containing All the Fights in the United States from 1816 to 1860* (New York: Dewitt, 1860), is a must for any student of antebellum boxing. John Ford, *Prizefighting: The Age of Regency Boximania* (New York: Great Albion, 1972), provides valuable information on the popularity and character of boxing in England during the late Georgian period.

There is no comprehensive study of animal sports and only a handful of historical works related to this theme. Martin and Herbert J. Kaufman, "Henry Bergh, Kit Burns, and the Sportsmen of New York," *New York Folklore Quarterly* 28 (1972): 15–29, discuss the conflict between Bergh and Burns, and Zula Steele, *Angel in Top Hat* (New York: Harper, 1942), provides a biographical look at Bergh. Gerald Carson, *Men, Beast and Gods: A History of Cruelty and Kindness to Animals* (New York: Scribner, 1972), contains useful information on blood sports. Jack Berryman, "The Ending of American Blood Sports" (paper presented at the 86th meeting of the American Historical Association, 1971), offered a solid discussion of the factors that led to the decline of animal sports.

Several other works were helpful in understanding the development of certain sports, including Henry Metzner, *A Brief History of the American Turnerbund*, rev. ed. (Pittsburgh: National Executive Committee of the American Turnerbund, 1924); Elizabeth Eliot, *Portrait of a Sport: The Study of Steeplechasing in Great Britain and the United States* (Woodstock, Vt.: Countryman, 1957); Reginald Rives, *The Coaching Club, Its History, Records and Activities* (New York, 1935); J. Brian Van Urk, *The Story of American Foxhunting: From Challenge to Full Cry*, 2 vols. (New York: Derrydale, 1940–41); Charles A. Peverelly, *The Book of American Pastimes* (New York, 1866). For the development of sports journalism, see John R. Betts, "Sporting Journalism in Nineteenth-Century America," *American Quarterly* 5 (1953): 39–64, and Jack W. Berryman, "The Tenuous Attempts of Americans to Catch up with *John Bull:* Specialty Magazines and Sporting Journalism, 1800–1835," *Canadian Journal of the History of Sport and Physical Education* 10 (May 1979): 40–61.

Index

Act to Prevent Horseracing, 28–29; modification of bill, 32; impact on harness racing, 56

Adams, Dr. Daniel D., 127–28

Admission fee: in horse racing, 39, 42, 49, 76–77, 78, 86–88; in baseball, 131, 148–49, 159, 168; in cricket, 148; to Caledonian games, 216; in billiards, 222, 228; in boxing, 232; to animal sports, 242

Akers, Dwight, 32, 66

All-England Eleven, 108–9

All-star games, 104, 131–32, 148, 157

Allen Street Court, 252, 253

Amateurs, 151–52, 154, 186–87, 285–86; in baseball, 166–68; in rowing, 194, 196–97; in yachting, 201; in track and field, 218, 219–20

America (yacht), 198–200, 206–7

American Billiard Players Association, 227, 245

American Cricket Club, 109

American Jockey Club, 75, 80, 81–82, 201; as racing innovators, 83–85; criticism of, 86–88; gambling, 89; sponsors of steeplechase racing, 264

American Skating Congress, 258

American Society for the Prevention of Cruelty to Animals, 241, 242–43, 249–50

American Turf Register and Sporting Magazine, 52

America's Cup, 185, 200, 205–8

Anglo-American community, 118, 208

Animal sports, 141, 185–86, 240–44

Ariel-Flirtilla (horse) race, 38

Artisans, 8, 18, 186, 255; in baseball, 92, 138–42, 153, 155–56, 175–78, 179–80, 182; in cricket, 113; in St. George Cricket Club, 103, 117; in pedestrianism, 212; in target shooting companies, 251. *See also* Eckford Base Ball Club; Butchers; Food market workers

Ashbury, James, 205–8

Aspinwall, Lloyd, 118, 195

Atalanta Boat Club, 195

Atlantic Base Ball Club (Brooklyn), 132, 138, 146, 153, 158, 163, 178–80; contest with Excelsiors, 132–33, 134; contest with Cincinnati Red Stockings, 171–72; as professional team, 157, 159–60, 172

Bachelor subculture, 185, 223–24, 232

Baptist, John, 190

Barlow, John, 213–14

Barnum, Phineas T., 77, 150

Baseball, 2, 8, 56, 91–94, 100, 106, 185, 194, 197, 211, 215, 216, 238, 247, 251, 252, 254, 265, 278, 281–82; comparison with fate of cricket, 107, 109–16, 129; debt to cricket, 118–19; developments of 1845–55, 121–26; developments of 1855–60, 126–38; fly rule, 127, 129–31; as America's preeminent sport, 134–37; developments of 1860–65, 145–54; developments of 1866–70, 154–74, 178–80; social class of ball players, 10,

A Note on the Author

Melvin L. Adelman is a faculty member at the Ohio State University, in the Department of Health, Physical Education, and Recreation. He received his Ph.D. degree in history from the University of Illinois at Urbana-Champaign in 1980 and has published several articles in the *Journal of Sport History* and the *Canadian Journal of the History of Sport*. This is his first book.